FREDERICK COUNTY [VIRGINIA] ROAD ORDERS

1743-1772

Virginia Genealogical Society
Richmond, Virginia

Published With Permission from the

Virginia Transportation Research Council
(A Cooperative Organization Sponsored Jointly by the Virginia
Department of Transportation and
the University of Virginia)

HERITAGE BOOKS
2007

HERITAGE BOOKS
AN IMPRINT OF HERITAGE BOOKS, INC.

Books, CDs, and more—Worldwide

For our listing of thousands of titles see our website
at
www.HeritageBooks.com

Published 2007 by
HERITAGE BOOKS, INC.
Publishing Division
65 East Main Street
Westminster, Maryland 21157-5026

Copyright © 2005 Virginia Genealogical Society

All rights reserved. No part of this book may be reproduced or transmitted in any form or by any means, electronic or mechanical, including photocopying, recording or by any information storage and retrieval system without written permission from the author, except for the inclusion of brief quotations in a review.

International Standard Book Number: 978-0-7884-4542-2

HISTORIC ROADS OF VIRGINIA

Louisa County Road Orders 1742-1748, by Nathaniel Mason Pawlett

Goochland County Road Orders 1728-1744, by Nathaniel Mason Pawlett

Albemarle County Road Orders 1744-1748, by Nathaniel Mason Pawlett

The Route of the Three Notch'd Road, by Nathaniel Mason Pawlett and Howard Newlon

An Index to Roads in the Albemarle County Surveyor's Books 1744-1853, by Nathaniel Mason Pawlett

A Brief History of the Staunton and James River Turnpike, by Douglas Young

Albemarle County Road Orders 1783-1816, by Nathaniel Mason Pawlett

A Brief History of Roads in Virginia 1607-1840, by Nathaniel Mason Pawlett

A Guide to the Preparation of County Road Histories, by Nathaniel Mason Pawlett

Early Road Location: Key to Discovering Historic Resources? by Nathaniel Mason Pawlett and K. Edward Lay

Albemarle County Roads 1725-1816, by Nathaniel Mason Pawlett

"Backsights," A Bibliography, by Nathaniel Mason Pawlett

Orange County Road Orders 1734-1749, by Ann Brush Miller

Spotsylvania County Road Orders 1722-1734, by Nathaniel Mason Pawlett

Brunswick County Road Orders 1732-1749, by Nathaniel Mason Pawlett

Orange County Road Orders 1750-1800, by Ann Brush Miller

Lunenburg County Road Orders 1746-1764, by Nathaniel Mason Pawlett and Tyler Jefferson Boyd

Culpeper County Road Orders 1763-1764, by Ann Brush Miller

Augusta County Road Orders 1745-1769, by Nathaniel Mason Pawlett, Ann Brush Miller, Kenneth Madison Clark and Thomas Llewellyn Samuel, Jr.

Amelia County Road Orders 1735-1753, by Nathaniel Mason Pawlett, Ann Brush Miller, and Kenneth Madison Clark

Fairfax County Road Orders 1749-1800, by Beth Mitchell

New Kent County and Hanover County Road Orders 1706-1743, Transcribed from the Vestry Book of St. Paul's Parish, by Ann Brush Miller

FOREWORD

by

Ann Brush Miller
Virginia Transportation Research Council

Frederick County Road Orders 1743-1772 is a cooperative project between Shenandoah University and the Virginia Transportation Research Council. It is the fifth volume of road orders produced cooperatively between a private group and the Virginia Transportation Research Council, following similar projects with the Orange County Historical Society (which sponsored the production of *Orange County Road Orders 1734-1749* and *Orange County Road Orders 1750-1800*); the Culpeper County Historical Society (which sponsored *Culpeper County Road Orders 1763-1764*); and the Fairfax County History Commission (which sponsored *Fairfax County Road Orders 1749-1800*).

The initial transcription of the county road orders was undertaken by Gene Luckman under the direction of Dr. Warren R. Hofstra of the Shenandoah University Department of History. Typing and correction of the original draft, and indexing were undertaken at the Virginia Transportation Research Council by Ann Brush Miller, with student assistants Silvana R. Del Castillo, Valerie B. Huber, and Sarah N. Coleman.

This volume covers the transportation records for the northwestern portion of Virginia for the mid-18th century. At its creation from Orange County in 1743, Frederick County included within its territory the present-day Virginia counties of Frederick, Shenandoah, Clarke, and Warren and the northern two-thirds of Page County. In addition, part of what is now northeastern West Virginia was within the original boundaries of Frederick County.

This volume is the twenty-third entry in the *Historic Roads of Virginia* series, initiated by the Virginia Transportation Research Council (then the Virginia Highway & Transportation Research Council) in 1973. *Frederick County Road Orders 1743-1772*, covering the northern portion of the Shenandoah Valley and what is now West Virginia, is the third volume of published road orders to be concerned with territory west of the Blue Ridge; portions of the Shenandoah Valley were covered by two previous publications, *Augusta County Road Orders 1745-1769* and *Orange County Road Orders 1734-1749*, which included the period during which the territory was part of Orange County, prior to 1745.

A NOTE ON THE METHODS, EDITING, AND DATING SYSTEM

by

Nathaniel Mason Pawlett
(Faculty Research Historian, Virginia Transportation Research Council, 1973-1995)

The road and bridge orders contained in the order books of an early Virginia county are the primary source of information for the study of its roads. When extracted, indexed, and published by the Virginia Transportation Research Council, they greatly facilitate this. All of the early county court order books are in manuscript, sometimes so damaged and faded as to be almost indecipherable. Usually rendered in the rather ornate script of the time, the phonetic spellings of this period often serve to complicate matters further for the researcher and recorder.

With these road orders available in an indexed and cross-indexed published form, it will be possible to produce chronological chains of road orders illustrating the development of many of the early roads of a vast area from the threshold of settlement through much of the eighteenth century. Immediate corroboration for these chains of road orders will usually be provided by other evidence such as deeds, plats, and the Confederate Engineers maps. Often, in fact, the principal roads will be found to survive in place under their early names.

With regard to the general editorial principles of the project, it has been our perception over the years as the road orders of Louisa, Hanover, Goochland, Albemarle, and other counties have been examined and recorded that road orders themselves are really a variety of "notes," often cryptic, incomplete, or based on assumptions concerning the level of knowledge of the reader. As such, any further abstracting or compression of them would tend to produce "notes" taken from "notes," making them even less comprehensible. The tendency has, therefore, been in the direction of restraint in editing, leaving any conclusions with regard to meaning up to the individual reader or researcher using these publications. In pursuing this course, we have attempted to present the reader with a typescript text that is as near a type facsimile of the manuscript itself as we can come.

Our objective is to produce a text that conveys as near the precise form of the original as we can, reproducing all the peculiarities of the eighteenth-century orthography. While some compromises have had to be made because of the modern keyboard, this was really not that difficult a task. Most of their symbols can be accommodated by modern typography, and most abbreviations are fairly clear as to meaning.

Punctuations may appear misleading at times, with unnecessary commas or commas placed where periods should be located; appropriate terminal punctuation is often missing or else takes the form of a symbol such as a dash or several dashes, etc. The original capitalization has been retained insofar as it was possible to determine from the original manuscript whether capitals were intended. No capitals have been inserted in place of those originally omitted. The original spelling and syntax have been retained throughout, even including the obvious errors in various places, such as repetitions of words and simple clerical errors. Ampersands have been retained throughout to include such forms as "&c" for "etc." Superscript letters have also been retained where used in y^e, y^t, s^d. The thorn symbol (y), pronounced as "th," has been retained in the aforesaid "y^e," pronounced "the," and "y^t" (that). The tailed "p" (resembling a capital "p" with the tail extended into a loop) has also been retained. This symbol has no counterpart in modern typography; given the limits of the modern keyboard, we have rendered it as a capital "p" (P). This should be taken to mean either "per" (by), "pre," or "pro" (sometimes "par" as in "Pish" for parish) as the context by the order may demand. For damaged and missing portions of the manuscripts we have used square brackets to denote the [missing], [torn] or [illegible] portions. Because of the large number of ancient forms of spelling, grammar, and syntax, it has been deemed impracticable to insert the form [sic] after each one to indicate a literal rendering. Therefore, the reader must assume that apparent errors are merely the result of our literal transcription of the road orders, barring the introduction of typographical errors, of course. If, in any case, this appears to present insuperable problems, resort should be made to the original records.

As to dating, most historians and genealogists who have worked with early Virginian records will be aware of the English dating system in use down to 1752. Although there was an eleven-day difference from our calendar in the day of the month, the principal difference lay in the fact that the beginning of the year was dated from March 25 rather than January 1, as was the case from 1752 onward to the present. Thus, January, February, and March (to the 25th) were the last three months in a given year, and the new year came in only on March 25.

Early Virginian records usually follow this practice, though in some cases dates during these three months will be shown in the form 1732/3, showing both the English date and that in use on the Continent, where the year began January 1. For researchers using material with dates in the English style, it is important to remember that under this system (for instance) a man might die in January 1734 yet convey property or serve in public office in June 1734, since June came *before* January in a given year under this system.

INTRODUCTION

by

Ann Brush Miller

> The roads are under the government of the county courts, subject to be controuled by the general court. They order whenever they think them necessary. The inhabitants of the county are by them laid off into precincts, to each of which they allot a convenient portion of the public roads to be kept in repair. Such bridges as may be built without the assistance of artificers, they are to be built. If the stream be such as to require a bridge of regular workmanship, the court employs workmen to build it, at the expense of the whole county. If it be too great for the county, application is made to the general assembly, who authorize individuals to build it, and to take a fixed toll from all passengers, or give sanction to such other proposition as to them appears reasonable.
>
> -- Thomas Jefferson, *Notes on the State of Virginia*, 1781

The establishment and maintenance of public roads were among the most important functions of the county court during the colonial period in Virginia. Each road was opened and maintained by an Overseer of the Highways appointed by the Gentlemen Justices yearly. He was usually assigned all the "Labouring Male Titheables" living on or near the road for this purpose. These individuals then furnished all their own tools, wagons, and teams and were required to labour for six days each year on the roads.

Major projects, such as bridges over rivers, demanding considerable expenditure were executed by commissioners appointed by the court to select the site and to contract with workmen for the construction. Where bridges connected two counties, a commission was appointed by each and they cooperated in executing the work.

At its creation from Orange County in 1743, Frederick County extended from the northwestern side of the Blue Ridge to "the utmost limits of Virginia." Although legislated into existence along with Augusta County in 1738, Frederick did not commence operation until 1743 when it was determined it had sufficient population to support a government.

Frederick lost much of its western territory to Hampshire County (now West Virginia) upon that county's creation in 1754. Its boundaries then remained unchanged until the creation of the counties of Dunmore (later renamed Shenandoah) and Berkeley (now West Virginia) in 1772. The county reached its present boundaries in 1836, with the creation of Clarke County (created from Frederick in that year) and the loss of slight additional territory to the new county of Warren (created from Shenandoah County).

The road orders contained in this volume cover the period from 1743, when Frederick's county government became operational, down to the creation of Dunmore and Berkeley counties from Frederick in 1772. As such, they comprise the principal extant evidence concerning the early development of roads over a large area of northwestern Virginia and northeastern West Virginia.

Frederick County Road Orders, 1743-1772

Frederick County Order Book 1 (1743-1745)

11 November 1743 Old Style, FOB 1, p. 3
Ordered that the Overseers of the Roads be Continued as they were untill the next Court --

9 December 1743 Old Style, FOB 1, p. 3
On the petition of John Wilcox and Others for a Road from John Funks Mill to Chesters Ferry and from thence to where the Road takes out of Chester's Road to Manasses's Run, its Order'd that Thomas Chester Gent John Wilcox & Jacob Funck, View Mark & lay off the Road petitioned for by the said Wilox &c. And make return of their proceedings to the next Court --

9 December 1743 Old Style, FOB 1, p. 4
John Kersey having by his Petition set forth that by an order of Orange County Court he had leave to keep fferry Over Shennandoe River near the Waggon Road /: where he liveth :/ And prayed leave To Continue the said fferry its ordered That the Same be Continued Accordingly --

9 December 1743 Old Style, FOB 1, p. 4
On the Petition of John Wood its Ordered that John Hardin, Samuel Simmons & Edward Rogers or any two of them View the Road from the Blue Ball to Ashbies bent branch & make return thereof to the next Court --

9 December 1743 Old Style, FOB 1, p. 4
On the Petition of Patrick Ryley its Ordered that the Road be Cleared from the head of the spring by the Chappel to John Evans's as it has been formerly laid off by Order of Orange County Court --

9 December 1743 Old Style, FOB 1, p. 5
On the Petition of Thomas Province & Others for a Road from John ffrost Mill to the Main Road between John Littlers plantation & John Milburns its Ordered that John Littler, William Dillan & Joseph Burckham or any two lay off the same & make return of their proceedings to the next Court --

13 January 1743/44 Old Style, FOB 1, p. 15
On the petition of Noah Hampton & Others for a Road from Noah Hamptons Mill, Into a Road on Great Cape Capon near James Coddy's Its Ordered that Jonathan Cobourn, Isaac Thomas, Peter Kuykendal & James Delheryea or any two of them do view mark & lay off the Road petitioned for by the said Hampton &c. & make return of their proceedings to the next Court --

13 January 1743/44 Old Style, FOB 1, p. 15
Ordered that Robert Ashby be Overseer of the Road from Howels ford to Ashby's bent Gap & that the Tithables Appointed by Orange Court be Continued to Work on the said Road --

13 January 1743/44 O. S., FOB 1, p. 15
Ordered that George Bowman, Andrew Falkenborough & Robt M^ckay Junr. or any two of them View & lay off the Road from John ffunks Mill cross Ceeder run Creek ford to the said Robert M^ckay Jun^rs. & to Branston Gap According to the petition of Jacob Teeter & Others & make return of their proceeding to the next Court --

13 January 1743/44 O. S., FOB 1, p. 16
John Hardin & Edward Rogers having Viewed the Road Petitioned for by John Wood between the Blue Ball & Ashby's bent Branch made their return that it was their Opinion that the said Road should be turned under the side of the Mountain along the Old Road as it was formerly Wherefore its Ordered that the said Wood have Liberty To Turn the said Road According to the Viewers report with his Own people --

13 January 1743/44 O. S., FOB 1, p. 16
The Order for Thomas Chester & Others to View & lay off a Road Petitioned for by John Wilcox & Others not being returned is Continued untill the next Court to be returned --

13 January 1743/44 O. S., FOB 1, p. 16
The Order for John Littler & Others to View & lay off a Road Petitioned for by Thos. Province & others not being returned is Continued untill ye next Court to be returned --

10 February 1743/44 O. S., FOB 1, p. 29
The Order for Jonathan Coburn & Others to View & Lay off a Road Petitioned for by Noah Hampton & Others not being returned is Continued untill the next Court to be returned --

10 February 1743/44 O. S., FOB 1, p. 29
George Bowman & Robert McCoy Junr having made their return on the Order for Viewing & Laying off the Road from John ffunks Mill Cross Ceedar Run Creek ford to the said Robert McCoy Jun^rs to Branstons Gapp in these words We the Subscribers have viewed and laid Out the Road from ffunks Mill back of George Teleners and from thence to Ceedar Creek ford & Robert McCoy's & from thence to Gregories ford upon the River & thereupon its Ordered that the s^d. Road be Cleared by the Petitioners Robert McCoy, George Dellener & George Bowman are hereby Appointed Overseers of the said Road & its further Ordered that they cause the said Road to be cleared According to Law.

10 February 1743/44 O. S., FOB 1, p. 29
Thomas Chester Gent. John Wilcox & Jacob Funk having made return on the Last Courts Order for Viewing Marking and laying off a Road from John Funks Mill to Chesters fferry & to where the Road takes Off to Manasses run, that they had Viewed Mark'd & laid off the said Road According to the said Order. Its Ordered that the most convenientest Tithables excepting those Tithables mentioned in the petition of Jacob Teeter work on the said Road & its further Ordered that Jacob Funk be Overseer from John Funks Mill to the North River & that William Tidwell be Overseer from the said River to the Haybottom & John Wilcox be Overseer from thence to where the Road takes off to Manasses Run & that they cause the said Road to be cleared According to Law --

10 February 1743/44 O. S., FOB 1, pp. 29-30
John Littler & William Dillon having made their return on the Order for Viewing & laying of the Road from John ffrosts Mill to the main Road between John Littlers & John Milbourns plantation in these Words, We have laid off the Road from Capt ffrost's Mill thence to Buffler lick thence to the Backside John Bossers field, thence to David Springers thence to the Usual ford thence on the East Side W^m. ffrosts plantation thence along a good Ridge by a Course of Marked Trees to Mathias Elmores thence along the said Elmors Creek to the head, the best Convenientest Way that can be had by Widow Dillons thence by the said Marked Trees to the main Road Leading to Rappahannock between John Littlers & John Milbourns which includes the whole, Its Ordered that the said Road be cleared by the Pet^{rs}. and Joseph Burkham & W^m. ffrost are hereby Appointed Overseers of the said Road & its further Ordered that they clear the same According to Law --

10 February 1743/44 O. S., FOB 1, p. 32
On the Petition of Richard Arnold & Others for a Road from the North Branch of Cape Capon to James Cody's Road its Ordered that the Petitioners have leave to Clear the same, And Benjamin Phipps & William Warden are hereby appointed Overseers of the same & its further Ordered that they cause the same to be Cleared, According to Law --

9 March 1743/44 O. S., FOB 1, pp. 48-49
Ordered that Thomas Rutherford Gent. W^m. Davis & Richard Stinson or any two of them do View Mark & Lay off a Road the best & Nighest Way from John Shepards to the Head of Bulskin & that John McCormick, Joseph Carter & John Neil or any two of them View Mark & lay off a road from the head of Bulskin Over ye said Neills Mill dam to the Court house & its Ordered that they make return of their proceeding to ye next Court --

9 March 1743/44 O. S., FOB 1, p. 49
Leonard Helms is hereby Appointed Overseer of the Road in the Room of John Hardin And its Ordered that the same hands Work on the said Road & that he Cause the same to be Cleared According to Law --

9 March 1743/44 O. S., FOB 1, p. 49
Isaac Perkins is hereby Appointed Overseer of the Road in the room of George Hoge Gent from Isaac Perkins Mill to Opecken And its Ordered that he Cause the same to be Cleared According to Law --

9 March 1743/44 O. S., FOB 1, p. 49
Ordered that a road be cleared from Israel Robinsons Gapp to Vestals Gapp According as its laid off by an Order of Orange County Court and that Andrew Campbell Gent. be Overseer of the said Road from the Mountain to Opecken Creek & that Thomas Hart & William Vestal be Overseers from Opecken Creek to Vestals Gapp & its further Ordered that they cause the same to be cleared According to Law --

13 April 1744 O. S., FOB 1, p. 72
The Order P Thomas Rutherford Gent & Others to View a Road &^{c} is Continued until the next Court to be returned --

13 April 1744 O. S., FOB 1, p. 72
The Order P Jonathan Cobourne & Others to View a Road &^{c} is Continued until the next Court to be returned --

14 April 1744 O. S., FOB 1, p. 77
On the Petition of Richard Morgan & Others for a Road from John Littlers to Thomas Shepards Mill its Ordered that John Littler John Ross Jacob Hite & Thomas Shepard View Mark & lay off the same & make return of their proceeding to the next Court --

14 April 1744 O. S., FOB 1, p. 77
John Beals & Patrick Gallasby is hereby Apponted Overseers of the Road from the head of the Spring by the Chapple to John Evans & from thence to Tuscorora & its Ordered that they cause the same to be Cleared According to Law --

14 April 1744 O. S., FOB 1, p. 78
Richard Beason is hereby Appointed Overseer of the Road from Robinsons Gap to Opecken in the Room of Andrew Campbell Gent & its Ordered that he Cause the same to be Cleared according to Law --

11 May 1744 O. S., FOB 1, p. 90
John Neil is hereby Appointed Overseer of the Road from Opecken Ford by ye said Neil's Mill to Kersey's ferry in the Room of John Littler & its Order'd that he Cause the same to the Kept in repair according to Law --

12 May 1744 O. S., FOB 1, p. 96
David Vance Gent. & Others having put in their Petition praying that they might have Leave to work on the Road Cleared by them wch Leads to Kersey's ferry Leave therefore is Granted them to work on the same & that they be Exempted from Working on the Other Road that goes to the said Ferry & its Ordered that John Hite be Overseer of the said Road & that he Cause the same to be Kept in good repair according to Law --

12 May 1744 O. S., FOB 1, p. 97
On the petition of Hugh Parrel Setting forth that he Labouring under great Hardship by reason of two Roads running thro' his Land & praying Leave to Stopp one of them. Leave therefore is granted him to Stop that Road which goes by Abraham Hollingsworth Accordingly --

12 May 1744 O. S., FOB 1, p. 97
Isaac Perkins is hereby appointed Overseer of the Road from John Littlers Old place by the Court house to Capt John Hites & that the Tithables which worked on the Road that went by Abraham

Hollingsworths work on the said Road & its Ordered that the said Isaac Perkins keep the same in good repair According to Law --

14 May 1744 O. S., FOB 1, p. 104
The Order P Thomas Rutherford G^t &^{c} to View a Road is Continued until the Next Court to be Returned --

14 May 1744 O. S., FOB 1, p. 104
The Order P Jonathan Cobourn & Others to View a Road &^{c} is Cont'd until the next Court to be returned --

14 May 1744 O. S., FOB 1, p. 104
Jacob Hite Gent John Littler John Ross & Thomas Shepard having made their return on the Last Courts Order for Viewing Marking and Laying off a Road from John Littlers to Thomas Shepards Mill in these Words We have Viewed & laid off a Road from John Littlers late Dwelling house by a Course of Marked Trees to the said Littlers new Design Thence to Opecken Creek Over Abrils ford thence to the late Dwelling place of John Smiths deced thence to Jacob Hites Thence to Thomas Shepards Mill and thereupon its Ordered that the said road be Cleared by the Petitioners & that Jacob Hite Gent Thomas Swearingham & Edward Thomas be Overseers of the same & its further Ordered that they cause y^e. s^d. Road to be Cleared according to Law --

8 June 1744 O. S., FOB 1, p. 119
Ordered that Thomas Reece be appointed Overseer of the Road from Opeken to Mill Creek in the Room of George Hobson & that he keep the said Road in repair According to Law --

8 June 1744 O. S., FOB 1, p. 119
On the petition of Meredith Helms Gent its Ordered that John Alford Hugh Ferguson & William McKee view Mark & Lay Off a Bridle Road from Scots Mill on Shanando the nearest & best way to the Courthouse of this County & make return of their proceedings to the next Court

8 June 1744 O. S., FOB 1, p. 119
Ordered that Benjamin Carter be Appointed Overseer of the Road From Perkins his Mill to Opecken in the Room of Isaac Perkins and Robert Wilson Overseer of the Road from the said Mill to Hites Mill in the Room of ye s^d. Isaac Perkins & that the said Isaac Perkins be Overseer of the Road from his Mill to John Littlers Old place --

8 June 1744 O. S., FOB 1, p. 120
The Order P Thos. Rutherford Gent. & Others to View a Road &^{c} is Cont^d until the next Court to be returned --

8 June 1744 O. S., FOB 1, p. 120
The order P Jon.^{a}. Cobourn & Others to View a Road &^{c} is Cont^d until the next Court to be returned --

8 June 1744 O. S., FOB 1, p. 122
On the petition of Jacob Hite Gent & others for a Road from the Chappel to Jays ferry it is Ordered that James Anderson, John Hampton, Jacob Hite & Thomas Rutherford Gent View Mark and lay off the same the Nearest & best way from the said Chappel by Andersons Mill from thence to fall into the Road from Capt Campbels to the said Ferry & to make return of their proceeding to the next Court --

9 June 1744 O. S., FOB 1, p. 122
Ordered that the Tithables Two miles on each side the Road in Jacob Hites & Edward Thomas precinct clear the Road from John Littlers to Thomas Sheppards Mill & work on the said Road --

13 July 1744 O. S., FOB 1, p. 137
On the motion of Samuel Earle it is Ordered that John Rout be Overseer of the Road from Gregorys Ford to the Top of the Ridge & that all the male labouring Tithables belonging to the Honble. Thomas Lord Fairfax's Quarter James Seabern Widow Borden William Remy Edward Rogers Jacob Peck Edwd Corder Thos Postgate John Painter James Burn Thomas Hooper John Gregory Rich^d. Gregory Benjn Gregory Saml Earle & John Oldrages work on the same & Observe the said Overseers Order & Directions in Clearing the same And its further Ordered that the said Rout keep the said Road in Good Repair According to Law --

14 July 1744 O. S., FOB 1, p. 142
Jonathan Cobourn & Peter Keykendal having made their return on an Order of this Court for Viewing Marking & laying off a Road from Noah Hamptons Mill into the Road on Great Cape Capon near James Cody's In these words Pursuant to the within Order we have Viewed Marked & lay'd off the road from James Coddy's to Hamptons Mill & thereupon its Ordered that the said Road be from hence forth established a Public Road, And Matthias Yoakam & John Colvin are hereby appointed overseers of the same & its further Ordered that they cause the said Road to be Cleared & when Cleared to keep the same in Repair according to Law & that the Titheables on the south Branch & Patersons Creek work on the said Road --

14 July 1744 O. S., FOB 1, pp. 142-143
Jacob Hite Thomas Rutherford Gent & John Hampton having made their return on the Last Courts Order for viewing & Laying off a Road from the Chapple to Jays ferry in these words In pursuance to the within Order to us Directed, we have Viewed Marked & laid of the within Mentioned Road from the Chapple to Thos Andersons & from thence by William Mitchells & Jacob Hite Gent into the Road that goes from the fferry to Captn Campbells near the plantation of Capt. Thomas Rutherford Whereupon its Ordered that the said Road be from henceforth established a public Road. And Wm Mitchell and Jacob Brooks are hereby appointed Overseers of the same And its further Ordered that they cause the said Road to be Cleared & when Cleared to Keep the same in repair according to Law And that the tithables living within three Miles on Each side the Road work on the same --

17 July 1744 O. S., FOB 1, pp. 153-154
Thomas Rutherford Gent & W^m. Davis having Viewed the Road from John Sheppards to the head of Bulskin according to an Order of this Court made their report in these words In Obediance to the within Order we have layed off & Marked the said Road from Potomack River the Nearest & best way from Sheppards fferry Thro' the Land of Thomas Rutherford & so over Walkers Mill Dam & so by the head of Pitts'es Marsh & so to the Head of Bulskin thro' the Lands of M^r. John McCormack Whereupon its Ordered that the said Road be from hence forth Established a public Road & Wm Davis is hereby Appointed Overseer of the same And its further Ordered that he Cause the said Road to be Cleared & when Cleared that he Keep the same in Repair according to the Law And that the Tithables living within three Miles on Each side the Road Work on the same --

17 July 1744 O. S., FOB 1, p. 154
John McCormack & [blank space in book] having viewed the Road from the head of Bulskin over John Neills mill Dam to the Courthouse according to an Order of this Court made their report in these words In Obedience to y^e. within Order we have laid Off & Marked the said Road from the head of Bulskin to Jno Neills Mill & so Over the Mill=damm the Nearest way to the Courthouse Whereupon its Ordered that the said Road be from henceforth Established a Public Road And John Neill is hereby Appointed overseer of the same And its further Ordered that he Cause the said Road to be Cleared & when Cleared that he Keep the same in Repair according to Law And that the Tithables Living within three Miles on Each side the road work on the same --

17 July 1744 O. S., FOB 1, p. 154
On the Petition of Lewis Hogg for leave to Keep a fferry & Clear a Road from Thomas Morgans Mill to his house & from thence to the Top of the Ridge Leave therefore is Granted him to Clear the same at his Own Costs & to Keep fferry & its Ordered that he be Allowed for Ferriages as is Allowed to Thos Chester Gent --

10 August 1744 O. S., FOB 1, p. 165
John Alford Hugh Ferguson & W^m McKee having viewed the Bridle Road from Scots Mill on Sharrando the Nearest & best way to the Courthouse of this County according to an Order of this Court made their report in these words In Obedience to the within Order of Court we have Viewed a Road from Scotts Mill to the Courthouse & Marked the same which we think very Convenient Whereupon it is Ordered that the said Road be from henceforth Established a Public Road & that Hugh Ferguson & John Alford be Overseers of the same & it is Ordered that they cause the same to be cleared & when cleared that they Keep the same in good repair According to Law & its further Ordered that he Tithables Living wth. in Two Miles on each side the said Road Work on the same --

10 August 1744 O. S., FOB 1, p. 165
On the Petition of David Vance Gent & Others its Ordered that a Road be Cleared from John Hites Mill into the Road that Comes from John Funks Mill to John Gregory's & John Niswanger & Robert Warth are hereby Appointed Overseers of the same & its Ordered that they cause the

same to be Cleared & when cleared that they keep the same in good repair According to Law & its further Ordered that the Tithables living within two Miles of the said Road work on the same –

11 August 1744 O. S., FOB 1, p. 170
On the Motion of Robert McKay Junr. its Ordered that James Bounds Ralph Weathers W^m. Rentfroe Charles Baker Robert M^{c}pherson, John Branson Thos Branson John Duckworth Thomas Thornton Christopher Gibson Willm. Smith Bathanay Haines, Spencer Jones, Thos Sharp, Thos Hankins, Marmaduke Vecory Robert Denton Saml Joredon & Thomas Alexander & the male labouring Tithables belonging to them work on the Road where the said McKay is now Overseer & that they Observe his Direction & Orders in Clearing the said Road as the Law Directs --

11 August 1744 O. S., FOB 1, p. 170
Thomas Postgate & John Gregory are hereby Appointed to View Mark and lay Off a Road from the said Postgate's Islands into the Road that comes from Thos Chesters Gent. & make return of their proceeding to the next Court --

11 August 1744 O. S., FOB 1, p. 177
Robert McCoy Junr. Lawrence Stephens & James Bounds are hereby Appointed to View Mark and lay Off a Road from the Mouth of Crooked Run the Nearest & best way to Capt John Hites --

14 September 1744 O. S., FOB 1, p. 188
The Order P Thomas Postgate & Others to View a Road &^{c} not being returned is Continued until the next Court to be returned --

14 September 1744 O. S., FOB 1, p. 188
The Order P Robt McKay Junr. & Others to view a Road &^{c} not being ret^d is Continued until the next Court to be returned --

15 September 1744 O. S., FOB 1, p. 197
Henry Vanmetre is hereby Appointed Overseer of the Road from Noah Hamptons Mill into the Road on Great Cape Capon near James Cody's in the Room of Matthias Yoakham & its Ordered that he Cause the same to be Cleared & when Cleared that he Keep the same in good repair According to Law --

15 September 1744 O. S., FOB 1, p. 199
Owen Thomas is hereby Appointed Overseer of the Road from Jeremiah Smiths to William Hogs in the Room of Joseph Edwards & its Ordered that he Keep the same in good repair According to Law --

12 October 1744 O. S., FOB 1, p. 208
The Order P Thomas Postgate & Others to View a Road &^{c} not being returned is Continued until the next Court to be Returned --

12 October 1744 O. S., FOB 1, p. 208
The Order P Robert McKay Junr & Others to View a Road &^c not being returned is Continued until the next Court to be returned --

9 November 1744 O. S., FOB 1, p. 222
On the Petition of George Hobson & Others for a Road from John Littlers Mill to William Gaddy's its Ordered that the said Road be Cleared by the Petitioners & that George Hobson & John Littler be Overseers of the same & its further Ordered that they keep said Road in good repair According to Law --

9 November 1744 O. S., FOB 1, p. 223
On the petition of Thomas Hankins Peter Woolf Edward Corder Darby Murphey Spencer Jons Isaac Gross Richard Pierceful John Read Marmaduke Vickory & John Nation for to have part of the Road which cometh from John Hites Mill Kersey's ford Cleared its Ordered that that part of the said Road from John Nations to the said ford be Cleared by the Petitioners & that John Nation be Overseer of the same & its further Ordered that he Keep the said Road in good repair according to Law --

10 November 1744 O. S., FOB 1, p. 226
On the motion of Samuel Earle Gent for Leave to Clear a Road from his Dwelling house to his Quarter Leave therefore is Granted him to Clear the same with this Own people as he think proper --

10 November 1744 O. S., FOB 1, p. 226
John Nation is hereby Appointed Overseer of the Road from the Run by his House to Kersey's ferry & its Ordered that he keep the said Road in good repair According to Law --

4 December 1744 O. S., FOB 1, p. 229
On the Petition of John Hardin & Others for a Road from John Nealands on Sherrando River to William Vestals its Ordered that Marquis Calmees John Linsey Gent & John Hardin View Mark & lay off the same & make return of their proceedings to the next Court --

4 December 1744 O. S., FOB 1, p. 229
On the Motion of Morgan Morgan Gent for a Road from his house to the Court house its Ordered that William McMachen Gent & George Hollingsworth View Mark & lay off the same & make return of their proceedings to the next Court --

4 December 1744 O. S., FOB 1, p. 229
Ordered that Thomas Chester David Vance Gent & Bathonia Haines View Mark & lay off a Road from the Mouth of Crooked Run the Nearest best way to the Courthouse & make return of their proceedings to the next Court & its further Ordered that the former Order for the said Road be reversed --

6 December 1744 O. S., FOB 1, p. 243
The Order P Thomas Postgate & Others to View a Road &c is Continued until the next Court to be returned --

6 December 1744 O. S., FOB 1, p. 243
The Order P Robert McKay & Others to View a Road from the Mouth of Crooked Run to Capt Jno Hites is Discontinued --

5 March 1744 O. S., FOB 1, p. 265
Ordered that Samuel Earle Gent in behalf of this Court Petition the Court of Prince William County for to meet this County with a Road from the Thorough fair at the Pignut Ridge to the top of the Blue Ridge at the head of Manasses Run --

5 March 1744 O. S., FOB 1, p. 265
Ordered that Robert Green Gent & John Newport petition the Court of Orange County for a Road from the County line of Frederick to the upper Inhabitants of Augusta on Woods River --

6 March 1744 O. S., FOB 1, pp. 275-276
Marquise Calmees John Linsey Gent. & John Hardin having viewed the Road from John Nealans on Sharrrando to William Vestals According to last Courts Order made their report in these words Pursuant to an Order of Court we have laid out & Viewed the Road from John Neelands on Sharoando to William Vestalls on the said River and have Concluded it to go as followeth from John Nealands down the said River to John Grimes's & thro' sum part of his fence still down the said River to Capt Striblings & then to leave the pond on the left side still down the said River to Timothy Haneys so thro' his fence by the Hillside so down the River to Darby Conelys & to Turn thro' a small part of his fence - to the right hand still to Continue down the River to Goldins as was - And to go thro' his field close to the River then down the said River to John Hammans there to go & there to go thro' his Tobacco Ground then down the said River to Thomas Hammans & there to go thro' a Small part of his fence & thro' his Yard & then down the said River to Elizabeth Pearsons there to turn to the Right hand & thro' sum of her fence & yard then across Pearsons Neck of Land to Jonathan Walkers & thro' his field & so the best way Over Bulskin & by Robert Hayes & along Hayes's path to Vestals. Whereupon it is Ordered that the said Road be from henceforth established a public Road and Enoch Pearson, Benj^a Frazier & John Brown are hereby Appointed Surveyors the same to be cleared & when cleared that they keep the same in good repair According to Law & its further Ordered that the Tithables living three Miles on Each side the said Road work on the same --

6 March 1744 O. S., FOB 1, p. 276
The Order for William M^{c}machen &^{c} to View a Road &^{c} is Continued until the next Court to be returned --

6 March 1744 O. S., FOB 1, p. 276
Thomas Chester & Bethony Haines having viewed the Road from the Mouth of Crooked Run to the Court=house according to last Courts Order made their report in these Words Pursuant to an Order of Court to us Directed we whose Names are under Written have Viewed Marked & laid

off a Road from the Mouth of Crooked Run & Crossing the said run the upper side of Thomas Bransons Plantation the Nearest & best way to the Courthouse Whereupon it is Ordered that the said Road be from henceforth established a public Road and Bathany Haines & Ralph Withers are hereby Appointed Surveyors theirof & it is Ordered that they cause the same to be in good repair according to Law & its further Ordered that the Tithables two Miles on each side of the Road work on the same --

6 March 1744 O. S., FOB 1, p. 276
The Order for Thomas Postgate &c to View a Road &c is Continued until the next Court to be returned --

9 March 1744 O. S., FOB 1, p. 283
On the Petition of Richard Crunk & Others for a Road from the County line thro' Howards Town to Joyn the New Road to this Courthouse its Ordered that a Road be Cleared accordingly & that the Tithables Convenient to the said Road work on the same And its further Ordered that Richard Crunk be Overseer & that he keep the said Road in good repair according to Law --

8 March 1744 O. S., FOB 1, p. 290
George Johnstone is hereby appointed Overseer of the Road from Scots Mill to the Court house in the room of Hugh Ferguson & Jn° Alford And its Ordered that he cause the said road to be Cleared & When Cleared that he keep the same in good repair According to Law --

9 March 1744 O. S., FOB 1, p. 298
John Littler is hereby Appointed Overseer of the Road in the Room of Jacob Hite Gent & its Ordered that he keep the said Road in good repair According to Law --

2 April 1744 O. S., FOB 1, p. 305
James Catlet is hereby Appointed Overseer of the Road from Howells ford to Ashby's Bent Gapp in the Room of Robert Ashby And its Ordered that he cause the same to be kept in Good repair According to Law --

2 April 1745 O. S., FOB 1, p. 315
The Order P Wm McMachen &c to View a Road &c is Continued until the next Court to be returned --

2 April 1745 O. S., FOB 1, p. 316
On the Petition of Thomas Branson Thomas Thorntown Thomas Sharp Jun[r] John Downton Edward Churchman John Branson Robert McKay Jun[r] Thomas Sharp Sen[r] Thomas Hankins Joseph Hankins Marmaduke Vickory Spencer Jones William Smith Bathany Haines William Ramor John Duckworth John Painter Thomas Postgate William Fearnley Hugh Caneday John Arledge James Sadin Thomas Alexander Edward Cordit John Gregory Abraham Crandon Robert Catlett William Remy James Kempes Benj[a] Gregory Christopher Nation John Nation for a Road from the Courthouse to Gregory's ford Its Ordered that the Petitioners Clear & Work on the same, And Samuel Earle is hereby Appointed Surveyor thereof And its further Ordered that he keep the said Road in good repair According to Law --

2 April 1745 O. S., FOB 1, p. 316
The Order P Thomas Postgate & Others to View a Road &^{c} is Continueed until the next Court to be returned --

2 April 1745 O. S., FOB 1, p. 323
John Linsey Gent Isaac Penington & Samuel Morris having returned that they had laid off a Road from this Courthouse to the top of the Blue Ridge of Mountains at William's Gap in these Words We report followeth That we have Viewed the Road road & think it most Convenient as it is Marked by us to go from Cap^n Neills off & on the Old Road to Joseph Wilkensons & Continuing thence Off on the same road to ffrancis Carney & from thence as mark to Edges Ford & from thence Off & On the Old Road to the Top of the said Mountain its therefore Ordered that the said Road be Cleared according to the said report & its further ordered that Thomas Colson be Appointed Overseer from Capt Lewis Neills to Francis Carneys Wm Jumpes from the said Carneys to Edges Ford on Shannadore River & Edward Garrett from ye s^d. ford to the Top of the Blue Ridge on W^{mss}. Gap & that all the Tithables wth in three Miles of each side ye Road from Neils to the River Clear ye said Road to the River & that all the tithables within five Miles of both sides of the River Clear ye same to the Top of the Mountain --

7 May 1745 O. S., FOB 1, p. 343
Grand Jury Presentments

We present Robert McCoy Junr for not Clearing the Road from Gregory's ford to West run According to Law within Six months past --

We present Jacob Brooks for not Clearing the Road from Opecken to Shanandore according to Law within Six months past --

We present Robert Wilson for not Clearing the Road whereof he is Surveyor according to Law within Six months past --

We present George Johnstone Gent for not Clearing the Road whereof he is Surveyor according to Law within Six months past --

We present Isaac Perkins for not Clearing the Road whereof he is Surveyor according to Law within Six months past --

8 May 1745 O. S., FOB 1, p. 349
James Bruce is hereby appointed Surveyor of the Road from the Courthouse to Lewis Neill Gent & its Ordered that the Tithables living two miles on Each side ye said Road Work on the same & that the same Bruce keep the said Road in good repair According to Law --

4 June 1745 O. S., FOB 1, p. 369
John Herrin is hereby Appointed Overseer of the Road from Potomack River to Thomas Rutherford Gent in the Room of Wm Davis, & the said William Davis is Cont^d. Overseer of the

Remaining part of the Road whereof he was formerly Appointed Surveyor & its Ordered that they keep the s^d. Road in Good repair According to Law –

4 June 1745 O. S., FOB 1, p. 369
John Littler & John Sheppard are hereby Overseers of the Road in the Room of Jacob Hite Gent And its Ordered that the said John Littler & John Sheppard cause the said Road to be Cleared & the Bridges repaired According to Law --

4 June 1745 O. S., FOB 1, p. 369
The Order P Thomas Postgate & Others to View a Road &^{c} Continued until the next Court to be returned --

5 June 1745 O. S., FOB 1, p. 374
Cobus Hogeland is hereby Appointed Overseer of the Road from Evan Watkins's Ferry to Tuscorora in the Room of John Shearer & its Ordered that he keep the said Road in good repair According to Law --

6 June 1745 O. S., FOB 1, p. 384
Ordered that the Tithables living within three Miles on each side the Road from the Courthouse to Lewis Neill Gent work on the Same under James Bruce who was last Court Appointed Surveyor thereof --

6 August 1745 O. S., FOB 1, p. 401
Ordered that all the Tithables living on this side of Opecken Creek within three Miles of the Road whereof James Bruce is Overseer Work on the same under the said James Bruce --

6 August 1745 O. S., FOB 1, p. 402
Thomas Postgate & John Gregory having Viewed the Road from the said Thomas Postgate's Island into the Road that comes from Thomas Chesters Gent according to an Order of this Court made their report in these Words, Viewed and Marked the Road within Mentioned Whereupon it is Ordered that the said Road be from henceforth Established a public Road & Samuel Earle is hereby Appointed Surveyor thereof & that the Tithables belonging to Thomas Postgate, Robert Halfpenny, James Burn, John Painter John Gregory & Thomas Alexander work on the same And it is further Ordered that the said Samuel Earle cause the said Road to be Cleared & when Cleared that he keep the same in good repair according to Law --

6 August 1745 O. S., FOB 1, p. 406
Ordered that William Miller & Jonathan Cobourn View Mark & lay off the Road Petitioned for by them John Rain & Solomon Hedges Gent & makes report of their proceedings to the said Court --

7 August 1745 O. S., FOB 1, p. 407
Ordered that the Sheriff sumons William Kersey to Appear at the next court to Answer the Petition of Joseph Edwards for not keeping the Road in repair whereof he is Overseer --

6 September 1745 O. S., FOB 1, p. 442
The Order of William Miller &c to View a Road &c is Continued until the next Court to be returned --

6 September 1745 O. S., FOB 1, p. 452
On the Motion of Thomas Chester Gent its Ordered that Thos Branson & Ralph Weathers View Mark & lay off the Nearest & best Way from Chesters fferry to Jno Hite & make return of their proceedings to the next Court --

6 September 1745 O. S., FOB 1, p. 452
On the Motion of Israel Robinson Gent its Ordered that Aaron Jenkins & Edward Robinson View Mark & Lay off a Road the nearest & best Way from the said Robinsons House into the Road that goes over Westalls Gapp & make return of there proceedings to the next Court --

6 September 1745 O. S., FOB 1, p. 453
On the motion of Thomas Rutherford Gent its Ordered that a Road be Cleared the nearest & best way from John McCormicks to Lewis Neil Gent & that the Tithables living within three Miles on each side of the said Road Work on the same. And its further Ordered that Jacob Penington be surveyor thereof & that he keep the said Road in good repair According to Law --

2 October 1745 O. S., FOB 1, p. 455
The Order for William Miller & Others to View & lay off a Road is continued until the next Court to be returned --

2 October 1745 O. S., FOB 1, p. 455
The Order for Thomas Branson & Others to View & lay Off a Road is Cont^d until the next Court to be returned --

2 October 1745 O. S., FOB 1, p. 445
The Order for Aaron Jenkins & Others to View & lay off a Road is Cont^d until the next Court to be returned --

3 October 1745 O. S., FOB 1, p. 466
Joseph Edwards
v.   On Petition
W^m. Kersey
The Road in the Petition Mentioned being Discontinued its Ordered that the said Pet^n be Dismis'd

3 October 1745 O. S., FOB 1, p. 466
Ordered that all the Tithables which work on the Road from Perkins Mill to Kerseys ferry be added to those formerly Ordered to Work on the Road from Johnstons Mill /: formerly Scots :/ to the Courthouse which said Road is hereby Established a Public Road And George Johnston is still continued Overseer of the same And it is further Ordered that the said Road from Perkins Mill to Kerseys ferry be discontinued --

3 October 1745 O. S., FOB 1, p. 466
Ordered that James Wood & William McMachen Gent View mark & lay off a Road from William Hoge Junr the Nearest and Best Way to the Courthouse & make return of their proceedings to the next Court.

Frederick County Order Book 2 (1745-1748)

5 November 1745 O. S., FOB 2, p. 2
Grand Jury Presentments

We present George Johnston Surveyor of the Road from the said Johnstons Mill to this Courthouse for not Clearing the said Road According to Law within Six Months last past by the Information of Meredith Helms Gent --
* * *
We present Leonard Helms for not Clearing the road According to Law -- within Six Months last past.
* * *
We present Robert McCoy for not Clearing the Road According to Law within Six Months last past --
* * *
We present George Bowman Surveyor of the Road from Ceder Creek to West Run for not clearing the said Road According to law within Six Months last past --
* * *
We present Thomas Rees Surveyor of the Road for not clearing the said Road According to Law within Six Months last past --
* * *
We present Robert Warf Surveyor of the Highway for not Clearing the same according to Law within six Months last past --
* * *
We present Jacob Nicewanger Surveyor of the highway for not clearing the same According to Law within six months last past --

[Note: Asterisks have been added to indicate portions skipped.]

6 November 1745 O. S., FOB 2, p. 4
Ordered that James Wood & William McMachen Gent View Mark & lay off a Road the Nearest & Best Way from the Courthouse to William Hoge Junr which said Road is from henceforth Establish a Public Road & William Rennolds is hereby Appointed Surveyor thereof And it is further Ordered that he with the Tithables living within three Miles of the said Road Clear & Work on the same According to Law --

6 November 1745 O. S., FOB 2, p. 4
On the Motion of Leonard Helms it is Ordered that the Tithables living on the Other Side Sharrando River above Marquis Calmes Gent work on the Road from ye River to the Top of the Ridge & that the Tithables on this Side of the Said River be exempted from working on the same

6 November 1745 O. S., FOB 2, p. 4
The Order P William Miller &^{c} to View a Road &^{c} not being returned to Same is Continued until the next Court to be returned --

6 November 1745 O. S., FOB 2, p. 4
The Order P Aaron Jenkins &^{c} to View a Road &^{c} not being returned the same is Continued until the next Court to be returned --

7 November 1745 O. S., FOB 2, p. 7
Thomas Shepard is hereby Appointed Overseer of the Road in the Room of Thomas Swearingham Gent & its Ordered that he keep the said Road in good repair According to Law --

7 November 1745 O. S., FOB 2, p. 8
Ralph Withers & John Branson having Viewed the Road from Chesters Ferry to the Courthouse according to an Order of Court made their report in these words Pursuant to an Order of Court to us directed we whose names are underwritten Have Viewed Marked & laid of a Road the Nearest & Best Way from Chesters Ferry to John Hites as follows from the Landing place at the point up the Bottom to the first Gapp in Guard Hill over ye Said Hill & Crooked Run to ye upper side Robert McKays Spring thence the nearest way to Crooked Run above Thos Bransons ther Crossing the said Run thence along ye Road laid of by Bethany Haines to John Hites Whereupon it is Ordered that the said Road be from henceforth established a Bridle Road And William Rentfroe & Bathany Haines are hereby Appointed Surveyors thereof And it is further Ordered that they wth. the Tithables living within three Miles on Each Side the said Road clear the same & make Bridges therein it is requisite according to Law --

5 December 1745 O. S., FOB 2, p. 22
Thomas Colson is hereby Appointed Overseer of the Road from Francis Carnaham to the Courthouse in the Room of James Bruce and it is Ordered that he keep the said Road in good repair according to Law --

5 December 1745 O. S., FOB 2, p. 23
On the motion of Solomon Hedges Gent for a Road from Buffintons to Carrols Place on Pattersons Creek Its Ordered that the Inhabitants of the said Creek Clear & work on the same under the said Solomon Hedges who is hereby Appointed Surveyor thereof And its further Ordered that he keep the said Road in good repair According to Law --

4 March 1745 O. S., FOB 2, p. 25
John Hite is hereby Appointed Surveyor of the Highways from the said John Hites to Isaac Perkins's Mill in the Room of the said Isaac Perkins And it is Order that the said John Hite cause the Highways to be Cleared & the Bridges Repaired According to Law --

4 March 1745 O. S., FOB 2, p. 25
Ralph Humfrey is hereby Appointed Surveyor of the Highways from Isaac Perkin's Mill to the said Ralph Humfreys in the Room of the said Isaac Perkins And it is Ordered that the said Ralph Humfrey cause the Highways to be cleared & the Bridges repaired According to Law --

4 March 1745 O. S., FOB 2, p. 26
John Neill is Continued Overseer of the Road from Opecken ford by his Mill to Kerseys ferry whereof he was formerly Appointed & it is Ordered that he cause the said Road to be kept in good repair According to Law --

4 March 1745 O. S., FOB 2, p. 28
On the Petition of Lewis Stephens, Martin Cartmell, Nathaniel Cartmell, Edward Cartmell, Benjamin Smith, Christopher Acklin, Samuel Vance, Samuel Glass, Joseph Glass, David Glass, Jacob Cooper, Joseph Fawcett, Thos Fawcett, John Fawcett, Richard Fawcett, [blank in book] Snapp for a Road from Lewis Stephens's Mills the Nearest & Best way to the Courthouse It is Ordered that David Glass & John Bullah [Beelah?] View Mark & lay of the same, And Paul ffroman & Nathaniel Cartmell are hereby Appointed Surveyors therof And its further Ordered that they with the Petitioners Clear & Work on the said Road & when Cleared that they Keep the said Road in good repair According to Law --

4 March 1745 O. S., FOB 2, p. 28
William Roberts and John Jones are hereby Appointed Overseers of the Road from the Courthouse to Johnston's Mill in the Room of George Johnston And it is Ordered that the said Wm Robert & John Jones cause the said Road to be kept in good repair According to Law --

4 March 1745 O. S., FOB 2, p. 28
George Dellener is hereby Appointed Overseer of the Road from Ceedar Creek to Funk's Mill & also Frederick Gabbert is hereby Appointed Overseer of the road from the said Funk's Mill to the County Line & its Ordered that the Tithables living within three miles of the said Road Work on the same And its further Ordered that the said George Dellener & Frederick Gabbert Cause the said Road to be Kept in good repair According to Law --

4 March 1745 O. S., FOB 2, p. 28
Ordered that W^m McMachen Gent, Alexander Ross & Josiah Ballinger View Mark & lay off a Road the Nearest & best Way from Morgan Morgan Gent to the Courthouse And George Hollingsworth is hereby Appointed Overseer from the Courthouse to the House of Josiah Ballinger And the said Josiah Ballenger from his House to the said Morgan Morgan's And it is further Ordered that the Tithables living within two Miles of Each side the said Road Clear & work on the same & that the said George Hollingsworth & Josiah Ballenger keep the said Road in good repair According to Law --

4 March 1745 O. S., FOB 2, p. 28
Ordered that Marquis Calmes Gent View Mark & lay off a Road the Nearest & best Way from the School House on the River to the Chapple at Cunninghams And the said Marq [torn] Appointed Surveyor thereof And it is further [torn] Tithables on both sides the River from

Hardins to John Madden /: Including the said Hardins Tithables:/ Clear & Work on the same And that said marquis Calmes cause the said Road to be Kept in good repair According to Law --

5 March 1745 O. S., FOB 2, p. 35
Colvert Anderson is hereby Appointed Overseer of the Road in the Room of William Mitchell And it is Ordered that he cause the said Road to be Kept in good repair According to Law --

6 March 1745 O. S., FOB 2, p. 45
Grandjury v. Geo:^{e} Johnston
The said George Johnston being presented for not clearing the Road whereof he was Surveyor & Appearing & saying nothing in Barr thereof at the motion of Gabriel Jones Attorney for the King, it is Ordered that he be fined fifteen shillings for the same according to Law & Costs & the Def^t in Mercy &^{c} --

6 March 1745 O. S., FOB 2, p. 45
Grandjury v. Leonard Helms
The Def^t failing to Appear & Answer the said Presentment ags^t him for not clearing the Road according to Law at the motion of Gabriel Jones Attorney for the King it is Ordered that he be fined fifteen shillings for the same according to Law & Costs --

6 March 1745 O. S., FOB 2, p. 45
Grandjury v. Robt McCoy
The Def^t failing to Appear & Answer the said Presentment ags^t him for not clearing the Road according to Law at the motion of Gabriel Jones Attorney for the King it is Ordered that he be fined fifteen shillings for the same according to Law & Costs --

6 March 1745 O. S., FOB 2, p. 45
Grandjury v. George Bowman
The Def^t failing to Appear & Answer the said Presentment ags^t him for not clearing the Road according to Law at the motion of Gabriel Jones Attorney for the King it is Ordered that he be fined fifteen shillings for the same according to Law & Costs --

6 March 1745 O. S., FOB 2, p. 46
Grandjury v. Thos Rees
The Def^t failing to Appear & Answer the said Presentment ags^t him for not clearing the Road according to Law at the motion of Gabriel Jones Attorney for the King it is Ordered that he be fined fifteen shillings for the same according to Law & Costs --

6 March 1745 O. S., FOB 2, p. 46
Grandjury v. Robt Warth
The Def^t failing to Appear & Answer the said Presentment ags^t him for not clearing the Road according to Law at the motion of Gabriel Jones Attorney for the King it is Ordered that he be fined for the same fifteen shillings according to Law & Costs --

6 March 1745 O. S., FOB 2, p. 46
Grandjury v. Jacob Nisewanger
The Def^t failing to Appear & Answer the said Presentment ags^t him for not clearing the Road whereof he is Surveyor according to Law at the motion of Gabriel Jones Attorney for the King it is Ordered that he be fined for the same fifteen shillings for the same according to Law & Costs --

1 April 1746 O. S., FOB 2, p. 70
John Neill & William McKee are hereby Appointed Overseer of the Road from Opecken ford by the said Neills Mill to Kerseys Ferry & its Ordered that the Tithables living within three Miles on Each side the said Road work on the same & its further Ordered that they keep the said Road in good repair According to Law --

1 April 1746 O. S., FOB 2, p. 70
Nicholas Handshaw is hereby Appointed Overseer of the Road in the Room of Thomas Reece & its Ordered that he keep the said Road in good repair According to Law --

1 April 1746 O. S., FOB 2, p. 70
Aaron Jenkins & Edward Robinson having Viewed the Road from Israel Robinsons Gent House into the Road that goes Over Vestals Gapp according to an Order of Court made their report in these Words executed & returned According to the within Order Directs whereupon its Ordered that the said Road be from henceforth established a Publick Road & Hugh Paul is hereby Appointed Surveyor thereof & it is further Ordered that Israel Robinson give the said Hugh Paul a List of the Tithables Convenient to the said Road which are Ordered to work on the same under the said Hugh Paul & it is likewise Ordered that he cause the said Road to be cleared & when cleared that he keep the same in Good repair According to Law --

1 April 1746 O. S., FOB 2, p. 71
George Bowman is on his Petition Discharged from being Overseer of the Road whereof he was formerly Appointed --

1 April 1746 O. S., Fob 2, p. 72
Thomas Brown & Mordecai Mendenhall are hereby Appointed Overseer of the Road in the Room of Patrick Gillaspy & John Bails & its Ordered that they cause the said Road to be kept in Good Repair According to Law --

2 April 1746 O. S., FOB 2, p. 79
Isaac Perkins is hereby Appointed Overseer of the Road from his Mill thro' the Town to the line thereof by Andrew Caldwells & it is Ordered that the Tithables within a Mile & half of the said Road Work on the same and it is further ordered that the said Isaac Perkins cause the Stumps and Grubbs in the Main Street of the said Town to be Cut up & the Holes filled from side to side & of the same & also to Clear the Drane which runs thro' the said Town --

6 May 1746 O. S., FOB 2, p. 80
On the motion of Isaac Perkins Its Ordered that he & his Tithables be exempted from working on any Road except the Road from his Mill to the North End of the Town whereof he is Overseer while he continues in the said Office --

6 May 1746 O. S., FOB 2, p. 80
On the motion of John Linsey Gent for a Road from his house into the Road which leads from the Courthouse to ffairfax County It is Ordered that he with Samuel Morris[?] View Mark & lay off the same And John Howard is hereby appointed surveyor thereof And its further Ordered that the Tithables living within four Miles of the said Road Clear & Work on the same & When Cleared the said John Howard cause the said Road to be kept in good repair According to Law --

6 May 1746, O. S., FOB 2, p. 81
Grand Jury Presentments

We present the Surveyors of the Road from Jacob Hites' to John Littlers for not keeping the same in repair According to Law --

7 May 1746 O. S., FOB 2, p. 88
Ordered that John Hampton & Thomas Low View Mark & lay off a Road the Nearest & best way from the Chaple to the Old Road which leads to William Mitchel's & Colvert Anderson is hereby Appointed Surveyor thereof And its further Ordered that the Tithables now under him Clear & work on the same & when Cleared that he cause the said Road to be Kept in good repair According to Law --

7 May 1746 O. S., FOB 2, p. 88
Ordered that John McCormack View Mark & lay off a Road the Nearest & best Way from his house to Opecken Creek & that Hugh Perrill William Albin & Simeon Taylor View Mark & lay of a Road from that part the said Creek were the said McCormack Ends the Nearest & best Way to the Courthouse & that they make report thereof to the next Court --

7 May 1746 O. S., FOB 2, p. 88
Ordered that Lewis Neill Gent & Patrick Rice View Mark & lay off a Road from [torn] the Nearest & best way to the Chapel at Cunningham's & make report thereof at the next Court --

3 June 1746 O. S., FOB 2, p. 102
William Dillon is hereby Appointed Overseer of the Road from Captn Frosts Mill to the Main Road between John Littler & John Milburns in the Room of William Frost & it is Ordered that the Tithables living within Two Miles on Each Side the said Road work on the same And it is further Ordered that the said Wm Dillon cause the said road to be kept in good repair According to Law --

3 June 1746 O. S., FOB 2, p. 102
Alexander Ross is hereby Appointed Overseer of the Road from his fence to the Corner of Smith's fence in the Room of Edward Thomas And it is Ordered that he keep the said Road in good repair According to Law --

3 June 1746 O. S., FOB 2, p. 103
David Lewis is hereby Appointed Overseer of the Road from Smith's fence to Jacob Hite Gent in the Room of John Littler And it is Ordered that he keep the said Road in good repair According to Law --

5 June 1746 O. S., FOB 2, p. 109
Thos Waters is hereby Appointed Overseer of the Road in the Room of William Roberts And it is Ordered that the Cause the said Road to be kept in good repair According to Law --

5 August 1746 O. S., FOB 2, p. 113
Ordered that Mordacai Mendenhall & Jacobus Hogeland join the Tithables Appointed to Work under them together & make a Sufficient Bridge Over Tuscarora Creek --

5 August 1746 O. S., FOB 2, p. 113
On the Petition of the Inhabitants of Potomack River it is Ordered that Israel Robinson Gent Thomas Berwick & Thos Cherry View Mark & lay off a Road from the Meeting house at the Gap of the Mountains above Hugh Pauls to the Warm Spring And James Boyl is hereby Appointed Overseer from the said Spring to Sleepy Creek & Edwd Robinson from Sleepy Creek to the Meeting house And it is further Ordered that the Tithables living within Six Miles on Each Side of the said Road Clear & Work on the same & when Cleared that the said James Boyl & Edward Robinson Keep the Said Road in Good repair According to Law --

5 August 1746 O. S., FOB 2, p. 114
Ordered that John Linsey Gent Isaac Pennington John Petite & Jacob Brooks View Mark & lay off a Road the Nearest & Best Way from Andrew Campbell Gent to Kersey's ferry & make Report thereof to the next Court --

6 August 1746 O. S., FOB 2, p. 129
On the motion of Edward Garrat it is Ordered that all the Tithables living within five miles of Edges ford work on the Road whereof he is now Overseer --

7 August 1746 O. S., FOB 2, p. 139
The Order for John McCormack & Others to View a Road &^{c} is Continued to be Returned --

7 August 1746 O. S., FOB 2, p. 139
The Order for Lewis Neill Gent & Others to View a Road &^{c} is continued until the next Court to be returned --

2 September 1746 O. S., FOB 2, p. 169
The Order P John McCormack & Others to View a Road is Continued until the next Court to be Returned --

2 September 1746 O. S., FOB 2, p. 169
The Order P Lewis Neill Gent & Others to View a Road &^c is Continued until the next Court to be Returned --

2 September 1746 O. S., FOB 2, p. 169
The Order P John Linsey Gent & Others to View a Road &^c is Continued until the next Court to be returned --

2 September 1746 O. S., FOB 2, p. 171
Jonathan Curtis presented his Petition to the Court for leave to Clear a Road from his house to Edward Beasons Mill, leave therefore is Granted the said Jonathan Curtis to Clear the same at his Own Expense The said Road having first laid off by Wm Baldwin & Benjamin Beason who are hereby Appointed to View the same --

7 October 1746 O. S., FOB 2, p. 181
On the Complaint of Thomas Colson its Ordered that all the Tithables living upon the long Marsh work on the Road from Lewis Neill Gent to Francis Carnies under the said Thomas Colson Overseer of the said Road --

9 October 1746 O. S., FOB 2, p. 187
John Linsey Isaac Penington John Peteat & Jacob Brooks having viewed the Road from Andrew Campbells Gent to the Chapple at Cunningham's according to an Order of this Court made their report in these Words In regard to an Order made at Frederick County Court in laying Out a Road from Maj^r Campbells to the Chapple at Cunninghams We viewed and marked as followeth along the main Road from Major Campbells to Joseph Evans's than thro' the Woods to William Mitchells than cross Opecken then thro' the woods to the head of the South fork of the Bulskin from thence as marked to Thomas Linseys'ses on the Long Marsh fromthence to Jno Linseys Gent & from thence to the Chapple at Cunninghams Whereupon It is Ordered that the said Road be from henceforth the Established Publicks Road And John Morris, John McCormack Jacob Penington Thos Linsey & James McKee are hereby Appointed Surveyors thereof Viz John Morris from Campbells to Opecken, John McCormack from Opecken to the head of Bulskin, Jacob Penington from the head of Bulskin to the Long Marsh Thomas Linsey from the Long marsh to Fairfax Road And James McKee from the Fairfax Road to the Chapple, And it is ordered that the Tithables living within five miles on Each side of the said Road Clear and Work on the same, And it is further Ordered that they the said John Morris John McCormack Jacob Penington Thomas Linsey & James McKee cause their several respective parts of the said Road to be Cleared & when Cleared that they cause the same to be kept in good repair According to Law--

9 October 1746 O. S., FOB 2, p. 187
Patrick Kersey is hereby Appointed Overseer of the Road in the Room of John Brown And it is Ordered that he Cause the said Road whereof he is new Appointed Overseer to be kept in good repair According to Law --

9 October 1746 O. S., FOB 2, p. 187
Ordered that that part of the Road which lead from Lewis Neills Gent to Kerseys ferry be Discontinued until the next Court --

4 November 1746 O. S., FOB 2, p. 193
Lewis Neill & Patrick Rice having Viewed the Road from Opecken Creek to the Chappel by James Cunnningham's according to an Order of this Court made their report in these words. We have marked & laid off a Road from Opecken Creek to the Chappel by James Cunninghams Beginning on the said Creek at John Neills ford by his House & so off on the Old Path that formerly went to James Hills until we came to the forks of the Old Waggon Road commonly called Littlers Waggon Road & from thence thro' the Woods along the S.W. side of Hills Marsh to Cunninghams house & so to the Chapple, Whereupon it is Ordered that the said Road be from henceforth established a publick Road And James Hill is hereby Appointed Surveyor thereof. And it is Ordered that the Tithables living within three miles of the said Road Clear & Work on the same & that the said James Hill cause the said Road to be kept in good Repair According to Law --

3 December 1746 O. S., FOB 2, p. 201
Ordered that George Johnston Gent Draw up a request to the Court of Prince William for a Road from Jefrey Johnstons at the Pignutt Ridge to the Top of the Ridge at Ashby bent --

3 March 1746 O. S., FOB 2, p. 202
Joseph Helms is hereby Appointed Overseer of the Road in the Room of Jacob Funk deced. And its Ordered that the said Joseph Helms Cause the said Road to be kept in good repair according to Law --

3 March 1746 O. S., FOB 2, p. 202
Thomas Branson is hereby Appointed Overseer of the Road in the room of Bathany Haines And its Ordered that the said Thomas Branson cause the said Road to be kept in good repairs according to Law --

3 March 1746 O. S., FOB 2, p. 203
Joseph Carter is hereby Appointed Overseer of the Road from Lewis Neills Gent to the Courthouse in the Room of Thomas Colson And its Ordered that the said Joseph Carter cause the said Road to be kept in good repair According to Law --

3 March 1746 O. S., FOB 2, p. 203
Thomas Colson is hereby Appointed Overseer of the Road from the Fairfax Road to John Linsey's Gent in the Room of John Howard And its Ordered that the said Thomas Calson cause the said Road to be kept in good repair According to Law --

3 March 1746 O. S., FOB 2, p. 204
John Mills is hereby Appointed Overseer of the Road from Middle Creek to Mill Creek in the Room of Thomas Brown & its Ordered that the said John Mills cause the said Road to be kept in good repair According to Law --

4 March 1746 O. S., FOB 2, p. 207
Charles Donahue is hereby Appointed Overseer of the Road from his house to Potomack River in the Room of Jacobus Hogeland & its Ordered that the said Charles Donahue cause the said Road to be kept in good repair according to Law --

4 March 1746 O. S., FOB 2, p. 207
John Wilson is hereby Appointed Overseer of the Road from Charles Donahues to Tuscorora Creek in the Room of Jacobus Hogeland And its Ordered that the said John Wilson cause the said Road to be in good repair according to Law --

4 March 1746 O. S., FOB 2, p. 207
Jeremiah Smith is hereby Appointed Overseer of the Road from his house to Wm Hoges Junr. in the room of Owen Thomas And its Ordered that the said Jeremiah Smith cause the said Road to be kept in good repair according to Law --

4 March 1746 O. S., FOB 2, p. 207
Nicholas Mercer is hereby Appointed Overseer of the Road from Opecken to David Loyd's in the Room of Thomas Hart And its Ordered that the said Nich^s Mercer cause the said Road to be kept in good Repair According to Law --

4 March 1746 O. S., FOB 2, p. 207
Jonas Hedge is hereby Appointed Overseer of the Road from Opecken to Robinson's Gap in the Room of Richard Beeson & its Ordered that the said Jonas Hedge cause the said Road to be Kept in good repair according to Law --

4 March 1746 O. S., FOB 2, p. 207
Joseph Hite is hereby Appointed Overseer of the Road from Thomas Rutherfords Spring to William Mitchels in the Room of Jacob Brooks And its Ordered that the said Joseph Hites cause the said Road to be kept in good repair according to Law --

4 March 1746 O. S., FOB 2, p. 207
Ordered that Thomas Lowe and Isaac Ewins View Mark & lay off a Bridle Road the nearest and best way from Morgan Morgan Gent to Andrew Campbell's Gent and make report of their proceedings to the next Court --

4 March 1746 O. S., FOB 2, p. 208
Ordered that Richard Stevenson, Overseer of the Road from Thomas Rutherford Gent to the Head of Bullskin, Clear the said Road according to the Direction of the said Thomas Rutherford --

5 March 1746 O. S., FOB 2, p. 208
On the Petition of James Coddy Thomas Smith John Parks William Naylor Josiah Arnold George Potts Darby McKeaver Samuel Farrington George Hoge Peter Foster & Walter Drening for a Road from Parks's Grave yard near Cape Capon Water, over Dellings Run into the Waggon Road on Joseph Edwards Land, It is Ordered, that the said Road be cleared by the said Petitioners & that they work on the same under James Coddy who is hereby Appointed Surveyor thereof. And it is further Ordered that the said James Coddy cause the said Road to be kept in good repair & make Bridges thereon where required according to Law --

5 March 1746 O. S., FOB 2, p. 208
John McCormack Hugh Parrel & Simeon Taylor having viewed the Road from Bullskins to the Courthouse according to an Order of this Court made their report in these words. In Regard to an Order of Court it was Appointed that John McCormick Hugh Parrel & Simeon Taylor should view a Road from Bullskin to the Courthouse which Road we have Marked as followeth from the head of the South fork of Bullskin to Opecken & thence to the Courthouse Whereupon it is Ordered that the said Road be from henceforth Established a Publick Road And John McCormack & Hugh Parrel are hereby Appointed Surveyors thereof And it is further Ordered that they Clear the same & make Bridges thereon where it is requisite According to Law --

5 March 1746 O. S., FOB 2, p. 212
Thomas Lowe is hereby Appointed Overseer of the Road from Morgan Morgans Chapple to William Mitchells in the Room Culbert Anderson and its Ordered that he keeps the said Road in Good Repair According to Law --

5 March 1746 O. S., FOB 2, p. 214
Samuel Morris is hereby Appointed Overseer of the Road from the Fairfax Road to the Chapple at Cunningham's in the Room of James McKee And its Ordered that the said Samuel Morris cause the said Road to be kept in good repair According to Law --

3 March 1746 O. S., FOB 2, p. 215
Christopher Beeler is hereby Appointed Overseer of the Road from the Head of Bullskin to the Long Marsh in the Room of Jacob Penington & Its Ordered that the said Christopher Beeler cause the said Road to be Kept in good repairs according to Law --

7 April 1747 O. S., FOB 2, p. 225
On the petition of Thomas Thornbur[torn] [E]dward Strode & Others for a Road from the said Thornbury's Mill to Opecken Creek by Edward Strouds & from thence into the Road that Leads[torn] Jacob Hite's to Vestal's ford on Sharando River. Its Ordered that G[torn] Hobson Junr. & Simon Moon View Mark & lay off the same & make report thereof to the next Court --

7 April 1747 O. S., FOB 2, p. 227
James McGrew is hereby Appointed Overseer of a Road in the Room of Simeon Taylor & its Ordered that the said James McGrew cause the said Road to be kept in good repair According to Law --

5 May 1747 O. S., FOB 2, p. 241
Grand Jury Presentments

We present Thomas Branson Surveyor of the Road from John Hites to Crooked Run for not Clearing Grubing & Keeping the said Road in repair According to Law within Six Months last past --

* * *

We present Enoch Pearson Surveyor of the Road from Vestals Gapp to the Long Marsh for not Clearing Grubing & Keeping the said Road in repair according to Law within Six Months last past --

* * *

(p. 242) We present George Dilliner Surveyor of the Road from John Funks Mill to Ceder Creek for not Clearing Grubing & Keeping the said Road in repair according to Law within Six Months last past --

* * *

-- it is Ordered that the Sheriff of this County Summon the Several persons presented to Appear at the next Court to Answer the several presentments ags^t them --

2 June 1747 O. S., FOB 2, p. 255
On the Petition of Thomas Berwick It is Ordered that Thomas Swearingen Gent William Mitchell and Robert Davis or any two of them View Mark and lay off a Road from the meeting house at the Gap of the Mountains to Hugh Pauls from thence to Thomas Cherrys & by Daniel Roses up the Bottom to Thomas Berwicks & from the said Berwicks to the Warm Springs, And that the Tithables living within Six Miles on Each side the said Road clear & work on the same, And Hugh Paul is hereby appointed Overseer from the said meeting house to Sleepy Creek and James Bayles from Sleepy Creek to the said Springs, And it is further Ordered that the said Hugh Paul & James Bayl cause the said Road to be cleared & when cleared that they cause the said Road to be kept in good repair according to Law --

2 June 1747 O. S., FOB 2, p. 255
Thomas Branson & Lawrence Stephens are hereby Appointed Overseers of the Road in the Room of Bathany Haines And it is Ordered that they cause the said road to be Kept in good repair according to Law --

4 August 1747 O. S., FOB 2, p. 259
On the motion of Lawrence Stephens it is Ordered that the Tithables living within four miles on Each side the Road whereof he is Overseer, work on the same --

1 September 1747 O. S., FOB 2, p. 313
Ordered that a Road be Cleared the Nearest & Bestway from the Chapple at James Cunninghams to the Chapple at Robert McCoys Spring And John Hardin & Samuel Earle are hereby Appointed Surveyors thereof the said Hardin from the said Chapple at Cunninghams to the Spring called Bordens Great Spring And the said Earle from the said Great Spring to the Chapple at McCoy's Spring And that the Tithables living within four Miles of Each side & Two Miles at Each End of the said Road /: Except the Tithables living on the South side of the River :/ Clear and Work on

the same, And it is further Ordered that the said Hardin & Earle Keep the said Road in good repair According to Law --

1 September 1747 O. S., FOB 2, p. 313
Ordered that the Tithables living within three Miles of the Road whereof John Nation is Overseer work on the said Road under the said Overseer --

1 September 1747 O. S., FOB 2, p. 313
Ordered that the sherif sumons John Morris, John McCormack Thomas Linsey Samuel Morris & Christopher Bealer to Appear at the next Court to Answer the Complaint of Jacob Hite Gent for not Clearing the Road whereof they are Overseers according to Law --

1 September 1747 O. S., FOB 2, p. 313
Ordered that the sherif sumons William McKee to Appear at the next Court to Answer the Complaint of John Neill for not Clearing the Road whereof he is Overseer According to Law --

2 September 1747 O. S., FOB 2, p. 323
William Hoge Junr came into Court & prayed leave to Open the Road Round his plantation which goes from the Court house to the South Branch the said Road as it now lies being of Great hurt to him & leave therefore is Granted him to Clear the same with his Own Hands according to the Opinion of James Wood & William McMachen Gent who are hereby Appointed to View the same --

2 September 1747 O. S., FOB 2, p. 330
Ordered that the Sherif Sumons the Overseers of the Road from John Littlers Old Place to Patrick Ryley's to Appear at the next Court to Answer the Complain of Andrew Campbell Gent ags^t them for not keeping the said Road in repair According to Law --

3 November 1747 O. S., FOB 2, p. 343
County Levy
To Samuel Earle for setting up Posts and &^{c} 50 [lb. Tobo]

3 November 1747 O. S., FOB 2, p. 343
On the motion of James Wood Gent for Leave to alter the Road which leads from the Court house to William Hoge Junr, Leave therefore is Granted him to alter the same the most Convenient way, And it is Ordered that the Inhabitants of the Town Clear the same --

3 November 1747 O. S., FOB 2, p. 343
Peter Woolf is hereby Appointed Overseer of the Road from Bordens Great Spring to James Cunninghams in the Room of John Hardin And it is Ordered that the said Peter Woolf cause the said Road to be Kept in good repair according to Law --

3 November 1747 O. S., FOB 2, p. 346
Robert McCoy and John Marley are hereby Appointed to view that part of the Road which leads from John Hites to the Chapple at McCoy's Springs which is turned by Thomas Branson and

make return to the next Court whether a better or more convenient Road may not be found to the said Chapple than what is made by the said Branson --

4 November 1747 O. S., FOB 2, p. 349
Ordered that John Linsey Gent & Patrick Matthews View Mark and lay off a Road the Nearest & Best way from the head of Pitts's Marsh to the Chapple at James Cunningham's & make report thereof to the next Court --

4 November 1747 O. S., FOB 2, p. 350
Ralph Withers is hereby Appointed Overseer of the Road from Thomas Branson's Mill to Thomas Chesters in the Room of William Rentfro and it is Ordered that the said Ralph Cause the said Road to be Kept in good repair according to Law --

4 November 1747 O. S., FOB 2, p. 351
Israel Robinson Gent & Robert Davis are hereby Appointed to View & Inspect whether the publick Road which leads from Andrew Campbells Gent to Watkins's Ferry can conveniently be turned by the Plantation formerly Jonathan Jayeas, deced now in the Possession of Elizabeth Dyer, & make report thereof to the next Court --

1 December 1747 O. S., FOB 2, p. 353
John Carsine is hereby Appointed Overseer of the Road from Francis Karney's to the River in the Room of William Jump deced And it is Ordered that the said John Carsine Cause the said Road to be Kept in good repair according to Law --

1 December 1747 O. S., FOB 2, p. 354
Robert McKay Junr & John Marley being Appointed last Court to View that part of the Road which leads from John Hites to the Chapple at McCoys Spring turned by Thomas Branson made their report in these words. In Obedience to the Court Consistent to the written Order having Viewed the said Road have Marked the same in the best Order; It is Ordered that the Tithables which work under Thomas Branson Clear the said Road as it is laid Off by the said Viewers & when cleared that the said Thomas Branson cause the said Road to be Kept in good repairs According to Law --

1 March 1747 O. S., FOB 2, p. 366
Henry Bowen Junr is hereby Appointed Overseer of the Road from Mill Creek to Opecken in the Room of Nicholas Hancher and it is Ordered that the said Henry Bowen Junr cause the said Road to be kept in good repair according to Law --

1 March 1747 O. S., FOB 2, p. 366
Thomas Provin is hereby Appointed Overseer of the Road from Jno Frosts Mill to the Main Road betwist John Littlers & John Milburns in the Room of William Dillon & it is Ordered that the said Thomas Provin cause the said Road to be kept in good repair according to Law --

1 March 1747 O. S., FOB 2, p. 366
Christopher Marr is hereby appointed Overseer of the Road from Howels ford to Foxtrap Point on the South Side of Shanando in the Room of James Cattlet & it is Ordered that the said Christopher cause the said Road to be kept in good repair according to Law --

1 March 1747 O. S., FOB 2, p. 367
On the Petition of George Hoge Matthew Harbinson Joseph Langdon George Lockmiller [blank in book], William Stephenson W^m. White William Blackburn Archibald Blackburn Isaac White William Wilson George Eger William Blackburn Junr James Blackburn James Young Matthew Young & Benjamin Blackburn for a Road from the County line by Thomas Little Gent to Lewis Stephens Mill It is Orderd that the said Road according as it is laid off by John Blackburn & George Seller who are hereby Appointed to View Mark & lay off the same And it is further Ordered that the Tithables living within two Miles on Each side the said Road together with the Petitioners clear & Work on the same And that the said John Blackburn & George Sellers be Overseers thereof who are also Ordered to Keep the said Road in good repairs according to Law

1 March 1747 O. S., FOB 2, p. 367
Thomas Sharp is hereby Appointed Overseer of the Road that lead from John Hite to Crooked Run in the Room Thomas Branson and it is ordered that the said Thomas Sharp cause the said Road to be Kept in good repair according to Law --

1 March 1747 O. S., FOB 2, p. 367
On the Petition of John Littler leave is granted him to clear a Road at his Own Costs from his Mill cross Opecken at the Mouth of his Mill run --

1 March 1747 O. S., FOB 2, p. 368
John Milburn is hereby Appointed Overseer of the Road from the Courthouse to Lewis Neill Gent & it is Ordered that the said John Milburn cause the said Road to be Kept in good repair according to Law --

1 March 1747 O. S., FOB 2, p. 368
John Melton is hereby appointed Overseer of the Road in the Room of Edward Garrat & it is Ordered that the said John Melton cause the said Road to be Kept in good repair according to Law --

2 March 1747 O. S., FOB 2, p. 370
John Evans is hereby Appointed Overseer of the Road from Tuscorora to Middle Creek in the Room of Mordecai Mendenhal & it is Ordered that the said John Evans cause the said Road to be Kept in good repair according to Law --

2 March 1747 O. S., FOB 2, p. 370
On the Petition of John Jones it is Ordered that all the Tithables above the road whereof the said Jones is now Overseer as high as Cabbin Run & all the Tithables living within three Miles of the Other side the said Road work on the same under the said John Jones

2 March 1747 O. S., FOB 2, p. 370
Ordered that Isaac Evans & John Bales View Mark & lay Off a Road the nearest & best way from Morgan Morgan Gent to Andrew Campbell Gent And that all the Tithables living between Opecken and the Mountain Clear & Work on the same under the said Morgan Morgan & Andrew Campbell who are hereby Appointed Overseers thereof And it is further Ordered that the said Overseers cause the said Road to be Cleared & when Cleared that they Keep the said Road in good repair According to Law --

3 March 1747 O. S., FOB 2, p. 385
Ordered that Lewis Neill & John Linsey Gent View alter and Amend the Road which leads from the Courthouse to the said Neills and that the Overseer of the said Road cause the same to be Cleared as laid off by them by the Tithables Ordered to Work thereon

5 March 1747 O. S., FOB 2, p. 406
Joseph Smith is hereby Appointed Overseer of the Road in the Room of John Hite, from the said Hites Mill to the Run at John Nations House & it is Ordered that the said Joseph Smith cause the said Road to be kept in good repair according to Law

5 April 1748 O. S., FOB 2, p. 408
John Collings is hereby Appointed Overseer of the Road from Andrew Campbell Gent to William Mitchells in the Room of John Morris And it is Ordered that the said John Collings cause the said Road to be Kept in good repair According to Law

5 April 1748 O. S., FOB 2, p. 410
On the Petition of John Hardin & Christopher Beeler to be released from working on that part of the Road which leads from the Court house to Robert Edges Whereof Thomas Colson is now Overseer, It is Ordered that the Sherif Sumons the said Colson to Appear at next Court to show cause why the said Hardin & Beeler shall not be released from working on the same

5 April 1748 O. S., FOB 2, p. 410
On the Petition of William Vance James Hoge Robert Warth William Evine Samuel Vance John Young James Colven James Vance Joseph Fawcit Edward Cartmell Hugh Pierce & Samuel Shinn for a Road from Robert Warths /: to be taken from the Head of the Road which leads from the Chapple at Robert McCoys Spring :/ to Lewis Stephens Mills, David Logan and Robert Warth are hereby Appointed to Lay Off the same And it is Ordered that the Petitioners aforesaid Clear the said Road & Work thereon under the said Logan & Warth who are also Appointed Overseers thereof And it is further Ordered that the said Logan & Worth cause the said Road to be cleared and when Cleared that they keep the same in good repair According to Law

6 April 1748 O. S., FOB 2, p. 424
The Petition of John Funks Junr & Others for the puting down the Road Granted last Court to the Upper Inhabitants of this County being heard & due consideration being thereupon had, the said Petition is Dismis'd & the Order for clearing the said Road is hereby confirmed --

7 April 1748 O. S., FOB 2, p. 425
Ordered that the Tithables living within three Miles on Each side the Road which leads from Bulskin to the Court house Clear & Work on the same under John McCormack & Hugh Parrell who were formerly Appointed Surveyor thereof

7 April 1748 O. S., FOB 2, p. 426
Liberty is hereby granted to Alexander Ross Overseer of the Road from John Littlers to Opecken to alter the said Road as he thinks proper

3 May 1748 O. S., FOB 2, p. 429
Hugh Paul having set forth by his Petition that the Road from the Meeting House to Warm Springs caused a great disturbance in the Neighborhood, And it appearing to the Court that the said Road is Useless is therefore Ordered to be discontinued

3 May 1748 O. S., FOB 2, pp. 429-30
Grand Jury Presentments

We present John McCormack Overseer of the Highway whereof he is Surveyor for not keeping the Road in repair according to Law within these Six Months last past from Oppecan to the Head of Bullskin

* * *

We present David Lewis Senr Surveyor of the Highway whereof he is Overseer for not keeping the Road in repair according to Law within these Six Months last past

3 May 1748 O. S., FOB 2, p. 430
On the motion of Thomas Colson Overseer of the Road from Francis Carneys to Opecken by Lewis Neill Gent It is Ordered that the Tithables living within five Miles on Each side the said Road, work on the same under the said Thomas Colson --

3 May 1748 O. S., FOB 2, p. 430
Henry Hardin is hereby Apponted Overser of the Road from the Haybottom to the Road which leads to Manasses Run in the Room of John Wilcox deced And it is Ordered that the said Henry Hardin cause the said road to be Kept in good repair according to Law And further that he cause the said Road to be Continued to Manasses Run --

3 May 1748 O. S., FOB 2, p. 430
William Stripling is hereby Appointed Overseer of the Road in the Room of Edward Garrets & it is Ordered that the said William cause the said road to be kept in good repair according to Law

3 May 1748 O. S., FOB 2, p. 431
John Alford is hereby Appointed Overseer of the Road from Johnston Run to John Sturmans in the Room of Leonard Helm And it is Ordered that the said John Alford cause the said Road to be Kept in good repair according to Law --

7 June 1748 O. S., FOB 2, p. 431
Edward Lucus is hereby Appointed Overseer of the Road from Thomas Shepherds Mill to Jacob Hites Gent in the Room of the said Thomas Shepherd, And it is Ordered that the said Edward Lucus cause the said Road to be Kept in good repair according to Law --

2 August 1748 O. S., FOB 2, p. 449
On the motion of Ralph Withers it is Ordered that all the Male Labouring Tithables living within three Miles of the Road from Bransons Mill to Thomas Chesters work on the same under the said Ralph Withers Overseer thereof --

2 August 1748 O. S., FOB 2, p. 450
On the Petition of Thomas Ashby Junr for a road from Howels ford to Gregory's Waggon Road It is Ordered that the Tithables from Thomas Hoopers to Mark Hardins on both sides of the River Clear & Work on the same under Thomas Ashby Junr who is hereby Appointed Overseer thereof And it is further Ordered that the said Thomas Ashby cause the said Road to be cleared & make Bridges thereon where it is requisite according to Law --

2 August 1748 O. S., FOB 2, p. 450
On the motion of John Jones it is Ordered that all the Male Labouring Tithables belonging to Col^o Burwell on the Island, Work on the Road whereof the said Jones is now Overseer

4 August 1748 O. S., FOB 2, p. 471
Ordered that all the Male Labouring Tithables living on the South side of the River from Howells ford to Burwells Quarter & Those living on the North side the River beginning at Seabins Quarter to Cabbin Run within a Mile & half of the same work on the Road from Howells ford to the Top of the Blue Ridge under Christopher Marr Overseer thereof.

4 October 1748 O. S., FOB 2, p. 497
William Ewing is hereby Appointed Overseer of the Road from Capt. John Hites to the Drafts of the Indian Run in the Room of Lawrence Stephens, And it is Ordered that the said William cause the said Road to be kept in good repair according to Law.

Frederick County Order Book 3 (1748-1751)

7 December 1748 O. S., FOB 3, p. 4
James Cromley is hereby Appointed Overseer of the Road from the Courthouse to Morgan Morgan in the Room of Josiah Ballenger deced & it is Ordered that the Tithables which worked under the said Ballenger work under the said Cromley & that the said Cromley cause the said road to be Kept in good repair according to Law

7 December 1748 O. S., FOB 3, p. 4
William Hiat is hereby Appointed Overseer of the Road from John Smith to John Littlers in the Room of Alexander Ross deced & it is Ordered that the Tithables which worked under the said Ross work under the said Hiat & that the said Hiat Cause the said Road to be Kept in good repair according to Law

7 December 1748 O. S., FOB 3, pp. 4-5
Andrew Caldwell is hereby Appointed Overseer of the Road from the Courthouse to John Littlers Old Place in the Room of Ralph Humfrey deced & it is Ordered that the Tithables which worked under the said Humfrey work under the said Caldwell & that the said Caldwell cause the said Road to be Kept in good repair according to Law --

3 January 1748 O. S., FOB 3, p. 11
John Sturman is hereby Appointed Overseer of the Road from John Meltons to his House & it is Ordered that he cause the said Road to be Kept in good repair according to Law --

3 January 1748 O. S., FOB 3, p. 11
John Madden is hereby Appointed Overseer of the Road from John Sturmans Run to Johnstons Mill in the Room of John Alford deced & it is Ordered that the Tithables which worked under the said Alford work under the said Madden & that the said Madden cause the said Road to be Kept in good repair according to Law --

3 January 1748 O. S., FOB 3, p. 11
Martin Cartmell is hereby Appointed Overseer of the Road from Isaac Perkins Gent Mill to Mr Gabriel Jones's Plantation on Opecken River And it is Ordered that all the Male Labouring Tithables living within two Miles on Each side the said Road Clear & Work on he same And that the said Martin Carmell cause the said Road to be Kept in good Repair according to Law --

4 January 1748 O. S., FOB 3, p. 13
Ordered that a Road be Cleared from Capt George Johnston's Plantation on the Long Marsh the Nearest & best way into the Road which leads from Williams's Gap to the Courthouse And that the Tithables living within Two Miles of Each side the said Road and two Miles of the Lower End thereof next the said Marsh Clear & work on the same under Isaac Penington who is hereby Appointed Surveyor thereof And it is further Ordered that the said Isaac Penington cause the said Road to be Kept in good repair according to Law --

4 January 1748 O. S., FOB 3, p. 13
Ordered that a Road be Cleared from the Chapple at Cuningham the Nearest & best way into the River Road And that John Sturman be Overseer thereof And it is further Ordered that the Tithables formerly Ordered to Work under the said Sturman Clear & work on the same And that the said John Sturman cause the said Road to be Kept in good repair according to Law --

4 January 1748 O. S., FOB 3, p. 13
John Neill is hereby Appointed Overseer of the Road from His House to the Chaple at Cuninghams in the room of James Hill And it is Ordered that all the Male Labouring Tithables living within three miles on Each side the said Road work on the same including Joseph Carter & Richard Carter's Tithables, And that the said John Neill cause the said Road to be Kept in good repair according to Law--

7 February 1748 O. S., FOB 3, p. 14
Lewis Neill Gent & William Glover are hereby Appointed Overseers of the Road from the Courthouse to Opecken Creek in the Room of John Milburn And it is Ordered that the Tithables which work under the said Milburn work under the said Neill & Glover & that the said Neill & Glover cause the said Road to be Kept in good repair According to Law

7 February 1748 O. S., FOB 3, p. 15
On the Petition of Thomas Ashby Junr a license is Granted him to keep Ferry at his House according to Law he having with George Johnston & Samuel Earle his Securities Entered into bond and Acknowledged the same & the said Bond is Admitted to Record And it is Ordered that the said Thomas Ashby Junr receive for the ferriage of a Man & Horse Seven Pence halfpenny

8 February 1748 O. S., FOB 3, p. 17
On the motion of Thomas Ashby Junr for a Road from James Seabins Gate to the said Ashby's ferry It is Ordered that Samuel Earle Gent & Thomas Hooper View Mark & lay off the same And make report thereof to the next Court --

8 February 1748 O. S., FOB 3, p. 18
John Duckworth is hereby Appointed Overseer of the Road from the County Road to the Chapple at McCoy's Spring in the Room of George Bowman And it is Ordered that the Tithables which work under the said Bowman work under the said Duckworth & that the said Duckworth cause the said Road to be Kept in good repair according to Law --

8 February 1748 O. S., FOB 3, p. 18
Robert Allan is hereby Appointed Overseer of the Road from John Hite Gent Mill to Jacob Christman's Spring in the Room of Jacob Nesewanger & it is Ordered that the Tithables which worked under the said Nesewanger work under the said Allan & that the said Allan cause the said Road to be Kept in good repair according to Law

8 February 1748 O. S., FOB 3, p. 18
Charles Burwell Esqr. Having set forth by his Petition that he labours under very great Hardships by reason that his People at his Quarters in his County worked upon five roads & prayed to be relieved therein, It is thereupon Ordered that the said Burwells Tithables under the care of John Ashby be Exempted from working on the Road from the Forks of the Road at Cuninghams Chapple to Opecken Creek whereof John Madden is now Overseer And they are hereby Exempted accordingly --

8 February 1748 O. S., FOB 3, p. 19
Ordered that all the Male Labouring Tithables living within Two Miles on the Southside the North River of the Sharrando work on the Road from the forks of the Hay Bottom Road to Manases Run under Henry Hardin Overseer --

9 February 1748 O. S., FOB 3, p. 34
On the motion of Martin Cartmell for an Addition of Tithables to work on the Road whereof he is Overseer, it is Ordered that the Tithables living within three Miles of the said Road Clear & Work on the Same

10 February 1748 O. S., FOB 3, p. 38
The Grandjury v. Thomas Branson Def^t
The Def^t not Appearing to Answer the said Presentment ags^t him for not Keeping the Road in Repair whereof he is Overseer according to Law At the motion of Gabriel Jones Attorney for the King it is Ordered that he be fined for the same fifteen Shillings Current Money & also that he pay Costs

10 February 1748 O. S., FOB 3, p. 39
The Grandjury v. Enoch Pearson Def^t
The Def^t failing to Appear & Answer the said Presentment ags^t him for not Clearing Grubing & Keeping the Road from Vestals Gap to the long Marsh in repair according to Law - whereof he is Surveyor. at the motion of Gabriel Jones Attorney for the King It is Ordered that he be fined for the same fifteen Shillings Current Money & also that he pay Costs

10 February 1748 O. S., FOB 3, p. 40
The Grandjury v. George Dellener Def^t
The Def^t failing to Appear & Answer the said Presentment ags^t him for not Keeping the Road from John Funks Mill to Cedar Creek in repair according to Law whereof he is Surveyor At the motion of Gabriel Jones Attorney for the King It is Ordered that he be fined for the same fifteen Shillings Current Money & also that he pay Costs

7 March 1748 O. S., FOB 3, p. 46
Samuel Vance is hereby Appointed Overseer of the Road from Lewis Stephen's Mill to M^r. Gabriel Jones his Place in the Room of Paul Froman And it is Ordered that the Tithables which worked under the said Froman work under the said Vance & that the said Vance cause the said Road to be Kept in good repair according to Law --

7 March 1748 O. S., FOB 3, p. 46
John Duckworth is hereby Appointed Overseer of the Road from Cedar Creek to Robert McCoy's Run in the Room of George Bowman & it is Ordered that the Tithables which worked under the said Bowman work under the said Duckworth & that the said Duckworth cause the said Road to be Kept in good repair according to Law

7 March 1748 O. S., FOB 3, p. 46
Ordered that Marquis Calmes Lewis Neill & Isaac Perkins Gent View the Road formerly appointed from Lewis Stephen's Mill to the County & make report thereof to the next Court

7 March 1748 O. S., FOB 3, p. 46
Thomas Waters is hereby Appointed Overseer of the Road from Opecken Creek to Sherando River in the Room of John Madden And it is ordered that the Tithables which worked under the

said Madden work under the said Waters And that the said Waters cause the said Road to be Kept in good repair according to Law --

7 March 1748 O. S., FOB 3, p. 46
John Bryant is hereby Appointed Overseer of the Road from Opecken Creek to the Courthouse in the Room of Thomas Waters And it is ordered that the Tithables which worked under the said Waters work under the said Bryant & that the said Bryant cause the said Road to be Kept in good repair according to Law --

7 March 1748 O. S., FOB 3, pp. 46-47
John Jones is hereby Appointed Overseer of the Road from Spout Run to M^r. John Sturmans in the Room of John Madden and it is Ordered that the Tithables which worked under the said Madden work under the said Jones & that the said Jones cause the said Road to be Kept in good repair according to Law --

7 March 1748 O. S., FOB 3, p. 47
William Gaddis is hereby Appointed Overseer of the Road from his Plantation to Littlers Mill in the Room of George Hobson And it is Ordered that the Tithables which worked under the said Hobson work under the said Gaddis & that the said Gaddis cause the said Road to be Kept in good repair according to Law

7 March 1748 O. S., FOB 3, p. 47
Abraham Hite is hereby Appointed Overseer of the Road from John Hites Mill to John Nations Run in the Room of Joseph Smith And it is Ordered that the Tithables which worked under the said Smith work under the said Hite & that the said Hite cause the said Road to be Kept in good repair according to Law

7 March 1748 O. S., FOB 3, p. 47
Henry Mills is hereby Appointed Overseer of the Road from Mills Creek to Littlers Old Place in the Room of Henry Bowen & it is Ordered that the Tithables which worked under the said Bowen work under the said Mills & that the said Mills cause the said Road to be Kept in good repair according to Law --

7 March 1748 O. S., FOB 3, p. 47
George Ross is hereby appointed Overseer of the Road from Littlers Old Place to Opecken in the Room Henry Bowen & it is Ordered that the Tithables which worked under the said Bowen work under the said Ross & that the said Ross cause the said Road to be Kept in good repair according to Law --

8 March 1748 O. S., FOB 3, p. 50
Ordered that all the Male Labouring Tithables living within three Miles on both sides the Road which leads from the Courthouse to Opecken including the Town work on the same under Lewis Neill Gent & William Glover Overseer thereof

8 March 1748 O. S., FOB 3, p. 53
[Margin note:] Order P. Helms to take the Bond of G. Johnston.
Ordered that Meredith Helm Gent. take Bond with the Security for the Sum of Two Hundred Pounds for the Keeping County Ferry Cross Shannando from the Plantation on which John Kersey now lives to Christopher Marrs Plantation for the Space of Eight Years the said Johnston to be Allowed for the same Twenty three Pounds P year to be levied on the Tithables of this County.

8 March 1748 O. S., FOB 3, p. 53
Ordered that Marquis Calmes & Samuel Earle Gent View Mark & lay off a Road to & from the Ferry in the County Road & make return thereof to the next Court --

8 March 1748 O. S., FOB 3, p. 53
Ordered that Robert Warth & David Logan View Mark & lay off a Road the Nearest & best way from Lewis Stephens Mill to the Road to McKoys Chapple And that the Tithables living within two miles of the said Road Clear & work on the same under the said Robert Warth who is hereby Appointed Surveyor thereof And it is further Ordered that the said Robert Warth cause the said Road to be cleared & when cleared that he keep the same in good repair according to Law

9 March 1748 O. S., FOB 3, p. 56
Abraham Vanmetre is hereby Appointed Overseer of the Road from Simon Linders to Old Loyds in the Room of Nicholas Mercer & it is Ordered that the Tithables which worked under the said Mercer work under the said Vanmetre & that the said Vanmetre cause the said Road to be kept in good repair According to Law --

9 March 1748 O. S., FOB 3, pp. 62-63
John Wood is hereby Appointed Overseer of the Road from Howels ford to the Top of the Ridge in the Room of Christopher Marr & it is Ordered that the Tithables which worked under the said Marr work under the said Wood & that the said Wood cause the said Road to be kept in good repair According to Law --

9 March 1748 O. S., FOB 3, p. 63
Thomas Rutherford is hereby Appointed Overseer of the Road from his House to John McCarmacks in the Room of Richard Stevenson And it is Ordered that the Tithables which worked under the said Stevenson work under the said Rutherford and that the said Rutherford cause the said Road to be Kept in good repair According to Law

9 March 1748 O. S., FOB 3, p. 63
Samuel Earle Gent is hereby Appointed Overseer of the Road from Cunninghams to Burdens Spring in the room of Peter Woolf & it is Ordered that the Tithables which worked under the said Woolf work under the said Earle & that the said Earle cause the said Road to be Kept in good repair according to Law --

9 March 1748 O. S., FOB 3, p. 63
Charles Buck is hereby appointed Overseer of the Road from Bransons Mill to Gregory's Ford in the Room of Samuel Earle Gent it is Ordered that the Tithables which worked under the said Earle work under the said Buck & that the said Buck cause the said road to be Kept in good repair according to Law

9 March 1748 O. S., FOB 3, p. 63
Thomas Rutherford is hereby Appointed Overseer of the Road from his House to Potomack in the Room of John Herin and it is Ordered that the Tithables which worked under the said Herin work under the said Rutherford & that the said Rutherford cause the said Road to be Kept in good repair according to Law --

9 March 1748 O. S., FOB 3, p. 64
Ordered that William Roberts & Edward Rogers View Mark & lay off a Road the nearest & best way from Mark Hardins Ford to Isaac Hollingsworth's & make return thereof to the next Court --

5 April 1749 O. S., FOB 3, p. 70
Stephen Hotzenbella is hereby Appointed Overseer of the Road in the Room of Robert Allan & it is Ordered that the Tithables which worked under the said Allan work under the said Hotzenbella & that the said Hotzenbella cause the said Road to be Kept in good repair According to Law --

2 May 1749 O. S., FOB 3, p. 72
On the Petition of John Snap. John Snap Junr. Joseph Fawcett, John Fawcett Richard Fawcett Andrew Longacre Richard Ireson & Nathaniel Carr for a Road from the Gap of the Little Mountain into the Road which leads from John Hites Gent to Kerseys ferry It is Ordered that the said Road be cleared by the Pet^{rs} & that they work on the same under the said John Snap who is hereby Appointed Surveyor thereof.

2 May 1749 O. S., FOB 3, p. 74
Grand Jury Presentments

We present the Overseer of the Road between Jacob Hites Gent & Littlers Mill for not Keeping the Road in repair according to Law within this Six Months last past --
* * *
We Present Isaac Perkins Gent for not Keeping the Road in repair whereof he is Overseer according to Law within these Six Months last Past

6 June 1749 O. S., FOB 3, p. 87
John Smith is hereby appointed Overseer of the Road in the Room of Alexander Ross deced & it is Ordered that the Tithables which worked under the said Ross work under the said Smith & that the said Smith cause the said Road to be Kept in good repair according to Law

6 June 1749 O. S., FOB 3, p. 87
Edward Musgrove is hereby Appointed Overseer of the Road from David Loyds to the top of the Blue Ridge at Vestals Gap in the Room of Reuben Rutherford & it is Ordered that the Tithables

which worked under the said Rutherford work under the said Musgrove & that the said Musgrove cause the said Road to be Kept in good repair According to Law --

6 June 1749 O. S., FOB 3, p. 87
William Rankins is hereby Appointed Overseer of a Road in the Room of William Hiat & it is Ordered that the Tithables which worked under the said Hiat work under the said Rankins & that the said Rankins cause the said Road to be Kept in good repair according to Law --

7 June 1749 O. S., FOB 3, p. 88
On the motion of John Neill Gent it is Ordered that the Road which leads from the Chapple at Cuninghems to the said Neills be Continued to the Run called Abrahams Run & that the Tithables which was formerly Ordered to work on the Road aforesaid Clear & Work on the same under the said John Neill Overseer thereof

7 June 1749 O. S., FOB 3, p. 88
Samuel Pritchard is hereby Appointed Overseer of the Road in the Room of Nathaniel Cartmell deced & It is Ordered that the Tithables which worked under the said Cartmell work under the said Pritchard & that the said Pritchard cause the said Road to be Cleared as laid Off by Abraham Wiseman & when Cleared that he Keep the same in good repair according to Law. --

7 June 1749 O. S., FOB 3, p. 96
Ordered that the Road which leads from Lewis Stephen's Gent Mill to the County Line be Discontinued on the motion of Gabriel Jones Gent --

8 June 1749 O. S., FOB 3, p. 101
Grandjury v. William Hiat. This Presentment ags^t the said Def^t for not Keep the Road in repair is Ordered to be Dismis'd

8 June 1749 O. S., FOB 3, p. 102
Grandjury v. Isaac Perkins Def^t. This Presentment ags^t the said Def^t for not keeping the Road in repair is Dismis'd & he Ordered to pay Costs --

8 August 1749 O. S., FOB 3, p. 119
On the Petition of Solomon Hedges, Abraham Richardson, Benjamin Parker, George Parker Junr John Radden John Rion Abra: Johnson, Theodore Davis, Isaac Johnson, Adam Warner Robert Lowder Vincent Williams James Patton, George Corn John Dowther Abra: Tegurden, Adam Stomp, John Adam Long, Cristana Long Gilles Sullivan, John Cokendal, Benjamin Cokendal, Nathl Cokendal, Abra: Cockendal, Abra: Cockendal Junr John Cockendal Peter Cockendal, David Tomson, Frank Tomson, Matthias Foman, James Cokendall John Dacker Luke Daker, William Earles, James ffannen, Henry Vanmetre Andrew Nowland James Williams Benjamin fforman Junr Richard ffreland John Colvin, Joseph Campbell, John Cinacome Job Pearall William Buffinton Daniel O Neal & Garrat Daker for a Road from the Mouth of Pattersons Creek to Job Pearsalls It is Ordered that Nicholas Raisner & George Parker View Mark & lay Off the same, and when laid off that the Petitioners Clear & Work on the same under the said Raisner & George Parker who is hereby Appointed Overseers thereof, And it is further Ordered

that the said Nicholas Raisner & George Parker cause the said Road to be Kept in good repair according to Law.

8 August 1749 O. S., FOB 3, p. 119
On the Petition of James Ross Edward Reeth Thomas Rumsey Jasper Sutten ffrancis Ross John Parker Simon Irishman Peter Peterson John Cuningham John Ross William Castleman Oliver Creamer Thomas McGuire Matthew Rogers, John Bauer [Baver?] Nich^l Crist Power Hazell, John ffinch [ffinel?] Richard Hazell William Fallon George Tebalt Joseph Robinson Abner Anderson William Johnston, John Large, Richard Doston Jacob Good Robert Bennett Caleb Doud, Christopher Bann Charles Keller George Undergrest, William Anderson, Peter Hart, Bagman Rogers ffred^k Jee, Thomas Hide Jacob Willf Michael Teebolt & Ebearm Breed for a Road from the lower part of Pattersons Creek by Power Hazels into the Waggon Road which leads from the Courthouse to the South Branch, It is Ordered that the said Power Hazel View Mark & lay Off the said Road & when laid Off that the Petitioners Clear & Work on the same under the said Power Hazel who is hereby Appointed Overseer thereof And it is further Ordered that the said Power Hazel cause the said Road to be Kept in good repair according to Law

8 August 1749 O. S., FOB 3, p. 121
Jeremiah Jack is hereby Appointed Overseer of the Road from Watkins fferry to the falling water in the Room of Charles Donahue And it is Ordered that the Tithables which worked under the said Donahue Work under the said Jack & that the said Jack cause the said Road to be Kept in good repair according to Law

9 August 1749 O. S., FOB 3, p. 124
Ordered that all the Male Labouring Tithables on the South Side of Sharrando from Manassus Run to Burwells Quarter including those on the Island Work on the Road from Howells ford to the Top of the Ridge under John Wood Overseer thereof --

9 August 1749 O. S., FOB 3, p. 124
On the Petition of Thomas Loftin & Others for the put in down the Road laid Off from Cuninghams Chapple to the main Road from the Court & from thence to Watkins ferry. It is Ordered that Jacob Hite John Hardin Gent & Isaac Penington View the said Road & the other Grounds & make report of their Opinions to the next Court --

9 August 1749 O. S., FOB 3, p. 124
The Complaint of Andrew Campbell against the Overseers from Littlers Old Place to Patrick Ryleys is Ordered to be Dismis'd --

9 August 1749 O. S., FOB 3, p. 124
Ordered that the Road which leads from Joseph Evans to Col^o Morgan Morgan be discontinued --

9 August 1749 O. S., FOB 3, p. 129
Jacob Brooks is hereby Appointed Overseer of the Road from Wm Hites Spring to the Middle of the Swamp in Smiths Marsh in the Room of David Lewis & William Rankin is also Appointed

Overseer from the said Swamp to Littlers Mill And it is Ordered that the Tithables living three Miles on each side of the said Road Clear & Work on the same & that the said Overseers joyn their gangs in making a Causeway over the Swamp. And it is further Ordered that the said Jacob Brooks & William Rankins Keep their respective parts of the said Road in good repair according to Law --

[Note: There are no Court orders from 11 August to 14 November 1749.]

14 November 1749 O. S., FOB 3, p. 167
Grand Jury Presentments

We present Samuel Earle Gent for not Clearing the Road under his care according to Law by his Own Confession to the Grand Jury.

15 November 1749 O. S., FOB 3, p. 168
George Ross is hereby Appointed Overseer of the Road from Littlers Old Place to Opecken Creek & it is Ordered that all the Male Labouring Tithables living within three Miles on Each side the said Road Clear & Work on the same. An that the said George Ross cause the said Road to be Kept in good repair according to Law --

16 November 1749 O. S., FOB 3, p. 172
Leonard Helms Samuel Timmons & Henry Hardin is hereby Appointed to View Mark & lay of a Road from the Hollow near Kerseys to the River the most convenient & best way to the Ferry commonly called Kerseys & make report thereof to the next Court --

6 November 1749 O. S., FOB 3, p. 172
John Kuykendal is hereby appointed Overseer of the Road from Stony Bridge to Parkers on the North River of Cacapon, in the Room of John Collins And it is Ordered that all the Male Labouring Tithables on the South Branch below the Trough & on Pattersons Creek Work on the same & that the said Kuykendal cause the said Road to be Kept in good repair according to Law --

16 November 1749 O. S., FOB 3, p. 174
Jonathan Cobourn & William Miller having returned that they laid out the Road Petitioned for by Henry Vanmetre from Hampton's Mill down the South Branch according to an Order of this Court Beginning below where the said Vanmetre did live from thence to where he now lives & so down by his Mill from thence Strait to Hamptons Mill, Leave therefore is granted & the said Vanmetre to Clear the same at his own Expense, according to the said Return --

16 November 1749 O. S., FOB 3, p. 174
The Order for Jacob Hite John Hardin & Isaac Penington to View a Road is Continued until the next Court for their return.

18 November 1749 O. S., FOB 3, p. 198
Thomas Doster is hereby Appointed Overseer of the Road from the Courthouse to Ballengers Plantation in the Room of George Hollingsworth & it is Ordered that the Tithables which worked under the said Hollingsworth Work under the said Doster & that the said Doster cause the said Road to be Kept in good repair According to Law

18 November 1749 O. S., FOB 3, p. 198
Richard Sturman is hereby Appointed Overseer of the Road from his House to Striblings Quarter & from that Road to Cuningham Chapple in the Room of John Sturman & it is ordered that the Tithables which worked under the said John work under the said Richard And that the said Richard Cause the said Road to be Kept in good Repair according to Law --

[Note: There are no Court records for December and January 1749. Entries for November (November 18) end at p. 198; entries for 13 February 1749 O. S. begin on p. 199.]

13 February 1749 O. S., FOB 3, p. 202
John Branson is hereby Appointed Overseer of the Road from Thomas Chester Gent to Bransons Mill in the Room of Ralph Withers & it is Ordered that the Tithables which worked under the said Withers work under the said Branson & that the said Branson cause the said Road to be Kept in good repair according to Law --

14 February 1749 O. S., FOB 3, p. 204
Lewis Stephens Gent Is hereby appointed Overseer of the Road from his mill to Mr Gabriel Jones Plantation in the room of James Vance and it is ordered that the Tithables that worked under the s^d Vance work under him and that the s^d Stephens Keep the s^d road in Repair according to Law.

14 February 1749 O. S., FOB 3, p. 204
Jacob Nisewanger is hereby appointed Overseer of the Road from Hites Mill to Nations Run in the room of Abraham Hite and it is Ordered that the Tithables that worked under the s^d Hite work under him and that he keep the s^d Road in Repair according to Law

14 February 1749 O. S., FOB 3, p. 204
John Funk Jn^r is hereby appointed Overseer of the Road from Funks Mill to Cedar Creek in the room of George Dillener And it is Ordered that the Tithables that worked under the s^d Dillener work under him & that the s^d Funk Keep the s^d Road in repair according to Law.

14 February 1749 O. S., FOB 3, p. 205
John Funk Junr is hereby appointed Overseer of the Road from from Funks Mill to Augusta Line in the room of Frederick Gabbert and it is Ordered that the Tithables that worked under the s^d Gabbert work under him and that the s^d Funk Keep the s^d Road in Repair according to Law.

14 February 1749 O. S., FOB 3, p. 205
Israel Robinson is hereby appointed Overseer of the Road from the Meeting house on the mountain to Hugh Liles on back Creek in the room of Hugh Paul and it is Ordered that all the

Tithables that did work under the s^d Paul work under him. And that the s^d Robinson keep the s^d Road in Repair according to Law.

14 February 1749 O. S., FOB 3, p. 208
On the Petition of William Mitchell and others It is Ordered that the Road from Evan's to Col° Morgans be discontinued and that the Tithables formerly Ordered to work thereon be discharged from the same.

15 February 1749 O. S., FOB 3, p. 210
On the Petition of Providence Williams, Samuel Hopkins Richd Poulson, Friend Cox, John Newton Joseph Newton John Hopkins William Smith Francis Spencer William Biggerstaff & John Friend for a Road to be laid off and Cleared from Frederick Town to the mouth of the South branch of Potomack Ordered that the s^d Williams lay off the same and be Overseer thereof and that the Petitioners Clear and Keep the Road in repair.

15 February 1749 O. S., FOB 3, p. 211
Ordered that Thomas Ashbey Thomas Ashbey Junr and Henry Hardin view and mark a Road the most convenient Way from Manasses Run Road to Chesters Old Road and from thence to Augusta Line and make Report of their Proceedings at the next Court.

16 February 1749 O. S., FOB 3, p. 213
The Grand Jury Plt ag^t Samuel Earle Dft. On Presentment the said Samuel Earle being Presented for not keeping the Road in repair whereof he is Overseer and appearing and Saying nothing in Bar of the s^d Presentment On the motion of Gabriel Jones Attor^y for our Soverign Lord the King It is ordered that he be Fined Fifteen Shill^s Current money and that he pay the Costs of this Presentment.

16 February 1749 O. S., FOB 3, p. 214
Henry Hardin Leonard Helms and Samuel Timmons having viewed the Road from the Hollow near Kerseys to Shanando River according to an Order of this Court made their Report in these words. We have viewed as within directed and find the Road must be Cleared along the Lower side of the Hollow to the River Whereupon it is Ordered That the s^d Road be from henceforth Established a Publick Road and Leonard Helm is hereby appointed Overseer thereof and that the hands formerly under him Clear and keep the same in repair according to Law.

16 February 1749 O. S., FOB 3, p. 214
Ordered that Samuel Timmons Leonard Helms and Henry Hardin lay off a Road from the landing place on the South Side of Shanando River at Kerseys Ferry to Fox Trap point Road and Leonard Helms is appointed Surveyor thereof and the hands formerly appointed to work under him is hereby Ordered to Clear the same and keep it in Repair according to Law.

16 February 1749 O. S., FOB 3, p. 214
Isaac Hollingsworth is hereby Appointed Surveyor of the Highway from Opeckon to the Town in the room of William Glover and Lewis Neal and the hands formerly Appointed to work under them are hereby Ordered to Work on the s^d Road and keep it in Repair according to Law.

21 February 1749 O. S., FOB 3, p. 237
Ordered that James Bruce and Henry Brinker be Surveyors of the Road from from the Town to Mr Briscoes in the Room of And^{rw} Caldwell and that the Tithables four miles on each side the s^d Road do assist and Observe the Directions of the s^d Surveyors in Clearing and keeping the s^d Road in Repair according to Law.

21 February 1749 O. S., FOB 3, p. 237
Lewis Stephens Gent is hereby appointed Surveyor of the Highway from his Mill to Mr Gabriel Jones's and it is Ordered that all the male labouring Tithables on the North side Cedar Creek and below the North Mountain together with the Tithables two miles on the Southside the s^d Road do assist and observe the Directions of the s^d Surveyor in Clearing and keeping the same in repair according to Law.

[Note: Court orders for February 1749 O. S. end with 21 February 1749 O. S. / FOB 3, p. 237. March 1749 O. S. Court orders consist of one (1) page only: 5 March, 3, p. 238, a called court for a murder charge. There are no court orders for April. May 1749 O. S. court orders begin on 8 May 1750, FOB 3, p. 239.]

8 May 1750 O. S., FOB 3, p. 239
Zacchariah Valentine is hereby appointed Surveyor of the Highway from the Long marsh Run to Vestals Iron works in the room of Enoch Pearson deceased and it is Ordered that all the Tithables formerly appointed to work on the s^d Road observe his Directions in keeping the s^d Road in repair according to Law.

8 May 1750 O. S., FOB 3, p. 243
Grand Jury Presentments

We present William Ewings Surveyor of the Road from Capt. John Hites mill to Widow Reeds path leading to Bransons Mill and McCoys Chapple for not Clearing and keeping the same according to law within six months

* * *

We present William Rankin Surveyor of the Road from from the Bridge on Smiths Creek to widow Littlers Mill for not keeping and Clearing the same according to Law.

9 May 1750 O. S., FOB 3, p. 244
Thomas Ashbey Thomas Ashbey Junr and Henry Hardin by a former Order of this Court having viewed the way from Manasses Run Road to Chesters Old Road made their Report in These words. We find it to be a very bad way. Where upon it is Ordered by the Court that the Petition for the s^d Road be dismissed. Present Mered. Helms Gent

9 May 1750 O. S., FOB 3, p. 245
It is hereby Ordered that Dennis Springer be Surveyor of the Highway from William Frosts to John Frosts Mill and that Thos Provin be surveyor of the other part of the s^d Road from William Frosts to Col^o Morgans Road and that all the male labouring Tithables formerly appointed assist

the s^d Surveyors and observe their Directions in Clearing and Keeping the s^d Road in repair according to law.

9 May 1750 O. S., FOB 3, p. 245
Ordered that Henry Enochs Evan Rogers and John Hopkins view the Ground for a Road from the Mouth of the S^o branch the most Convenient and best way to this Courthouse and make their Report to the next Court and also what number of Tithables are convenient to Work on the s^d Road.

9 May 1750 O. S., FOB 3, p. 245
Jacob Hite John Hardin &^c not having made their report in complyance to a former Order of this Court for them to view a Road the same is continued for them to make their Report.

9 May 1750 O. S., FOB 3, p. 249
Ordered that John Melton keep a County Ferry over Shanando River from William Francoms to the s^d Meltons Plantation And that he be allowed for the same as shall be agreed by the next Court. On Condition there is not now in force an Act of Assembly for keeping a public Ferry at the s^d place. And that he be allowed from the time he has a Boat in Order until the Law be known.

12 May 1750 O. S., FOB 3, p. 267
John Thomas is hereby appointed Overseer of a Road from from Ross's fence by the great Road to Opeckon Creek in the room of William Ranking And it is Ordered that all the male Tithables within Three miles on each Side of the s^d Road work under him as their Overseer And that he keep the s^d Road in Repair according to Law.

12 May 1750 O. S., FOB 3, p. 268
It is Ordered that Thomas Marks and Nathaniel Cartmell Mark and lay off a Road the most Convenient and best way from Hoop Petticoat Gap to Hites Mill. And that Thomas Marks be Surveyor thereof and that all the male labouring Tithables Two miles on each side the s^d Road assist in Clearing and keeping the s^d Road in repair according to Law.

12 May 1750 O. S., FOB 3, p. 268
Jacob Nisewanger is hereby appointed Surveyor of the Road from Hites Mill to Nations Run And that all the male labouring Tithables two miles on each side the s^d Road from the s^d Run as far as Hoop Petticoat Gap assist the Surveyor in keeping the same in Repair according to Law.

14 May 1750 O. S., FOB 3, p. 272
(Grand Jury ag^t David Lewis) Presentment The Dft failing to appear and answer the s^d Presentm^t against him for not keeping the Road in repair according to Law whereof he is Overseer On the motion of Gabriel Jones atorney for Our Lord the King It is Ordered that he be fined fifteen shillings according to Law.

14 May 1750 O. S., FOB 3, p. 273
(Grand Jury Plt ag^t John McCormack Dft.) Presentment The Dft failing to appear to answer the s^d presentment against him for not keeping the Road in Repair according to Law of which he was appointed Overseer On the motion of Gabriel Jones Atorney for Our Lord the King It is Ordered that he be fined Fifteen Shillings according to Law.

15 May 1750 O. S., FOB 3, p. 283
(Grand Jury Plt v Thomas Branson. Dft.) On Presentment for stopping a Road The Dft failing to appear On the motion of Gabriel Jones Atorney for Our Lord the King It is Ordered that he be fined Five shillings

16 May 1750 O. S., FOB 3, p. 290
It is Ordered that George Johnston Gent. Be Surveyor of the Highway from his House to the Road from Town to Fairfax County in the Room of Isaac Pennington and It is further Ordered that the Tithables formerly appointed to work on the s^d Road keep the same in repair according to Law.

16 May 1750 O. S., FOB 3, p. 290
Ordered that Thomas Sharp be Overseer of the Road from Bransons Mill to the dividing Branch and Lawrence Stephens Overseer of the Road from the s^d Branch to Hites Mill and it is further Ordered that the Tithables formerly appointed to work on the s^d Road keep the same in Repair according to Law.

16 May 1750 O. S., FOB 3, p. 290
On the Petition of George Pemberton It is Ordered that he have liberty to lay off and Clear a Road from his Dwelling house to the Road that leads from Capt Rutherfords to Doctor McCormacks.

16 May 1750 O. S., FOB 3, p. 292
It is Ordered that Thomas Low formerly appointed Overseer of the Road from William Mitchells to Cunninghams Chapple Continue the Road to the Creek and that he Cause the Tithables appointed to work under him to Cut down the Bank where the s^d Road was laid off.

[Note: There are no Court orders for June or July 1750.]

14 August 1750 O. S., FOB 3, p. 294
On the motion of Power Hasel and George Parker it is Ordered that all the Tithables from the mouth of Pattersons Creek upwards and also the Tithables on the north branch above the mouth of Pattersons Creek upwards work on the Road from the s^d Creek to Job Pearsals as formerly laid off.

15 August 1750 O. S., FOB 3, p. 299
Ordered that Samuel Pritchard John Hite Gent and Robert Allen or any two of them mark and lay off a Road the most convenient and best way from Hoop Petticoat Gap to Hites Mill and it is further Ordered that Thomas Marks be Overseer of the s^d Road and the Tithables two miles on each side the s^d Road Clear and keep the same in repair according to Law.

15 August 1750 O. S., FOB 3, p. 301
Ordered that John Shearer and Van Swearengen mark and lay off a Road the most Convenient and best Way from Watkins Ferry to Vestals Gap and that William Sheppard be Surveyor of that part of the s^d Road lying on the West side of Opeckon and Thomas Caton Surveyor from Opeckon to the Gap and it is further Ordered that all the male Labouring Tithables Three miles on each side of the s^d Road clear and keep the same in Repair according to Law.

15 August 1750 O. S., FOB 3, p. 301
Ordered that Thomas Caton be Surveyor of the Road from his House to Mr Jacob Hites and it is further Ordered that the male Labouring Tithables three Miles on each Side the s^d Road Clear the same and keep it in Repair according to Law.

17 August 1750 O. S., FOB 3, p. 314
(The Grand Jury Plt ag^t The Overseer of the Road from Hites to Littlers Dft) On Presentment The Sheriff having returned on the Summons Not found this presentment is Ordered to be Dismissed

(The Grand Jury Plt ag^t The Overseer of the Road from Sheppards Mill Dft) On Presentment The Sheriff having returned on the Summons not found this Presentment is Ordered to be Dismissed

18 August 1750 O. S., FOB 3, p. 316
Ordered that Samuel Earle Gent Edward Rogers and John Nation mark and lay off a Road the most convenient and best way from Gregorys Ford thence near his Ld Ships Seat and into Hites Waggon Road

18 August 1750 O. S., FOB 3, p. 316
On the Petition of Jacob Racklies Michael White, John Thomas and Ellis Thomas It is Ordered that Ellis Thomas mark and lay off a Road the most Convenient and best way from John Racklies to John Fossets and that the petitioners Clear and keep the same in Repair according to Law and it is further Ordered that the s^d Ellis Thomas be Overseer of the s^d Road.

18 August 1750 O. S., FOB 3, p. 320
Ordered that Meredith Helm John Lindsey and John Hardin Gent. agree with John Melton to keep a County Ferry over Shanando at his plantation and make their Report to next Court

21 August 1750 O. S., FOB 3, pp. 335-336
Ordered that William Stevenson and Augustine Windle mark and lay off a Road the most Convenient way from Lewis Stephens Mill to the widow Littles and that the Tithables two miles

on each side of the s^d Road Clear and keep the said Road in Repair according to Law. And it is further Ordered that the s^d William Stevenson and Augustine Windle be Overseers of the Road.

[Note: There are no Court orders for September or October 1750.]

16 November 1750 O. S., FOB 3, p. 367
Ordered that Marquis Calmes Gent Set up advertisements of a Pistole reward for any person who shall make discovery of the Offender or Offenders concerned in the pulling down any One of the Direction boards for the Roads in this County.

16 November 1750 O. S., FOB 3, p. 369
Ordered that William Stevens keep Ferry over Shanando River from William Francoms Plantation to Meltons Plantation on the same terms formerly agreed on with John Melton deceased.

16 November 1750 O. S., FOB 3, p. 369
Ordered that William Stevens be Overseer of the Road of which John Meton [Melton] deced was formerly Overseer.

[Note: There are no Court orders for December or January 1750 O. S.]

12 February 1750 O. S., FOB 3, p. 372
Thomas Cooper is appointed Surveyor of the Road from Chesters to Bransons Mill in the Room of Thomas Branson

12 February 1750 O. S., FOB 3, p. 373
Joseph Edwards is appointed Surveyor of the Road from the North River of Great Ca Capon and It is Ordered that the Tithables Eight Miles on Each side of the s^d Road Clear and keep the same in repair according to Law.

12 February 1750 O. S., FOB 3, p. 374
It is ordered that Job Pearsall have liberty to Place Gates for his Conveniency so they do not Obstruct the passage on the main Road leading through his Plantation at the South Branch

13 February 1750 O. S., FOB 3, p. 378
Ordered that Nicholas Osbourn be Overseer of the Road from the Chapple at Cunninghams to Mr Lewis Neills ford on Opeckon in the room of John Neill dec'd.

13 February 1750 O. S., FOB 3, p. 378
Ordered that James Hoge be Overseer of the Road from Cedar Creek to the Cross Road at John Duckworths and that he keep the same in repair according to Law and it is further Ordered that the Tithables Three miles on each Side of the s^d Road work on the same.

14 February 1750/1 O. S., FOB 3, p. 383
Ordered that Gersham Keys Thomas Rutherford and Richard Stephenson View and lay off a Road the most Convenient & best way from Mr Rutherfords towards Cunninghams Chappel and make report of their proceedings to next Court.

15 February 1750/1 O. S., FOB 3, p. 385
Benjamin Grub is hereby appointed overseer of the Road from John McCormacks to the main Road to Town in the room of Hugh Parrel and John McCormack and it is Ordered that he together with the Tithables formerly appointed keep the s^d Road in Repair according to Law.

15 February 1750/1 O. S., FOB 3, p. 385
Ordered that John Hardin Gent be Overseer of the Road on the River Side from the long marsh to Vestals in the Room of Zacchariah Valentine

15 February 1750/1 O. S., FOB 3, p. 387
Ordered that Robert Worthington John Smith & Benjamin Rutherford View and lay off a Road from the great Road leading from Mr Jacob Hites to John Smiths to the head of Worthingtons Marsh thence down the s^d Marsh the nearest and best way into the Road near John Swims called Keys's Road and into the Road leading by Tho: Rutherfords to Vestal's Ferry And that Robert Worthington be Overseer thereof And it is further Ordered that the Tithables within Two miles on each side the s^d Road Clear and keep the same in Repair according to Law.

15 February 1750/1 O. S., FOB 3, p. 387
Ordered that Josiah Huls be Overseer of the Road from Sleepy Creek to the Widow Pauls in the room of Hugh Paul decd.

18 February 1750/1 O. S., FOB 3, p. 403
Meredith Helm and John Hardin Gent being appointed by the Court to Agree with John Melton to keep Ferry not having made their Report to the Court the same is Continued to the next Court.

14 May 1751 O. S., FOB 3, p. 424
Ordered that Patrick Reiley be Overseer of the Road from Morgans Chapple to Opeckon Creek in the Room of Thomas Low.

15 May 1751 O. S., FOB 3, p. 430
Ordered that Joseph Coombs be Overseer of the Road from Kerseys to the Ferry Road on the s^o side of Shanando in the room of Leonard Helm

15 May 1751 O. S., FOB 3, p. 431
Gersham Keyes Gent is appointed Overseer of the Road from David Loyds Crossing Shannando River and from thence to the top of the ridge in the room of Edward Musgrove and the Tithables formerly appointed are Ordered to keep the same in repair according to Law.

15 May 1751 O. S., FOB 3, pp. 435-438
Grand Jury Presentments

We present Jacob Nisenwanger Surveyor of the Road from John Hites to a branch of Opeckon for not Clearing the s^d Road according to Law within this six months last past.

We present Leonard Helms Surveyor of the Road from Col^o Burwells Mill Foxtrap point for not Clearing neither the Ford nor Ferry Road according to Law within six months last past
* * *
We present John Hite G^t Surveyor of the Road from his House to Isaac Parkins Gent for not Clearing the s^d Road according to Law within this six months last past.

We present Thomas Waters Surveyor of the Road from Opeckon Creek to Col^o Burwells Mill for not Clearing the s^d Road according to Law within this six months last past
* * *
We present John Hite Gent for not keeping the Bridge at his mill in order according to Law within this six months last past.

We present John Keykendal Surveyor of the Road from the South branch to the North River within this County for not clearing the s^d Road according to Law within this six months last past.
* * *
We present Robert Worthington Surveyor of the Road from John Smiths to Vestals Ford for not clearing the Road according to Law within this six months last past.

17 May 1751 O. S., FOB 3, p. 449
George Bruce is appointed Overseer of the Road from Town to Opeckon in the room of Isaac Hollingsworth.

17 May 1751 O. S., FOB 3, p. 452
Edward Sniggers is appointed Overseer of the Road from the River at Edges Ford to Francis Carneys in the room of John Cassine.

17 May 1751 O. S., FOB 3, pp. 452-453
Edward Sniggers is appointed Overseer of the Road from the Head of the Pond on Shanando River to Wormleys Quarter in the room of Benoni Frasier and it is Ordered that the Tithables on the Opposite Side the River as far as the Road extends be added to the former tithables appointed and that they keep the said Road in repair according to Law.

17 May 1751 O. S., FOB 3, p. 453
Mark Matterley is appointed Overseer of the Road from the Bridge to the Head of the Great Pond on Shanando in the Room of Richard Sturman.

17 May 1751 O. S., FOB 3, p. 453
John Madden is appointed Overseer of ye Road from Sturmans Bridge to Burwells Mill in the room of John Jones.

20 May 1751 O. S., FOB 3, p. 462
Ordered that Joseph Roberts be Surveyor of the Road from the Run by Nations to Kerseys ferry in the room of John Nation

20 May 1751 O. S., FOB 3, p. 462
Ordered that the R^t Honble Thomas L^d. Fairfax Baron of Cameron be Surveyor of the Road from Nations Run to Captain Hites in the Room of Jacob Nisewanger

20 May 1751 O. S., FOB 3, p. 462
Ordered that Robert Ashbey and Edward Rogers lay off a Road the most convenient and best way from Mark Hardins ford on Shanando River to Isaac Hollingsworths and make their Report to the next Court.

21 May 1751 O. S., FOB 3, p. 464
By a former Order of this Court for John Hardin and Meredith Helms to agree wth John Melton to keep a County Ferry the s^d John being dead the Order discontinued.

13 August 1751 O. S., FOB 3, p. 493
Edward Rogers and Robert Ashbey having returned that they have marked and laid off a Road from Mark Hardins Ford to Isaac Hollingsworth the most Convenient and best way in Complyance to an Order of this Court. Ordered that Robert Ashbey be Overseer of that part of the s^d Road from the River to Opeckon and that He with the Tithables within Two miles of the s^d Road below the Southwest Marsh Clear and keep the s^d Road in Repair according to Law. And that Thomas Low be Overseer of the other part from Opeckon to Isaac Hollingsworths and that He with the Tithables Two miles on each side the Road on that side Opeckon Clear the same and keep it in repair according to Law.

13 August 1751 O. S., FOB 3, p. 494
Ordered that all the Tithables within Three Miles of the Road above Nations Branch work on the Road from the s^d Branch to Hites mill under Tho: L^d. Fairfax Surveyor of the s^d Road.

13 August 1751 O. S., FOB 3, p. 494
Ordered that Mark Matterley be Overseer of the Road from the head of the pond at Striblings Quarter to Mr Sturmans and from thence to Cunninghams Chapple in the room of Richard Sturman and that the Tithables formerly appointed work on the same.

Frederick County Order Book 4 (1751-1753)

16 August 1751 O. S., FOB 4, p. 3
(Grand Jury Plt ag^t Jacob Nisewanger Deft - On presentment for not Clearing a road)
The deft failing to appear On the motion of Gabriel Jones attorney for our Lord the King It is ordered that he be fined fifteen shillings and Costs

17 August 1751 O. S., FOB 4, p. 4
(Grand Jury Plt ag^t John Keykendal Deft - on presentment)
The Deft John Keykendal being presented for not clearing the Road whereof he was Surveyor, appeared by John Sturman his attorney and being heard, On the Motion of Gabriel Jones attorney for Our Lord the King, It is ordered that he be fined fifteen shillings

17 August 1751 O. S., FOB 4, p. 5
(Grand Jury Plt ag^t John Hite Gent Dft - On presentment)
The deft being solemnly called and appearing, It is ordered on the motion of the said Deft that this presentment, at his Cost, be continued untill next Court

17 August 1751 O. S., FOB 4, p. 8
(Grand Jury Plt ag^t Robt Worthington Deft on presentment for not clearing a Road)
The deft being called appeared and being heard It is ordered that this Presentment be dismiss'd

20 August 1751 O. S., FOB 4, p. 14
(Grand Jury Plt ag^t John Hite Dft - Presentment)
This presentment is ordered to be continued to the next Court

[Note: There are no Court orders for September or October 1751.]

12 November 1751 O. S., FOB 4, p. 55
Ordered that John Hardin agree with some person to blow the Rocks in the Road through Williams's Gap and bring in his Charge at laying the next Levy

13 November 1751 O. S., FOB 4, p. 57
Ordered that Christopher Marr mark and lay off a Road from from the County line to happy Creek and that he be overseer thereof and that the tythables betw^n the County Line and Happy Creek on the East side of the s^d River work on the same

13 November 1751 O. S., FOB 4, p. 60
Grand Jury Presentments

Isaac Hollingsworth hath cut a Mill Race across the publick Road and doth not keep a sufficient Bridge over the same for either Carriages or even man and horse to pass the same safely
* * *
William Shepherd for not opening & Clearing a Road from William Richeys to John Vestals Gap at Shanandoah River for wch he was appointed overseer by this Court of Fredericks Order
* * *
We present John Wilson overseer of the Road from Beesons Mill to Peter Tostie's

13 November 1751 O. S., FOB 4, p. 62
{Grand Jury Plt ag^t John Hite Deft) - on presentment
    The Deft being called appeared and being heard It is ordered by the Court that this presentment be dismissed

[Note: There are no court orders for December 1751 or January 1752.]

12 February 1752 New Style, FOB 4, p. 113
Ordered that Gershom Keyes John Hardin and Richard Stevenson or any two of them being first sworn before a magistrate of this County do view & lay off a Road from Vestals ford to Captain Johnstons Road and make report to next Court

13 February 1752 New Style, FOB 4, p. 116
Ordered that the Overseers of the Road from Thomas Harts to Linders ford and the overseers of the Road from the s^d Ford to the mountain join their gangs and repair the ford -- cross the s^d Creek

13 February 1752 N. S., FOB 4, p. 116
Ordered that John Lindsey Gent be continued overseer of the Road from the end of Johnstons Road to Cunninghams Chapple

13 February 1752 N. S., FOB 4, p. 117
Nicholas Osbourn is hereby appointed surveyor of the Road crossing Opeckon at John Neills ford to Cunninghams Chaple in the Room of John Neill Deced and that the Tithables formerly appointed work on the same

2 June 1752 N. S., FOB 4, p. 140
On the petition of Martin Cryder Adam Hunter Jam^s Sears Michael Poker John Fauhelm Jacob Disponet Barnet Disponet Jacob Breakley Junr Jacob Breakly sen^r John Dyer Jacob Cooper William Dyer Christopher Disponet Rodolph Wiseman Philip Cross John Bachelder Robt Marney William Russel Nicholas Counts for a Road from Disponets Gap to Lewis Stephens mill It is ordered that Lewis Stephens Martin Cryder & William Russell being first sworn before a Justice of the Peace for this County Mark the said Road & make report to the next Court

3 June 1752, FOB 4, p. 152
(Grand Jury Plts ag^t William Shepherd Deft) on presentment for not clearing a road
The Deft failing to appear on ye motion of Gabriel Jones Attorney for our Lord the King It is ordered that he be fined fifteen shillings & Costs

3 June 1752, FOB 4, p. 152
(Grand Jury Plt ag^t Is^c Hollingsworth Deft) on presentment for cutting a mill race across the Road & not keeping it in Repair
The Deft failing to appear on the motion of Gabriel Jones attorney for our Lord the King It is ordered that he be fined fifteen shillings & Costs

3 June 1752, FOB 4, p. 152
(Grand Jury Ptf ag^t John Wilson Dfd) on presentment for not Clearing a Road
The deft being Called appeared and being heard it is ordered that this presentment be dismis'd

3 June 1752, FOB 4, p. 152
Andrew Campbell is hereby appointed overseer of the Road from Tuscarora to William Richeys and it is ordered that the said Andrew Campbell cause the said Road to be cleared & the Bridges Repaired in the s^d precint

4 June 1752, FOB 4, p. 167
Ordered that Richard Stevenson and Gershom Keyes being first sworn before a Justice of the peace for this County do view & mark a Road from the Ferry at Vestals Gap to the main Road leading to Robinsons Gap and make report to next Court

17 July 1752, FOB 4, p. 215
Ordered that Joseph Edwards be overseer of the Road from Jeremiah Smiths to the North River and that the tithables within Eight miles of the s^d Road keep the same in Repair according to Law

7 July 1752, FOB 4, p. 215
Ordered that John Davis be overseer of the Road from Mr George Johnstons long marsh to the Court house Road in the Room of Geo Johnston Gent

4 August 1752, FOB 4, p. 218
John Milbourn is hereby appointed Overseer of the Road from Opeckan at Hugh Hainses to the Indian Grave on the Main Road and it is ordered that all the Tithables formerly appointed to work on the said, work under him as their Overseer and that he keep the same in repair according to Law

4 August 1752, FOB 4, p. 218
Benjamin Grub is hereby appointed Overseer of the Road from Hugh Hainses to John McCormacks And it is ordered that all the Tithables formerly appointed to work on the said Road work under him as their Overseer & that he keep the same in repair according to Law

4 August 1752, FOB 4, p. 218
Robert Cunningham is hereby appointed Overseer of the Road from Morgans Chapple to Opeckan in the Room of Patrick Reily And it is Ordered that all the Tithables formerly appointed to work on the said r^d work under him as their Overseer and that he keep the same in repair according to Law

4 August 1752, FOB 4, p. 219
Lawrence Snap is hereby appointed overseer of the Road from Crooked Run to Captain John Hite's in the Room of William Ewings and it is ordered that the Tithables formerly appointed to work on the said Road work under him as their Overseer and that he keep the said Road in Repair according to Law

5 August 1752, FOB 4, p. 226
John Ashby is hereby appointed overseer of the Road from Shannando River at the school house to Cunninghams Chapple in the room of Marquis Calmes Gent And it is ordered that all the Tithables formerly appointed to work on the said Road, work under him as their overseer and that he keep the same in Repair according to Law

5 August 1752, FOB 4, p. 226
Edward Rogers is hereby appointed overseer of the Road from McKays Chapple to Bordens Spring in the room of Samuel Earle and it is ordered that the Tithables formerly appointed to work on the said Road, Work under him as their overseer and that he keep the said Road in Repair according to Law

5 August 1752, FOB 4, p. 226
William Quintin is hereby appointed overseer of the Road from Burdens Spring to Cunninghams Chapple in the Room of Samuel Earle And it is ordered that all ye Tithables formerly appointed to work on the said Road work under him as their Overseer and that he keep the same in repair according to Law

5 August 1752, FOB 4, p. 226
Ordered that Neals Friend William Demose John Rogers and Peter Julian being first sworn before a Justice of the peace for this County do mark and lay off a Road from the mouth of the South Branch and also from Neals Friends the nearest & best way to the town of Winchester and make report thereof to ye next Court

5 August 1752, FOB 4, p. 226
Christopher Marr is hereby appointed overseer of the Road from the fork of the Road going to the Hay Bottom from to Manasses Run and also of the Road to the County Line through Chesters Gap in the Room of Henry Hardin and it is ordered that all the Tithables formerly appointed to work on the said Road work under him as their overseer and that he keep the same in repair according to Law

5 August 1752, FOB 4, p. 226
Ordered that all the Tithables within five miles on each side of the Road from Loyds to the Top of the mountain at Vestals Gap work on the Road from the River to the top of the mountain under Gresham Keys Overseer of the said Road

5 August 1752, FOB 4, p. 235
Henry Fry and Darby McKever are hereby appointed overseers of ye Road from Hews's to the south Branch Road above Jeremiah Smiths and it is ordered that the Tithables within Six miles on each side of the said Road work on the same under the said Fry & McKever as their overseers and that they keep the same in repair according to Law and it is further ordered that the said overseers divide the said Tithables between them

6 August 1752, FOB 4, p. 242
Richard Stevenson & Gershom Keys being formerly appointed to lay off a Road further time is granted them untill next Court to make their Report

1 September 1752, FOB 4, p. 266
Ordered that Thomas Hart & John Shearer being first sworn before a Justice of the peace for this County lay of a Road from Watkin's Ferry to vestals Gap the most convenient & best way and make report to the next Court

1 September 1752, FOB 4, p. 266
Nathaniel Cartmill is hereby appointed overseer of the Road from Sandy ford on Opeckon to Isaac Parkins mill &^{c} and it is ordered that John Becket Nathaniel Cartmill Benjamin Smith Charles Parkins Enoch Pearson Thomas Doster, Robert Lemon & William Williams work under him as their overseer and keep the same in repair according to Law

1 September 1752, FOB 4, p. 266
William Quintin is hereby appointed is hereby appointed Overseer of the Road from Burdens Marsh to Cuninghams Chapple in the Room of Samuel Earle And it is ordered that the Tithables formerly appointed to work on the said Road work under him as their overseer & that he keep the same in Repair according to Law

2 September 1752, FOB 4, p. 289
Richard Stevenson & Gershom Keys being formerly appointed to lay of a Road further time is granted them untill next Court to make their report

15 September 1752, FOB 4, p. 310
Bartholomew Bryant is hereby appointed overseer of the Road from Cuninghams to middle Creek in the Room of John Mills, and it is ordered that all the tithables formerly appointed to work on the s^d Road work under him as their overseer & that he keep the same in repair according to Law

5 October 1752, FOB 4, p. 328
Ordered that John Shearer William Shepherd Jonas Hedge and William Richey or any three of them being first sworn before a Justice of the peace for this County do meet and view the Road Landings at Watkins's ferry and make report to the next [court] and it is further ordered that in the meantime Joseph Williams have leave to Land at the most landing for himself & Travellers In their Passage from Maryland

8 November 1752, FOB 4, p. 340
Ordered that the Right Honb^{le} Thomas Lord Fairfax Marquis Calmes & Thomas Bryan Martin Gent being first sworn before a Justice of the peace for this County do meet & view the most convenient way for a Road from Howells ford to Ashbys Gap & make report thereof to the next Court

8 November 1752, FOB 4, p. 340
Ordered that Jonas Hedge Peter Hedge & George Harman being first sworn before a Justice of the peace for this County do lay of a Road from Rachell Hoods to the Race grounds & make report to the next Court

8 November 1752, FOB 4, p. 341
Adam Hunter is appointed overseer of the Road from Desponets Gap to Stevens's mill And it Is ordered that the Tithables three miles on each side the said Road work on the same under him as their overseer & that he clear & keep it in repair according to Law

8 November 1752, FOB 4, p. 342
Grand Jury Presentments

We of the Grand Jury do present the overseer of the Road between Robert Cuninghams and where Doctor John Brisco now lives.
* * *
We of the Grand Jury do present the overseer of the Road leading into Shanandore River on the west side It being the Road that leads through Ashbys Gap below where Thomas Ashby now keeps Ferry over the s^d River

9 November 1752, FOB 4, p. 343
A former order of this Court for Gersham Keys Gent & Richard Stevenson to lay of a Road not being complyd with the same is ordered to be continued to the next Court

9 November 1752, FOB 4, p. 345
James Stinson is appointed overseer of the Road from Opeckon where Joseph Robbins lived to Burwells Mill on Shanando in the Room of Thomas Waters and it is ordered that the tithables formerly appointed to work on the same work under him as their overseer & that he keep the same in repair according to Law

9 November 1752, FOB 4, p. 347
John Shearer William Shepherd & Jonas Hodge being ordered to view the landings at Watkins ferry & having failed to return their Report the Petition of Joseph Williams was considered by the Court and it is ordered that the old landings & Road be continued

6 December 1752, FOB 4, p. 360
The Right Honble Thomas Lord Fairfax Marquis Calmes and Thomas Bryan Martin Gent having returned that they have laid off the Road from the widow Woods mill to the Ferry Ordered that it be cleared according to the Return and John Timmons is hereby appointed overseer thereof and It is further Ordered that the Tithables formerly appointed to work on the same work under him as their overseer and that he keep the same in repair according to Law

6 December 1752, FOB 4, p. 361
Ordered that the Right Honb^le Thomas Lord Fairfax Marquis Calmes & Meredith Helm Gent being first sworn before a Justice of the peace for this County do view the Landings a Carseys Ferry and make report to the next Court

6 December 1752, FOB 4, p. 368
Peter Hedge Jonas Hedge & George Harman having failed to lay of a Road according to a former order of this Court Ordered that a new order Issue to them to lay of the s^d road and that they make report to the next [Court]

6 December 1752, FOB 4, p. 369
(Grand Jury Plts ag^t An overseer of a Road Deft) on Presentment
The Grand Jury not being particular in their presentment It is ordered that the same be dismisd

6 December 1752, FOB 4, p. 369
Joseph Roberts is appointed overseer of the Road from Nations Plantation to the River in the Room of John Nation and it is ordered that the Tythables two miles on each side the Road do work on the same under him as their overseer & that he keep the same in Repair according to Law

6 December 1752, FOB 4, p. 369
Thomas Ashby is appointed overseer of the Road from Burwills Mill to the Fork of the Road at Fox Trap point and also of the Road to the waggon Ford in the Room of Joseph Combs and it is ordered that the Tythables formerly appointed to work on the said Roads work under him as their overseer & that he keep the same in Repair according to Law

6 December 1752, FOB 4, p. 369
George Shunaman is appointed overseer of the Road from Opeckon to the sign Post at Quintins and it is ordered that the tithables two miles on each side the s^d Road work on the same under him as their overseer & that he keep the same in repair according to Law

6 December 1752, FOB 4, p. 370
John Armstrong is appointed overseer of the Road from the Signpost at Quintins to the River and it is ordered that the tythables two miles on each side the s^d Road work under him as their overseer & that he keep the same in Repair according to Law

[Note: There are no Court orders for January 1753.]

6 February 1753, FOB 4, p. 377
William Quintin is appointed overseer of the Road from Burdens Spring to Cuninghams Chapple and it is ordered that the tithables four miles on each side the Road & two miles on each end thereof work on the same under him as their overseer and that he keep it in repair according to Law

6 March 1753, FOB 4, p. 403
John Bryan is appointed overseer of the Road from Winchester Town to Opeckon where Joseph Robins formerly lived and it is ordered that the Tithables formerly appointed to work on the said Road work on the same under him as their overseer and that he clear and Keep the same in Repair according to Law

6 March 1753, FOB 4, p. 403
James Stevenson is appointed overseer of the Road from Opeckon where Joseph Robins formerly lived to Burwells Spout Run and it is ordered that the Tithables formerly appointed to work on s^d Road work on the same under him as their Overseer & that he Clear & Keep it in Repair according to Law

6 March 1753, FOB 4, p. 403
Stephen Pilcher is appointed overseer of the Road from Winchester Town to Lewis Neills ford on Opeckon and it is ordered that the Tithables formerly appointed to work on ye said Road work on the same under him as their overseer and that he clear & keep it in Repair according to Law

6 March 1753, FOB 4, p. 403
Lewis Neill Gent is appointed overseer of the Road from the ford at his House to Littlers Road and it is ordered that the Tithables three miles on each side the s Road work on the same under him as their overseer and that he clear and keep it in Repair according to Law

6 March 1753, FOB 4, p. 403
Thomas Colson is appointed overseer of the Road from from Littlers Road to Carneys Old House and it is ordered that the Tithables formerly appointed to work on said Road work under him as their Overseer and that he clear & keep it is Repair according to Law

6 March 1753, FOB 4, p. 403
Edward Sniggers is appointed overseer of the Road from from Carneys Old House to the River and it is ordered that the Tithables formerly appointed to work on the said Road work on the same under him as their Overseer and that he clear & keep it in Repair according to Law --

6 March 1753, FOB 4, p. 404
Mr Michael Pike is appointed overseer of the Road from from the River to the Top of the mountain at Williams's Gap and it is ordered that the Tithables formerly appointed to work on the said Road work on the same under him as their Overseer and that he clear & keep it in Repair according to Law

6 March 1753, FOB 4, p. 404
Thomas Colson is appointed overseer of the Road from The Fairfax Road to Mr John Lindseys and it is ordered that the Tithables formerly appointed to work on the s^d Road work on the same under him as their overseer and that he clear & keep it in Repair according to Law

6 March 1753, FOB 4, p. 404
Moses Guess is appointed overseer of the Road from Burwells Spout Run to Mr Jno Sturmans Old Place and it is ordered that the Tithables formerly appointed to work on the s^d Road work on the same under him as their Overseer and that he clear & keep It in repair according to Law

6 March 1753, FOB 4, p. 404
Mark Matterly is appointed Overseer of the Road from Mr John Sturmans Old place to the Fairfax Road and it is ordered that the Tithables formerly appointed to work on the said Road Work on the same under him as their overseer and that he clear & keep it in Repair according to Law

6 March 1753, FOB 4, p. 404
Stephen Emry is appointed overseer of the Road from the Fairfax Road to the Northside of the Long Marsh And it is ordered that the Tithables formerly appointed to work on the said Road work on the same under him as their overseer & that he clear & keep it in Repair according to Law

6 March 1753, FOB 4, p. 404
John Hardin is appointed overseer of the Road from the North side of the Long Marsh to Vestalls Ford and it is ordered that the Tithables formerly appointed to work on the s^d Road work under him as their overseer and that he clear & keep it in Repair according to Law

6 March 1753, FOB 4, p. 404
Gersham Keys Gent is appointed Overseer of the Road from Vestalls Ford to the Top of the Ridge and it is ordered that the Tithables formerly appointed to work on the said Road work on the same under him as their overseer and that he clear & keep the same in Repair according to Law

6 March 1753, FOB 4, p. 405
Neils Friend William Demosse Owen Rogers & Peter Julian having made their Report that they have marked a Road the most convenient way from Winchester Town to Potomack River in order for a Road to be cleared to the mouth of the south Branch Ordered that the said Road be cleared according to Law

6 March 1753, FOB 4, p. 405
Neals Friend is appointed overseer of the Road from Potowmack River at Neals Friends to the falling springs and that the Tithables Eight miles on each side of the said Road work on the same under him as their overseer and that he clear & keep the same in Repair according to Law

6 March 1753, FOB 4, p. 405
William Demose is appointed Overseer of the Road from the falling springs to the Bear Garden Ridge and it is ordered that the Tithables Eight miles on each side the said Road work on the same under him as their overseer & that he clear & keep the same in Repair according to Law

6 March 1753, FOB 4, p. 405
Owen Rogers is appointed overseer of the Road from the Beargarden Ridge to George Potts his Plantation and It is ordered that the Tithables two miles on each side of the s^d road work on the same under him as their overseer and that he clear & keep the same in Repair according to Law

6 March 1753, FOB 4, p. 405
Peter Julian is appointed overseer of the Road from George Potts's to the south Branch Road and it is ordered that the Tithables three miles on each side the said Road work on the same under him as their Overseer and that he clear and keep the same in Repair according [to law]

6 March 1753, FOB 4, p. 405
Ordered that Thomas Bryan Martin Lewis Stevens Gents and Jacob Nisewanger or any two of them being first sworn before a magistrate of this County mark and lay off a Road from Peter stevens Lane the most convenient way to the Dutch Road at Kerseys Ferry and make report to the next Court

6 March 1753, FOB 4, p. 405
William Duckworth is appointed overseer of the Road from Littlers old Place to Mill Creek in the Room of Henry Mills and it is ordered that the Tithables three miles on each side the said Road work on the same under him as overseer and that he clear & keep the same in repair according to Law

6 March 1753, FOB 4, p. 405
Frances Lilburn is appointed overseer of the Road from Mill Creek to Tuscarora in the Room of John Evans and it is ordered that the Tithables three miles on each side the s^d Road work on the same under him as their overseer and that he clear & keep the same in Repair according to Law

6 March 1753, FOB 4, p. 405
Richard Beason is appointed overseer of the Road from Tuscarora to Tostees in the Room of Andrew Campbell and it is ordered that the Tithables three miles on Each side the s^d Road work on the same under him as their overseer and that he clear & keep it in Repair according to Law

6 March 1753, FOB 4, p. 406
Robert Lemen is appointed Overseer of the Road from Peter Tostees to Watkins's Ferry in the Room of Jeremiah Jack and it is ordered that the Tithables three miles on each side the said Road work on the same under him as their overseer and that he clear & keep it in Repair according to Law And it is further Ordered that if the s^d overseer see it necessary he cause Watkins's Fence to be moved further from the River

6 March 1753, FOB 4, p. 406
Matthew Brooks is appointed overseer of the Road from Ross's to John Smiths old place in the Room of John Thomas and it is ordered that the Tithables three miles on each side the s^d Road work on the same under him as their overseer and that he clear & keep it in Repair according to Law

6 March 1753, FOB 4, p. 406
Edward Thomas is appointed overseer of the Road from from John Smiths Old place to Jacob Hites in the room of Jacob Brooks and it is ordered that the Tithables three miles on each side the s^d Road work on the same under him as their Overseer and that he clear & keep it in Repair according to law

6 March 1753, FOB 4, p. 406
Captn Richard Morgan is appointed overseer of the Road from Jacob Hites to Mr Swearingens Ferry in the Room of Edward Lucas and it is ordered that the Tithables three miles on each side the said Road work on the same under him as their Overseer and that he keep the same in Repair according to Law

6 March 1753, FOB 4, p. 406
Henry Heath is appointed overseer of the Road from Winchester Town to Robert Pearis's Plantation and it is ordered that the Tithables three miles on each side the said Road work on the same under him as their Overseer and that he clear & keep the same in Repair according to Law

6 March 1753, FOB 4, p. 406
Captn Jeremiah Smith is appointed Overseer of the Road from Robert Pearis's to his own House & it is ordered that the Tithables three miles on each side the s^d Road work on ye same under him as their overseer and that he clear & keep the same in Repair according to Law

6 March 1753, FOB 4, p. 406
Joseph Edwards is appointed overseer of the Road from Jeremiah Smiths to ye north River near Tho Parkers and It is Ordered that the Tithables eight miles on each side the s^d Road clear & keep it in Repair according to Law

6 March 1753, FOB 4, p. 407
Mr. Charles Buck is appointed overseer of the Road from Bransons Mill place to the main Road from McCoys Chapple and it is ordered that the Tithables one mile on each side the said Road work on the same under him as their overseer & that he clear & keep it in Repair according to Law

6 March 1753, FOB 4, p. 407
James Lemen is appointed overseer of the Road from Littlers old Plantation to Winchester Town and it is ordered that he a Road from each of the streets in the said Town into the s^d Road and that all the Tithables in the Town and two miles on each side the said Road work on the same under him as their overseer and that he clear & keep the same in repair according to Law

6 March 1753, FOB 4, p. 407
John Kuykendall is appointed overseer of the Road from the North River near Thomas Parkers to Peter Tostees Plantation and it is ordered that all the Tithables on the south Branch below the Trough and all the Tithables from Frees mill to the north Branch work on the same under him as their overseer and that he clear and keep it in Repair according to Law

6 March 1753, FOB 4, p. 407
Henry Vanmeter is appointed overseer of the Road from Peter Tostees Plantation to Hamptons mill and it is ordered that all the Tithables on Pattersons Creek above Frees Mill and all the above the Trough to the County line on the Branch work on the same under him as their overseer and that he clear & keep it in Repair according to Law

6 March 1753, FOB 4, p. 407
Peter Casey is appointed Overseer of the Road from the Mannor Line to the County Line and it is ordered that all the Tithables on Pattersons Creek above Frees Mill and all the Tithables on the south Branch above the Trough work on the same under him as their overseer and that he clear and keep it in Repair according to Law

6 March 1753, FOB 4, p. 407
Solomon Hedge is appointed overseer of the Road from Willm Buffingtons to Pattersons Creek and It is ordered that the Tithables formerly appointed to work on s^d Road work on the same under him as their overseer and that he clear & keep it in repair according to Law

6 March 1753, FOB 4, p. 407
Joseph McDowell is appointed overseer of the Road from Hites Mill to Cedar Creek and it is ordered that the Tithables three miles on each side the s^d Road work on the same under him as Their overseer and that he clear & keep the same in Repair according to Law

6 March 1753, FOB 4, p. 407
Captain John Funk is appointed overseer of the Road from Cedar Creek to the County Line and it is ordered that the tithables three miles on each side the s^d Road work on the same under him as their Overseer and that he clear & keep the same in repair according to Law

6 March 1753, FOB 4, p. 408
James Brown is appointed overseer of the Road from the main Road near Robert Warths to Crooked Run and it is ordered that the Tithables four miles on each side the said Road work on the same under him as their overseer and that he clear & keep the same in repair according to Law

6 March 1753, FOB 4, p. 408
Robert McCoy is appointed overseer of the Road from Crooked Run to Gregorys Ford and it is ordered that the Tithables two miles on each side the s^d Road work on the same under him as their overseer and that he keep the same in repair according to Law

6 March 1753, FOB 4, p. 408
William Evans is appointed overseer of the Road from the County Road near Robert Warths to Stevens Mill and it is ordered that the Tithables three miles on each side the said Road work on the same under him as their overseer and that he clear & keep the same in repair according to Law

6 March 1753, FOB 4, p. 408
Samuel Prichard is appointed overseer of the Road from Mr Perkins Mill to Mr Gabriel Jones's and it is ordered that the Tithables one mile on ye East side and three miles on the West Side of the s^d Road work on the same under him as their overseer and that he clear and keep it in repair according to Law

6 March 1753, FOB 4, p. 408
Lewis Stevens Gent is appointed overseer of the Road from Mr Gabriel Jones's to s^d Stevens's Mill And it is ordered that the Tithables three miles on each side the said Road work on the same under him as their overseer and that he clear & keep it in repair according to Law

6 March 1753, FOB 4, p. 408
William Blackburn Junr is appointed overseer of the Road from Stevens's mill to the Head of Funks mill Creek and it is ordered that the Tithables three miles on each side the s^d Road work on the same under him as their overseer and that he clear & keep it in Repair according to Law

6 March 1753, FOB 4, p. 408
Christopher Windle is appointed overseer of the Road from the Head of Funks Mill Creek to the County Line and it is ordered that the Tithables three miles on each side of the said Road work on the same under him as their overseer & that he clear & keep the same in Repair according to Law

6 March 1753, FOB 4, p. 408
Isaac Parkins Gent is appointed overseer of the Road from Andrew Caldwells to his mill and it is ordered that all the Tithables one mile on each side the s^d Road work on the same under him as their overseer and clear & keep it in repair according to Law

6 March 1753, FOB 4, p. 408
John Hite Gent is appointed overseer of the Road from Mr Isaac Parkins's to his own Mill and it is ordered that the tithables four miles on each side the s^d Road clear & keep it in Repair according to Law

6 March 1753, FOB 4, p. 409
The Right Honble Thomas Ld Fairfax is appointed overseer of the Road from Mr Hites to Nations Run and it is ordered that the Tithables three miles on each side the said Road work on the same under him as their overseer and clear & keep it in repair according to Law

6 March 1753, FOB 4, p. 409
Joseph Roberts is appointed overseer of the Road from Nations Run to Ashbys Ferry and it is ordered that the Tithables three miles on each side the s^d Road work on the same under him as their overseer and clear & keep it in Repair according to law

6 March 1753, FOB 4, p. 409
David Vance is appointed overseer of the Road from Mr Hites to Branson's mill place and it is ordered that the tithables three miles on each side the s^d Road work on the same under him as their overseer and clear & keep it in Repair according to Law

6 March 1753, FOB 4, p. 409
Francis Baldwin is appointed overseer of the Road from Jno Frosts mill to William Frosts ford and it is ordered that the Tithables formerly appointed to work on s^d road work on the same under him as their overseer and clear & keep it in Repair according to law

6 March 1753, FOB 4, p. 409
Jacob Vanmeter is appointed overseer of the Road from Mr Jacob Hites to Thomas Catons in the Room of Thomas Caton and it is ordered that the Tithables three miles on each side the said Road work on the same under him as their overseer and clear & keep it in repair according to Law

7 March 1753, FOB 4, p. 413
Ordered that Isaac Parkins Lewis Stevens Gent and Nathaniel Cartmill being first sworn before a Justice of the peace for this County do view the Ground for a Road from Fromas mill to the sand Ford on Opeckon and make report to the next Court whether it be necessary that a Road be cleared there

7 March 1753, FOB 4, p. 417
A former order of this Court for Mr Gershom Keys and Richd Stevenson to Lay off a Road not being complyd with Ordered that the same be continued to the next Court

7 March 1753, FOB 4, p. 418
(Grand Jury Plt ag^t Henry Mills Deft) On Presentment for not clearing a Road
The Deft being called & failing to appear on the motion of Mr Gab^l Jones Deputy attorney for Lord the King It is ordered that he be fined fifteen shillings & costs according to Law

3 April 1753, FOB 4, p. 451
Thomas Bryan Martin Lewis Stevens Gent & Jacob Nisewanger having made their report that they have laid off a Road from Peter Stevens's Lane to the Dutch Road leading to Kerseys Ferry Ordered that the same be cleared and Jacob Niswanger is appointed overseer of the same and it is ordered that the tithables three miles on the southside and one mile on the northside of the s^d Road work on the same under him as their overseer & that they clear & keep the same in Repair according to Law

1 May 1753, FOB 4, p. 472
On the motion of William Jollyffe praying for leave to turn the main road from the town of Winchester to Watkins's ferry where it passeth thro' his land Ordered that Isaac Parkins Gent and John Millburn being first sworn before a Justice of the Peace for this County view the same and make report to the next Court.

1 May 1753, FOB 4, pp. 472-473
Grand Jury Presentments

We of the Grand Jury do present the Overseer of the Road from town to Robert Pearis's for not keeping the s^d Road in Good repair according to Law

* * *

We of the Jury do present Samuel Prichard by the Information of Lewis Stevens for not Clearing of the Road from Gabriel Jones's to Isaac Parkins's Mill of wch he is overseer & for not Keeping of the s^d Road in repair according to Law within these six months last past

2 May 1753, FOB 4, p. 490
John Millburn George Hollingsworth being ordered to lay of a Road from Winchester town to Robert Moselys place and having made their return Ordered that the said Road be cleared according to the s^d Return.

2 May 1753, FOB 4, p. 498
Ordered that Jacob Hite John Briscoe & William Jones being first sworn before a Justice of the peace for this County mark and lay of a Road from Mitchells Ford to the Head of Bullskin & make report to the next Court

2 May 1753, FOB 4, p. 498
Thomas Lindsey is appointed overseer of the Road from the head of Bullskin to Penningtons Marsh and it is ordered that the Tithables three miles on each side the s^d Road work on the same under him as their overseer and that he Clear and Keep the same in repair according to Law

2 May 1753, FOB 4, p. 498
Thomas Hampton is appointed Overseer of the Road from Penningtons Marsh to Mr Calmes's and it is ordered that the tithables three miles on each side the s^d Road work under him as their overseer & that he clear & keep it in repair according to Law

2 May 1753, FOB 4, p. 499
Ordered that the Right Honb^{le} Thomas Lord Fairfax John Hite & Lewis Stevens being first sworn before a Justice of the peace for this County lay off a Road the most convenient way from Mr Hites to the Road from Stevens Lane to Kerseys ferry and make report to the next Court

2 May 1753, FOB 4, p. 499
George Wright is appointed overseer of the Road from Mr Hites to the Road from Stevens's Lane to Kerseys Ferry and it is ordered that the tithables two miles on each side the s^d Road work on the same under him as their Overseer & Clear & keep it in repair according to Law

Frederick County Order Book 5 (1753-1754)

5 June 1753, FOB 5, p. 2
George Ross is appointed overseer of the Road from Robert Moselys to Opeckon Creek where John Neils old mill formerly stood and it is Ordered that the Tithables three miles on each side

the s^d Road work on the same under him as their Overseer and that he clear & keep the same in repair according to Law

6 June 1753, FOB 5, p. 28
Isaac Parkins & John Millburn having viewed the Road which William Jollyffe Junr Petitioned to have altered & having returned that it is sufficient Ordered that the s^d William Jollyffe clear the same & that from henceforth it be established a publick Road

7 June 1753, FOB 5, p. 44
(Grand Jury Plt v Henry Heath Deft) On Presentment for not Clearing a Road
The Deft being called appeared and being heard this presentment is ordered to be dismissed

8 June 1753, FOB 5, p. 49
(Grand Jury Plt ag^t Samuel Prichard Deft) on Presentment for not clearing a Road
The sheriff having returned on the sumons not executed & the Deft being called & failing to appear on the motion of Gabriel Jones Gent Deputy Attorney for our Lord the King ordered that he be fined fifteen shillings according to Law & Costs

8 August 1753, FOB 5, p. 85
John Hite and Robert Allen in pursuance to a former Order of this Court that they have marked and laid off a Road the most Convenient way from Hoop Petticoat Gap to Hites Mill Ordered that it be cleared according to Law and that Thomas Marques be Overseer thereof and it is further Ordered that the Tithables Two miles on each Side the s^d Road clear and keep the Same in Repair according to Law.

4 Oct 1753, FOB 5, p. 238
Ordered that the Road from Jacob Hites to Thomas Catons be discontinued

6 November 1753, FOB 5, p. 256
Grand Jury Presentments

Richard Beason overseer of the Road from Tusegroro to Peter Tostees on the Oath of James Wood for not keeping the s^d Road in repair according to Law within Six months past

Stephen Pilcher overseer of the Road from Opeckon Creek from Capt Lewis Neills to Winchester Town for not keeping the Road in repair according to Law by the Oath of Mr William Elsey within Six months last past.

We of the Grand Jury present Benjamin Grubb Overseer of the Road from Mr John McCormacks to Opeckon Creek which leads to this Town for not keeping the same in repair according to Law within Six months last past

We of the Grand Jury present Samuel Pritchard Overseer of the Road from Capt Isaac Parkins to Mr Gabriel Jones's by the Information of Mr Leonard Helms for not keeping the said Road in Repair according to Law within Six months last past

We of the Grand Jury present Capt. Lewis Stevens Overseer of the Road from Mr Gabriel Jones's to the s^d Stevens own House for not keeping the same in repair according to Law by the oath of the s^d Leonard Helms within Six months last past

6 November 1753, FOB 5, p. 257
Grand Jury Presentments continued

We of the Grand Jury present M^r. David Vance overseer of the Road from Capt John Hites to Crooked Run for not keeping the s^d Road in repair according to Law within Six months last past

* * *

We of the Grand Jury present William Duckworth Overseer of the Road from Mr Robert Cunninghams to Mr Robert Moseleys for not keeping the said Road in Repair according to Law within Six months past

* * *

We of the Grand Jury present Gershom Keys Gent Overseer of the Road from the Blue Ridge to Thomas Rutherfords for not keeping the same in Repair according to Law within Six months last past

6 November 1753, FOB 5, p. 258
Ordered that James Wood John Lindsey and Lewis Stevens being first sworn do meet and view the Roads from Winchester Town to Kerseys Ferry and report to next Court which in their Judgments is the most convenient to be kept Open.

5 March 1754, FOB 5, p. 304
Ordered that John Hammer and George Hoge being first sworn before a Justice of this County do mark and lay off a Road the most Convenient way from from the lower part of the south Branch to the main Road near Thomas Parkers and make a report to the next Court

5 March 1754, FOB 5, p. 304
William Reynolds is appointed overseer of the Road from the Fork of the Road on his own Land to Babbs Creek in the Room of Peter Julian and it is ordered that the Tithables formerly appointed keep the same in repair according to Law

5 March 1754, FOB 5, p. 304
George Julian is appointed Overseer of the Road from Babbs Creek to George Potts's Plantation in the room of Peter Julian and It is Ordered that the Tithables formerly appointed keep the same in repair according to Law

5 March 1754, FOB 5, p. 305
John Chenowith is appointed Overseer of the Road from William Gaddis's house to Littlers mill in the room of William Gaddis and it is ordered that the Tithables formerly appointed keep the said Road in repair according to Law

5 March 1754, FOB 5, p. 322
Martin Grider is appointed Overseer of the Road from Disponet's Gap to Lewis Stevens's mill in the room of Adam Hunter and it is ordered that the Tithables formerly appointed keep the s^d Road in repair according to Law.

5 March 1754, FOB 5, p. 322
Isaac Beason is appointed overseer of the Road from Tuscorora Creek to Robert Lemons in the Room of Richard Beason and it is ordered that the Tithables formerly appointed keep the said Road in repair according to Law.

5 March 1754, FOB 5, p. 322
Francis Fowler is appointed Overseer of the Road from Morgans Chapple to Opeckon in the room of Robert Cunningham and it is ordered that the Tithables formerly appointed keep the s^d Road in repair according to law.

5 March 1754, FOB 5, pp. 322-323
Ordered that Solomon Hedge Benjamin Rutherford Benjamin Forman & Abraham Johnson or any three of them being first sworn before a Majestrate of this County do meet and view the Roads as first marked and now used from Benjamin Kuykendals to the Trough hill and make report to the next Court

5 March 1754, FOB 5, p. 323
Ordered that Samuel Pritchard Steven Hotsenpella and Robert Allen being first sworn before a Magestrate of this County do meet and lay off a Road from Sandy ford on Opeckon to Fromans mill and make Report to the next Court

5 March 1754, FOB 5, p. 323
Ordered that William Buffington be overseer of the Road from the plantation late Peter Tostees to the North River in the Room of John Kuykendal and it is ordered that the Tithables formerly appointed keep the same in Repair according to Law.

5 March 1754, FOB 5, p. 323
George Huddle is appointed overseer of the Road from the head of Funks mill Creek to the County Line in the Room of Christopher Windle and it is ordered that the Tithables formerly appointed keep the same in Repair according to Law.

5 March 1754, FOB 5, p. 323
James Stroud is appointed Overseer of the Road from Cunninghams mill to Tuscorora in the room of Francis Lilbourn and it is Ordered that the Tithables formerly appointed keep the s^d Road in repair according to Law.

5 March 1754, FOB 5, p. 323
Simeon Rice is appointed overseer of the Road from Thomas Harts to the top of the mountain at Vestals Gap in the room of Gershom Keys Gent and it is Ordered that the Tithables formerly appointed keep the said Road in repair according to Law.

5 March 1754, FOB 5, p. 323
John Abril is appointed Overseer of the Road from Ross's field to the other side of Opeckon Creek and that the Tithables formerly appointed keep the same in repair according to Law.

5 March 1754, FOB 5, p. 324
Joseph Edwards is appointed Overseer of the Road from Opeckon to the middle of Smiths Bridge and it is ordered that the Tithables formerly appointed keep the same in repair according to Law.

5 March 1754, FOB 5, p. 325
Joseph M^c.Dowell is appointed Overseer of the Road from Crismans Spring to Cedar Creek and it is ordered that the Tithables formerly appointed keep the said Road in repair according to Law.

5 March 1754, FOB 5, p. 325
Lawrence Stevens is appointed Overseer of the Road from Crismans Spring to Hites Mill and it is Ordered that the Tithables formerly appointed keep the said Road in Repair according to Law.

6 March 1754, FOB 5, p. 330
Peter Hedges is appointed Overseer of the Road from Lemons to Watkins's ferry in the room of Robert Lemon and it is Ordered that the Tithables formerly appointed keep the said Road in repair according to Law.

7 March 1754, FOB 5, p. 337
Ordered that George Johnston Gent in the name of this Court apply to the Justice of Prince William County for an Order for a Road to be cleared in the said County of Prince William from the fork of the Road below Watts's Ordinary to meet a Road cleared in this County leading through Manassas Run Gap

7 March 1754, FOB 5, p. 338
Adam Pain is appointed Overseer of the Road from the Warm Springs to the mouth of Sleepy Creek in the room of James Boyle and it is Ordered that the Tithables formerly appointed keep the same in repair according to Law

7 March 1754, FOB 5, p. 338
Samuel Stroud is appointed Overseer of the Road from the Meeting house to Opeckon in the room of Jonas Hedge and it ordered that the Tithables formerly appointed keep the said Road in repair according to Law.

7 March 1754, FOB 5, p. 338
Edward Teague is appointed Overseer of the Road from Mr Jacob Hites to Swearengens Ferry in the room of Richard Morgan and it is Ordered that the Tithables formerly appointed keep the same in Repair according to Law.

7 March 1754, FOB 5, pp. 338-339
Ordered that Peter Julian Thomas Low and James Cromley being first Sworn before a Justice of this County do meet and lay off a Road the most Convenient and best way from Captain Jeremiah Smiths to Col° Morgans and thence into the Main County Road near Patrick Reileys.

2 April 1754, FOB 5, p. 345
Lewis Stevens Gent is appointed Overseer of the Road from from his old plantation to his L^{d}ships Quarter in the room of Jacob Nisewanger and it is ordered that the Tithables formerly appointed keep the same in repair according to Law.

2 April 1754, FOB 5, p. 345
Thomas Bryan Martin Esq is appointed Overseer of of the Road from his L^{d}ships Quarter into the Dutch Road in the room of Jacob Nisewanger and it is Ordered that the Tithables formerly appointed keep the same in repair according to Law.

2 April 1754, FOB 5, p. 347
Michael Harper is appointed overseer of the Road from Edward Snickers's to Moses Guess's in the room of Mark Matterly and it is Ordered that the Tithables formerly appointed keep the same in repair according to Law

2 April 1754, FOB 5, p. 347
Ordered that Thomas Low Peter Julian and James Cromley being first sworn before a Justice of this County do mark and lay off a Road from Jeremiah Smiths to Morgan Morgans thence into the main County Road the most convenient and best way and make report to next Court

2 April 1754, FOB 5, p. 348
Samuel Mount is appointed overseer of the Road from from Opeckon to the widow Cunninghams in the room of Nicholas Osbourn and it is ordered that the Tithables formerly appointed keep the same in repair according to Law.

2 April 1754, FOB 5, p. 348
Stephen Hotsenpella Robert Allan and Samuel Pritchard having in Complyance to an Order of of this Court returned that they have marked a Road from Sandy ford to Fromans mill Ordered that Robert Glass, Nathaniel Cartmill Nathan Cartmill John Thomas Robert Hodgson Jacob Cooper Jacob Frey Joseph Frey Martin Grider John Cook Samuel Vance Benjamin Frey Abra^m Frey Paul Froman, John Tuckerman, Peter Miller John Capper, Joseph Fosset Phillip Harihill And^w Longacre, Richard Ireson Richard Fosset Nathl Carr Joseph Glass John Becket Adam Hunter Phillip Cross Samuel Glass John Dyer clear and keep the same in Repair according to the prayer of their petition and it is further ordered that Paul Froman Junr be overseer of the s^d Road.

2 April 1754, FOB 5, p. 349
Jonathan Taylor is appointed Overseer of the Road from Littlers old place to Opeckon Creek in the room of George Ross and it is Ordered that the Tithables Three miles on each side the said Road keep the same in Repair according to Law.

2 April 1754, FOB 5, p. 349
Gershom Keys Gent is Ordered to enter into Bond with one security as the Law directs for keeping Ferry on his Land cross Shanando river to the Land of the Honble. William Fairfax Esq. And it is further ordered that he keep two able hands and a Boat sufficient to take over wheel carriages

2 April 1754, FOB 5, p. 349
Edward Snigers is Ordered to enter into Bond with one Security as the Law directs from the Land of Ld Fairfax Crossing Shanando River to the Land of John Mercer Gen^t

3 April 1754, FOB 5, p. 376
Gershom Keys and Thomas Rutherford his Security having in Open Court acknowledged their Bond for the s^d Greshom his keeping Ferry cross Shanando River the same is admitted to Record.

3 April 1754, FOB 5, p. 376
Edward Snigers and John Ashbey his Security having in Open Court acknowledged their Bond for the s^d Edward his keeping Ferry cross Shanando River the same is admitted to Record

5 April 1754, FOB 5, p. 416
Ordered that James Lemon with the Tithables appointed to work under him as overseer of the Road clear a Road from the end of the new Street in Winchester into the main Road leading to Parkins Mill and also to clear from the end of the s^d Street into the Road leading to the River

7 May 1754, FOB 5, p. 424
Ordered that John Vestal William Hall and John Croles being first sworn before a Justice of this County do mark and lay off a Road from Robert Harpers at the mouth of Shanando the most convenient and best way to William Halls mill and from thence into the Road to Winchester and make report to next Court

7 May 1754, FOB 5, p. 426
William Draper is appointed Overseer of the Road from from the great Plain to Selsers Mill run where the Road crosseth the same and it is Ordered that all the Tithables from Stoney Creek upwards keep the same in repair according to Law

7 May 1754, FOB 5, p. 426
Matthias Selser is appointed Overseer of the Road from Selsers Mill run to the South River ford and it is Ordered that the Tithables within three Miles on each side the said Road and on the same side the River keep the same in Repair according to Law

7 May 1754, FOB 5, p. 426
Peter Ruckner is appointed Overseer of the Road from the South River ford to the Top of the Blue Ridge and it is Ordered that the Tithables formerly appointed to work under Phillip Long keep the said road in repair according to Law.

7 May 1754, FOB 5, p. 426
William Bethell is appointed Overseer of the Road from the Top of the Blue Ridge to Calebs Run and and it is Ordered that the Tithables formerly appointed keep the same in repair according to Law.

7 May 1754, FOB 5, pp. 427-428
Grand Jury Presentments

We present the overseer of the Road from Lewis Neills to Winchester Town for not keeping the same in repair according to Law.

We present the overseer of the Road from Edward Snickers's on Shanando to Carneys pond for not keeping the same in repair according to Law

We present the overseer of the Road from Peter Tostees to Watkins's ferry for not keeping the same in repair according to Law

We present the overseer of the Road from Robt Cunninghams to Samuel Pattons for not keeping the same in repair according to Law

* * *

We present the overseer of the Road from Geo. Wrights to Capt John Hites for not keeping the same in repair according to Law

7 May 1754, FOB 5, p. 428
Ordered that Charles Buck and Ralph Withers being first sworn by this County do view and lay off a Road from his L^d.ships house into M^c.Coys Chapple Road and from thence to his L^d.ships Quarter in the long Bottom and make report to next Court

9 May 1754, FOB 5, p. 455
Ordered that Lewis Neill John Milbourn and William Jolliffe Junr being first sworn before Justices of this county do view the Road from Littlers old place to Opeckon Creek and mark such places where they see a necessity for altering the s^d Road and make report to next Court

4 June 1754, FOB 5, p. 474
Henry Brinker is appointed overseer of the Fairfax Road and it is further ordered that all the Tithables in Winchester together with the Tithables formerly appointed keep the same in repair according to Law and that the s^d Henry be exempted from working on any other Road during the time he is overseer

4 June 1754, FOB 5, p. 474
Lewis Neill William Jolliffe Junr and John Milbourn having viewed the Road from Littlers Old place to Opeckon in complyance to a former Order of this Court and marked where the s^d. Road in their Opi[nion] is necessary to be altered. Ordered that the s^d. Road as now marked be established and that the old Road continue until further Orders for Clearing the new part.

4 June 1754, FOB 5, p. 475
Ordered that William Whitson Henry Nelson and Moses M^c.Coy being first sworn before a magestrate of this County do view and mark a Road the most convenient and best way from Calebs Run to the Brushbottom Ford from thence to the Percimmon Pond above James M^c.Coys and make report to next Court.

5 June 1754, FOB 5, p. 485
Ordered that Thomas Swearengen Gent Jonas Hedge and Isaac Beason being first sworn do view the Ford at Linders and the Creek above and below and make report to next Court

5 June 1754, FOB 5, p. 490
Ordered that Cornelius Ruddle be Overseer of the Road from his Lordships line to Allens mill Creek and that the Tithables formerly appointed keep the s^d Road in repair according to Law.

5 June 1754, FOB 5, p. 490
Ordered that Abraham Collet be overseer of the Road from Allens Mill Creek to Stoney Creek and that the Tithables formerly appointed keep the s^d Road in repair according to Law.

5 June 1754, FOB 5, p. 490
Joseph Langdon is appointed Overseer of the Road from Stoney Creek to millers foot path and that the Tithables formerly appointed keep the said Road in repair according to Law

5 June 1754, FOB 5, p. 491
Abraham Denton is appointed overseer of the Road from Millers foot path to the Old County Line and it is Ordered that all the Tithables formerly appointed keep the s^d. Road in repair according to Law.

Frederick County Order Book 6 (1754-1755)

6 June 1754, FOB 6, p. 2
Ordered that all the Tithables in Winchester work on the Fairfax Road under Henry Brinker the Overseer thereof and that the said Henry be exempted from working on any other Road during the time he is Overseer.

6 June 1754, FOB 6, p. 15
(Grand Jury Plt ag^t Edward Snigers Dft) On presentment for not keeping the Road in repair whereof he is Overseer. The Dft being solemnly called and failing to appear Ordered he be fined Fifteen shillings Current money to be appropriated according to Law.

6 June 1754, FOB 6, p. 15
(Grand Jury Plt ag^t Peter Hedge Dft) On presentment for not Keeping the Road in repair of which he is Overseer. The Dft being solemnly called and failing to appear Ordered that he be fined Fifteen shillings to be appropriated according to Law.

6 June 1754, FOB 6, p. 15
(G. Jury Plt ag^t James Stroud Dft) On Presentment For not keeping the Road in repair of which he is Overseer. The Dft being solemnly called and failing to appear Ordered that he be fined Fifteen shillings to be appropriated according to Law.

6 August 1754, FOB 6, p. 23
Thomas Low is appointed Overseer of the Road from Marquis Calmes's to Opeckon Run in the room of James Stinson and it is Ordered that the Tithables three miles on each side the s^d. Road keep the same in repair according to Law

6 August 1754, FOB 6, p. 24
Ordered that Jeremiah Smith be Overseer of the Road from the County Line to his House in the Room of Joseph Edwards and that the Tithables Five miles on each side the said Road keep the same in repair according to Law.

6 August 1754, FOB 6, p. 24
Ordered that Henry Spears be Overseer of the Road from Calebs Run to the Percimmon Pond and that the Tithables Three miles on each side Clear and keep the same in repair according to Law.

6 August 1754, FOB 6, p. 25
Ordered that John Painter James Rainey and John Branson being first sworn before a Justice of this County do mark and lay off a Road the most convenient and best way from Crooked Run to Capt. Hites and make report to next Court.

7 August 1754, FOB 6, p. 33
Ordered that Abraham Vanmeter and Samuel Stroud with their respective Gangs open the Road at Linders to a place below the Old fording place where it is marked by the viewers appointed by this Court.

8 August 1754, FOB 6, p. 33
Ordered that the Tithables belonging to the R^t. Honble. Thos. L^d. Fairfax clear a Road as laid off by Charles Buck and Ralph Withers from his L^d.ships house to his Quarter in the long Bottom and that they keep the same in repair according to Law

8 August 1754, FOB 6, p. 36
Ordered that Peter Hedge with the Tithables of which he is Overseer clear the Road through the main Street of maidstone to Potomack River and to the Main Road.

8 August 1754, FOB 6, p. 36
Ordered that James Forman be overseer of the Road from William Richeys to Opeckon and that the Tithables three miles on each side the Road work on the same.

8 August 1754, FOB 6, p. 36
Ordered that Thomas Shepard Jacob Vanmeter and Robert Buckles being first sworn do view and mark a Road from Catons Ford the most convenient and best way to Vestals Gap and make report to next Court.

3 September 1754, FOB 6, p. 65
Ordered that Francis Lilbourn Samuel Holliday & Benjamin Richardson being first sworn do view the Road and ford from Morgans Chapple to Mill Creek and the Ground the most convenient to the main Road and report to next Court their Opinion of the same

5 September 1754, FOB 6, p. 81
(Grand Jury Plt v Benjamin Grub Dft) On Presentment for not keeping a Road in Repair whereof he is Overseer. The Dft appeared and being heard Ordered that he be fined Fifteen Shillings for the same and that he pay Cost

5 September 1754, FOB 6, p. 81
(Grand Jury Plt ag^t Samuel Pritchard Dft) On Presentment for not keeping the Road whereof he is Overseer in Repair The Dft being summoned and failing to Appear Ordered that he be fined Fifteen Shillings for the same and that he pay Cost.

5 September 1754, FOB 6, p. 81
(Grand Jury Plt ag^t Lewis Stevens Dft) On presentment for not keeping the Road in repair whereof he is Overseer The Dft appeared and being heard Ordered that he be fined Fifteen Shillings for the same and that he pay Cost.

5 September 1754, FOB 6, p. 82
(Grand Jury Plt ag^t Gershom Keys Dft) On presentment for not keeping a Road in repair whereof he is Overseer the Dft being summoned and failing to appear Ordered that he be Fined Fifteen Shillings and that he pay Cost.

5 September 1754, FOB 6, p. 89
Ordered that John Rout Senr be Overseer of the Road from Gregorys ford to Ashbeys Ford in the Room of Thomas Ashbey and it is Ordered that the Tithables formerly appointed keep the same in repair according to Law

5 September 1754, FOB 6, p. 90
Ordered that Mercy Calmes be Overseer of the Road from the old School house on Shanando to Cunninghams Chapple in the room of John Ashbey and that the Tithables formerly appointed keep the same in repair according to Law.

1 October 1754, FOB 6, p. 91
Ordered that M^r. Michael Pike be continued overseer of the Road from Edward Snigers's to the Top of the Mountain at Williams's Gap and that the Tithables formerly appointed Keep the same in Repair according to Law

1 October 1754, FOB 6, p. 97
Francis Lilbourn &c having made their Report that they have viewed the Road from Morgans Chapple to the Main Road in Complyance to an Order of this Court and find there is a necessity for altering the same and that they have marked from the said Chappel to Robert Cunninghams house Ordered that it be cleared accordingly and that the Tithables formerly appointed Keep the same in Repair according to Law.

1 October 1754, FOB 6, p. 108
Stephen Emrey is Continued Overseer of the Road from the Bridge at the Long marsh to Edward Snigers's and it is Ordered that the Tithables formerly appointed to keep the s^d Road in repair according to Law

2 October 1754, FOB 6, p. 109
Ordered that William Hand and Christopher Marr being first Sworn view and mark a Road the most Convenient and best way from the Culpepper Road at Chesters Gap to Chesters Ford and make report to next Court

6 November 1754, FOB 6, p. 135
(Grand Jury Plt ag^t William Duckworth Dft) On presentment for not keeping the Road in Repair and being heard Ordered that he be fined Fifteen Shillings and that he pay Costs

7 November 1754, FOB 6, p. 145
Ordered that Thomas Caton Gent Jonas Hedge & Peter Hedge being first sworn before a majestrate of this County do view and lay off a Road from Hoglands Neck by Barnet Newkirks and into the great Road and make report to next Court.

4 February 1755, FOB 6, p. 166
Jeremiah Smith is continued Overseer of the Road from his House to Robert Pearis's and it is Ordered that the Tithables Five miles on each side of the s^d. Road keep the same in Repair according to Law

5 February 1755, FOB 6, p. 167
Ordered that Thomas Caton Jacob Hite and John Lindsey G^t. being first sworn do view and mark a Road from the Head of Bullskin to Watkin's Ferry the most convenient and best way and make report to next Court

5 February 1755, FOB 6, p. 167
Ordered that William Bethell James M^c.Coy and Charles Buck being first Sworn do view and mark a Road the most convenient way from the Sign Post at the Hawks bill down the South River into the Road leading to Winchester and make Report to the next Court.

5 February 1755, FOB 6, p. 167
Ordered that Daniel Holman William White and Jonas Little being first Sworn do view and mark a Road the most convenient way from Stevens's mill at the narrow passage to the main Road near Reiley Moors and make report to next Court

5 February 1755, FOB 6, p. 167
Stephen Cannil and John Ashbey Robert Ashbey and Marquis Calmes his Securitys in Open Court acknowledged their Bond for the s^d. Stephen keeping Ferry over Shanando River at Col^o. Burwells Land according to Law.

7 February 1755, FOB 6, p. 177
Thomas Caton Gent and Enoch Pearson are appointed Overseers of the Road from Enoch Pearson's to Watkins's Ferry in the room of Peter Hedge and it is ordered that the Tithables formerly appointed keep the same in repair according to Law

4 March 1755, FOB 6, p. 193
Isaac Evans is Appointed overseer of the Road from Mendenalls mill to Cunninghams mill in the Room of James Stroud and it is Ordered that the Tithables between Opeckon Creek and the foot of the mountain keep the same in Repair according to Law.

4 March 1755, FOB 6, p. 194
Joseph Glass is appointed Overseer of the Road from John Beckets house to Capt. Hites mill in the room of Thomas Marquis and it is Ordered that the Tithables formerly appointed keep the s^d. Road in repair according to Law.

4 March 1755, FOB 6, p. 194
Ordered that William Crawford Benjamin Grubb and Richard Stevenson being first sworn do view and lay off such Roads as they shall find needful on both sides the River from Keys ferry into the Main Roads near the same and make report to next Court.

4 March 1755, FOB 6, p. 194
Ordered that Daniel Holman William White and Jonas Little being first sworn do view and mark a Road from Lewis Stevens mill to the next best ford on the River above Reily Moors and from thence into the main Road and make report to next Court.

1 April 1755, FOB 6, p. 198
Michael Harper is continued overseer of the Road from Snigers's house to Moses Gess's and it is further ordered that all the Tithables within Five miles of the s^d. Road keep the same in repair according to Law.

1 April 1755, FOB 6, p. 199
Thomas Buck is appointed overseer of the Road from the North River to the Hay-Bottom in the room of Gervas Dothertay and it is further Ordered that the Tithables two miles on each side of the s^d. Road keep the same in Repair according to Law.

1 April 1755, FOB 6, p. 199
Leonard Helm is appointed overseer of the Road from Opeckon to the sign post near Quintons in the room of Thomas Low and it is further ordered that the Tithables Three miles on each side keep the same in repair according to Law.

1 April 1755, FOB 6, p. 199
Ordered that Edward Cartmill and Joseph Vance being first sworn do view the Road from Lewis Stephens's to M^c.Coys Chapple and mark where it is needful to make alteration in the same and make report to next Court.

1 April 1755, FOB 6, p. 199
On the petition of Walter Shirley it is Ordered that Gershom Keys Nathaniel Thomas and Samuel Pearson being first sworn do meet and Review that part of the Road from Harpers ferry to Winchester where the s^d. Road passeth through the Land of the s^d. Shirley and Report to next Court if it be necessary to alter the same.

2 April 1755, FOB 6, p. 200
Ordered that Edward Thomas and Morgan Morgan lay off a Road from the new Bridge at Opeckon the most convenient way into the Road leading from Winchester to Henry Enochs' and that they be overseers thereof and it is further ordered that the tithables Four miles on each side of the said Road clear and keep the same in repair according to Law

2 April 1755, FOB 6, p. 200
Ordered that Peter Julian be overseer of the Road leading from Winchester to Henry Enochs' from the beginning of the s^d new Road as far as the County Line and that the Tithables Four miles on each side of the s^d Road clear and keep the same in Repair according to Law.

2 April 1755, FOB 6, p. 200
Ordered that Thomas Wadlington be Overseer of the Road from the River at Snigers' to the County Line at Williams's gap and that the Tithables formerly appointed keep the same in Repair

2 April 1755, FOB 6, p. 201
Ordered that James M^c.Kenney Christian Stickley and John Lewis being first sworn do mark a Road the nearest and best way from Jeremiah Lewis's to Stevens' mill at the narrow passage and make report to next Court.

2 April 1755, FOB 6, p. 201
Ordered that Peter Stover be Overseer of the Road from Funk Mill to the North River and that the Tithables formerly appointed keep the same in Repair according to law.

2 April 1755, FOB 6, p. 201
George Wright is Ordered to continue Overseer of the Road from Captain Hites to the new Road near the said Wrights house and that the Tithables three miles on each side the s^d. Road keep it in repair according to Law.

2 April 1755, FOB 6, p. 201
Ordered that Zebulon Thorp continue Overseer of the Road from Captain Hites to Crooked Run and it is ordered that the Tithables three miles on each side the s^d. Road keep the same according to Law in Repair.

2 April 1755, FOB 6, p. 201
Ordered that Humphrey Keys be overseer of the Roads from the main Roads to Keys's Ferry and that the Tithables two miles on each side clear and keep them in Repair according to Law.

2 April 1755, FOB 6, p. 207
Ordered that Robert Pearis be overseer of the Road from Winchester to Hogs Creek and that the Tithables on the west side of Winchester old street and Three miles on the southside the s^d. Road work on the same and that the s^d. Tithables in Winchester be exempted from working on Neills Road.

2 April 1755, FOB 6, p. 207
Ordered that William Stroop be continued Overseer of the Road from Buckles' marsh to where it intercepts the Road leading to Reubin Rutherfords and it is further Ordered that the Tithables within the following bounds keep the same in Repair according to Law viz up Buckles marsh to the old Wagon Road at Thomas Harts and down the Belhaven Road to Shanando, down Shanando to the mouth, up Potomack to Buckles' marsh.

2 April 1755, FOB 6, p. 207
Ordered that Jeremiah Smith be Overseer of the Road from Hogs Creek to M^c.Coys Ridge and it is further Ordered that the Tithables Two miles on each side the s^d. Road keep the same in Repair according to Law.

2 April 1755, FOB 6, p. 213
Ordered that John Bryan be continued Overseer of the Road from Opeckon near his house to Winchester and it is further Ordered that he mark and clear the said Road on the Top of the Ridge to avoid as much as possable the swampey part of the s^d. Road and that the Tithables Three miles on each side of the Road and also the Tithables on the East side of the Old Street in Winchester keep the same in repair according to Law.

2 April 1755, FOB 6, p. 214
Ordered that John Reno be Overseer of the Road from the sign post to Cannills ferry in the room of John Armstrong and it is furthered Ordered that the Tithables Three miles on each Side the s^d. Road keep the same in repair according to Law.

3 April 1755, FOB 6, p. 231
Ordered that Thomas Cordery be Overseer of the Road from Tuscorora Creek to Peter Tostees in the room of Isaac Beason and that the Tithables formerly appointed keep the same in Repair according to Law.

3 April 1755, FOB 6, p. 231
Ordered that John Beason be overseer of the Road from the mountain to Opeckon in the room of Samuel Stroud and that the Tithables formerly appointed keep the same in repair according to Law

4 April 1755, FOB 6, p. 234
Ordered that Enoch Pearson Robert Davis and Jonas Hedge being first sworn do lay off a Road from Enoch Pearsons to the mouth of Back Creek and it is further Ordered that Enoch Pearson be overseer thereof and that the Tithables Three miles on each side the s^d. Road Clear & keep the same in Repair according to Law

5 April 1755, FOB 6, p. 238
Ordered that Reuben Rutherford John Vestal & William Crawford being first sworn do lay off a Road from John Hardins to vestals wagon Road and make report to next Court.

6 May 1755, FOB 6, p. 246
Grand Jury Presentments
We . . . present the Overseer of the Road from the Top of the Ridge to Snigers's ford.
Also the overseer of the Road from Captain Lewis Niells to Winchester by the Information of Mr William Seale for not keeping the s^d. Roads according to Law
* * *
We of the Grand Jury present the Surveyor of the Road from Jacob Cristmans to Capt John Hites mill

We of the Jury present the Overseer of the Road from the North River ford to the ford of Crooked Run

7 May 1755, FOB 6, p. 256
Ordered that John Jones be Overseer of the Road beginning at the County Line near $Jerem^h$ Lewis's to Christian Dilliners and that the Tithables between the north mountain and two miles on the Southside the Road clear and keep the same in repair according to Law.

7 May 1755, FOB 6, p. 256
Ordered that Adolph Ilor be Overseer of the Road from Christian Dilleners to Lewis Stevens mill at the narrow passage that the Tithables between the North mountain and two miles on the south side the Road clear and keep the same in repair.

5 June 1755, FOB 6, p. 310
Ordered that James M^c.Coy be overseer of the Road from the Road crossing the River at his ford to Captain Jacob Funks & that the tithables in the ford below Mason Combs and John Morrice his old plantation keep the same in repair according to Law

5 June 1755, FOB 6, p. 311
Ordered that John Duckworth be overseer of the Road from Captain Jacob Funks to his house and that the Tithables two miles on each side the s^d Road keep the same in Repair according to Law

6 June 1755, FOB 6, p. 315
Ordered that Simeon Rice with the Hands that work under him as overseer of the Road Clear the Roads to and from Keys's ferry into the main Roads in the room of Humphrey Keys formerly appointed

6 June 1755, FOB 6, p. 315
Ordered that William Evans be Overseer of the Road from Steven's mill to M^c.Coys Chapple Road near Cartmills and that the Tithables two miles on each side the s^d. Road keep the same in Repair according to Law.

8 June 1755, FOB 6, p. 338
On the motion of Lewis Stevens Gent Ordered that the Sheriff summon Daniel Holman & William White to show cause why they have not laid off a Road and made their Report in Pursuance of an Order of this Court

8 June 1755, FOB 6, p. 339
Ordered that Thomas Caton Gent George Harland and Robert Davis being first sworn do mark and lay off a Road from Gillilands mill to Andrew Campbells and make their Report to next Court

1 July 1755, FOB 6, p. 341
Jacob Cristman is appointed Overseer of the Road from Capt. Hites mill dam to the s^d Cristmans Spring in the Room of Lawrence Stephens and it is further ordered that the Tithables formerly appointed keep the s^d Road in Repair according to Law.

1 July 1755, FOB 6, p. 341
Thomas Colson is continued Overseer of the Road from Carneys Spring to Opeckon at Neills ford and that the Tithables formerly appointed keep the s^d Road in Repair according to Law.

5 August 1755, FOB 6, p. 373
(Grand Jury Plt ag^t Thomas Wadlington Dft) On Presentment
For not keeping a Road in repair whereof he is Overseer. The Dft being solemnly called and failing to appear Judgment is granted ag^t him for the Sum of Fifteen shillings and the Costs of this Prosecution.

3 September 1755, FOB 6, p. 380
Anthony Turner is appointed Overseer of the Road in the Room of William Chaplin

3 September 1755, FOB 6, p. 386
Ordered that the Road through the Land of Walter Shirley be continued as first cleared.

7 October 1755, FOB 6, p. 405
Ordered that Lewis Neill Gent be Overseer of the Road from his House at Opeckon to the Sign post and that the Tithables Four miles on each side the said Road keep the same in repair according to Law

7 October 1755, FOB 6, p. 405
Peter Wolf is appointed Overseer of the Road in the Room of William Quinton

Frederick County Order Book 7 (1755-1758)

4 February 1756, FOB 7, p. 15
Ordered that Edward Snigers be Overseer of the Road from the Ferry Road to the Top of the Ridge at Williams's Gap in the room of Thomas Wadlington and that the tithables six miles on each side of the River above and below keep the same in Repair according to Law

4 February 1756, FOB 7, p. 15
Ordered that Thomas Wadlington be Overseer of the Road from Shanando River to Carneys Spring in the Room of Edward Snigers and that the Tithables three miles on each side the Road keep the same in repair according to Law

4 February 1756, FOB 7, p. 15
Ordered that John Lindsey Gent William Calmes & Thomas Wadlington being first sworn before a majestrate of this County do view and lay off a Road from the Fairfax Road to the Ferry Landing and from thence to the Fairfax Road on the other side the River and make report to next Court.

4 February 1756, FOB 7, p. 15
Ordered that John Lindsey Gent agree with some person to blow up the Rock or Rocks at Williams's Gap and make report to next in Order to be allowed at laying the next County Levy.

4 February 1756, FOB 7, p. 16
Ordered that John Vestal be overseer of the Road from Vestals Ford to Col° Fairfax's Quarter and that the Tithables Four miles on each side of the s^d. road and also Four miles on the North end thereof keep the same in Repair according to Law.

4 February 1756, FOB 7, p. 16
Ordered that Michael Pike be Overseer of the Road from Col° Fairfax's Quarter to the Fairfax Road and that the Tithables Three miles on each side the s^d. Road keep the same in repair according to Law.

2 March 1756, FOB 7, p. 17
Ordered that Thomas Speake John M^c.Cormack John Davis and John Lindsey or any three of these being first sworn before a Justice of this County do meet view and lay off a Road from the Main Road near Sebastians Quarter to Hardin and Keys Mill from thence to the Iron Works and make a report to next Court

2 March 1756, FOB 7, p. 20
Ordered that Richard Fallis, William Duckworth and William Holbrook, being sworn do mark a Road from Joseph Edwards Junr to the main Road at the Bridge over Opeckon Creek and make report to next Court

2 March 1756, FOB 7, p. 20
John Davis is appointed Overseer of the Road from the top of the blue ridge at Thorns Gap to Caleb Jobs mill in the room of William Bethell deceased and it is ordered that the Tithables formerly appointed keep the same in repair according to Law.

3 March 1756, FOB 7, p. 30
Jonas Seaman is appointed Overseer of the Road from Morgans Chapple to Opeckon in the room of Francis Fowler and it is Ordered that the Tithables formerly appointed keep the same in repair according to Law

3 March 1756, FOB 7, p. 30
Evan Thomas is appointed Overseer of the Road from William Jolliffs to Mary Ballangers in the room of Edward Thomas and it is Ordered that the Tithables formerly appointed keep the same in repair according to Law

4 March 1756, FOB 7, p. 39
Peter Wolf is appointed Overseer of the Road from Burdens Run to Cunninghams Chapple in the room of William Quinton and that the Tithables formerly appointed keep the same in repair according to Law.

5 March 1756, FOB 7, p. 42
Ordered that Adam Funk be Overseer of the Road from M^c.Nishes Run to Stoney Run in the room of Joseph Langdon and that the Tithables formerly appointed keep the same in repair

6 April 1756, FOB 7, p. 57
Ordered that John Lindsey Gent Thomas Speake, John Davis John M^c.Cormack being first Sworn do view from the Bridge at Worthingtons marsh to the main road to Vestals Gap and make report to next Court the most convenient way.

5 August 1756, FOB 7, p. 101
Ordered that Thomas Swearengen John Lindsey Henry Moore and Michael Pike Gent being first sworn do view and report to next Court the most convenient way from the Inhabitants on Worthingtons marsh to Hardin & Keys mill

5 August 1756, FOB 7, p. 103
Ordered that the order for Thomas Speake, John Lindsey, John McCormack and John Davis to view a Road from the main Road near Sebastians Quarter to Hardin & Keys mill be discontinued

8 September 1756, FOB 7, p. 121
Ordered that John Lindsey and Thomas Speake Gent agree wth. workmen to blow up the Rocks in Williams's Gap that obstruct the Road and make report to next Court

5 October 1756, FOB 7, p. 125
Ordered that Richard Sturman William Roberts & Thomas Waters being first Sworn do view the Road from the Lower Corner of John Reno's Plantation to some part of the Road above the said Plantation and report to next Court if the same can be altered without prejudice to the Publick.

6 October 1756, FOB 7, p. 128
Ordered that George Bounds, Caleb Odell and Benjamin Denton being first Sworn do mark and lay off a Road from George Julians on passage Creek to Bucks mill and make report to next Court

[Note: There are no Court orders for December 1756 or January 1757.]

1 February 1757, FOB 7, p. 159
Ordered that John Reno have leave to clear a Road from the Corner of his Fence into the main Road according to the return made by Thomas Waters and William Roberts and that the same hereafter be established

1 March 1757, FOB 7, p. 190
On the motion of Josiah Ridgway for leave to alter the main road running through his Land towards Watkins Ferry Ordered that Lewis Moore and Robert Cunningham being first Sworn do view the way proposed by him and make their report next Court.

1 March 1757, FOB 7, p. 190
On the motion of John Lewis and others praying they may be exempted from working on the Messanuting Road Ordered that John Jones William Bailey and George Nicholls be Summoned to appear at next Court to be examined concerning the s^d motion

1 March 1757, FOB 7, p. 190
The following persons are appointed Overseers of the Several Roads the ensuing year to wit

From the head of Funks Mill Run to the County line Ulrick Stone in the room of Geo. Huddle.

From Swearangens Ferry to Jacob Hites, Thomas Shepard in the room of Abraham Teague.

From Stephens's Mill to the Head of Funks Mill Creek Daniel Currey in the room of William Blackbourn.

From Allans Mill Creek to his Lordships Line Daniel Holman in the room of Cornelius Ruddle

From Stoney Creek to Mill Creek John Skean in the room of Abraham Collet.

From Desponets Gap to Stephens's Mill Jacob Brake in the room of Martin Grider

1 March 1757, FOB 7, p. 192
On the motion of Joseph Vance and Peter Stephens for leave to alter the main Road running through their Lands Ordered that Charles Barnes John Nisewanger and Joseph M^c.dowell being first sworn do view how they propose to alter the same and make report to next Court

3 March 1757, FOB 7, p. 212
On the motion of Joseph Roberts he is discharged from being Overseer of the dutch Road from Kerseys ferry to Wrights branch.

5 April 1757, FOB 7, p. 222
Joseph Vance is appointed Overseer of the Road from Crismans Spring to Cedar Creek in the room of Joseph M^c.dowell

5 April 1756, FOB 7, p. 222
On the motion of Thomas Wadlington praying viewers of the work done by him on the Road at Williams' Gap Ordered that Michael Pike William Calmes & Henry Hurst view the same and make report to next Court

5 April 1757, FOB 7, p. 222
Thomas Reece is appointed Overseer of the Road from Col^o. Morgans to Ballengers Meadow in the room of James Cromley

6 April 1757, FOB 7, p. 230
On the motion of John Lewis and others praying they may be relieved from keeping the Massanuting Road in repair Ordered that such of the Petitioners who live above a mile on the Northside of the N^o. River be exempted from working on the s^d. Road

6 April 1757, FOB 7, p. 230
James Bruce is appointed Overseer of the Road from Winchester to Robert Moseleys Plantation in the room of James Lemon and it is Ordered that he with the Tithables formerly appointed keep the same in Repair according to Law.

3 May 1757, FOB 7, p. 238
Grand Jury Presentments

We of the grand Jury do present Henry Brinker Overseer of the Road leading from Winchester to Opeckon Creek by Lewis Neills for not keeping the said Road in repair according to Law within six months by the knowledge of two of us.

3 May 1757, FOB 7, p. 239
Thomas Waters is appointed Overseer of the Road from Opeckon Creek to Winchester in the room of John Bryan and it is Ordered that the Tithables formerly appointed do keep the s^d. Road in repair according to Law.

3 May 1757, FOB 7, p. 239
William Helm is appointed Overseer of the Road from the Sign Post to Opeckon Creek in the room of Leonard Helm and it is Ordered that the Tithables formerly appointed do keep the s^d. Road in repair according to Law.

3 May 1757, FOB 7, p. 239
Henry Stevens is appointed Overseer of the Road from Lawrence Stevens's by Lewis Stephens's Old Plantation to Col^o. Martins Road in the room of Lewis Stephens and it is Ordered that the Tithables formerly appointed keep the said Road in Repair according to Law.

3 May 1757, FOB 7, p. 239
Joseph Bealer is appointed Overseer of the Road from Opeckon Creek to Capt Rutherfords Plantation in the room of Joseph Hite and it is Ordered that the Tithables Three miles on each side of the s^d. Road keep the same in repair according to Law.

2 August 1757, FOB 7, p. 266
Michael Pike William Hurst and William Calmes having reported to the Court they have viewed the work done by Thomas Wadlington on the Road at Williams's gap in complyance to this Court Order and find it is compleated according to agreement on the motion of said Thomas it is Ordered that the Sum of Thirty eight pounds fourteen shillings be made an article for his use at the laying the next Levy.

4 October 1757, FOB 7, p. 280
Ordered that Marquis Calmes be Overseer of the Road from Burwells Mill to Cunninghams Chapple and that the Tithables on the River below Coombs's Ford to Moses Guess's upper Quarter keep the same in Repair according to Law.

4 October 1757, FOB 7, p. 285
Ordered that Lawrence Harrison be Overseer of the Road from from Worthingtons Marsh to Thomas Lindsays and that the Tithables three miles on each side the said Road keep the same in repair according to Law.

4 October 1757, FOB 7, p. 285
Ordered that Thomas Lindsey be Overseer of the Road from his House to Marquis Calmes's and that the Tithables Three miles on each side the said Road keep the same in repair according to Law.

1 November 1757, FOB 7, p. 293
Ordered that John Gardener be Overseer of the Road from John M^c.Cormacks to Opeckon Creek in the room of Benjamin Grub and that the tithables formerly appointed keep the same in repair according to Law

1 November 1757, FOB 7, p. 293
Ordered that Robert Milbourn be Overseer of the Road from Opeckon Creek to the main County Road in the room of John Milbourn and that the Tithables formerly appointed keep the same in repair according to Law.

1 November 1757, FOB 7, p. 294
Ordered that Edward Robinson be Overseer of the Road from from Snickers Ferry up the Riverside to Cunninghams Chapple in the room of Michael Harper and that the Tithables within two miles on each side keep the same in Repair according to Law.

1 November 1757, FOB 7, p. 294
Grand Jury Presentments

We of the granjury do present John Abrell Overseer of the Road from Opeckon Bridge to William Jolliffs for not keeping the said Road in repair according to Law within Twelve months past by the knowledge of Two of us
* * *
We of the granjury do present Henry Brinker Overseer of the Road from Lewis Neills to Winchester for not keeping the said Road in repair according to Law by the knowledge of Two of us.
* * *
We of the granjury do present James Bruce Overseer of the Road from Winchester to Robert Moseleys by the Information of Lewis Moore.

3 November 1757, FOB 7, p. 306
County Levy
Thomas Wadlington for work done on a Road   [£] 38.14. 0

5 November 1757, FOB 7, p. 320
John Funk Gent is appointed Overseer of the Roads through the Town to Parkins's Mill and it is Ordered that the Tithables in Town together wth. Mr Parkins's Tithables keep the same in Repair according to Law

5 November 1757, FOB 7, p. 320
George Wright Senr. is appointed Overseer of the Road Hite's house to Lewis Stevens's new Road

5 November 1757, FOB 7, p. 320
Martin Funk is appointed Overseer of the Road from Bowmans Mill to the Old County Line in the room of John Funk.

7 December 1757, FOB 7, p. 330
(Grand Jury Plt ag^t John Abrell Dft) On Presentment for not keeping
a Road in Repair. The Dft being summoned and failing to appear It is Ordered that he be fined the Sum of Fifteen Shillings Current money and Cost.

(Grand Jury Plt ag^t James Bruce Deft) On Presentment for not keeping a Road in repair. The Dft appeared and the Witnesses being sworn and arguments heard it is Ordered that the Dft be fined the Sum of Fifteen Shill^s. Current money and that he pay Cost

7 December 1757, FOB 7, p. 332
Ordered that Thomas Robinson be Overseer of the Road from Snickers's Ferry up the River side to Cunninghams Chapple in the room of Michael Harper and that the Tithables three miles on each Side the Road keep the same in repair according to Law.

7 December 1757, FOB 7, p. 333
Ordered that William Jolliffe Evan Thomas and Robert Stewart mark and lay off a Bridle Road from Edward Dodds to the main Road and on the motion of the said Edward leave is given him to clear the same.

7 December 1757, FOB 7, p. 333
Ordered that the new Road as formerly laid off through the Common from Winchester to Robert Moselys be cleared and that James Bruce be Overseer thereof and that the Tithables appointed to work on the Old Road clear and keep the same in Repair according to Law and when the same is compleated the said Old Road is to be discontinued.

7 March 1758, FOB 7, p. 382
Ordered that James Bruce William Reynolds and Peter Ruble being first Sworn before a Justice of this County do view and lay off a Road the most convenient & best way from the Lanes through the Common of Winchester to William Jolliffs and make report to next Court

8 March 1758, FOB 7, p. 390
On the motion of Sundry Persons Ordered that John Hite Robt Allen and Samuel Pritchard being first sworn do mark a Road from Col^o. Hites through the Town laid out on Lewis Stephens Plantation and from thence into the Main road and make report to next Court.

9 March 1758, FOB 7, p. 405
(Grand Jury Plt ag^t Henry Brinker Deft) On Presentment
The Plt appeared and being heard Ordered that the suit be dism^d.

(Grand Jury Plt ag^t Henry Brinker Dft) On Pre_____ *[Note: The pen appears to have run out of ink.]*
The Dft being heard Ordered that the suite be dismissed.

10 March 1758, FOB 7, p. 406
Ordered that Josiah Ridgway have leave to alter the main Road in the manner laid off by Lewis Moore and Robt. Cunningham and that the other part of the Road be discontinued.

Frederick County Order Book 8 (1758-1760)

4 April 1758, FOB 8, p. 1
Ordered that John Briscoe be Overseer of the Road from Edward Thomas's to Mr Jacob Hites in the Room of Edward Thomas and it is further Ordered that the Tithables formerly appointed Keep the same in repair according to Law.

4 April 1758, FOB 8, p. 2
Ordered that John Skean Joseph Allen and Jackson Allen being first Sworn do meet and lay off a Road from Isaac Ruddells Mill into the Main Road between the s^d Jackson Allens and John Skeans and make report of their proceedings to next Court.

4 April 1758, FOB 8, p. 3
Ordered that John Snap Senr Joseph Fry John Snap Jun John Fosset and Joseph Powell work on the Road from Paul Fromans mill by the Head of Opeckon into the Road leading to Winchester.

5 April 1758, FOB 8, p. 7
Michael Handley is appointed Overseer of the Road from Stoney Creek to Mill Creek in the room of John Skean and it is Ordered that the Tithables formerly appointed keep the s^d. Road in repair according to Law.

5 April 1758, FOB 8, p. 8
Ordered that the Road from Winchester to Robt Moseley be cleared according to the return of James Bruce and William Reynolds

5 April 1758, FOB 8, p. 11
Ordered that the Road from Col^o. Hites through Stephens Town from thence to the Main Road be cleared according to the Return and that the Tithables appointed to work on the Old Road clear and keep the same in repair under Samuel Boyd who is appointed Overseer thereof.

5 April 1758, FOB 8, p. 12
Ordered that the Overseer with the Tithables formerly appointed keep the Old Road from Col^o. Hites to Crismans Spring in repair according to Law.

2 May 1758, FOB 8, p. 29
Grand Jury Presentments

We of the Grand Jury do present the Overseer of the Road leading from Winchester and crossing Col^o. Hites Mill dam for not keeping the same in Repair according to Law within Two months past by the knowledge of two of us.

* * *

We of the Grand Jury do present Henry Moore Gent for turning the Kings Highway without having an Order of Court for the same within Two months past by the knowledge of two of us.

3 May 1758, FOB 8, p. 36
Ordered that Jacob Crisman be Overseer of the Old Road from Col°. Hites to Crismans Spring in the room of Lawrence Stephens and that the Tithables formerly appointed keep the same in Repair according to Law.

3 May 1758, FOB 8, p. 42
On the motion of Cornelius Ruddle leave is given him to open a Road and to keep it in repair from Jackson Allens crossing the mouth of Smiths Creek thence through Whites Bottom to William Clarks at Mount Pleasant.

4 July 1758, FOB 8, p. 46
William Hurst is appointed Overseer of the Road from Caleb Job's Run to the Culpepper Line at Chesters gap in the room of Richard Harrold and it is Ordered that the Tithables on the South Side of the River work on the part of the Road on the South Side and the Tithables on the Northside the River on the part of the Road on the North Side

5 July 1758, FOB 8, p. 62
(Grand Jury Plt ag^t Henry Moore G^t Dft) On presentment for Stoping a Road. The Dft being heard it is Ordered that the Suit be dismiss'd

5 July 1758, FOB 8, p. 63
Ordered that John Greenfield be Overseer of the Streets in Town Viz. Loudon Cameron & Piccadilley and that the Tithables in the s^d Town of Winchester clear and keep the said Streets in Repair

1 August 1758, FOB 8, p. 87
Ordered that John Timmons be Overseer of the Road from Howells Ford to the Top of the Ridge also from the Ferry Landing at Combs's to the Main Road also from the Wagon Ford into the said Road, and it is also Ordered that the Tithables a mile and a half on each side the River including Burwells quarter where Peter Catlet is Overseer and up the River to Howells ford keep the same in repair according to Law

1 August 1758, FOB 8, p. 88
Ordered that Thomas Cooper be Overseer of the Road from Gregorys Ford to the Top of the Ridge and that the Tithables formerly appointed keep the same in Repair according to Law.

1 August 1758, FOB 8, p. 88
Ordered that Robert Steward be Overseer of the Road from Ross's Field crossing Opeckon to the middle of Smith's Bridge in the Room of John Abrill and Joseph Edwards and it is further Ordered that the Tithables Three miles on each side the s^d. Road keep the same in repair accord^g. to Law

1 August 1758, FOB 8, p. 88
Ordered that John Timmons be Overseer of the Road from Shanando at the Wagon Ford to the Fork of the Road to Stephens town and that the Tithables Three Miles on each side of the Road keep the same in Repair accord^g to Law.

1 August 1758, FOB 8, p. 89
Ordered that Jeremiah Stroud be Overseer of the Road from Opeckon Creek to Lucas's Marsh in the Room of Anthony Turner and that the Tithables formerly appointed keep the said Road in Repair according to Law.

1 August 1758, FOB 8, p. 89
John North is appointed Overseer of the Road from the New Town to Nations's and that the Tithables One Mile and an half on the Northside and Three miles on the South side together with the Tithables in the s^d. Town keep the same in repair according to Law.

5 September 1758, FOB 8, p. 95
Ordered that the Tithables on the Westside of the River Shanando be exempted from working on the Road from Howells Ford to the Top of the Ridge under John Timmons Overseer of the said Road

7 September 1758, FOB 8, p. 106
Ordered that William Miller John Hite John Painter and Robert Mackoy being first sworn do view Chesters Road and from the new town into the said Road and make report to the next Court which way is the most convenient

7 September 1758, FOB 8, p. 106
Ordered that Van Swearengen Gent John Mendenal & William Campbell being first Sworn do view the Road passing through the Plantation of Thomas Caton Gent and see if it may be conveniently altered and make Report to next Court.

3 October 1758, FOB 8, p. 128
William Tapp is appointed Overseer of the Road from Spout Run to Cunninghams Chapple in the room of William Quinton and it is Ordered that the Tithables formerly appointed keep the same in repair according to Law.

7 November 1758, FOB 8, p. 134
Ordered that Henry Moore Gent have leave to alter the main Road near his Plantation according to the return of the viewers and that it be Established the main Road

7 November 1758, FOB 8, p. 134
Ordered that Peter Stoufer John Funk and George Bowman being first Sworn do meet and lay off a Road the most convenient & best way from Peter Stoufers to George Bowman's Mill and make report to next Court

8 November 1758, FOB 8, p. 146
Ordered that Lawrence Snap be Overseer of the Road from Col°. John Hites to Stephensburgh in the room of Samuel Boyd and it is further Ordered that the Tithables formerly appointed Keep the s^d Road in repair according to Law.

11 November 1758, FOB 8, p. 169
Ordered that William Jolliffe Junr be Overseer of the Road from Cunninghams Mill to Robert Moseleys in the Room of William Duckworth and that the Tithables formerly appointed keep the same in repair according to Law.

6 February 1759, FOB 8, p. 188
John Snap Junr is appointed Overseer of the Road from the Gap on the Little Mountain to John Hites Mill in the Room of John Snap Senr. and it is Ordered that the Tithables formerly appointed keep the same in Repair according to Law.

6 February 1759, FOB 8, p. 188
Ordered that John Skeane Gent. be Overseer of the Road from the Main County Road to August where the Messnuting Road Crosseth the same to Messanuting Run in the Room of Samuel Newman. And that the Tithables formerly appointed Keep the same in Repair according to Law.

6 February 1759, FOB 8, p. 189
On the motion of Noah Hampton praying leave to Alter the Road above his House from Coombs's Ferry up Shanando River It being considered by the Court the motion is Rejected.

3 April 1759, FOB 8, p. 212
Jacob Bowman is appointed Overseer of the back Road from Funks Mill Run to the County Line in the room of Ulrick Stone and it is Ordered that the Tithables formerly appointed keep the same in Repair according to Law.

3 April 1759, FOB 8, p. 212
George Farrow is appointed Overseer of the Road from Howells Ford to the Top of the Ridge, also from the Ferry Landing at Coombs's into the said Road, also from the Waggon Ford into the said Road. And it is Ordered that the Tithables on the Southside the River including Burwells Quarter where Peter Catlet is Overseer and the Island and up the River to Howells Ford work on the said Roads and keep them in repair according to Law.

5 April 1759, FOB 8, p. 227
Ordered that Phillip Bush be Overseer of Cameron Street and it is Ordered that the Tithables in the Town on the East side of Loudon Street keep the same in repair And it is further Ordered that the same Tithables be exempted from Working on Loudon Street.

1 May 1759, FOB 8, pp. 232-233
On the Petition of Isaac Hite and others for a Road from Henry Spears's to go by the said Isaac Hites and thence into the main County Road. Ordered that William Miller Peter Rufner Ephraim

Leith and Joseph McDowell or any three of them being first Sworn by a Justice of this County do view and mark the said Road and make report to next Court.

1 May 1759, FOB 8, pp. 234-235
Grand Jury Presentments

We of the Grand Jury do present Henry Brinker Overseer of the Road leading from Winchester to Opeckon Creek by Captain Lewis Neills for not keeping the said Road in Repair according to Law within Two months past by the knowledge of two of us.
* * *
We of the Grand Jury do present James Bruce Overseer of the Road leading from Winchester by Richard McMachens for not keeping the same in repair according to Law within Two months past by the knowledge of Two of us
* * *
We of the Grand Jury do present the Overseer of the Road between Col^o John Hites and the new Town called Stephensburgh for not keeping the same in repair according to Law within Two months past by the knowledge of Two of us
* * *
We of the Grand Jury do present Robert Steward Overseer of the Road from William Jolliffs to the middle of the Bridge between Edward Thomas^s. and John Smith's Fences for not keeping the same in repair according to Law within Two months past by the knowledge of Two of us
* * *
We of the Grand Jury do present John Greenfield Gent Overseer of Loudon Street through Winchester for not keeping the same in repair according to Law within two months past by the knowledge of Two of us

1 May 1759, FOB 8, p. 236
Ordered that Henry Spears be Overseer of the Road from Ephram Leiths hollow to Clauds ford and it is Ordered that the Tithables on the North side of the River keep the same in repair according to Law

2 May 1759, FOB 8, p. 240
Daniel Bush is appointed Overseer of the Road through Loudon Street and Peccadilley and it is Ordered that all the Tithables on the West side of Cameron Street keep the same in repair according to Law

2 May 1759, FOB 8, p. 241
John Skeane Gent is appointed Overseer of the Road from Selsers Mill Run to the County Line at Woods Plain and it is Ordered that the Tithables from Pennewiths Mill Creek up the North River to Smiths Creek up Smiths Creek to the County Line with the County Line to the Timber Ridge and with the Timber Ridge to Pennewiths Mill keep the same in repair according to Law

2 May 1759, FOB 8, p. 241
John Shearer is appointed Overseer of the Road from Mr Catons to Maidston and it is Ordered that the Tithables between Opeckon and the North Mountain keep the same in repair

3 May 1759, FOB 8, p. 252
Phillip Bush is appointed Overseer of Cameron Street and it is Ordered that he clear from the end of the said Street into the main Road and it is further Ordered that the Tithables in Winchester to the Eastward of Loudon Street Clear and keep the same in repair according to Law.

5 June 1759, FOB 8, p. 257
Ordered that Joseph Coombs Ferry keeper keep a Boat sufficient to Carry a Waggon and Two Horses with Two able hands and that he enter into Bond according to Law.
* * *
Joseph Coombs with John Ashbey his Security enterd into Bond according to Law for keeping Ferry cross Sha^{do}

6 June 1759, FOB 8, pp. 263-264
(Rex v Henry Brinker) On Presentment for not keeping a Road in Repair. The Dft failing to appear Ordered that the Dft be Fined Fifteen Shillings and pay Cost
* * *
(Rex Plt ag^t James Bruce Dft) On Presentment for not keeping a Road in Repair. The Dft failing to appear Ordered that the Dft be Fined Fifteen Shillings and pay Cost
* * *
(Rex Plt ag^t John Greenfield Dft) On Presentment for not keeping a Road in repair. The Deft being heard Ordered that he be fined Fifteen Shillings and pay Cost
* * *
(Rex Plt ag^t Lawrence Snap Dft) On Presentment for not keeping a Road in Repair. The Dft failing to appear Ordered that He be Fined Fifteen Shillings and pay Cost.

6 June 1759, FOB 8, p. 266
Ordered that William Roberts Thomas Waters, John Reno and Edward Rogers or any three of them being first Sworn do lay off a Road from the Glebe to M^{c}koys Chapple, and also from the Glebe to Cunningham Chapple and make report to next Court

6 June 1759, FOB 8, p. 267
On the Petition of William Reynolds and others for a Road from Sir Johns Road by the Quakers Meeting house and through the Lane between the said William Reynolds and Phillip Babb. Ordered that John Nevill Henry Rinker Alexander McDaniel and Henry Heath or any three of them being first Sworn do view and lay off the same and make report to next Court.

7 August 1759, FOB 8, p. 282
Ordered that William White Cornelius Ruddell John Skean and Daniel Holman or any three of them being first sworn do mark a Road the most convenient way from the Old field formerly Benja: Allens to the Narrow Passage.

7 August 1759, FOB 8, p. 284
John Denton is appointed Overseer of the Road from George Julians in Powells fort to Bucks mill and it is Ordered that the Tithables in the s^d Fort clear & keep the same in Repair according to Law.

7 August 1759, FOB 8, p. 285
On the return of the Viewers appointed by this Court Ordered that a Road be cleared between the Plantations of William Reynolds and Thomas Babb Junr and into Sr Johns Road in the same manner as heretofore & that the Spring be left open to the said Road and it is further Ordered that Edward Mercer be Overseer thereof and that the Tithables a mile on each side the s^d Road Clear and keep the same in repair according to Law.

4 September 1759, FOB 8, p. 305
Ordered that Edward Mercer be Overseer of S^r. John's Road from Winchester to the Plantation where Isaac Thomas did live and that the Tithables Three miles on each side of the said Road keep the same in repair according to Law.

4 September 1759, FOB 8, p. 305
Ordered that Owen Rogers be Overseer of S^r. John's Road from the Plantation where Isaac Thomas did live to the County Line and that the Tithables Six miles on each side the said Road keep the same in repair according to Law

5 September 1759, FOB 8, p. 313
Grand Jury Presentments

Robert Stewart On Presentment.
The Dfts demurred to the Evidence the Grand Jury presenting of their own knowledge and the Demurrer being argued and Judged good by the Court the Suits are ordered to be dismisd.

6 February 1760, FOB 8, p. 340
It is ordered that William Glover be appointed Surveyor of the Road that leads from Winchester to Opeckon in the Room of Thomas Waters deceased and that the Male Tithables for four Miles on each side the said Creek work on the said Road under him

6 February 1760, FOB 8, p. 342
Ordered that Henry Earnest be appointed Surveyor of the Road from Stevensburgh to a place called Nations's.

4 March 1760, FOB 8, p. 346
Abraham Miller is appointed Surveyor of the Road in in the Room of Henry Spears

4 March 1760, FOB 8, p. 347
Ordered that John Hite Lewis Stephens & John Snapp view the Road that leads thru David Diddricks Land & report the convenience & inconvenience that may attend turning the same to the Court

5 March 1760, FOB 8, p. 350
Ordered that James McGill be appointed Surveyor of the Road known by the name of Sir Johns Road from the Hunting Ridge to Isaac's Creek at Pritchets place and that the Male Tythables between the said Ridge and Creek for six miles on each side the Road work under him

5 March 1760, FOB 8, p. 350
Ordered that William Morgan be appointed Surveyor of the Road from Jacob Hites to Swearingens Ferry in the Room of Thomas Shepherd

4 March 1760, FOB 8, p. 355
Ordered that Samuel Newman be appointed Surveyor of the Road in the Room of John Skeen Gent

1 April 1760, FOB 8, p. 358
Upon the Petition of Samuel Pritchard and others It is Ordered that John Allen Robert Glass and Joseph Jones they being first sworn view the ground mentioned in the said Petition & Report whether a good Road can be made according to the prayer of the Petitioners to the next Court

1 April 1760, FOB 8, p. 358
Ordered that Jacob Chandler be appointed Surveyor of the Road that leads from Littlers Run to Mill Creek in the Room of William Jolliffe

1 April 1760, FOB 8, p. 358
Ordered that John Flemming Rober Felson and John Hogeland they being first sworn view the Ground from Hogelands Ferry to Thomas Catons & Report their Oppinion thereof to the next Court

Frederick County Order Book 9 (1760-1762)

6 May 1760, FOB 9, p. 8
Upon a petition of Samuel Pritchard and others to Turn a road upon a report thereof Made to the Court it is Ordered that the said Road be Turned according to the Prayer of the Petition

6 May 1760, FOB 9, p. 8
Upon a report made to this Court it is ordered that the road Leading through David Dedricks Land be Turned Agreeable to the Prayer of the Petition

6 May 1760, FOB 9, p. 9
Upon the Petition of Sundry of the Inhabitants of this County Praying that a road May Be opened from Robert Cunninghams Mill and Morgans Chapple into the road Called Sir John's Road it is Ordered that Zac'quell Morgan Peter Ruble and Robert Cunningham View the Ground and Report their Opinion thereof to the Court

6 May 1760, FOB 9, p. 10
Ordered that William Helm William Roberts Senr Benjamin Rutherford and Edward Rogers View the Road from the Glebe to Cunningham and M^{c}kay's Chappels and from the Glebe into the Main road that Leads to Winchester and report their Opinion thereof to the Court

7 May 1760, FOB 9, pp. 20-21
Grand Jury Presentments

We of the Grand Jury do Present Daniel Bush overseer of the road Leading through Winchester and Loudon Street for not keeping the same in repair according to Law within two months Past by the knowledge of two of us

* * *

We of the Grand Jury do Present Robert Stewart Overseer of the road Leading from Opeckon Creek to to Smiths Bridge for not keeping the same in repair according to Law within two months Past by the knowledge of two of us

* * *

We of the Grand Jury do Present William Jolliffe Overseer of the road from Robert Cunninghams mill to Littlers Branch for not keeping the same in Repair according to Law within two months Past by the knowledge of two of us

* * *

We of the Grand Jury do Present Major Lewis Stephens Overseer of the Road Leading from his mill to Opeckon Creek for not keeping the same in repair according to Law within two months Past by the knowledge of two of us

* * *

We of the Grand Jury do Present Paul Froman Junr Overseer of the Road Leading from his Mill to the Sandy Ford on Opeckon Creek for not keeping the same in Repair according to Law within two months Past by the knowledge of two of us

* * *

We of the Grand Jury do Present Nathaniel Cartmill Overseer of the Road Leading from the Sandy Ford on Opeckon Creek to Parkins's Mill for not keeping the same in repair according to Law within two months Past by the knowledge of two of us

3 June 1760, FOB 9, p. 56
On the Petition of Simon Carson to Turn a road upon a report made. Ordered that the said Petition be Continued until the next Court for hearing

3 June 1760, FOB 9, p. 56
Upon the Petition of Sundry of the Inhabitants of this County to Open a road from the Head of Bullskin Marsh to run by the Head of Long Marsh into the road at the Dry Marsh below Captain Lewis Neills It is Ordered that John Lindsey Thomas Speake Gen^t. And Thomas Colson view the ground & report their opinion thereof to the Court

3 June 1760, FOB 9, p. 57
On the Petition of Sundry of the Inhabitants of this County to open a road from Richard Hoglands Ferry to go by John Hogland Mill to Capt. Thomas Caton's it is ordered that Barnet Newkirk Evan Watkins and John Hogland view the ground & report their Opinion thereof to the Court

3 June 1760, FOB 9, p. 57
Henry Loyd is appointed Overseer of the road from his House to the top of the ridge in the room of Simeon Rice Deceased Ordered that the Tithables Formerly Appointed keep the same in repair According to Law

3 June 1760, FOB 9, pp. 74-75
(Grand Jury Plt ag^t Daniel Bush Dft) on Presentment for not keep^g. the Street in repair
The Defend^t failing to appear Ordered that he be fined Fifteen Shillings and that he Pay the same to the Church Wardens of Frederick Parish to be Appropriated According to Law and that he pay the Costs of the Prosecution

(Grand Jury Plt ag^t Robert Stewart Dft) on Presentment for not keeping a road in repair
The summons not being Executed ordered that an Alias Issue returnable to next Court

(Grand Jury Plt ag^t William Jolliffe Dft) on Presentment for not keeping a road in repair
The summons not being Executed It is Ordered that an Alias Issue returnable to next Court

(Grand Jury Plt ag^t Lewis Stephens Dft) on Pres^t for not keeping a road in repair
The Dft failing to appear Ordered that he be fined Fifteen Shillings and that he Pay the same to the Church Wardens of Frederick Parish to be appropriated according to Law & that he pay the Cost of the Prosecution

(Grand Jury Plt ag^t Paul Froman Junr Dft) on Pres^t for not keep^g a road in repair
The summons not being Executed, It is ordered that an Alias Issue Returnable to next Court

(Grand Jury Plt ag^t Nathaniel Cartmill Dft) on Presentm^t, for not keep^g a road in repair
The summons not being Executed It is ordered that an Alias Issue returnable to next Court

1 July 1760, FOB 9, p. 91
Upon the Petition of Sundry of the Inhabitants of this County It is ordered that the Inhabitants one mile and a half on the S^o. side, two miles & a half on the N^o. side and three miles above, Work on the road from Paul Fromans mill to the Sandy Ford on Opeckon under the said Paul Froman their overseer

1 July 1760, FOB 9, p. 91
Mounts Bird is hereby appointed Overseer of the road from Benjamin Allins Mill Creek to Stoney Creek in the room of Michael Hentine and it is ordered that the Tithables Formerly appointed keep the same in repair According to Law

1 July 1760, FOB 9, p. 91
Isaac Ruddell is Appointed Overseer of the road from Stoney Creek to McNishes run, and it is ordered that the Tithables formerly appointed keep the Same in repair according to Law

1 July 1760, FOB 9, p. 92
Owen Wingfield is appointed overseer of the road from Col^o Fielding Lewis's Quarter to the Ferry Landing at Combs's in the room of Moses Gess Deceased. Ordered that the Tithables one mile on Each side of the said road keep the same in repair according to Law

5 August 1760, FOB 9, p. 93
William Calmes is appointed Overseer of the Road from Carney's Spring to Opeckon Creek by Capt Neills. Ordered that the Tithables formerly appointed work under him and keep the Same in repair according to Law

5 August 1760, FOB 9, p. 101
Henry Hogland is appointed Overseer of the road from Richard Hoglands Ferry to go by John Hoglands Mill to Capt. Thomas Catons and it is ordered that the Tithables three miles on Each side of the said road, open & keep the same in Repair according to Law

7 August 1760, FOB 9, p. 117
Upon the Petition of Jacob Hite It is ordered that Isaac Evans and James Stroud View and Lay off a road from his mill to the Main road Leading to Watkins's Ferry at John Evans's, and that Joseph Beeler and James Morriss View and Lay off a road from the said Hites Mill each way into the Main Road leading to Swearingen's Ferry and report their Opinion thereof to the Court

7 August 1760, FOB 9, p. 117
Ordered that Samuel Pearson and George Pemberton view and Lay off a road from Jacob Hites Mill to the main road Leading from Winchester to Vestals Gap near the head of Worthingtons Marsh and report their opinion thereof to the Court

7 August 1760, FOB 9, p. 118
The Report made by William Miller Thomas Chester & James Miller to Turn the road round Simon Carsons Fence Not Appearing to the Court, It is Ordered that they make a new Report being first Sworn before a magistrate to next Court

7 August 1760, FOB 9, p. 122
Alexander Wodron James Craik Charles Smith & Henry Heath are appointed Overseers of all the Streets in the Town of Winchester, and it is Ordered that all the male Labouring Tithables Living in the said Town Work under them & keep the same in Repair according to Law

7 August 1760, FOB 9, p. 126
William Neill is appointed overseer of the Road called Littlers Road from Opeckon Creek to the fork where it joins Winchester Road Leading to Spout Run and It is Ordered that the Tithables three miles on Each side Work on and keep the same in Repair according to Law

7 August 1760, FOB 9, p. 127
William Duckworth is Appointed Overseer of the Road from Samuel Littler's to Robert Cunningham's in the Room of Jacob Chandler and It is ordered that the Tithables formerly appointed keep the same in repair according to Law

7 August 1760, FOB 9, p. 129
William Patterson is appointed Overseer of the road from Mandanhalls Mill Run to Capt. Thomas Catons, In the room of Thomas Cordery, Ordered that the Tithables formerly appointed keep the same in repair according to Law

2 September 1760, FOB 9, p. 139
James Stinson is appointed overseer of the Road from the Glebe to Cunnninghams Chapple and It is ordered that the Tithables three miles and a half on Each side keep the same in Repair according to Law

2 September 1760, FOB 9, p. 139
William Roberts Senr is appointed overseer of the Road from the Glebe as far as the Dutch Road towards M^{c}kays Chapple and it is ordered that the Tithables three Miles on Each side keep the same in Repair according to Law

2 September 1760, FOB 9, p. 139
Ordered that John Prince, Edward Rogers, James Knight and John Painter or any three of them being first sworn before a Justice, View the Road from the Dutch Road to M^{c}kays Chapple and Report their Opinion thereof to the Court.

2 September 1760, FOB 9, p. 139
William Duckworth is appointed Overseer of the Road from Samuel Littler's to Robert Cunningham's Mill in the Room of Jacob Chandler, and It is Ordered that all the Tithables Between Opeckon and the North Mountain keep the same in Repair According to Law

2 September 1760, FOB 9, p. 140
John Prince is appointed overseer of the Road from Lord Fairfax's Quarter where Nation Formerly Lived to the Ford at Comb's in the room of Thomas Bryan Martin Gent. and It is ordered that the Tithables formerly appointed keep the same in Repair According to Law

3 September 1760, FOB 9, p. 157
Lewis Neill is Appointed Overseer of the Road Called Littlers Road from Opeckon Creek to the Fork where It Joins Winchester Road Leading to Spout Run, in the Room of William Neill, & It is Ordered that the Tithables three Miles on Each side keep the same in Repair according to Law

7 October 1760, FOB 9, p. 187
A Report made by William Miller James Miller & David Chester to Turn a road round Simon Carson's Fence being Returned Ordered that the said Road be Turned Accordingly

7 October 1760, FOB 9, p. 187
Upon the Petition of Sundry of the Inhabitants of this County It is ordered that Richard Morgan Thomas Shepherd George Myles and Thomas Swearingen or any three of them being Sworn View the road from Hoglands Ferry to the Road Leading to Winchester, and report their Opinion thereof to the Court

7 October 1760, FOB 9, p. 188
Peter Stoufer is appointed Overseer of the Road from Cedar Creek to Stoufers Town in the room of Martin Funk, and It is Ordered that the Tithables two Miles on Each side of the road keep the same in Repair according to Law.

8 October 1760, FOB 9, p. 191
Samuel Pearson is appointed Overseer of the Road from Jacob Hites Mill to the Main Road Leading from Winchester to Vestals Gap Near the Head of Worthingtons Marsh and It is Ordered that the Tithables three Miles on Each side keep the same in Repair According to Law

8 October 1760, FOB 9, p. 191
Joseph Beeler is Appointed Overseer of the Road from Jacob Hites' Mill Leading Each way into the Main Road from Winchester to Swearingens, and It is Ordered that the Tithables three miles on Each side keep the same in Repair according to Law

8 October 1760, FOB 9, p. 191
Mounts Bird is Continued Overseer of the Road from Stoney Creek to the County Line and It is ordered that all the Tithables Between Stoney Creek and Mill Creek keep the same in Repair according to Law.

8 October 1760, FOB 9, p. 191
Samuel Newman is Continued Overseer of the Mountain Road from Wood's Plains Over the Mountains to Selser's Mill run and It is Ordered that all the Tithables Between Mill Creek & the County Line keep the same in Repair

4 November 1760, FOB 9, p. 196
Ordered that John Prince, Edward Rogers, and Thomas Sharpe Senr. being first sworn, do View the Road from the Dutch Road where William Roberts & Others Leaves off, to M^{c}kay's Chapple, and Report their Opinion thereof to the Court

4 November 1760, FOB 9, pp. 198-199
Grand Jury Presentments

We the Grand Jury do present Henry Brinker for not keeping the Road in order according to Law, from Winchester to Lewis Neills by the knowledge of two of us at this Present time
* * *
Also Edward Mercer for not Opening the Road from Cap. Pearis's to Sir John's Road at the Quaker meeting by the knowledge of Two of us at this Present time
* * *

Also Thomas Doster for not keeping the Road in Order according to Law from Winchester to Col°. Morgans within this month by the knowledge of two of us

5 November 1760, FOB 9, p. 201
John M^cmachen is appointed Overseer of the Road from Winchester to Lewis Neill's in the Room of Henry Brinker and It is ordered that the Tithables three Miles on Each side (the Town Excepted) Work on the same

5 November 1760, FOB 9, p. 201
James Stroud is appointed Overseer of the Road from Jacob Hites Mill to the main Road Leading to Watkin's Ferry at John Evans's and It is ordered that the Tithables three Miles on Each side work on the same

5 November 1760, FOB 9, p. 203
Ordered that Thomas Speake John McCormick Richard Stinson & Valentine Crawford or any three of them being first sworn View the Ground from the Head of Worthingtons Marsh to Thomas Speaks & Report their Opinion thereof to the Court

2 December 1760, FOB 9, p. 206
Upon the Petition of Sundry of the Inhabitants of this County, It is Ordered that John Parks, David Miller and James Robinson or any two of them being first Sworn do View the ground from Hugh Lyles Plantation on Back Creek thro' Curtis's Gap, to Robert Cunninghams and report their Opinion thereof to the Court

3 December 1760, FOB 9, p. 210
Owen Wingfield is appointed Overseer of the Road from Col° Fielding Lewis's Quarter to the Ferry Landing at Combs's in the room of Moses Gess Deceased, Ordered that the Tithables two miles on Each Side work on the same

5 December 1760, FOB 9, p. 256
(Grand Jury ag^t Henry Brinker) on Presentment
By Consent this Suit is Continued untill next Court

5 December 1760, FOB 9, p. 256
(Grand Jury Plt ag^t Thomas Doster Dft) On Presentment
The Summons not being Executed, Ordered that an Alias Issue Returnable to next Court

5 December 1760, FOB 9, p. 257
(Grand Jury Plt ag^t Edward Mercer Dft) On Presentment
The Summons not being Executed, Ordered that an Alias Issue Returnable to next Court

3 March 1761, FOB 9, p. 262
Ordered that Charles Buck Lawrence Snapp & George Bounds or any two of them being first sworn do View the Ground from Charles Bucks Mill to Christian Blanks ford on the North River, and from thence to Stephensburg and report their Opinion thereof to the Court

3 March 1761, FOB 9, p. 264
Ordered that Jeremiah Smith, Robert White & William Chambers or any two of them being first sworn, do View the Ground from the South Branch road near Capt. Smiths through Hooppettycoat Gap to Winchester & report their opinion thereof to the Court

3 March 1761, FOB 9, p. 265
Elijah Isaac is appointed Overseer of the Road from Lewis Neills to Carneys Spring in the room of William Calmes, Ordered the Tithables formerly appointed work on the same

3 March 1761, FOB 9, p. 265
William Cook is appointed Overseer of the road from Snickers's Ferry to Cunninghams Ferry in the room of Thomas Robinson, Ordered that the Tithables formerly appointed work on the same

3 March 1761, FOB 9, p. 265
Barnet Siver is appointed Overseer of the road from George Sellers's to Lewis Stephens's Mill in the room of Jacob Bowman Ordered that the Tithables formerly appointed work on the same

4 March 1761, FOB 9, p. 267
John Larick Junr is Appointed overseer of the Road from M^{c}kays Chapple to the Widow Duckworths in the room of Robert M^{c}kay. Ordered that the Tithables Formerly Appointed work on the same

4 March 1761, FOB 9, p. 267
Caleb Odell is appointed Overseer of the road from Bucks Mill to Powells fort in the room of John Denton and It is ordered that the Tithables formerly Appointed work On the Same

4 March 1761, FOB 9, p. 268
Ordered that Abraham Fry, Joseph Fry, Barnet Disponet and William Russell or any three of them being first Sworn do View the Road from Winchester to the South Branch at the County Line on the North Mountain and Report the Conveniancy and Inconveniancy thereof to the Court

4 March 1761, FOB 9, p. 269
David Miller is Appointed Overseer of the road from Robert Cunninghams to his Plantation, John Parks from David Miller's to the Foot of the North Mountain, & James Robinson from the Foot of the North Mountain to Hugh Lyles on back Creek, Ordered that the Tithables living Between the Road leading to Watkins's Ferry & the Mountain work & keep the same in Repair according to Law

4 March 1761, FOB 9, p. 270
John Lewis is Appointed Overseer of the road from the County line to Stephens's Mill upon the Narrow Passage in the room of John Jones, Ordered that the Tithables formerly appointed Work on the same

4 March 1761, FOB 9, p. 274
Thomas Rees Junr is Appointed Overseer of the road from Col°. Morgans to the widow Ballingers in the Room of Thomas Rees, Ordered that the Tithables formerly appointed work on the same

4 March 1761, FOB 9, p. 274
George Cunningham is appointed overseer of the Road from Robert Cunninghams to Littlers Mill in the room of William Duckworth Deceased, Ordered that the Tithables formerly appointed work on the same

4 March 1761, FOB 9, p. 275
Thomas Helm is Appointed Overseer of the Road called Littlers Road from the Beginning to Opeckon Creek in the room of Jonathan Taylor Ordered that the Tithables Formerly Appointed Work on the Same

4 March 1761, FOB 9, p. 275
William M^cmachan is Appointed Overseer of the road from Winchester to Col°. Morgans in the room of Thomas Doster Ordered that the Tithables formerly appointed Work on the same according to Law

5 March 1761, FOB 9, p. 276
William Cherry is Appointed Overseer of the road from Sleepy Creek to the Widow Pauls in the room of Josiah Hulse, Ordered that the Tithables formerly appointed work on the same

5 March 1761, FOB 9, p. 276
Ordered that Richard Stephenson William Crawford and Frederick Beeler or any two of them being first Sworn do View the ground from John McCormicks to the Iron Works and report their opinion thereof to the Court

7 April 1761, FOB 9, p. 297
Jonathan Seaman is appointed Overseer of the Road from Morgans Chaple Opeckon Creek at his House in the room of Jonas Seaman Ordered that the Tithables formerly appointed work on the Same

7 April 1761, FOB 9, p. 298
Jeremiah Smith is appointed Overseer of the road from Hoge Creek to the County Line, Ordered that the Tithables six miles on Each side work on the Same

5 May 1761, FOB 9, p. 301
Ordered that Jacob Hite, John Hardin, & John Hartley being first Sworn do View the road which runs thro' Charles Dicks Land, & report to the next Court the Conveniency or Inconveniency that may attend Turning the Road

5 May 1761, FOB 9, p. 302
Joseph Fry is Appointed Overseer of the Road from the Place Marked by the viewers to the County Line on the North Mountain, Ordered that the Tithables within Ten miles of the said Road work on the same

5 May 1761, FOB 9, p. 303
Grand Jury Presentments

We of the Grand Jury do present the Overseer of the Road from M^r. Jacob Hites to Edward Thomas's Bridge Between the said Edward Thomas's fences & John Smiths Fences for not keeping the same in Repair According to Law, within one month past by the knowledge of two of us

We of the Grand Jury do present the several Overseers of the Road Leading from Winchester to Edward Snickers's ford over Shanando River for not keeping the same in Repair according to Law one month past by the knowledge of two of us

We of the Grand Jury do Present the Present Possessor of the mill formerly Belonging to John Neill dec^d on the Road leading from Winchester to Edward Snickers's ford over Shanando River for suffering the water at Sundry times to overflow the Mill dam which Causes the Main Road Leading by the Dam & Mill to be Continually in disrepair by the Knowledge of two of us

5 May 1761, FOB 9, p. 305
Ordered that Jonas Hedges James Davis, Robert Paul and Henry Newkirk or any three of them being first sworn do view the Ground from Hoglands Ferry to John Parks's & report their Opinion thereof to the Court

5 May 1761, FOB 9, p. 305
Robert White is appointed Overseer of the Road from the South Branch Road near Jeremiah Smiths to Winchester, Ordered that the Tithables three miles on Each Side work on the same

5 May 1761, FOB 9, p. 305
John Davis is appointed Overseer of the road from Thorn's Gap to Jeremiah's run Ordered that the Tithables formerly appointed keep the same in Repair according to Law

5 May 1761, FOB 9, p. 305
Shadraik Parlour is appointed Overseer of the road from Jeremiah's run to the Brush Bottom ford Ordered that the Tithables for two miles on Each side work on the same

6 May 1761, FOB 9, p. 307
Joseph Combs is Appointed Overseer of the Road from the Forks of the River to the Ferry Landing in the room of John Reno Ordered that the Tithables three miles on Each side of the said Road work on the same

6 May 1761, FOB 9, p. 307
Patrick Rice is Appointed Overseer of the Road from the Long Marsh Below Capt. Neills to his House Ordered that the Petitioners Keep the Same in Repair

6 May 1761, FOB 9, p. 307
Edmond Lindsey Junr. is Appointed Overseer of the Road from Patrick Rice's to John McCormick's, Ordered that the Petitioners Keep the same in Repair

7 May 1761, FOB 9, p. 311
John McCormick is Appointed overseer of the road from his house to Crawford's Muster Ground in the room of Thomas Rutherford deceased Ordered that the Tithables formerly appointed work on the same

7 May 1761, FOB 9, p. 311
Hugh Haines is appointed Overseer of the road from John McCormicks to Opeckon Creek Ordered that the Tithables formerly appointed work on the same

7 May 1761, FOB 9, p. 311
William Neill is Appointed Overseer of the road from Opeckon Creek to the Main Road Leading to Winchester Ordered that the tithables formerly appointed work on the same according to Law

7 July 1761, FOB 9, p. 326
Robert Lemen is appointed Overseer of the Road from Jacob Hite's to his House, Ordered that the Tithables formerly appointed work on the same

7 July 1761, FOB 9, p. 326
William Morgan is appointed Overseer of the Road from Robert Lemen's to Swearingen's ferry, Ordered that the Tithables formerly appointed work on the same according to Law

7 July 1761, FOB 9, p. 327
William Cochran is appointed Overseer of the Road from Winchester to Samuel Littlers, Ordered that the said Road be opened as Laid Off by James Carter & George Hollingsworth, and that the Tithables formerly appointed (the Town Excepted) work on the same

7 July 1761, FOB 9, p. 327
Ordered that Robert Rutherford & George Hollingsworth view and Lay Off a road from the Place where the Bullskin Road Intercepts Littlers Old Road to fall into the Potomack Road before it Comes to Benjamin Blackburns Plantation and make report to next Court

4 August 1761, FOB 9, p. 328
Henry Childs is appointed Overseer of the Road in the room of Owen Wingfield, Ordered that the Tithables formerly Appointed work on the same

4 August 1761, FOB 9, p. 330
Ordered that a Road be opened from Swearingen's ferry thro' Shepherds Town to the Old Road that Leads to Winchester Ordered that the same Tithables that work'd on the old road Open the same

4 August 1761, FOB 9, p. 330
Walter Davis is Appointed Overseer of the Road from Crooked Run to Howells ford, Ordered that the Tithables formerly appointed work on the same

4 August 1761, FOB 9, p. 330
Thomas Berry is Appointed Overseer of the road from Howells ford, Ordered that the Tithables formerly Appointed work on the same

4 August 1761, FOB 9, p. 330
Ordered that Edward Snickers, Benjamin Southard Benja[n] Berry and Talliaferro Stribling or any three of them, View the road which runs thro' Col[o] George Mercers Land and report to the Court the Conveniency & Inconveniencys that may attend Turning the said road

4 August 1761, FOB 9, p. 331
Ordered that Bryan Bruin, Edward M[c]Guire, Philip Bush and Godfrey Humbert be overseers of the Streets in Winchester. Ordered that the Tithables formerly App[d] Keep the Same in Repair

5 August 1761, FOB 9, p. 334
George Cunningham is appointed Overseer of the road from Cunningham's Mill to Samuel Littlers Run. Ordered that the Tithables three miles on Each side work on the same

1 September 1761, FOB 9, p. 334
Thomas Berry is Appointed Overseer of the Road from Seaburn's ford to Combs's ferry. Ordered that the Tithables According to a List Returned work on the same

1 September 1761, FOB 9, p. 335
John Timmons is Appointed Overseer of The road from Combs's Ferry to the Top of the Ridge, Ordered that the Tithables According to a List returned work on the Same

1 September 1761, FOB 9, p. 335
Ordered that John Prince Ralph Withers Joseph Borden and Peter Woolf or any three of them being first Sworn, View the road from Samuel Earle's House to his Quarter & report the Conveniency & Inconveniency that may attend Turning the said Road to the Court

2 September 1761, FOB 9, p. 336
Samuel Beam is Appointed Overseer of the Road from the white house Thorns Gap in the room of Peter Rufner. Ordered that the Tithables formerly Appointed work on the same

2 September 1761, FOB 9, p. 336
James Seaburn is Appointed Overseer of the road from Gregory's ford to the Top of the Blue ridge at the head of Menasses run Ordered that the Tithables five miles above & two miles below the Ford work on the same

2 September 1761, FOB 9, p. 337
Nathaniel Curry is Appointed Overseer of the Road from from Spout run to Cunningham's Chapple Ordered that the Tithables formerly appointed work on the same

1 December 1761, FOB 9, p. 344
On the motion of Robert McKay, Ordered that Lewis Stephens Isaac Hite William Miller & James Hoge or any three of them being first sworn do meet & view the road from M^{c}kays Chapple to Edward Cartmills and Report to the Court of the Conveniency & Inconveniency that may attend turning the said Road.

1 December 1761, FOB 9, p. 345
John Beckett is Appointed Overseer of the road from Col^o. Hites to his House Ordered that the Tithables formerly appointed work on the same

2 December 1761, FOB 9, p. 350
Jacob Hite is appointed Overseer of the Road from Alexander Fryers to Swearingens Road in the room of Joseph Beeler Ordered that the Tithables formerly Appointed work on the Same

2 December 1761, FOB 9, p. 352
James Fowler is appointed Overseer of the Road from his house to the head of Bullskin. Ordered that the Tithables formerly appointed work on the same

2 December 1761, FOB 9, p. 352
David Castleman is Appointed Overseer of the Road from the Head of Bull Skin to the main Road by Fryers. Ordered that the Tithables formerly Appointed work on the same

2 December 1761, FOB 9, p. 352
James Lindsey is Appointed Overseer of the Road from James Fowlers to Marquis Calmes's Ordered that the Tithables formerly appointed work on the same

2 February 1762, FOB 9, p. 360
Thomas Netherton is appointed Overseer of the road from Capt. Spears to the fork of the Road that Leads to Charles Bucks Ordered that the Tithables three miles on Each Side work on the Same

2 February 1762, FOB 9, p. 361
Thomas Chester is Appointed Overseer of the Road from the S^o. River to the fork of the Road that Leads to Charles Bucks. Ordered that the Tithables three Miles on Each Side work on the same

3 February 1762, FOB 9, p. 362
James Carter is Appointed Overseer of the Road from Winchester to Lewis Neill's, Ordered that The Tithables formerly appointed work on the same

2 March 1762, FOB 9, p. 365
At the motion of Thomas Doster to Turn a road which Runs thro' his Plantation Ordered that Lewis Moore Robert Cunningham, Zacquell Morgan, & Thomas Provan or any three of them being first Sworn do View the said road & report to the Court the Conveniency or Inconveniency that may attend Turning the said Road

2 March 1762, FOB 9, p. 366
Ordered That Lewis Moore Robert Cunningham Zacquell Morgan and Thomas Provan or any three of them being first Sworn do view the Road from Thomas Doster's to the main Road near the widow Ballenger's, & Report their Opinion thereof to the next Court

4 March 1762, FOB 9, p. 388
Richard Pearis is Appointed Overseer of the road from Tuscorora to Captain Caton's in the room of William Patterson's. Ordered that all the Tithables Between the mountain & Opeckon Work on the Same

4 March 1762, FOB 9, p. 388
Stephen Rawlings is Appointed Overseer of the Road from the top of the Mountain to Sleepy Creek. Ordered that the Tithables Six Miles on Each side work on the same

4 March 1762, FOB 9, p. 388
Ordered that Richard Pearis, Henry Vanmeter, James Blair & Robert Stogdon or any three of them being first Sworn do view the ground from Opeckon Creek to the Mountain & report their Opinion thereof to the Court

4 March 1762, FOB 9, p. 398
John Routt is Appointed Overseer of the Road from Gregorys ford to Menasses run at the County Line in the room of Thomas Cooper. Ordered that the Tithables formerly Appointed work under him and Keep the same in Repair According to Law

5 March 1762, FOB 9, p. 416
Ordered that the Road Running thro' Charles Dick's Land be Turned according to the Report made by Jacob Hite, John Hardin and John Hartley. Viewers Appointed by Order of Court

6 April 1762, FOB 9, p. 431
John Provan is Appointed Overseer of ye Road from William Frosts to William Dillons in the room of Thomas Provan. Ordered that the Tithables formerly Appointed work on the Same

6 April 1762, FOB 9, p. 432
On the Motion of Samuel Earle Leave is Granted him to Hang a Gate Across the Road Leading from Crooked Run to Gregorys ford

7 April 1762, FOB 9, p. 450
Ordered that all the Tithables four miles on Each side of the Road (the Town Excepted) from Winchester to Hoge Creek work under Robert Pearis the Overseer

1 June 1762, FOB 9, pp. 467-468
On the petition of Sundry of the Inhabitants Living about Mills's Gap praying to have a Road opened from thence to Follis's mill and the main Road at Jane Caldwells Plantation Ordered that John Chinworth Zacquil Morgan Enoch Nash & Thomas Rees or any three of them being first sworn do view the Ground Layed Off & make report to next Court

Frederick County Order Book 10 (1762-1763)

2 June 1762, FOB 10, p. 16
Ordered that Gersham Keyes be appointed Overseer of the Road in the room of Henry Loyd

3 June 1762, FOB 10, p. 67
Zacquel Morgan, Peter Ruble & Robert Cunningham being appointed by an Order of Court to view the Ground from Cunninghams Mill & Morgan's Chapel to S^r. Johns Road and Report whether a good Road can be opened returned their Oppinion Ordered that the said Road be opened as Laid Off by the said Viewers and that the Inhabitants two miles on each side work thereon under Henry Bower who is appointed Overseer

3 June 1762, FOB 10, p. 68
It is Ordered that Robert Cunningham Peter Ruble Asariah Pugh & Thomas Doster or any three being first sworn do view the Ground from Thomas Dosters to the main Road and Report their Oppinions to the Court

4 August 1762, FOB 10, p. 78
It is Ordered that James Littler, Abraham Denton, Rynard Bardin & George Seller or any three of them being first sworn do view the Ground from Stony Lick by Christopher Windles in the main Road by Mr Pughs & mark the same and Report their Opinion to the next Court

4 August 1762, FOB 10, p. 78
Ordered that William Calfee be appointed Overseer of the Road from Chesters ford to Manassehs Run and that the Inhabitants five miles on Each side of the Road work on the same

4 August 1762, FOB 10, p. 78
It is Ordered that John Timmons be appointed Overseer of the Road from Howells Ford to the Top of the Ridge and that he clear and keep the Road open to the Waggon Ford and Ferry Landing and that the Tithables who formerly were appointed to work upon It work under him

4 August 1762, FOB 10, p. 79
It is Ordered that John Briscoe John Abril William Rankins and David Rankin or any three of them being first Sworn do view the Ground and see whether the main Road can be turned to Run upon the Line between Edward Thomas and John Smith and Make Report thereof to Court

4 August 1762, FOB 10, p. 93
Richard Pearis, Henry Van Meter, James Blair, & Robert Stogdon, being appointed to view the ground from Opeckon Creek to the Mountain having made their Report It is Ordered to be that a Road be opened as marked & Laid off by the said Viewers And that James Blair be Overseer thereof and that the Tithables Three miles on each side the said Road work thereon under him

5 August 1762, FOB 10, p. 113
It is Ordered that John Morgan be appointed Overseer of the Road from Sleepy Creek to the warm springs & that the Tithables as far as the River on one side of the Road and Ten miles on the Other side including Pearce Butlers work thereon under him

7 September 1762, FOB 10, p. 152
Henry Brinker is appointed Overseer of the Road leading to Connigocheague from the Town of Winchester to Littlers place in the room of William Cochrain and the usual Tithables work under him

7 September 1762, FOB 10, p. 152
It is Ordered that Burr Harrison be appointed overseer of the Road leading from Augusta to Winchester from the County Line to Stony Creek in the room of Moses Bird and the usual Tithables work under him

7 September 1762, FOB 10, p. 152
It is Ordered that Robert Stockdon Senr be appointed Overseer of the Road Leading from Winchester to Watkins Ferry from Tuscarora to Mr Thomas Catons Plantation in the room of Richard Pearis Gent. And that the usual Tithables work under him

7 September 1762, FOB 10, p. 153
John Chinwoth, Enoch Nash & Zacquil Morgan being appointed to View mark and Lay off the ground from Mills's Gap to Follis's Mill and main road at Jane Caldwells Plantation having made their Report Ordered that the said Road be opened according as Laid off and that the Tithables one Mile on each side the said road work thereon under George Follis who is appointed overseer thereof

8 September 1762, FOB 10, p. 165
On the Petition of sundry inhabitants of this praying that a road may be opened from the top of the mountain at Mills Gap into the most convenient part of Sir John Sinclairs road ordered that Thomas Robinson Josias Springer Thomas Sharp and James Robinson or any three being first sworn do view the ground and report the conveniences and inconveniences that will attend the opening the same

9 September 1762, FOB 10, p. 176
Upon the motion of Robert McCoy praying an order for persons to be appointed, to View the road leading from John Funks to McCoys Chappel and report the conveniences and inconveniences that will attend the turning the same round his fence. Ordered that Thomas Cooper, John Branson, Robert Haines, and John Painter or any Three of them being first sworn do view the same and make report thereof to the Court

9 September 1762, FOB 10, p. 176
Upon the motion of Samuel Earle praying that a road may be opened from his house unto the road Leading from Chesters Gap at Manassers run. It is ordered that Lawrence Snapp, John Painter, Thomas Harrison, and Robert McCoy, or any three of them being first sworn do view the ground and Lay off the same in the most convenient manner and make report thereof to the Court

9 September 1762, FOB 10, p. 195
Ordered that Humphrey Keyes be appointed overseer of the Road from the Ferry at Keyses to the top of the Mountain in the room of Gersham Keyes and the usual Tithables work under him that worked under Simeon Rice

9 September 1762, FOB 10, p. 195
Ordered that Edward Snickers be appointed Overseer of the Road from the ferry at his House to the top of the Ridge and that the Usual Tithables work under him

9 September 1762, FOB 10, p. 196
Ordered that Robert Buckles be appointed Overseer of the Road leading from Swearingens Ferry to Keyses Ferry, from Swearingens to Melchiah Inglis Branch and Thomas Hart from the said branch to Keyses Ferry and that the Tithables two miles on each side the said road work thereon under them

2 November 1762, FOB 10, p. 297
It is Ordered that Joseph Manfield be appointed overseer of the road Leading from Charles Dicks mill to Thomas Lindsey's, in the room of Lawrence Harrison and that the usual Tithables work under him

2 November 1762, FOB 10, pp. 297-298
It is Ordered that Joseph Morris be appointed Overseer of the road called Sir John's Road Leading from the timber Ridge to Isaac's Creek and that the Tithables within five miles on Each side thereof work thereon under him

2 November 1762, FOB 10, p. 301
It is Ordered that Thomas Bryan Martin Gent. Be appointed Overseer of the road Leading from the Right Honourable Thomas Lord Fairfax's Quarter to Combe's Ferry in the room of John Prince and that the usual Tithables work thereon under him

2 November 1762, FOB 10, p. 301
It is Ordered that John Tyler be appointed Overseer of the road Leading to Messanutting from the White house to the dry run and that the Tithables three miles on each side thereof work thereon under him

2 November 1762, FOB 10, p. 302
It is Ordered that John Armstrong be Appointed Overseer of the road leading from Opeckon ford at the said Armstrongs house to Winchester in the room of William Glover and the usual Tithables work thereon under him

2 November 1762, FOB 10, p. 302
Daniel Bush Gent. Robert Rutherford, George Michael Laubinger and Robert Aldridge are appointed Overseers of the streets in Winchester, in the room of Philip Bush, Godfrey Humbart Bryan Bruin & Edward McGuire & It is Ordered that the usual Tithables work thereon under them

2 November 1762, FOB 10, p. 302
On the motion of Thomas Perry It is Ordered that Andrew Freitley Christopher Aldred James Bruce and Richard Carter or any three of them being first sworn do view the ground from the Town of Winchester, to the said Thomas Perry's mill and make report whether a good road may be had

2 November 1762, FOB 10, p. 302
It is Ordered that the Tithables five miles on each side of the road in Humphrey Keye's District work thereon under him

3 November 1762, FOB 10, p. 315
Archibald Wager is appointed Appointed Overseer of Road Leading from Stephensburgh to the Right Honourable Thomas Lord Fairfax Fairfax's plantation called Nations in the Room of Charles Darnald Bradford and It is Ordered that the usual tithables work thereon Under him

3 November 1762, FOB 10, p. 315
It is Ordered that Joseph Pugh be appointed Overseer of the Road Leading from the Town of Woodstock To Toms Brook and that the Tithables from the River to the Road and three Miles on the other side of the Road work thereon under him

3 November 1762, FOB 10, p. 315
It is Ordered that Martin Funk be appointed overseer of the Road Leading from Toms Brook to Stover Town and that the tithables from the River on one side and three Miles on the other side work thereon under him

3 November 1762, FOB 10, p. 315
It is Ordered that Peter Stephens be appointed Overseer of the Road Leading from Jacob Christmans plantation to the Widow Duckworth's plantation and that the usual Tithables work thereon under him

3 November 1762, FOB 10, p. 315
It is Ordered that Peter Stover be appointed Overseer of the Road Leading from the plantation of the Widow Duckworth to Stover's Town and that the Tithables Three Miles on Each side thereof work thereon under him -

3 November 1762, FOB 10, p. 315
John Hite is Appointed Overseer of the Road Leading from his house to the Town of Winchester and It is Ordered that the Tithables Three miles on Each side thereof Work thereon under him

3 November 1762, FOB 10, p. 315
It is Ordered that David Shepherd be appointed Overseer Road Leading from Shepherds Town to the plantation of Robert Lemon and that the tithables four miles on Each Side thereof work thereon under him

7 December 1762, FOB 10, p. 400
James Bruce, Andrew Freitley and Christopher Aldrick being appointed to View the Ground Leading from the Town of Winchester to Perries mill made their Report. Whereupon It is Ordered that a Road be opened from the Town to the said Mill and that the Petitioners work thereon under Thomas Perry who is appointed Overseer of the same.

7 December 1762, FOB 10, p. 401
Upon the Petition of Sundry Inhabitants of the County praying that a Road may be opened from the Baptist meeting house to the Road Leading from Morgan Morgans to the Town of Winchester It is Ordered that Morgan Morgan Junr William Connel John Watson and Thomas Berry or any three of them being first sworn do View the Ground Leading from the said meeting house to the said road and make Report of the Conveniences and Inconveniences attending oppening the same [blank space from erasure] at the Next Court

7 December 1762, FOB 10, p. 401
It is Ordered that Ezekiel Hickman be appointed Overseer of that part of the Road Leading from Thomas Catons to Vestals Gap and from Opeckon Creek to Shepherds Town in the Room of Anthony Turner Deceased that the usual Tithables work thereon under him

7 December 1762, FOB 10, p. 402
John Painter Thomas Harrison and Robert McKay having been appointed to View the Ground Leading from Samuel Earls House in to the Road called Chesters Road Manaseh's Run made their Report Where upon It is Ordered that a Road be opened from the said Samuel Earles to the said Chesters Road and that the Tithables three miles on each side thereof work thereon under Thomas Cooper who is appointed Overseer of the same

7 December 1762, FOB 10, p. 402
It is Ordered that George Leith be appointed Overseer of that part of the Road Leading from the White House to Thorns Gap and from Suttons Run to a Mill above Charles Thompsons on Colonel Carlyles Land and the Tithables four Miles on each side thereof work thereon under him

2 February 1763, FOB 10, p. 408
It is Ordered that the Tithables three miles on Each side the Road (which Thomas Bryan Martin Gent and Archibald Wager were appointed Overseers of by a former Order of this Court) work thereon under them

1 March 1763, FOB 10, p. 413
Abraham Denton Reynold Borden and George Seller having by a former Order of this Court been been appointed to View the Ground from Stoney Lick by Christopher Windels into the main Road at Mr Pughs Plantation, made their Report, Whereupon It is Ordered that a Road be opened as Laid off and marked by the Said Viewers & that the Tithables Three miles on Each Side thereof work thereon under Christopher Widell who is appointed Overseer of the same

2 March 1763, FOB 10, p. 417
Thomas Robinson Josias Springer and Thomas Sharpe having been appointed to View the Ground from the top of the Mountain at Mill's Gap into the most Convenient Left part of Sir, John Sinclair's road made their Report Whereupon It is Ordered that a Road be Opened as Laid off by the said Viewers and that the Tithables four Miles on Each side thereof work so far thereon under Richard Stephens as from Sir, John Sinclairs Road to the Mouth of Lick branch & to the top of the Mountain under James Wright who are appointed Overseers of the same

2 March 1763, FOB 10, p. 417
It is Ordered that Edward Dodd be appointed Overseer of the Road Leading from the Bridge on Opeckon Creek to William Jolliffe's Junr and that the Tithables Three Miles on Each side thereof work thereon under him

2 March 1763, FOB 10, p. 418
John Prince Ralph Withers and Peter Wolfe being appointed to View the Road Leading from Samuel Earles house and Report the Inconveniences attending opening the same made their Report Whereupon It is Ordered that the old Road be Continued and that the Road Lately opened by the said Samuel be Stoped up

2 March 1763, FOB 10, p. 418
Upon the petition of sundry Inhabitants of this County praying that a Road may be opened from Joseph Langdons to the Town of Woodstock and It is Ordered that Jonathan Langdon Charles Devinner Jacob Rief and Jesse Broughten or any Three of them (being first sworn) do View the said Ground and make Report of the Conveniences and Inconveniences attending opening the same, at the Next Court

Frederick County Order Book 11 (1763-1764)

5 March 1763, FOB 11, p. 76
It is Ordered that Jacob Vanmetre Morgan Morgan John Whison & Thomas Thornberry or any three of them being first sworn do View the Road from Mecklinburgh to Lynders ford on

Opeken Creek, or to the most convenient Ford on the said Creek and make report thereof at the Next Court

5 March 1763, FOB 11, p. 76
Henry Brinker is appointed Overseer of the Road leading from the Town of Winchester to Litlers old place & It is Ordered that the Tithables Four miles on Each side thereof work thereon under him

3 May 1763, FOB 11, p. 81
Morgan Morgan Junr William Crumley and John Watson having been appointed to View from the Baptist meeting house into the Great Road Leading from Morgan Morgans to the Town of Winchester made their report, Whereupon It is Ordered that a Road be opened as Opened as Laid off by them and that the Tithables Two [blank space from erasure] Miles on each Side thereof work thereon under William Chinoth who is appointed Overseer of the same

3 May 1763, FOB 11, p. 82
Upon the petition of Sundry Inhabitants of this County praying that a road may be opened from Thomas Humes Mill upon Sugar Tree Creek into the road Leading to Chesters Gap, It is Ordered that Ezekiel Morgan Randolph Fugett Darby McCarty and John Callfee (or any three of them do View the Ground and make Report of the Conveniences and Inconveniences attending the same

4 May 1763, FOB 11, p. 82
William Russell is appointed Overseer of the Road Leading from Barnett Desponet's to Stephens Mill & It is Ordered that the usual Tithables work thereon under him

4 May 1763, FOB 11, p. 92
Upon the petition of John Houghland praying that a road may be opened from his Mill to Shannandah River, It is Ordered that George Myles James Davis and Jonas Hedges or any three of them do View the Ground and make Report of the Conveniences and Inconveniences Attending opening the same

4 May 1763, FOB 11, p. 96
Jonathan Langdon Charles Deveney and Jesse Braughton having been appointed to View the Ground from Joseph Langdons plantation to the Town of Woodstock made their report Whereupon it is Ordered that a road be opened as Laid off by them and the Tithables Two Miles on each side thereof work thereon under Jonathan Langdon who is appointed Overseer of the same

4 May 1763, FOB 11, p. 96
Jacob Vanmetre Morgan Morgan and Thomas Thornberry having been appointed to View the ground from the Town of Mecklinbugh to the most convenient ford on Opeckon Creek made their report Whereupon It is Ordered that a road be opened as by them Laid off and that the Tithables three miles on Each side thereof work thereon under Edward Mercer who is appointed overseer of the same

5 May 1763, FOB 11, p. 117
It is Ordered that William Crawford Valentine Crawford Robert Worthington Junr. & Alexander Vance or any three of them (being first sworn) do view the ground from Jacob Hites plantation to nearest and best way to Keyes'es Ferry and make Report of the conveniences and Inconveniences attending opening a Road from the said Jacob's plantation to the said ferry

7 June 1763, FOB 11, p. 186
It is Ordered that Hugh Bayes be appointed Overseer of the Road leading from Lewis Stephen's Mill to the house of Phillip Peter Backer in the room of Daniel Curry and that the usual Tithables work thereon under him

7 June 1763, FOB 11, p. 186
It is Ordered that Joseph Berry be appointed Overseer of the Road leading from Seaburns Ford to Combes ferry and that the Tithables from William Woods upward work Thereon under him

7 June 1763, FOB 11, p. 191
It is Ordered that Isaac Johnston Senr be appointed overseer of the Road Leading from Littlers old place to Cunninghams Mill & that the Tithables three Miles on each side thereof work thereon under him

7 June 1763, FOB 11, p. 191
It is Ordered that Lewis Moore & Charles Smith Gent. do agree with some person to build a Bridge over Bruise's Millrun where the main Road crosses

9 June 1763, FOB 11, p. 237
It is Ordered that Joseph Fry Samuel Fry Joseph Fawcett and John Fawcett or any three of them being first Sworn do view the Ground from Joseph Fry's plantation on Cedar Creek to the Furnace Erecting on the north branch of pembroke & make Report of the Conveniences and Inconveniences attending opening a Road from the said plantation to the said Furnace

4 October 1763, FOB 11, p. 279
Henry Heath is appointed overseer of Road from the end of Cameron Street in the Town of Winchester to where it Joins the Road Leading from the end of Loudon street and It is Ordered that the Tithables which worked under Henry Brinker work thereon under the Said Henry Heath

7 October 1763, FOB 11, p. 333
Upon the presentment of the Grand jury against James Lindsay overseer of the Road from John Lindseys to the ford at Combses ferry for not keeping the same in Repair, This day came the Attorney of our Lord the King & the said James Lindsey being duly summoned & not appearing Tho' solemnly called It is Considered by the Court that for the said Offence he forfeit & pay to the Church Wardens of Frederick Parish Fifteen shilling to the use of the poor of the said parish that he pay the Costs of this prosecution & may be taken &^{c}

1 November 1763, FOB 11, p. 342
Jacob Burner is appointed Overseer of the Road in the Room of Matthais Selser Deceased and It is Ordered that the usual Tithables work thereon under him

2 November 1763, FOB 11, p. 344
It is Ordered that Thomas Lindsey Patrick Rice Isaac Lahew & Edmond Lindsey or any three of them being first Sworn do View the Ground from Lewis Neills Mill to Edmond Lindsey's Junr plantation and make Report of the Conveniences & Inconveniences attending opening a Road from the Said Mill to the said plantation at the Next Court

2 November 1763, FOB 11, p. 344
It is Ordered that William Catlett Benjamin Rutherford and Owin Wingfied or any two of them being first sworn do View the Ground from Lewis Neills Mill to Owin Wingfields Land & make Report at the Next Court of the Conveniences and Inconveniences attending opening a Road from the Said Mill to the said Land

2 November 1763, FOB 11, p. 346
It is Ordered that William Albin John Parrell Peter Shipley & Joseph Parrell or any three of them being first sworn do View the Ground from Lewis Neills mill into Perry's road and make Report of the Conveniences and Inconveniences attending opening a Road from the said Mill to the said Road at the Next Court

2 November 1763, FOB 11, p. 346
It is Ordered that Alexander Fryer Jonathan Simmons and Patrick Dowley or any Two of them being first sworn do View the Ground from the said Alexander Fryers to Jacob Hites Mill and make Report at the Next Court of Conveniences and Inconveniences attending opening a Road from the said Alexander Fryer's to the said Mill

2 November 1763, FOB 11, p. 346
It is Ordered that Thomas Shepherd Thomas Swearingen Henry Pedinger and William Morgan or any three of them being first sworn do View the Ground from the Town of Mecklinburgh to the meeting House between Buckles and Lucas' and make Report at the Next Court of the Conveniences & Inconveniences attending opening a Road from the said Town to the said meeting house

2 November 1763, FOB 11, p. 350
Thomas Babb is appointed overseer of the Road called Sir John Sinclaire's road in the room of Edward Mercer from the forks to James McGills and It is Ordered that the usual Tithables work thereon under him.

2 November 1763, FOB 11, p. 350
Jonathan Lupton is appointed overseer of the road Called the Southbranch road from the Town of Winchester to Hoge Creek in the room of Robert Pearis and It is ordered that the usual Tithables work thereon under him.

2 November 1763, FOB 11, p. 350
Jonathan Tayler is appointed Overseer of the Road from William Neill's upon Opecon into the Great Road that runs by William Joleff's in the room of Robert Millburne & It is Ordered that the usual Tithables work thereon under him

7 December 1763, FOB 11, p. 442
David Wright is appointed Overseer of the Road Leading from Colonel John Hites to the forks of the Road leadging from Lord Fairfax to Stephensburgh in the room of George Wright and It is Ordered that the usual Tithables work thereon under him

7 December 1763, FOB 11, p. 442
Jacob Miller is appointed Overseer of the road Leading from Magneturs run to Moses Birds and It is Ordered that the usual Tithables work thereon under him

7 December 1763, FOB 11, p. 442
Burr Harrison is appointed overseer of the road Leading from Moses Birds to the County Line. It is Ordered that the Tithables on Each side the North river be Exempted from working on the Messanutting road, And that they together with the usual Tithables working on the said road from Moses Birds to the County Line work thereon under the said Overseer

3 January 1764, FOB 11, p. 475
William Albin John Parrell and Joseph Parrell having been appointed by a former Order of this Court to View the Ground Leading from Lewis Neills Mill the Nearest and most Convenient way into the Road Leading from Thomas Sperrys mill to the Town of Winchester made their Report Whereupon It is Ordered that a road be opened as by them Laid off and that that the tithables two miles and an an half Each side thereof work thereon under William Albin who is appointed Overseer of the same
[Note: The name is written Thomas Sperry in this order; however, this appears to be Thomas Perry's [not Sperry's] mill; see FOB 10, p. 302; FOB 10, p. 400.]

3 January 1764, FOB 11, p. 475
Adam Stephen Gent is appointed Overseer of the road from Jonathan Seamons to Jacob Hites and It is Ordered that the Tithables two miles on Each side thereof work thereon under him

4 January 1764, FOB 11, p. 476
It is Ordered that Thomas Rutherford Jame Wood Charles smith and Gerard [Smith?] be appointed Overseers of the Streets in the Town of Winchester & that the Inhabitants of the said Town work thereon under them

Frederick County Order Book 12 (1764-1765)

6 March 1764, FOB 12, p. 27
Ordered that William Bilbroaw be Appointed Overseer of the Road from Coombes's Ferry to Lewis's Mill in the Room of Henry Giles the Ensuing Year and that the Tithables that formerly Worked under him Work under the present Overseer

6 March 1764, FOB 12, p. 27
Ordered that Joseph Wilkinson be Appointed Overseer of the Road from Hog Creek to the County Line the Ensuing Year and that the former Tithables that used to Work under John Smith work under him.

7 March 1764, FOB 12, p. 29
Upon the petition of Sundry Inhabitants praying that a Road may be opened from Sr Johns Road by Thomas Babbs down by William McMachen Angus McDonalds and down to Berry's Mill It is Ordered that Thomas Babb William McMachen John Parrell and Joseph Parrell or any three of them view said Ground and make report thereof to the next Court.

7 March 1764, FOB 12, p. 29
John Calfee Randolph Fugate and Ezekiel Morgan being Appointed to View the Ground from Hume's Mill on Sugar Tree Run into the Road Leading to Chesters Gap made their report It is Ordered that a Road be Opened as laid off by them and that the Tithables Three Miles on Each side of said Road work thereon under Ezekiel Morgan who is Appointed Overseer

2 May 1764, FOB 12, p. 72
Upon the Petition of Sundry Inhabitants praying that a Road may be opened from Sir John's Road above Thomas Babbs Plantation the nearest and best way to Thomas Perry's Mill. Ordered that William Reynolds Benjamin Blackburn George Hollingsworth and Joseph Neavill or any three of them being first sworn do view the Ground and Report to the Court the Conveniences and Inconveniences that may attend the opening of a Road according to the Prayer of the Petition

5 May 1764, FOB 12, p. 102
Ordered that George Rice James McCormack Thomas Speakes William Crawford or any Three of them being first sworn do view the best and most Convenient way from Vestals ford to Christopher Beelor's mill & the best & most convenient way from the Long Marsh to Christopher Beelor's Mill & make Report Thereof to Court

7 August 1764, FOB 12, p. 140
James Jones is Appointed overseer of the Road from Chesters Ford to the Top of the Ridge in the Room of David Chester & ordered that the usael Tithes work Thereon under him

7 August 1764, FOB 12, p. 140
John Prince is Appointed overseer of McKays Chapel Road from the Forks of Earls Mill Runn to George Henry [?] in the Room of Edward Rogers & ordered that the usael Tithes work under him

7 August 1764, FOB 12, p. 140
Joseph George is Appointed Overseer of the Road from Howells Ford to the Top of the Ridge & It is Ordered that the usael Tithables work Thereon under him

7 November 1764, FOB 12, p. 249
Ordered that the Tithables within five miles of Keys Ford work under Humphrey Keys Overseer of the Road from The foard to the Top of the Mountain

5 December 1764, FOB 12, p. 278
Henry Pedinger is Appointed Overseer of the streets of Mecklenburgh & Ordered that the Inhabitants work Thereon under him

5 December 1764, FOB 12, p. 279
Upon the Complaint of Burr Harrison Gent. against Jacob Moore for Abusing him & Insulting him when he was Acting as an Overseer of the highway, It is Ordered that he be Summoned to Appear & answer the Said Complaint

5 December 1764, FOB 12, p. 279
Ordered that Henry Brinker & John McKamie be Appointed Overseers of the Streets in Westchester in the Room of Charles Smith & Gerrard Smith

5 December 1764, FOB 12, p. 279
Joseph Combs Overseer of the Road from Combs Ferry at the Town of Winchester who stands presented by the Grand Jury for not Keeping the same in Repair This day Came the Attorney of our Lord the King & the said Joseph being duly Summoned & failing to appear tho Solemnly Called. It is therefore Considered by the Court that the said Joseph do forfeit & pay to the Church Wardens the Sum of Fifteen Shillings or One hundred Fifty pounds of Tobacco for the use of the poor of the parish & that he pay the Costs of this prosecution & may be Taken &^c.

5 March 1765, FOB 12, p. 315
Thomas Lindsey is Appointed Overseer of the Road from James Fowlers to Thomas Lindseys in the Room of James Fowler & It is Ordered that the Usael Tithables work Thereon under him

3 April 1765, FOB 12, p. 358
Luke Collins & Adam Haymaker is Appointed Overseers of the Streets in Winchester in the Room of James Wood & Thomas Rutherford Gent.

5 April 1765, FOB 12, p. 396
Joseph Lupton is Appointed Overseer of the Road from Winchester to Opeckon at Armstrongs ford & It is Ordered that the Tithables within five miles on Each Side of the Road work Thereon under him

April 5, 1765, FOB 12, p. 396
Ordered that the Tithables on Each Side of the Road from Armstrongs ford upon Opeckon to the Signpost at Littlers Road work Thereon under William Helms

6 June 1765, FOB 12, p. 463
Ordered that William Neill Isaac Lerew Edmond Lindsey Junr. & Thomas Lindsey or any Three of Them do view the Ground from Lewis Neills Mill the nearest & best way to Thomas Lindsey's & make Report Thereof to Court

6 June 1765, FOB 12, p. 463
John Parrell is Appointed overseer of the Road Lewis Neills Mill to Thomas Perry's Mill in the Room of William Alebin deceased Ordered that the usael Tithables work Thereon under him

6 June 1765, FOB 12, p. 463
John M^c.Kamurs Appointed overseer of Loudon Street & the Streets Lanes behind it & the Commons Ordered that the Tithables Living There work thereon under him

7 June 1765, FOB 12, p. 482
Joseph Hawkins is Appointed Overseer of the Road in the Room of Burr Harrison Gent. & It is Ordered that the Same Tithables work Thereon under him.

6 August 1765, FOB 12, p. 497
Ordered that John Gram Frederick Comber Jacob Pences & Philip Long or any Three of them being first sworn do view the Ground from the Augusta Line on the South River above John Breedings fence the Nearest and Best way to the Road to Crosses Thorns Gap & make Report Thereon to the Court

7 August 1765, FOB 12, p. 499
Ordered that David Castleman be Appointed Overseer of the Road from the head of Bulskin to the main Road from Winchester to M^c.Lenburgh & that the Tithables Three miles on Each Side work Thereon under him.

8 August 1765, FOB 12, p. 511
Ordered that John Saveir be Appointed Overseer of the Road from the The Massanutten Mountain to the County Line Leading to Brocks Gap in the room of Samuel Newman & that the usael Tithables do work thereon under him

3 September 1765, FOB 12, p. 540
Upon the petition of Robert M^c.Coy Leave is granted him to Turn the Road from the Chappell to Cedar Creek as it formerly went & hang Gates across it

3 September 1765, FOB 12, p. 540
Thomas Farnley is Appointed Overseer of the Road in the room of John Prince & It is Ordered that the Same Tithables work Thereon under him

Frederick County Order Book 13 (1765-1767)

2 October 1765, FOB 13, p. 11
Upon the petition of Sundry Inhabitants of Mecklenburgh & the parts Adjoining praying that a Road may be Opened from that place into the Warm Spring Road at Richard Pearis's Plantation by the head of the Swann Ponds It is Ordered that Robert Stogdon James Jones Jacob Morgan & William Morgan or any three of them being first sworn do View the Ground & Report their Opinion to the Court

2 October 1765, FOB 13, p. 12
John Parrell is appointed Overseer of the Road from Perry's Mill to Winchester in the Room of Thomas Perry & It is Ordered that the same Tithables work thereon under him

2 October 1765, FOB 13, p. 12
Ordered that the Tithables five miles on Each Side to the Top of the mountain work under Humphrey Keys Overseer of the Road from Keye's ferry to the Top of the mountain

2 October 1765, FOB 13, p. 13
Ordered that Van Swearingen ju^r William Morgan Thomas Swearingen and Jacob Vanmetre or any Three of them being first Sworn do View the Ground from the High Street in Mecklenburgh to Joseph Barnes ford & return their Opinion of the same to the Court

4 March 1766, FOB 13, p. 49
Upon the Petition of John Hites Praying that a Road may be Opened from the Race Grounds below his House to the Swift Shoal Ford on Shanondoah & from thence down the River to the County Road It is Ordered that Peter Catlett Joseph Berry Baylis Earle & Robert Willson or any Three of them being first sworn do view the Ground & make a Report of their Opinion to the Court

4 March 1766, FOB 13, p. 49
Robert Stogdon James Jones & Jacob Morgan having been appointed to view the ground from Mecklenburgh to the warm Spring Road at Pearis's Plantation made their Report It is Ordered that a Road be Opened as Laid Off by the Viewers and that the Tithables three miles on Each Side thereof work thereon under George Neilly who is appointed Overseer of the same

4 March 1766, FOB 13, p. 50
Upon the Petition of Charles Smith Praying that a road may be Opened from Doct^r. Wells to Fielding Lewis's Mill and It is Ordered that John Lindsey Humphrey Wells Thomas Colson & William Calmees & George Hampton or any three of them being first sworn do View the Ground & Report their Opinion of the same to the next Court

1 April 1766, FOB 13, p. 51
Humphrey Wells John Lindsey William Calmees Thomas Colson and George Hampton having been Appointed to View the Ground from the Place where Humphrey Wells Lives to Fielding Lewis's Mill made their Report It is Ordered that a Road be Opened as Laid Off by them and that the Tithables within Two miles thereof do work thereon under Humphrey Wells who is by the Court appointed Overseer thereof

6 May 1766, FOB 13, p. 52
Peter Hanger is appointed Overseer of the Highway from Woodstock to Mounts Birds in the Room of Jacob Miller dec^d and it is Ordered that the usual Tithables work Thereon under him

6 May 1766, FOB 13, p. 53
Richard Pearis is Appointed Overseer of the Road from Winchester to Hoge Creek in the Room of Jonathan Lupton It is Ordered that the usual Tithables work Thereon under him

7 May 1766, FOB 13, p. 53
Ordered that the Tithables Three miles of Littlers Road from the Beginning to Opeckon Creek work thereon under Thomas Helm the Overseer

7 May 1766, FOB 13, p. 54
John Reed is appointed Overseer of the Road from Col^o Hites to Chrismans Spring in the room of Lawrence Snapp and It is Ordered that the Tithables Three miles on each Side work thereon under him

3 June 1766, FOB 13, p. 59
Upon the Petition of George Bruce praying to have a Road Opened from the horse Pond in McCormacks Road to his mill Ordered that William Jolliffe Isaac Johnson John Reese & Edward Dodd or any three of them being first Sworn do view the ground & Report to the Court their Opinion of the Same

3 June 1766, FOB 13, p. 59
Ordered that John Neavill & William Jolliffe Gent do agree with Some Person to Build a Bridge over Bruces Mill Run and Bring in the Charge at Laying the next Levy

3 June 1766, FOB 13, p. 59
Magness Tate is Appointed Overseer of the Road from Keyes's Ferry to the Top of the mountain in the Room of Humphrey Keyes & It is Ordered that the Tithables five miles on each Side as far as Henry Loyds work thereon under him

3 June 1766, FOB 13, p. 59
Andrew Tillery is Appointed overseer of the Road from Keys ford & the ferry to Henry Loyds & It is Ordered that the Tithables Three miles on Each Side work thereon under him

3 June 1766, FOB 13, p. 63
Upon the motion of John Smith Praying that a Road Leading from Alexander Fryers to the Head of Bulskin through his Land may be turned & It is Ordered that William Rankin John Dawkins & John Briscoe & David Rankins jn^r or any three of them being first sworn do view they ground & Report there Opinion to the next Court

4 June 1766, FOB 13, p. 78
Robert Harper Entered into & Acknowledged a Bond for Keeping a ferry Over Potowmack River which is Ordered to be Certified

5 June 1766, FOB 13, p. 116
Henry Pedinger is appointed Overseer of the Road from the Streets of McLenburgh to the ferry & It is Ordered that the Tithables of the Town work thereon under him

1 July 1766, FOB 13, p. 122
William Rankin David Rankin ju^r & John Dawkins having been appointed to View the Ground from Alexander Fryers to the head of Bulskin & Report the Conveniences & Inconveniences that will attend the Turning of the Road as it now Runs through the Land of John Smith made their Report It is Ordered that the said Road be Turned as is marked by the Viewers

5 August 1766, FOB 13, p. 124
Upon the Petition of Joseph Wilkinson George Hoge is appointed overseer of the Road from the Timber Ridge to Hoge Creek in the Room of the said Wilkinson It is Ordered that the usual Tithables work thereon under him

5 August 1766, FOB 13, p. 124
Upon the Petition of Joseph Dillon Leave is Granted him to Turn the Road from Frosts to Dillons Plantation Round the North side of Dillons Plantation into a Lane he Clearing It at his Own Expense

2 September 1766, FOB 13, p. 173
Robert Willson is appointed Overseer of the Road from Winchester to Opeckon at Armstrongs Place in the Room of Joseph Lupton Itis Ordered that the usual Tithables work thereon under him

5 September 1766, 13, p. 213
It is Ordered that James Daugherty William Pikering Achebud Ashcraft Evan Rogers & John Province or any Three of them being first Sworne do View the Ground from Pughs & Barretts Mill by the End of the Sleepy Creek mountain to the warm Springs & Lay off and mark a Road the best & most Convenient way & make Report of their opinion of the same to next Court

5 September 1766, 13, p. 214
Isaac Dawson is Appointed overseer of the Road of Sr Johns from the end of the Sleepy Creek mountain where the warm Spring Road Crosses it to James Daughertys Ordered that the Inhabitants Six miles on Each Side thereof work thereon under him

5 September 1766, 13, p. 214
James Lindsey is appointed Overseer of Loudon Street & the Cross streets and Commons as far as Cameron Street in the Room of John McKamie and It is Ordered that Tithables within that Distance do work under him

5 September 1766, 13, p. 214
George Sexton is Appointed overseer of Cameron Street and all the Streets to the Eastward thereof and the Commons in the Room of Adam Haymaker It is Ordered that the Tithables within that Compass work Thereon under him

7 October 1766, 13, p. 230
Upon the Petitioner of the Inhabitants praying that the Road may be Opened from John Dentons Jacob Rushes Plantation in the upper end of Powels fort Ordered that John Denton Elijah Odell Abraham Dillback & Jacob Rush or any Three of them being first sworn do view the same and make Report of their Opinion to the next Court

7 October 1766, FOB 13, p. 230
Jacob Burner is Appointed Overseer of the Road from the White House in Masanutting to the Top of Masanutting mountain Ordered that the Tithables Six miles on one side and to the County Line on the Other Side work thereon under him

4 November 1766, FOB 13, p. 248
Upon the Petition of John Briscoe Setting forth that a Road Leading through his Plantation to Keyes Ferry was very Prejudicial to him & Praying that it may be Turned Ordered that Magnes Tates Robert Worthington jn^r James McKey & Edward Willett do View the Ground & Report the Inconveniences that will attend the Turning the same

4 November 1766, FOB 13, p. 249
Upon the Petition of John Briscoe praying that a Road may be opened from his mill upon Opeckon to the settlement under the mountain by William Cockraines Ordered that Frances Lilbourne Charles Demoss and Bartholomew Fryatt do View the same and make Report of their Opinion of the same to the Court

4 November 1766, FOB 13, p. 249
Also that a Road may be opened into the mountain Road by Murty Handleys Ordered that William Merchants David Lewis & Joseph Edwards jn^r do veiw the Ground & Report thier opinion of the same to the next Court

4 November 1766, FOB 13, p. 249
Also that a Road may be Opened from Samuel Mounts upon Bullskins to the Road Leading to Ashbys Gap. Ordered that James McCormack John Grantom & John Smith do Veiw the ground & Report their opinion of the Same to the next Court

4 November 1766, FOB 13, p. 249
John Grantom is Appointed Overseer of the Road from Edward Thomas's Plantation to Jacob Hites in the Room of John Briscoe Ordered that the Tithables Three miles on Each side work Thereon under him

4 November 1766, FOB 13, p. 249
Jacob Burner is Appointed Overseer of the Road from the White House to the Top of Massanutting mountain Ordered that the Tithables from the mouth of Hawk's Bill on the one Side and to the County Line on the Other Side work thereon under him

4 November 1766, FOB 13, p. 250
Daniel Morgan is appointed Overseer of the Road from Comb's Ferry to the Forks leading to Winchester Ordered that the Tithables three miles on Each Side work thereon under him

4 November 1766, FOB 13, p. 250
John Reese Edward Dodd & Isaac Johnson being appointed to View the Ground from the Horse Ponds in Doctor McCormacks Road to Bruces Mill made their Report Ordered that a Road be Opened as Laid off by them and that the Tithables within three miles work thereon under Edward Dodd who is appointed Overseer thereof

4 November 1766, FOB 13, p. 250
Ordered that the Road Leading from Doctor Wells to Col^o Lewis's mill which was opened Last Spring be Stoped up

4 November 1766, FOB 13, p. 251
William Guest is Appointed Overseer of the Road from Col^o Mercers upper Quarter to Cunninghams Chapell Ordered that the usual Tithables work thereon under him

4 November 1766, FOB 13, p. 251
Humphrey Wells is Appointed Overseer of the Road from his House to Capt. Calmees's. Ordered that the usael Tithables work thereon under him

4 November 1766, FOB 13, p. 251
George Hampton is Appointed Overseer of the Road from Doctor Wells to Snickers Ferry Ordered that the Tithables three miles on Each Side work thereon under him

6 November 1766, FOB 13, p. 258
County Levy
Towards the Building a Bridge at Bruce's Mill   [£] 30. 0. 0

3 March 1767, FOB 13, p. 277
Joseph Glass is Appointed Overseer of the Road from Paul Fromans Mill to the sandy ford on Opeckon in the room of Paul Froman Ordered that the Tithables one mile & an half on the South Side Two miles & an half on the north side & Three miles at the upper End work thereon under him

3 March 1767, FOB 13, p. 279
Samuel Littler is appointed Overseer of the Road called Littlers in the Room of Thomas Helm Ordered that the usael Tithables work thereon under him

3 March 1767, FOB 13, p. 279
Ordered that Jacob Frey Samuel Frey Joseph Fawcett & John Fawcett or any Three of them do view the ground from the furnace Erecting on the north Branch of Pembroke to the Forge Erecting on Cedar Creek & Report their Opinion to the next Court

3 March 1767, FOB 13, p. 280
Ordered that James Knight David Brown John Bell & William Kearfoot do View the Ground from the Southwest Pond to Hites mill & Report their Opinion of the same to the next Court

3 March 1767, FOB 13, p. 280
James McCormack John Grantom & John Smith being appointed to view the Ground from John Briscoes Mill upon Opeckon to Ashbys Gap made their Report Ordered a Road be Opened as marked by them and that the Tithables three miles on Each Side thereof work thereon under William Rankin who is appointed Overseer thereof

3 March 1767, FOB 13, p. 281
Lewis Pence is appointed Overseer of the Road from Dry Run to the Top of the Ridge at Thorntons Gap in the Room of Samuel Beam Ordered that the usael Tithables work thereon under him

5 March 1767, FOB 13, p. 293
Jacob Fry John Fawcett & Joseph Fawcett being appointed to view the ground from the furnace Erecting on the north Branch of Pembroke to the forge Erecting on Cedar Creek made their Report Ordered that the same be Opened as laid off by them and that John Fawcet be Appointed Overseer of the same from the furnace to Devault Hulbergers and that the Inhabitants six miles on Each Side & above work thereon under him and Lewis Stephens is appointed overseer from Hulbergers to the forge and that the Tithables six miles on Each Side and at the uper End work thereon under him

7 April 1767, FOB 13, p. 330
Abraham Nisewanger is appointed Overseer of the Road from Col^o Hites to Chrismans Spring in the Room of John Reed Ordered that the usael Tithables work thereon under him.

7 April 1767, FOB 13, p. 332
William Gist is Appointed Overseer of the Road from Col° Mercers upper Quarter to Cunninghames Chappell Ordered that the Tithables one & one half miles on Each side work thereon under him

10 April 1767, FOB 13, p. 381
Thomas Bryan Martin is Appointed Overseer of the Roads from Nations Plantation to the ford at Ashbys Gap Ordered that the Tithables three miles on Each Side thereof work thereon under him

10 April 1767, FOB 13, p. 382
Bayles Earle is Appointed overseer of the Road from Cunninghams Chappell to George Henrys. Ordered that the Tithables Two miles on Each Side work thereon under him

7 May 1767, FOB 13, p. 382
John Crane is Appointed Overseer of the Road from Snickers ferry to Bullskin Ordered that the Tithables three miles on Each Side work thereon under him

7 May 1767, FOB 13, p. 382
Benjamine Rankin is Appointed Overseer of the Road from Bullskin to the Bloomery Ordered that the Tithables three miles on Each Side work thereon under him

7 May 1767, FOB 13, p. 384
John Shely, Alexander Burnett, & Benjamin Beelor being appointed to view the Ground from Beelors mill into the main Road at Bradleys made their report & that it was Necessary to Continue the Road along the old Road to the mill which would go through a Corner of Briscoes new ground. Ordered that the Road be Opened as Viewed & Laid off by them and that the Tithables Two miles on Each Side work thereon under Benjamin Beelor who is Appointed overseer

7 May 1767, FOB 13, p. 384
William Baldwin is Appointed overseer of the Road from Cunninghams mill to that part of the Road Opposite to Samuel Wilsons House Ordered that the Tithables from Opeckon on one Side of the said Road & from the mountain on the Other work thereon under him

[Note: Entries for 6 May 1767 are entered in the order book between the entries for May 7 and May 8.]

6 May 1767, FOB 13, p. 387
Upon the petition of John Lisher praying that a Road may be Opened from John Snaps to the furnace Ordered that a Road be Opened & that Tithables four miles on Each Side work thereon under John Snapp who is appointed Overseer & from the furnace to the mill Seat

6 May 1767, FOB 13, p. 387
Magness Tate Edward Violett & James M°Kee having been appointed to view the Road Running through Briscoes Plantation to Keyes Ferry & Report whether the Conveniences or

Inconveniences of the Said Road made their Report Ordered that the Road be Turned as marked and Laid off by them

6 May 1767, FOB 13, p. 391
William Hancher is Appointed Overseer of the Road from Cunninghams Mill to Henry Bowens. Ordered that the Tithables Two miles on Each Side work thereon under him

8 May 1767, FOB 13, p. 426
Ordered that William Doster, Thomas Babb, Ichebud Ashcraft, James Daugherty & Zadock Springer or any Three of them being first Sworn do view the nearest & best way from the warm Springs to Barretts mill & Report the Conveniences & Inconveniences that will attend the Opening a Road on the Same

2 June 1767, FOB 13, p. 430
William Doster Zadock Springer James Daugherty & Ichebud Ashcraft being Appointed to View the Ground from the warm Springs to Barretts Mill made their Report Ordered that a Road be opened as Laid off by them and that the Tithables five miles on Each Side work thereon under James Daugherty from the Springs to Ichebud Ashcrafts & five miles on Each Side from Ashcrafts to the Buffaloe Run work under Ichebud Ashcraft & five miles on Each Side & on the Lower End work thereon from the Buffaloe Run to the End and Zadock Springer

2 June 1767, FOB 13, p. 431
Ordered that Jeremiah Stroade Jonas Hedges, Henry Newkirk & Tunis Hood do view the Ground from the fork [ford?] of Opeckon on the main Road at Edward Stroades to Hoglands Ferry & make Report of the Conveniences & Inconveniences that will attend Opening a Road on the same

Frederick County Order Book 14 (1767-1770) Parts 1 and 2

4 June 1767, FOB 14 Part 1, p. 17
Henry Fravell is Appointed Overseer of the Road from the Narrow Passage to Mounts Birds. Ordered that the usael Tithables that worked on the same under Peter Hanger from the said Passage work thereon under him

4 June 1767, FOB 14 Part 1, p. 18
Jonathan Seaman is Appointed Overseer of the Road from his House on Opeckon to Jacob Hites It is Ordered that the Tithables Two Myles on Each Side work thereon under him

7 June 1767, FOB 14 Part 1, p. 52
Jeremiah Stroad, Jonas Hedges Henry Newkird & Tunis Hood being Appointed to View the Ground from the ford of Opeckon on the main Road at Edward Stroads to Hoglands Ferry made their Report. Ordered that a Road be Opened as Laid off by them and that the Tithables Three miles on each Side thereof work thereon under Henry Newkirk who is Appointed Overseer

7 June 1767, FOB 14 Part 1, p. 59
Peter Babb is Appointed Overseer of Sir John's Road from the Place where the Road from Robert Cunninghames falls into it to the forks where the Road Leads to Winchester Ordered that the Tithables Three miles on each Side work thereon under him

7 June 1767, FOB 14 Part 1, p. 59
Jeremiah Smith is Appointed Overseer of the Road from Jesse Pughes to Jeremiah Smiths Ordered that the Tithables three Miles on each Side thereof & on the upper end work thereon under him

7 June 1767, FOB 14 Part 1, p. 59
Joseph Berry, Baylis Earle & Peter Catlett having been appointed to View the Ground from the Race Ground below John Hites to the Swift Shoal foard on Shannandoah & from thence into the County Road made their Report Ordered that the Tithables Three miles on each Side work thereon under James Catlett who is Appointed Overseer thereof.

5 August 1767, FOB 14 Part 1, p. 61
Upon the Petition of the Inhabitants praying that a Road may be Opened from the County Line in Massanutting to Mauks mill Ordered that Joseph Strickler Jacob Burner Daniel Stover & Martin Coffman or any Three of Them do View the said Ground & Report the Conveniences & Inconveniences that will attend the Opening of a Road

5 August 1767, FOB 14 Part 1, p. 61
Benjamin Rufner is Appointed overseer of the Road from the White House to the Dry Run in the Room of John Taylor Ordered that the usual Tithables work thereon under him

5 August 1767, FOB 14 Part 1, p. 62
Thomas Berry is Appointed Overseer of the Road from Snickers Ford to Cunninghams Chappel in the Room of William Cooke Ordered that the usual Tithables work thereon under him

6 August 1767, FOB 14 Part 1, p. 72
Francis Lilbourne Charles Demoss & Bartholomew Fryett having been Appointed to View the Ground from John Briscoes Mill on Opeckon to the Settlement under the mountain by William Cockrains having made their Report Ordered that a Road be opened as Laid off by them & that the Tithables Three Miles on each Side thereof work thereon under Jonathan Osburn who is Appointed Overseer thereof

6 August 1767, FOB 14 Part 1, p. 72
David Lewis William Merchant & Joseph Edwards being appointed to View the Ground from John Briscoe's Mill upon Opeckon into the main Road by Murty Handleys made their Report Ordered that a Road be Opened as Laid off by them and that the Tithables Three miles on each Side thereof work thereon under David Lewis who is appointed overseer thereof

1 September 1767, FOB 14 Part 1, p. 99
Elijah Odell John Denton & Jacob Rush having been Appointed to View the Ground from John Denton's to Jacob Rushe's made their Report Ordered that a Road be Opened as Laid off by them & that the Tithables belonging to the Great Fort of Powell's work thereon under Elijah Odell who is appointed overseer thereof

1 September 1767, FOB 14 Part 1, p. 99
Upon the petition of Sundry Inhabitants praying that a Road may be opened from the white Post to the Cross Roads near Cunninghams Chapell, Ordered that Peter Catlett Daniel Morgan Samuel Blackburne & Baylis Earle or any Three of them being first Sworn do view the Same & Report their Opinion to the Court

1 September 1767, FOB 14 Part 1, p. 99
Upon the petition of Sundry Inhabitants praying to have a Road opened from the main Road Leading from Winchester to Watkins ferry at Peter Fusseys bigg Spring to the upper Side of the mouth of Opeckon Creek Ordered that Jeremiah Stroade Robert Fillson William Porterfeild Andrew Bowman or any three of them do view the same & Report the Conveniences & Inconveniences that will attend the Opening of a Road on the Same, to the next Court

1 September 1767, FOB 14 Part 1, p. 100
Upon the Petition of Cutlip Sink praying to have a Road opened from Christian Dellingers to his mill on Stoney Creek Ordered that Taverner Beall George Harrison Jacob Wolfe & Peter Coffield or any three do view the Ground & Report their Opinion of the same to the next Court

3 November 1767, FOB 14 Part 1, p. 144
William Morgan Van Swearingen & Jacob Vanmetre having been appointed to View the ground from Mecklenburg to Barnes Foard made their Report Ordered that a Road be opened as Laid off by them & that the Tithables Three miles on each side Work thereon under Nicholas McIntire who is Appointed overseer thereof

3 November 1767, FOB 14 Part 1, p. 144
Joseph Strickler Jacob Burner Daniel Stover & Martin Cofman being appointed to view the Ground from the County Line in Massanutting to Mauks Mill made their Report Ordered that the Road be opened as Laid off by them and that the Tithables four miles on each side thereof work thereon under Nicholas Long who is Appointed overseer

3 November 1767, FOB 14 Part 1, p. 145
Semion Hiatt is appointed overseer of the Road from Jacob Hites Bridge to the Bridge at Edward Thomas's in the Room of John Grantum Ordered that the usael Tithables Work thereon under him

3 November 1767, FOB 14 Part 1, p. 146
Jeremiah Strode William Porterfeild & Andrew Bowman having been Appointed to View the Ground from Fusseys Large Spring to the upper side of Opeckon Creek at the mouth made their

Report Ordered that the tithables Three miles on each side Work thereon under Jeremiah Strode who is appointed overseer thereof

3 November 1767, FOB 14 Part 1, p. 146
Ordered that Edward Snickers Toliaferro Stribling Thomas Speake & Daniel Johnston or any Three of them being first sworn do View the Ground from Thomas Speaks's to Sniggers's ferry & Report the Conveniences that will attend the opening a Road on the same

3 November 1767, FOB 14 Part 1, p. 146
Ordered that Samuel Mounts Samuel Worthington James Pearson & Moses Walton or any Three of them being first sworn do View the Road from Samuel Mounts the Nearest & best way to Jacob Hites mill & Report the Conveniences & Inconveniences that may attend the opening a Road thereon

4 November 1767, FOB 14 Part 1, p. 148
Robert Blackburn is Appointed overseer of the Road from the Horse Ponds to Bruce's Mill in the Room of Edward Dodd Ordered that the former Tithables work thereon under him

4 November 1767, FOB 14 Part 1, p. 148
Ordered that the Road from the late Glebe to Cunninghams Chappel be Discontinued

5 November 1767, FOB 14 Part 1, p. 158
John Vestall is Appointed overseer of the Road from the musterground to the foard. Ordered that the Tithables Three miles on each side work thereon under him

5 November 1767, FOB 14 Part 1, p. 159
Robert Worthington jn.^{r} is Appointed overseer of the Road from the Muster Ground to the forks by John Smiths Ordered that the Tithables Three miles each side work thereon under him

5 November 1767, FOB 14 Part 1, p. 160
Christopher Lambert is appointed overseer of Loudoun Street & the Cross-Streets in it in the Room of James Lindsey Ordered that the usael Tithables work thereon under him

7 November 1767, FOB 14 Part 1, p. 184
Abraham Kendrick is Appointed overseer of the Road from Tidwells ford to Chesters Ford in the Fork in the Room of Thomas Buck Ordered that the usael Tithables work thereon under him

7 November 1767, FOB 14 Part 1, p. 184
James Hoge is Appointed overseer of the Road from the Great Road to the Fork of the Road that Leads to Henry Spears Road in the Room of Isaac Hite Ordered that the usael Tithables work thereon under him

November 7th 1767, FOB 14 Part 1, p. 184
Francis McCormack is Appointed overseer of the Road from William Frosts Plantation on Back Creek to Bridgers Mill Ordered that the usael Tithables work thereon under him

November 7th 1767, FOB 14 Part 1, p. 185
Mercer Babb is Appointed overseer of the Road from Joseph Bridges Mill to William Dillons Plantation Ordered that the usael Tithables work thereon under him

7 November 1767, FOB 14 Part 1, p. 185
Joseph Berry is Appointed overseer of the Road from the Top of a Ridge to the Top of the Bank of the River on the opposite at the Ferry at the Ford. And Ordered that the Tithables three miles on each side & the upper end Work thereon under him.

1 March 1768, FOB 14 Part 1, p. 188
Pearce Butler is Appointed overseer of the Road from Ichebud Ashcrofts to the warm Springs in the Room of James Daugherty. Ordered that the Tithables five myles on each side Work thereon under him.

1 March 1768, FOB 14 Part 1, p. 189
Robert Jackson is Appointed overseer of the Road from Mill Creek to Sir Johns Road in the Room of Richard Stepenson. Ordered that the usael Tithables work thereon under him

2 March 1768, FOB 14 Part 1, p. 193
Upon the Petition of James Hoge Praying that the Road Leading through his Plantation to Massenutting may be Turned from that part of his Plantation where it now Runs to a Different Part and that Viewers may be Appointed to Veiw the same. Ordered that the Same be Rejected the Court knowing the Road as it now Runs to be good and not being acquainted with any good cause for Appointing a Veiw.

2 March 1768, FOB 14 Part 1, p. 193
Upon the Petition of Sundry Inhabitants praying that a Road from John Evan's fence to Jacob Hites mill may be altered. Ordered that Hugh Hysle James Stroad Issac Evans & Abraham Vanmetre or any Three of them being first Swore do Veiw the Same and Report the Conveniences & Inconveniences that may attend the opening a Road on the same

2 March 1768, FOB 14 Part 1, p. 193
Upon the Petition of Sundry Inhabitants praying that a Road may be opened from Abraham Dursts Shop to the Road on this side of the massanuting mountain Ordered that George Harrison George Riddle Jacob Holdman & Curtis Alderson or any Three of them being first Swore do view the same & Report to the Court the Conveniences & Inconveniences that may attend the same

2 March 1768, FOB 14 Part 1, p. 194
Edward Snickers Toliafero Stribling & Daniel Johnston being appointed to View the Ground from Thomas Speakes Plantation to Snickers Ferry made their Report. Ordered that a Road be opened as Laid off by them & that the Tithables Two miles on each side Work thereon under Toliaferro Stribling who is Appointed overseer

2 March 1768, FOB 14 Part 1, p. 195
Edward Violet is appointed overseer of the Road from the musterground to Vestalls Foard. Ordered that the Tithables Three miles on each side Work thereon under him

2 March 1768, FOB 14 Part 1, p. 195
Bayles Earles is Appointed overseer of the Road from Nations Plantation to the Foard & Ferry at Berrys in the Room of Thomas Bryan Martin Ordered that the usael Tithables work thereon under him

3 March 1768, FOB 14 Part 1, p. 197
Samuel Worthington Samuel Pearson & Moses Walton being appointed to Veiw the Ground from Samuel Mounts to Jacob Hites Mill made their Report ordered that a Road be opened as Laid off by them and that the Tithables Two miles on eachside work thereon under Isaiah Pemberton who is Appointed overseer

3 March 1768, FOB 14 Part 1, p. 197
Upon the Petition of Thomas Rutherford praying to have the Warm Spring Road viewed from Andrew Tilleroys the Nearest & Best Way to Henry Lloyds Ordered that Thomas Hart Thomas Lloyd James Shirly & Richard Bowen or any Three of them being first Sworne do Veiw the same & Report the Convenience & Inconviniene that attend the same

5 March 1768, FOB 14 Part 1, p. 222
A Supersedeas to Stop the opening of the Road from the Race Ground below John Hites to the Swift Shoal Foard was Produced. Ordered that the Proceedings of the Same to the Secretaries Office

5 April 1768, FOB 14 Part 1, p. 235
Edmond Lindsey jn^r is Appointed overseer of the Road from the Cross Roads at Carneys Spring to the Head of Bulskin. Ordered that the Tithables Two miles on each side thereof work thereon under him

5 April 1768, FOB 14 Part 1, p. 235
Thomas Mason is Appointed overseer of the Road from the Flatt Rock to the Ford upon Bulskin above Mr Pykes. Ordered that the Tithables Two miles on each side work thereon under him

6 April 1768, FOB 14 Part 1, p. 235
David Brown overseer of the Road from Opeckon to Winchester in the Room of John Hite ordered that the Tithables as usael Work thereon under him

3 May 1768, FOB 14 Part 1, p. 237
Thomas Hart. James Lloyd James Shirley & Richard Bowers having been appointed to Veiw the ground leading to the Warm Springs from Andrews Tilleroys to Henry Lloyds made their Report. Ordered that a Road be opened as laid off by them, and that the Tithables Two miles on each side work thereon under Thomas Hart who is Appointed Overseer

3 May 1768, FOB 14 Part 1, p. 238
Ordered that Jacob Hite John Neavill & Daniel Sturges Gent. do Veiw the Ground from the Musterground the Nearest & Best way to Keyes Ferry & Report the Conveniences & Inconveniences that may Attend the altering any of the Roads that are at Present established and that all Road in the mean Time be Continued

3 May 1768, FOB 14 Part 1, p. 240
William Shepherd is appointed overseer of the Streets of Mecklenburg and the Road leading to the River in the Room of Henry Bedinger Ordered that the usael Tithables work thereon under him

3 May 1768, FOB 14 Part 1, p. 240
Laurence Snapp is appointed overseer of the Road from his House to Toms Brook. Ordered that the usael Tithables work thereon under him

3 May 1768, FOB 14 Part 1, p. 240
Abraham Kendrick is Appointed overseer of the Road from the North River Leading to Chesters Gap to the South River. Ordered that the Tithables four miles on each side work thereon under him

4 May 1768, FOB 14 Part 1, p. 243
Hugh Lyle Abraham Vanmetre James Stroade & Isaac Evans having been Appointed to Veiw the Ground from John Evans's Fence to Jacob Hite Mill and Report whether the same Coud be Turned with Advantage to the Publick made their Report. Ordered that the Road be Continued as it formerly Run

4 May 1768, FOB 14 Part 1, p. 243
Thomas Black is appointed overseer of the Road from Chrismas Spring to Ceedar Creek Ordered that the usael Tithables work thereon under him

4 May 1768, FOB 14 Part 1, p. 243
George Ruddull Jacob Holdman & Curtis Alderson having been appointed to View the ground from Abraham Darst's Smith's Shop to the Top of the Massanutting mountain made their Report Ordered that the Road be opened as laid off by them and that the Tithables from where the Road Crosses Smiths Creek up the Creek to John Nisewangers and across by John Dauvens to the River thence up Holmans Creek to Caspere Branners thence to Henry Brooks thence to Mark Oilers thence a Straightline to Smiths Creek Work thereon under Daniel Holdman who is appointed overseer thereof

4 May 1768, FOB 14 Part 1, p. 244
Henry Gore is Appointed overseer of the Road from the Massanutting mountain to the County line Ordered that the Tithables from John Newmans up Smiths Creek to the County line with the line to Joseph Sivelys from thence with the lines of the other District Work thereon under him

4 May 1768, FOB 14 Part 1, p. 254
Ordered that Daniel Holdman Christian Stickley Christian Dellinger & Jacob Rinker or any Three of them being first Swore do Veiw the ground from the County line on Cape Capon Mountain by Sinks Mill to Abraham Darst's Smith Shop & Report the Conveniences & Inconveniences that may Attend the opening the Road on the Same to the Next Court

6 May 1768, FOB 14 Part 1, p. 262
George Helmes is Appointed overseer of Cameron Street in the Room of George Sexton Ordered that the usael Tithables do Work thereon under him

7 May 1768, FOB 14 Part 1, p. 292
Ordered that James Barrett Benjamin Barrett Thomas Doster & Joseph Bridges or any Three of them being first Swore do Veiw the Ground from where Morgans Road Crosses Sir Johns Road, the Nearest & Best Way to the Warm Springs Road at Joseph Bridges and Report the Conveniences & Inconveniences that may Attend the opening a Road on the same to the Next Court

2 August 1768, FOB 14 Part 1, p. 293
Ordered that Ralph Withers John Painter Sr James & Thomas Cooper or any Three of them being first swore do Veiw the Ground from Lord Fairfax's upper Quarter to the land Office & Report the Inconveniences & Conveniences that may attend the opening a Road on the same

2 August 1768, FOB 14 Part 1, p. 295
James Burns is appointed overseer of the Road from McKay's Chappel to Gregorys Ford in the Room of Robert McKay Ordered that the usael Tithables work thereon under him

2 August 1768, FOB 14 Part 1, p. 295
Thomas Doster is Appointed overseer of the Road from the Buffaloe run as far as Laid off by the Veiwers from the Warm Springs in the Room of Zadock Springer and that the Tithables five miles on each side & at the Lower end work thereon under him

2 August 1768, FOB 14 Part 1, p. 296
Henry Reese is appointed overseer of the Road from Littlers Lane to Robert Cunninghams in the Room Isaac Johnson Ordered that the usael Tithables work thereon under him

3 August 1768, FOB 14 Part 1, p. 300
Ordered that Philip Bush do agree with some person to Build a Stone Bridge in Cameron Street Eighteen feet wide and that he bring in the Acc^t for the same at Laying the Next levy
[Note: "Depositum" of £ 21. 3. 7 for this bridge was noted in the levy, 1 November 1768, FOB 14 Part 1, p. 347.]

4 August 1768, FOB 14 Part 1, p. 310
Jonathan Lupton is appointed overseer of the Road from the furnace to the Gap of the little mountain Ordered that the Tithables Three miles on each side & at the upper end Work thereon & under him

4 August 1768, FOB 14 Part 1, p. 310
George Rice is appointed overseer of the Road from Doctor M{{c}}Cormacks to Thomas Lindseys House Ordered that the Tithables Two miles each side work thereon under him

4 August 1768, FOB 14 Part 1, p. 310
William M{{c}}Cormack is appointed overseer of the Road from Docter M{{c}}Cormacks to the Muster Ground Including the Bridge Ordered that the Tithables two miles each side thereof work under him

5 August 1768, FOB 14 Part 1, p. 318
William Roberts is appointed Overseer of the Road from Jacob Hites Mill to John Evans's fence in the Room of William Burns. Ordered that the usael Tithables work thereon under him

5 August 1768, FOB 14 Part 1, p. 318
Ordered that John Hardinger ju{{r}} Henry Heath, John Geestin [Gustin?] & Josiah Hulls or any Three of them being first Sworne do View the Ground from the Warm Springs to the County line & make Report of the Conveniences & Inconveniences that may attend the opening a Road on the same to the Next Court.

1 November 1768, FOB 14 Part 1, p. 346
Lewis Wolfe is appointed overseer of Loudon Street in the room of Christopher Lambert Ordered that the usael Tithables work thereon under him

1 November 1768, FOB 14 Part 1, p. 347
County Levy
To a Depositum in the Sherifs Hands   [£] 21. 3. 7
[Note: For the stone bridge in Cameron Street: order, 3 August 1768, FOB 14 Part 1, p. 300.]

1 November 1768, FOB 14 Part 1, p. 348
William Vandeveir is appointed overseer of the Road from the Top of the Blue Ridge to Keyes Ferry Including the Foard in the Room of Magnes Tate Ordered that the Tithables on the Southside the River Five miles up & down and five miles up and Down the River on the Northside and half a mile from the Banks of the Northside work thereon under him And that they be Exempted from all other Roads.

1 November 1768, FOB 14 Part 1, p. 348
Upon the Petition of James Keith praying for a Road from the Head of Long Marsh to his Mill upon Bulskin. Ordered that George Rice Edmond Rice Owen Thomas and Samuel Mounts or any Three of them being first Swore do veiw the Same and Report the Conveniences and Inconveniences that may attend the Opening a Road on the Same

1 November 1768, FOB 14 Part 1, p. 348
Upon the Petition of James Keith praying for a Road from his Mill to Vestals Foard Ordered that John Vance John Vestall Hugh Stephenson & James M{{c}}Cormack or any Three of them being

first Swore do view the same and Report the Conveniences and Inconveniences that may Attend the opening a Road on the Same --

1 November 1768, FOB 14 Part 1, p. 348
William Baldwin ju^r. is appointed overseer of the Road from Mill Run to Mills Gap. Ordered that the Tithables three miles on each side Work thereon under him

1 November 1768, FOB 14 Part 1, p. 349
Robert Jackson is appointed overseer of a Road from Mill Run to Sir Johns Road. Ordered that the Tithables three Miles on each side Work thereon under him

1 November 1768, FOB 14 Part 1, p. 349
Ordered that Henry Newkirk John Hougland George Myles and James Davis or any Three of them being first Swore do veiw the ground from Sir Johns Road near George Pauls to Houglands Ferry and to Van Swearingens mill on Tunises Branch and report the Conveniences and Inconveniences that may Attend the opening a Road on the same to the Next Court

1 November 1768, FOB 14 Part 1, p. 349
Ordered that James Forman, Edward Tyler Thomas Turner, and Joseph Franceway or any Three of them being first Swore do view the ground from M.^{c}lenburgh to Andrew Swearingen's Mill and from thence to the Maine Road that Leads to the mouth of Opeckon and report the Conveniences and Inconveniences that may attend the opening a road on the Same.

1 November 1768, FOB 14 Part 1, p. 349
Ordered that David Castleman David Kennedy Samuel Mounts and John Dawkins or any three of them being first Swore do Veiw the ground from the Widow McCormacks to the Head Spring of Bulskin and report the Conveniences and Inconveniences that may attend the Turning the road.

2 November 1768, FOB 14 Part 1, p. 351
Ordered that the Tithables between the Three top mountain & the Road and two miles on the West Side of the Road work under Lawrence Snapp from his House to Tom's Brook.

2 November 1768, FOB 14 Part 1, p. 354
Peter Catlett is Appointed overseer of the Road from Nations Plantation to Berrys Ferry & ford in the Room of Baylis Earle. Ordered that the usael Tithables work Thereon under him

2 November 1768, FOB 14 Part 1, p. 354
Peter Catlett Daniel Morgan & Baylis Earle having been appointed to view the Ground from the white Post to the Crossroads near Cunninghams Chapple made their Report Ordered that a Road be opened as laid off by them and that the Tithables Two miles on each side work thereon under Baylis Earle who is appointed overseer.

2 November 1768, FOB 14 Part 1, p. 356
Ordered that Ralph Withers John Painter ju.ʳ James Burner & Thomas Cooper who were appointed to Veiw the ground from the Land Office to Lord Fairfax's upper Quarter be Summoned to Show why they have not Returned their Report.

5 November 1768, FOB 14 Part 2, p. 379
George Rice Edmund Rice & Samuel Mounts being appointed to Veiw the Ground from the Head of Long Marsh to Keiths Mill made their Report Ordered that the Road be opened as laid off by them and that the Tithables Two Miles on each side work thereon under George Rice who is appointed overseer thereof.

5 November 1768, FOB 14 Part 2, p. 380
Ordered that Joseph Steer Thomas Babb Angus MᶜDonald & John MᶜDonald or any Three of them being first Swore do Veiw the Ground from Richard Pearis to the Quaker Meeting House & report the Conveniences and Inconveniences that may Attend the opening a road on the same to the Next Court.

7 February 1769, FOB 14 Part 2, p. 407
Upon the Petition of Sundry Inhabitants of Back Creek praying that the Road from Eaton's Mill through Mill's Gap to Fallis's Mill may be reviewed, ordered that Zadock Springer Levy Springer Abraham Sutton & Isaac Stanly or any Three of them being first Sworne do Veiw the same & Lay off & Alter it as is most convenient & make a Report thereof to the Next Court.

7 February 1769, FOB 14 Part 2, p. 408
Ordered that Benjamin Thornberry Dugal Campbell Jonah Seaman & Jonathon Seaman or any Three of them being first Swore do Veiw the ground from the head of Mills Creek to the causeway by Onans & report the Conveniences & Inconveniences that may attend the opening a Road on the same.

7 February 1769, FOB 14 Part 2, p. 408
Upon the motion of Thomas Cowen Ordered that Caleb Booth, William Robinson William Boyd, & Benjamin Thornberry or any Three of them being first Swore do view the Road thate Runs through Thomas Cowens Meadow & Report to the Next Court the Conveniences & Inconveniences that may attend the Turning of the same.

8 February 1769, FOB 14 Part 2, p. 409
Ordered that William Miller Andrew MᶜKay Robert Painter & Robert Hains or any Three of them being first Swore do veiw the Ground from Lord Fairfax's upper Quarter to the Land Office & report to the next Court the Conveniences and Inconveniences that may attend the opening a Road on the same.

8 February 1769, FOB 14 Part 2, p. 409
Upon the petition of Sundry Inhabitants that a Road may be opened from Semples furnace to the Warm Springs Road above Peter Burrs Ordered that Thomas Hart William Dark James Lloyd &

Henry Lloyd or any Three of them being first Sworne do Veiw the same & Report the conveniences & Inconveniences that may attend the opening a Road on the same.

8 February 1769, FOB 14 Part 2, p. 411
Upon the Petition of Robert Allen praying for a Road from his House to the Road leading to Winchester Ordered that Nathaniel Cartmill James Marquis Joseph Colvill & William Marquis or any Three of them being first Swore do Veiw the same & make Report of the conveniences and Inconveniences that may attend the Same.

8 February 1769, FOB 14 Part 2, p. 415
Ordered that Jonas Hedge Henry Newkirk John Hougland & George Myles or any Three of them being first swore do Veiw the Ground from Van Swearingens Mill upon Tunis's Branch to the Warm Springs Road near Hedges & Report the Conveniences & Inconveniences that may attend the opening a Road on the Same to the Next Court.

8 February 1769, FOB 14 Part 2, p. 415
David Ashby is appointed overseer of the Road from the Head of Buck Marsh to Marquis Calmes in the Room of Humphrey Wells. Ordered that the usual Tithables work thereon under him

8 February 1769, FOB 14 Part 2, p. 415
Valentine Crawford is appointed to View the ground from Keiths Mill to Vestals ford in the Room of John Vestall one of the Viewers appointed by a former order of this Court

8 February 1769, FOB 14 Part 2, p. 415
James Foreman, Edward Tyler & Joseph Franceway being appointed to veiw the ground from Mecklinburgh to Andrew Swearingen's Mill made their Report Ordered that a Road be opened as Laid off by them and that the Tithables on the east side to the River and on the West one mile & an half work thereon under James Forman who is appointed overseer.

9 February 1769, FOB 14 Part 2, p. 433
Joseph Steer John McDonald & Thomas Babb being appointed to Veiw the ground from Richard Pearis's into Sir Johns Road made their Report. Ordered that the Road be opened as Laid off by them and that the Tithables two miles on each side work thereon under Thomas Babb who is appointed overseer.

4 April 1769, FOB 14 Part 2, p. 448
Peter Helphingston is appointed overseer of Cameron Street Ordered that the usual Tithables Work thereon under him

4 April 1769, FOB 14 Part 2, p. 448
Isaac Zane is Appointed overseer of the Road from the Forge upon Cedar Creek to Opeckon in the Room of Lewis Stephens Ordered that the Tithables Three miles on each side Work thereon under him.

4 April 1769, FOB 14 Part 2, p. 448
Isaac Zane is Appointed overseer of the Road from Opeckon to the Winchester Road in the Room of Samuel Pritchard Ordered that the Tithables a mile & an Half on each side work thereon under him

4 April 1769, FOB 14 Part 2, p. 448
Upon the Petition of Isaac Evans Ordered that James Strode James Grayham William Campbell & Andrew Campbell or any three of them being first swore do veiw the Ground at his Plantation whereon a Road now goes & Report the Conveniences & Inconveniences that may attend the Turning the Same.

4 April 1769, FOB 14 Part 2, p. 449
George Briscoe is Appointed overseer from Briscoes Mill to the Settlement under the North Mountain in the Room of Jonathon Osborne. Ordered that the usual Tithables Work thereon under him

4 April 1769, FOB 14 Part 2, p. 450
Upon the Petition of Sundry Inhabitants Praying for a Road from Houghlands Ferry by Hugh Lysles William Baldwins & William Hancheires to Fall into Morgans Road Leading to Winchester Ordered that James Davis John Hays Jonas Hedges & George Ruble or any Three of them do Veiw the same & make Report of the Conveniences & Inconveniences that may attend the opening a Road on the Same.

4 April 1769, FOB 14 Part 2, p. 450
Jonathon Rose is appointed overseer of the Road from the Top of the Mountain to Sleepy Creek. Ordered that the Tithables Six Miles on each side thereof work thereon under him

April 1769, FOB 14 Part 2, p. 451
Ordered that Thomas Thornbrough Jonathon Rose Lucas Hood & Josiah Hults or any Three of them being first Sworne do Veiw the Ground from Thomas Cherrys ford to the Warm Springs Road by Lucas Hoods & Report the Conveniences & Inconveniences that may Attend the turning the same.

4 April 1769, FOB 14 Part 2, p. 451
James Hagan is Appointed overseer of the Road from William Jolliffs to Opeckon in the Room of Edward Dodd. Ordered that the usual Tithables work thereon under him

4 April 1769, FOB 14 Part 2, p. 452
James Lloyd is Appointed overseer of the Road from Henry Moors to the Elk Branch in the Room of Thomas Hart. Ordered that the Tithables Two Miles on each side work thereon under him

4 April 1769, FOB 14 Part 2, p. 452
Thomas Hart Henry Lloyd Godwin Swift & Francis Hamilton are appointed to Veiw the ground from Semples furnace to the Warm Spring Road & Report the Conveniences & Inconveniences that may attend the opening a Road on the same.

5 April 1769, FOB 14 Part 2, p. 453
Isaac Zane is Appointed overseer of the Road from Stephensburgh to Nations Plantation. Ordered that the Tithables Three miles on each side Work thereon under him

5 April 1769, FOB 14 Part 2, p. 457
Zadock Springer Levi Springer & Abraham Sutton being appointed to View the Road from Eatons Mill to Fallis's Mill made their Report. Ordered that the Road be Altered as Marked by them from the Place Opposite to Sutherlands Ford to the Mountain Run and that the Tithables five Miles on each side Work thereon under Abraham Sutton who is Appointed overseer.

6 April 1769, FOB 14 Part 2, p. 465
John Vance Hugh Stephenson & James McCormack being appointed to Veiw the Ground from Keiths Mill to Vestalls foard made their Report. Ordered that a Road be opened as Laid off by them and that the Tithables Three Miles on each side work as far as Beelors Mill under Henry Hurst & from thence to Vestalls ford under Benjamin Beelor who are appointed overseers

6 April 1769, FOB 14 Part 2, p. 465
Upon the Petition of James Keith Praying for a Road from his Mill into the main Road Leading from Sniggers Ferry to fall into the same at Jonathon Osborns Plantation Ordered that David Kennedy Hugh Stephenson Henry Hurst & Owen Thomas or any Three of them being first Sworne do Veiw the same & Report the Conveniences & Inconveniences that may attend the opening a Road on the Same to the Next Court

6 April 1769, FOB 14 Part 2, p. 466
Benjamin Thornberry William Robinson & Caleb Booth being appointed to veiw the road through Thomas Cowens Plantation made their Report. Ordered that the Road be altered upon Condition that the said Thomas keep it in proper Repair

7 April 1769, FOB 14 Part 2, p. 469
Isaac Eaton is Appointed overseer of the Road from the Widow Calwells to the Mountain Ordered that the usual Tithables Work thereon under him

2 May 1769, FOB 14 Part 2, p. 502
Ordered that all the Tithables within Three Miles of the Road (every way) from the Forge upon Cedar Creek to Opeckon work thereon under Isaac Zane the overseer thereof

1 August 1769, FOB 14 Part 2, p. 506
Upon the Petition of Sundry Inhabitants Praying for a Road from the Head of John Luptons Meadow to the South Branch Road above David Dennys Ordered that Robert Hutchins John

Lupton George Hoge & Isaac Perkins ju.^r do veiw the same & report the Conveniences & Inconveniences of opening a Road on the same

1 August 1769, FOB 14 Part 2, p. 507
Joseph Covill William Marquis & James Marquis having been appointed to view the ground from Robert Allens House to the Road leading to Winchester made their Report Ordered that a Road be opened as laid off by them and that the Tithables half a mile on each thereof Work thereon under John Allen who is appointed overseer

1 August 1769, FOB 14 Part 2, p. 507
Upon the Petition of Sundry Inhabitants praying for a Road from John Spears's to Van Swearingen's Mill at Houghlands Ordered that James Jack Robert Fillson John Fleming & William Porterfeild or any three of them being first Sworne do veiw the same & Report the Conveniences & Inconveniences that may attend the opening a Road on the same.

1 August 1769, FOB 14 Part 2, p. 508
Upon the Petition of Sundry Inhabitants praying for a Road from Matthew Smith's Plantation to McCoys Chappell Ordered that Benjamin Oney Edward Rogers Edward Corder & Ralph Withers or any three of them being first sworne do Veiw the same & report the Conveniences & Inconveniences that may attend the opening a Road on the same

1 August 1769, FOB 14 Part 2, p. 509
Upon the Petition of Sundry Inhabitants praying that a Road may be opened from Swearingens Mill into the Warm Springs Road at Lucas Hoods Ordered that Henry Newkirk, George Myles John Houghland and John Champion or any Three of them being first sworne do veiw the same & Report the Conveniences & Inconveniences that may attend the opening a Road on the same

1 August 1769, FOB 14 Part 2, p. 509
Godwin Swift Henry Lloyd and Thomas Hart having been appointed to veiw the ground from Semples Furnace to the Warm Spring Road made their Report. Ordered that a Road be opened as Laid off by them and that the Tithables Three Miles on Each side work thereon under James Hendricks who is appointed overseer thereof --.

1 August 1769, FOB 14 Part 2, p. 509
Upon the motion of Thomas Cowen leave is Granted him to Turn the Road which leads through his Plantation around the same It appearing that this may be done without any Inconvenience

2 August 1769, FOB 14 Part 2, p. 510
Upon the Petition of Isaac Zane ordered that John Hite David Brown William Hough or any three of them being first Sworne do veiw the Ground from Stephensburgh to Nations Plantation & Report the Conveniences & Inconveniences that may attend the opening a Road on the same.

2 August 1769, FOB 14 Part 2, p. 511
Ordered that the Sherif do pay Philip Bush Twenty one pounds Three Shillings & Seven pence. The Depositum in his Hands for Building a Bridge over Cameron Street.

3 August 1769, FOB 14 Part 2, p. 527
Isaac Zane is appointed overseer of the Road from the Forge to the furnace in the Room of Lewis Stephens. Ordered that the usual Tithables Work thereon under him.

3 August 1769, FOB 14 Part 2, p. 529
Upon the petition of George Michael Laubinger & several others Praying that a Lane which was Laid out by James Wood dec.^{d} Close & Joining the back Line of Loudon Street & which has been stopt up, may be opened again Upon hearing the same It is ordered that the said Lane be opened & so from time to time be kept by the overseer of Loudon Street for the time being .

5 September 1769, FOB 14 Part 2, p. 562
Upon the petition of Jacob Hite & others Praying for a Road from John Wisecarvers to Coopers Mill by Benjamin Frys. Ordered that Heronimus Baker Woolrick Sobinger Samuel Beam & John Fawcett or any Three of them being first sworne do veiw the same & report the Conveniences & Inconveniences that may attend the same to the Next Court

5 September 1769, FOB 14 Part 2, p. 562
Upon the Petition of Sundry Inhabitants Praying for a road from the baptist meeting House to William Hancheirs. Ordered that Morgan Morgan William Boyd John Watson & David Garrett or any three of them being first swore do view the same & report the Conveniences & Inconveniences of the same to the Next Court.

5 September 1769, FOB 14 Part 2, p. 563
John Lupton Robert Hodgson & Isaac Perkins ju^r having been appointed to veiw the ground from John Lupton's Meadow to the South Branch Road above David Denny's made their Report. Ordered that a Road be opened as laid of by them & that the Tithables two miles on each side work thereon under David Denny who is appointed overseer

6 September 1769, FOB 14 Part 2, p. 567
Harmon Levingood is appointed overseer of the Road from Millers Town to Stoney Creek in the Room of Peter Hanger ordered that the Usual Tithables work thereon under him

6 September 1769, FOB 14 Part 2, p. 567
Ordered that the Tithables above Happy Creek be Exempted from Working on Manassits run Road.

6 September 1769, FOB 14 Part 2, p. 567
Ordered that the Tithables on the South side of the south River of Shannondoah be Exempted from Working in the forks of the River.

6 September 1769, FOB 14 Part 2, p. 568
Ordered that the Tithables up the North River under Kendrick be exempted from working on the S.^{o} Side of the South River

6 September 1769, FOB 14 Part 2, p. 568
Ordered that John Reed be appointed overseer of the road from Pasage Creek to the North river & that the Tithables from Pasage Creek to the N.º River work thereon under him

6 September 1769, FOB 14 Part 2, p. 568
Ordered that William Morgan Thomas Rutherford John Taylor & Samuel Taylor or any Three of them being first Swore do veiw the Ground from Semples Furnace to the Warm Spring Road & report the Conveniences & Inconveniences that may attend the opening a Road on the same.

6 September 1769, FOB 14 Part 2, p. 570
Ordered that James Ballenger Mordecai Walker Mercer Babb & Henry Heath or any three of them being first Sworne do Veiw the Ground from Winchester to Mercer Babbs & report the Conveniences & Inconveniences that may attend opening a Road on the same.

6 February 1770, FOB 14 Part 2, p. 574
William Boyd David Watson & David Gerrard having been appointed to Veiw the Ground from the Baptist Meeting House to William Hancheirs made their report Ordered that a Road be opened as laid off by them & that the Tithables two Miles on each side Work thereon under Nathaniel Bell who is appointed overseer thereof.

7 February 1770, FOB 14 Part 2, p. 577
County Levy
To Edward Dodd the Balance for Building a Bridge over Bruces Mill Run   [£] 20. 0. 0.

7 February 1770, FOB 14 Part 2, p. 577
John Helm is appointed overseer of the Road from the Forks of the road leading from Winchester to William Jolliffs to opeckon Creek in the Room of Jonathon Tayler Ordered that the Tithables two Miles on each side thereof work thereon under him

7 February 1770, FOB 14 Part 2, p. 577
John Rees is appointed overseer of the Road from the Ford on Opeckon to Doc.ʳ McCormacks. Ordered that the Tithables Three Miles on each side thereof work thereon under him

7 February 1770, FOB 14 Part 2, p. 578
Ordered that Barack Fisher Robert White David Denny & John Lupton or any Three of them being first Swore do Veiw the Ground from Isaac Perkins's to Hoge Creek where the Road Leading from Winchester to the South Branch Crosses it

7 February 1770, FOB 14 Part 2, p. 578
Upon the motion of William Marks Leave is granted him to turn the Road at his Plantation as he has now opened it

7 February 1770, FOB 14 Part 2, p. 578
James Davis Jonah Hedges & George Ruble having been appointed to veiw the ground from Hoglands ferry to Hugh Lysles William Baldwins & William Hancheirs to fall into Morgans

Road Leading to Winchester made their Report. Ordered that a Road be opened as Laid off by them & that the Tithables two Miles each side work from the Ferry to John Parks under Jonas Hedge & from Hugh Lysles to Mill Creek under Hugh Lysle from Mill Creek to William Hancheirs under Thomas Rees & from thence to Morgans Road under George Ruble who are appointed overseers thereof

7 February 1770, FOB 14 Part 2, p. 579
Robert Wood is appointed overseer of the Road from Winchester to Hoge Creek in the Room of Richard Pearis Ordered that the usual Tithables Work thereon under him

8 February 1770, FOB 14 Part 2, p. 582
Ordered that Richard Pearis Henry Heth John Boyd & William Lupton or any Three of them being first swore do Veiw the ground from the End of the Common to Henry Heaths & report the Conveniences & Inconveniences that may attend opening a road on the Same.

6 March 1770, FOB 14 Part 2, p. 584
William Warren is appointed overseer of the Road from the North River to the forks of Henry Spears Road Ordered that the Tithables Three Miles on each side thereof Work thereon under him

6 March 1770, FOB 14 Part 2, p. 585
Heronimus Baker Samuel Beam & Woolrick Sobinger having been appointed to Veiw the Ground from John Wisecarvers to Coopers Mill made their Report ordered that a Road be opened as Laid off by them and that the Tithables one mile on each side work thereon under Jonathon Lupton who is appointed overseer thereof

6 March 1770, FOB 14 Part 2, p. 587
Job Pugh is appointed overseer of the Road from Isaac's Creek to the County line in the Room of Joseph Morris Ordered that the usual Tithables Work thereon under him.

6 March 1770, FOB 14 Part 2, p. 590
Upon the Petition of Samuel Beall praying that a Road may be opened out of the main Road Leading from Jacob Hites to Mecklenburg through Fosters Land to the Ferrying Water & also to the Ford of Potomack. Ordered that John Taylor John Wright James Hendricks & William Dark or any Three of them being first sworne do veiw the same & report the Conveniences & Inconveniences that may attend the same.

7 March 1770, FOB 14 Part 2, p. 591
William Ashby is appointed overseer of the Road from Gregorys Ford to the Top of the blue Ridge in the Room of Joseph King Ordered that the Tithables Two Miles up & down the River Including those in the forks Work on the same under him

7 March 1770, FOB 14 Part 2, p. 591
George Myles Henry Newkirk & John Hougland having been appointed to veiw the ground from Swearingen's Mill into the Warm Spring Road at Lucas Hoods made their Report Ordered that a

Road be opened as Laid off by by them and that the Tithables Two Miles on each side thereof work thereon from the Mill to Cherrys Run under Tunis Hood who is appointed overseer & from thence to the Warm Spring Road under Lucas Hood who is appointed overseer thereof

7 March 1770, FOB 14 Part 2, p. 592
Upon the Petition of sundry Inhabitants Praying that a road may be opened from Isaac Evans to Henry Vanmetres Mill on Tuscarora & from the said Mill to the Warm Springs Road. Ordered that James Strode Isaac Evans William Burns & Abraham Vanmetre or any Three of them being first Sworne do veiw the same & report the Conveniences & Inconveniences that may attend opening the said Road.

7 March 1770, FOB 14 Part 2, p. 592
John Watson ju[r] is appointed overseer of the Road from Buffaloe Run to Howards old Feild in the Room of Thomas Doster. Ordered that the usual Tithables do work thereon under him

7 March 1770, FOB 14 Part 2, p. 593
Barack Fisher Robert White David Denny & John Lupton having been appointed to Veiw the ground from Isaac Perkins's to Hoge Creek where the Road from Winchester Crosses it made their Report. Ordered that a Road be opened as Laid off by them & that the said Isaac Perkins do the same

8 March 1770, FOB 14 Part 2, p. 595
Richard Jackman is appointed overseer of the Road from Abraham Durst's Smith Shop to the top of the Massanutting Mountain from the North river to the County Line in the Room of David [Daniel?] Holman. Ordered that the usual Tithables work thereon under him.

8 March 1770, FOB 14 Part 2, p. 595
Ordered that the Tithables that work on the Road from the County Line as the main Road now goes till it Intersects the road leading from the said Smiths Shop to the top of the s.[d] Mountain

8 March 1770, FOB 14 Part 2, p. 595
The report made by Henry Newkirk & others appointed to veiw a Road being objected to is set aside And It is Ordered that the same be Reveiwed by Edward Davis John Davis John Burckam & John Doke who are to make their Report of the Conveniences & Inconveniences attending the same to the Next Court.

9 March 1770, FOB 14 Part 2, p. 601
Upon the Petition of sundry Inhabitants Praying for a road from Hogs Creek where the South Branch road Crosses it to go by the Plantation of Isaac Perkins to Jessee Pughs Mill Ordered that George Hoge William Hoge Barack Fisher & Casper Rinker or any three of them being first sworne do Veiw the same & Report the Conveniences & Inconveniences of the same to the Next Court.

10 March 1770, FOB 14 Part 2, p. 634
Upon the Petition John Allen Praying that the Road leading from Winchester to Marlbrough Forge may be turned Round his feild Ordered that John Hite Robert Glass Joseph Glass & Nathaniel Cartmill or any Three of them being first Sworne do Veiw the same & Report the Conveniences & Inconveniences of turning the same.

1 May 1770, FOB 14 Part 2, p. 636
Upon the Petition of Benjamin Thornbrough & Enos Ellis seting forth that the Road Leading from Winchester to Houghlands Ferry is very Injurious to their Plantation & that the same may be altered without any Inconveniences to the Publick & so as to be less Prejudicial to them Ordered that Hugh Lysle Dugal Campbell David Miller & Jacob Moon or any Three of them being first Sworne do Veiw the same & Report the Conveniences & Inconveniences that may attend the altering the Same.

2 May 1770, FOB 14 Part 2, p. 638
Ordered that Richard Campbell Taverner Beale Joseph Watson & Philip Peter Baker or any Three of them being first Swore do Veiw the ground from John Littles to Millers Town & report the Conveniences & Inconveniences that may attend the opening a Road on the same.

2 May 1770, FOB 14 Part 2, p. 639
William Ashby is Appointed overseer of the Road from the Forks of Shanondoah to the top of the mountain in the Room of James Jones Ordered that the usual Tithables Work thereon under him

2 May 1770, FOB 14 Part 2, p. 641
Mordecai Waker Henry Heth & Mercer Babb having been appointed to Veiw the ground from Winchester to Mercer Babbs Plantation made their Report It is ordered that a Road be opened as Laid off by them & that the Tithables two Miles on each side work thereon under Mordecai Walker who is appointed overseer thereof

2 May 1770, FOB 14 Part 2, p. 642
Upon the Petition of Isaac Zane ju.ʳ Praying for a Road from Marlborough forge to Manasset's Gap upon the Blue Ridge Ordered that John Hite Baylis Earle John Fawcett & Henry Richards or any Three of them being first Sworne do Veiw the same & Report the Conveniences & Inconveniences that may Attend the opening a Road on the same

2 May 1770, FOB 14 Part 2, p. 644
The Veiwers appointed to veiw the Ground from Winchester to Marlborough Forge round John Allens Plantation made their Report which being Examined & found to be wrongly made is set aside

3 May 1770, FOB 14 Part 2, p. 646
Ordered that the Hands working under Henry Gore do keep the Road in Order from the County Line at the foot of the River to the top of the Massanutting Mountain

3 May 1770, FOB 14 Part 2, p. 653
Upon the Petition of Sundry Inhabitants Praying for a Road from Marlborough Forge to Pughs Mill Ordered that Robert White William Pickering Job Pugh & Jeremiah Smith or any Three of them being first Sworne do Veiw the same & report the Conveniences & Inconveniences that may attend the opening the same to the Next Court.

3 May 1770, FOB 14 Part 2, p. 655
George Hoge William Hoge & Barack Fisher having been appointed to Veiw the Ground from Hoge Creek where the Winchester Road Crosses it to go by Isaac Perkin's Plantation to Jessee Pughs Mill made their Report Ordered that a Road be opened as Laid off by them & that the Tithables Three Miles on each side work thereon under Isaac Perkins who is appointed overseer thereof.

3 May 1770, FOB 14 Part 1, p. 655
Ordered that the Tithables on each side of the Road from the top of the Hunting ridge to the County Line work under James McGill who is Appointed overseer of the same.

3 May 1770, FOB 14 Part 2, p. 655
Thomas White is Appointed overseer of the Road from the Winchester Common to Littlers run in the Room of Henry Brinker Ordered that the Tithables four Miles on each side thereof work thereon under him

3 May 1770, FOB 14 Part 2, p. 657
Philip Carver is appointed overseer of the Road from Winchester to Lewis Neills in the Room of James Carter Ordered that the usual Tithables work thereon under him

7 August 1770, FOB 14 Part 2, p. 663
Henry Nelson is Appointed overseer of the Road from Moody's run to Thorns Gap Ordered that the Tithables Three Miles on each side thereof work thereon under him

7 August 1770, FOB 14 Part 2, p. 663
Adam Cunningham is Appointed overseer of the road from Moody's run to Kellors Ford. Ordered that the Tithables three Miles on each side work thereon under him

7 August 1770, FOB 14 Part 2, p. 663
Upon the Petition of the Inhabitants Praying that a road may be opened from the Main road near Mauks Mill to the County line. Ordered that Benjamin Strickler Francis Slaughter Gabriel Jones & David Loudeback or any three of them being first Sworne do Veiw the Same and report the Conveniences & Inconveniences that may attend the same

7 August 1770, FOB 14 Part 2, p. 664
Upon the petition of John Spencely praying that a mill road may be opened from his house to the County road leading over the Mountain Ordered that John Vestall, Humphrey Keyes, William Vandevere & Simon Dayle or any Three of them being first Sworne do Veiw the Same and report the Conveniences & Inconveniences that may attend the same

7 August 1770, FOB 14 Part 2, p. 665
An Order having been made at September Court Last directing a Veiw of the road from Semples furnace to the Warm Spring road, and the same, appearing by a petition from the Inhabitants of that Neighborhood to be unnecessary. Ordered that the same be Discontinued

7 August 1770, FOB 14 Part 2, p. 665
John McCormack is Appointed overseer of the road from Toliafero Striblings to Bulskin Including the whole bridge over the run and that the usual Tithables Three Miles on each side Work thereon under him

8 August 1770, FOB 14 Part 2, p. 667
James Strode Isaac Evans & Abraham Vanmetre having been appointed to Veiw the ground from Isaac Evans to Henry Vanmetres Mill and from thence to Warm Spring road made their report. Ordered that a road be opened as laid off by them and that the Tithables Two Miles & ahalf on each side work thereon under him

8 August 1770, FOB 14 Part 2, p. 670
Richard Fawcett sen.^{r} is appointed overseer of the road from the Top of the Little Mountain to Marlbro furnace in the room of Jonathon Lupton. Ordered that the usual tithables work thereon under him.

8 August 1770, FOB 14 Part 2, p. 670
Henry Heath is Appointed overseer of the road from the Winchester Common to Sir Johns Road. Ordered that the Tithables three Miles on each side thereof work thereon under him

8 August 1770, FOB 14 Part 2, p. 670
Robert Beckett is Appointed overseer of the road from Col.^{o} Hites to Robert Becketts. Ordered that the Tithables a mile on each side work thereon under him

8 August 1770, FOB 14 Part 2, p. 671
It appearing to the Court that a former order of this Court directing a Lane running thro the Town on the back of Loudoun Street to be opened had not been Complied with the same having been obstructed by some of the persons who had Stopd it up. It is Ordered that the Surveyor of the Streets do open the said Lane & keep the same Open.

8 August 1770, FOB 14 Part 2, p. 672
Upon the petition of Thomas Rutherford It is Ordered that the County Surveyor do lay off & ascertain the Just bounds of the Lane which is Ordered to be opened back of Loudoun Street be paying the Costs of it

Frederick County Order Book 15 (1770-1772)

6 November 1770, FOB 15, p. 32
Upon the Petition of Sundry Inhabitants praying that a Road may be opened from Goony run ford into M^r. Hite's Road by the three Miles Lick, Ordered that Darby M^c.Carty Joseph McKay, & Thomas Hume do view the Ground And report the Conveniences & Inconveniences that may attend the clearing and Opening a road thereon to the next Court.

6 November 1770, FOB 15, p. 32
Upon the Petition of Sundry Inhabitants praying that a road may be opened from the Presbyterian Meeting House at the head of Tuscarora to the Meeting House on Back Creek Ordered that James Robinson John Kennedy, John Parker & David Snodgrass or any three of them do view the Ground and report the Conveniences and Inconveniences that may attend the clearing and Opening a road thereon to the next Court.

6 November 1770, FOB 15, p. 36
Upon the Petition of Joseph Baker praying that the Road leading from Isaac Hite's to Henry Funk's Mill, which runs through his plantation, may be turned Round it. Ordered that Isaac Hite, Charles Buck, Thomas Allen and William Miller Junr or any Three of them, do view the Ground and report the Conveniences & Inconveniences that may attend the turning the same, to the next Court

6 November 1770, FOB 15, p. 37
David Ashbey is appointed Overseer of the road from the Forks of the Road leading to Berry's Ferry, to Cunningham's Chapel in the room of William Gist And It is Ordered that the usual Tithables work thereon under him

7 November 1770, FOB 15, p. 40
Joseph Watson is Appointed Overseer of the Road from Marlbro Forge to Philip Peter Bakers in the room of Daniel Curry, Ordered that the Tithables within three Miles of the said Road on each side do work thereon under him --

7 November 1770, FOB 15, p. 40
John Grigsby is appointed Overseer of the Road from George Henry's Spring to James Burner's run in the Room of Thomas Farnley, and It is Ordered that the usual Tithables work thereon under him --

7 November 1770, FOB 15, p. 41
George Riddle is Appointed Overseer of the road from Jumping run Bridge to Stony Creek, And It is Ordered that the Tithables from the North River at the Mouth of the run, to the North Mountain, Work thereon under him --

7 November 1770, FOB 15, p. 42
Daniel Morgan is appointed Overseer of the Road from Cunningham's Chapel to Lord Fairfax's in the room of Baylis Earle, Ordered that the usual Tithables work thereon under him

8 November 1770, FOB 15, p. 54
Ordered that Jeremiah Smith, Samuel Smith, Jesse Pugh, and Joseph Pugh or any three of them being first sworn, do view the Ground from Jeremiah Smith's Plantation to the Line of Hampshire County, and report the conveniencys and inconveniencys that may attend the Opening & Clearing a road thereon --

8 November 1770, FOB 15, p. 57
Ordered that Robert Wood, John Lupton, Jeremiah Smith and John Thomas or any three of them being first sworn, do view the Road leading from Hog's Creek to Jessee Pughs Mill, and the road petitioned for from the said Mill to Marlbro Furnace and report which will be the most proper road to Establish, or whether both of them will be Necessary for the Publick, to the next Court

4 December 1770, FOB 15, p. 97
Upon the Petition of Elizabeth Jolliffe praying to have a Road opened from James Hagan's to her Mill and from the Mill into the Bull Skin Road, Ordered that Samuel Littler, Edward Dodd, James Hogan and John Littler or any three of them being first Sworn do view the ground and make report of the conveniences and inconveniencies that may attend the opening a road thereon, to the next Court

4 December 1770, FOB 15, p. 99
Robert Wood, John Lupton and John Thomas having been appointed to View the Ground from Hogs Creek to Jesse Pugh's Mill & from the said Mill to Marlbro Furnace, and report which of the said Road will be proper to Establish or whether both of them will be Necessary for the convenience of the Publick, make their Report that the road leading from Hog's Creek to Jesse Pugh's Mill is only necessary for the Convenience of Isaac Perkins, George Hoge & William Hoge, and that the Road leading from the said Mill to the Marlbro furnace is of publick Utility and may be easily Opened. It is Ordered that the said Road be opened as laid off by the viewers. and that the Tithables within three Miles on each side of the said Road Work thereon from the said Mill to John Whites, under John McCool who is appointed Overseer of that part, and that the Tithables within three Miles on each side of the said Road from John White's Run to the said Furnace, work thereon under John Thomas, who is appointed Overseer of that part, and that the first mentioned Road be Discontinued --

4 December 1770, FOB 15, p. 99
Robert Wood is appointed Overseer of the road from Winchester through Hoop Pettycoat Gap, as far as Allen's Cabbin, and It is Ordered that the Tithables within three Miles on each side thereof, work thereon under him --

4 December 1770, FOB 15, p. 99
Robert White is appointed Overseer of the road from Winchester though Hoop Petticoat Gap from Allens Cabbin to the Road leading from Winchester to Jeremiah Smith's, and It is Ordered that the Tithables within three Miles on each side thereof work thereon under him --

4 December 1770, FOB 15, p. 100
David Davis is appointed Overseer of the road from Winchester to Hogs Creek in the room of Robert Wood, And it is Ordered that the Tithables within two and an half Miles on each side thereof, Work thereon under him --

4 December 1770, FOB 15, p. 100
Humphrey Keyes, John Vestal & Simon Doyle having been appointed to View the ground from John Spenceley's to the main Road leading over the mountain, It is Ordered that a road be opened as laid off by them, And that the Tithables within half a Mile on each side of the said Road who live on the East side of Shennadoah River, Work thereon under Robert Goldsberry who is Appointed Overseer of the same --

4 December 1770, FOB 15, p. 100
Ordered that John Lupton, Robert White, David Brown & Joseph Calvin or any three of them being first sworn, do view the Ground from the Ford of Opeckon by David Browns near Col.º Hites Tanyard to the Hoop Petticoat Gap and report the Conveniences and Inconveniences that may attend the opening a Road --

4 December 1770, FOB 15, p. 100
Richard Campbell, Joseph Wattson and Philip Peter Baker being appointed to view the Ground from John Little's to Miller Town made their Report and It is Ordered that a Road be opened as laid off by them and that the Tithables within three Miles on each side thereof (so as they do not Cross the River) Work thereon under Richard Campbell who is appointed Overseer of the same -

4 December 1770, FOB 15, p. 100
Upon the Petition of John Neavill praying that a Road may be Opened from the Muster Ground above the Widow Caldwells to his Mill and from his Mill into the Main Road by Jonah Seaman's. It is Ordered that George Cunninghame, Robert Aldridge, Francis Lillburn and Jacob Chew or any three of them being first sworn, do view the ground and report the Conveniences & Inconveniences that may attend the Opening a Road thereon --

4 December 1770, FOB 15, p. 101
Upon the Petition of Thomas Helm praying that a Road may be opened from the dry Marsh to his Mill, Ordered that Thomas Blackmore, James Barnett, Humphrey Wells and Peter Luke, or any three of them being first Sworn do view the ground, and Report the Conveniences & Inconveniences that may attend the opening a road thereon --

5 February 1771, FOB 15, p. 102
James Hagan, John Littler and Edward Dodd having been appointed to view the Ground from James Hagan's by the Widow Jolliffe's Mill into the Bull Skin Road made their report, And It is Ordered that a Road be opened as laid off by them, And that the Tithables within two Miles from the said Mill do work thereon under Edward Dodd who is Appointed Overseer of the same

5 February 1771, FOB 15, p. 102
Upon the Petition of Isaac Hite praying that a road may be opened from his Mill to the road leading to Massinutting, It is Ordered that Edward Cartmill Nicholas Sperry, John Worth & George Brinker, or any three of them being first sworn do view the ground and report the conveniences and Inconveniences that may attend the opening a road thereon, to the Court.

5 February 1771, FOB 15, p. 103
James Chew, Francis Lillburne, & George Cunninghame having been appointed to view the ground from the Muster ground above the Widow Calwells by Neavills Mill, into the main road by Jonah Seaman's made their report, And It is Ordered that a Road be opened as laid off by them, and that the Tithables within two miles on each side side thereof, Work thereon, under James Chew who is appointed Overseer of the same --

6 February 1771, FOB 15, p. 103
Upon the Petition of Isaac Zane -- praying to have a road Opened from his Forge through Manassip's Run Gap, It is Ordered that John Rout, Joseph King, John Hite, John Fawcett, Baylis Earle and Henry Richards or any three of them being first sworn do view the ground, report to the court the Conveniences & Inconveniences that may attend the Opening a Road thereon --

6 February 1771, FOB 15, p. 104
Benjamin Thornbrugh is appointed Overseer of the Road from Cunningham's Mill to Samuel Willson's in the room of William Baldwin & It is Ordered that the ususal Tithables work thereon under him --

5 March 1771, FOB 15, p. 105
Upon the Petition of Sundry Inhabitants praying that a Road may be opened from the Warm spring road at Joseph Bridges' to George Bruce's Mill, It is Ordered that Alexander Ross, Thomas Butherfield, Zophar Johnson and Thomas Baldwin or any three of them being first sworn do view the Ground, and report the Conveniences and Inconveniences that may attend the opening a Road thereon to the Court.

5 March 1771, FOB 15, p. 109
Dougall Campbell, Jacob Moon and David Miller having been appointed to review that part of the Road leading from Winchester to Hougland's Ferry, which Leads through Benjamin Thornbrugh's & Enos Ellis's Land, Ordered that the Road be altered as marked at Benjamin Thornbrugh's Plantation, but that it be continued as first laid out at Enos Ellis's Plantation, and that the Tithables within three Miles on each side thereof, work thereon under Andrew McDonald from David Miller's old Plantation to Isaac Eaton's --

6 March 1771, FOB 15, p. 114
Upon the Petition of Sundry Inhabitants praying that a Road may be opened from John Lyles by James Morrison's, John Miller's, John Glenn's and William Glenn's Plantations, to Patterson's Mill and from thence into the Warm Springs Road, It is Ordered that Leonard Rush, William Glenn, James Morrison and Hugh Lyle or any three of them being first sworn, do view the

Ground and report the Conveniences & Inconveniences that may attend the opening a Road thereon to the Court.

6 March 1771, FOB 15, p. 114
James Barnett, Thomas Blackmore and Peter Luke having been appointed to view the Ground from the dry Marsh to Helm's Mill made their report And It is Ordered that a Road be opened as laid off by them and that the Tithables within one Mile and a half thereof, work thereon under Thomas Helm who is appointed Overseer of the same --

6 March 1771, FOB 15, p. 116
Upon the Petition of Sundry Inhabitants praying to have a Road Opened from John Little's to the Augusta line, It is Ordered that Evan Jones, Thomas Hinton, Jacob Holdman, William Jones Taverner Beall, Peter Hollow, Augustine Coffman, and Christopher Windle, or any four of them being first Sworn do view the Ground, and report the Conveniences and Inconveniences that may attend the opening a Road thereon to the Court.

6 March 1771, FOB 15, p. 117
Henry Ghosney is appointed Overseer of the Road from Lewis's Mill to Berry's Ferry, Ordered that the Usual Tithables work thereon under him --
[Note: There are three spellings of this name: "Gosney" in the margin, "Ghosney" in the text, and "Gosne" in the order book index.]

6 March 1771, FOB 15, p. 118
Upon the Petition of Jesse Felkner &c. praying that the part of the road leading from Hougland's Ferry to Winchester and the one that goes by Hancher's, which passes through their plantations where they enter at the Branch Road, may be altered or entirely stopped, Ordered that Morgan Morgan, James Seaton, John McDonald & Henry Heath being first Sworn, do view the said Roads, and report whether they are both necessary, and which is the most convenient, to the Court --

6 March 1771, FOB 15, p. 119
John Rout is appointed overseer of the Chapel Road from Samuel Earl's Meadows to Gregory's Ford and Seaborn's ford. Ordered that the usual Tithables work thereon under him, and that he keep the fords in repair --

8 March 1771, FOB 15, p. 135
Upon the Presentment of the Grand Jury against David Castleman for not keeping the Road in repair whereof he is Surveyor. This day came the Attorney for our Lord the King and the Deft having been duly summoned was by the Court that the said Deft. be fined fifteen Shillings for the same --

8 March 1771, FOB 15, p. 135
Upon the Presentment of the Grand Jury against William Rankin for not keeping the road in repair whereof he is surveyor. This Day came the Attorney for our Lord the King, and the Deft

having been duly summoned was Solemnly called but came not. It is therefore Considered by the Court that the said Deft. be fined fifteen shillings for the same.

8 March 1771, FOB 15, p. 141
George Burket is appointed Overseer of the Road from Lewis Neil's Mill to John McMachen's old place, Ordered that the usual Tithables work thereon under him --

9 March 1771, FOB 15, p. 165
Philip Carver is appointed Overseer of the Road from Lewis Neill's Mill. Ordered that the Tithables from the Fredericksburg Road down Opeckon to Lewis Neill's and the Tithables between Opeckon and the road leading to Mr Jolliffe's work thereon under him --

2 April 1771, FOB 15, p. 181
Gasper Rinker is Appointed Overseer of the Road from the Hunting Ridge to the County line in the room of James McGill, Ordered that the Tithables within five Miles on each side thereof do work thereon under him --

7 May 1771, FOB 15, p. 183
Alexander Ross, Thomas Butterfield, and Thomas Baldwin having been appointed to view the Ground from Joseph Bridges to Bruces Mill made their Report. Ordered that a Road be opened as laid off by them, and that the Tithables within two Miles on each side thereof do work thereon under Alexander Ross who is appointed Overseer of the same --

7 May 1771, FOB 15, p. 184
Henry Heath, Morgan Morgan, and Joseph Seaton, having been appointed to view the ground from Houghlands Ferry and thru' Falkner's Land made their report Ordered that the Road be turned as marked out by them --

7 May 1771, FOB 15, p. 187
Ordered that the Tithables within three and a half miles on each side of the Road whereof William Ashby is Surveyor, do work thereon under him --

7 May 1771, FOB 15, p. 188
John Nicholas is appointed Overseer of the Road from the North River ford to Crooked Run and It is Ordered that the Tithables within two Miles on each side of the Road do work thereon under him

7 May 1771, FOB 15, p. 188
Robert Haines is appointed Overseer of the Road from Crooked Run to the main County Road leading from Augusta. Ordered that the Tithables within two miles on each side thereof do work thereon under him --

7 May 1771, FOB 15, p. 188
Upon the Petition of Henry Funk praying that a Road may be opened from his Mill on Passage Creek to Abraham Kendrick's upper ford and from thence to William Ashby's. Ordered that

William Miller, Thomas Allen, William Kearfoot and Joseph Baker or any three of them being first sworne, do view the Ground and report the conveniences and inconveniences that may attend the opening a road thereon --

7 May 1771, FOB 15, p. 188
George Brinker George Warth and Nicholas Sperry having been appointed to view the Ground from Isaac Hites Mill to the Massenutting Road made their report Ordered that the Tithables within two Miles on each side thereof and at each end do work thereon under Isaac Hite who is appointed Overseer of the same --

7 May 1771, FOB 15, p. 188
Benjamin Rutherford is appointed Overseer of Littler's Road from Opeckon Creek to the fork of the Road leading from Winchester to Spout Run in the room of Lewis Neill. Ordered that the Tithables withing three Miles on each side thereof do work thereon under him --

8 May 1771, FOB 15, p. 190
John Moore is appointed Overseer of the Road from Jumping Run Bridge to the North River Ford in the room of Edwin Young. Ordered that the usual Tithables work thereon under him --

8 May 1771, FOB 15, p. 191
The report of the viewers made from William Patterson's Mill to John Lyle's is Ordered to be set aside, and that James Strode Benjamin Thornberry, John Parks and Joseph McCoy or any three of them being first sworn do view the next and best way from John Lyle's to the said Mill and report the conveniences and inconveniences that may attend the opening and clearing a Road thereon --

8 May 1771, FOB 15, p. 191
Evan Jones, Jacob Holdman, Peter Holler and Augustine Coffman having been appointed to view the ground from the County Line below Brocks Gap to John Littles made their report. and It is Ordered that the Road be opened as laid off by them and that the Tithables within three Miles on each side thereof do work thereon from Littles to Narrow passage Creek under George Mafuse who is appointed overseer of that part, and that the Tithables within five Miles on each side thereof from Passage Creek to Stoney Creek do work thereon under Peter Holler who is appointed overseer of that part, And that the Tithables within five Miles on each side thereof from Stoney Creek to Christian Dellinger's do work thereon under Jacob Helsley who is appointed overseer of that part, And that the Tithables within five Miles on each side thereof from Christian Dellingers to Mill Creek do work thereon under Jacob Rinker who is appointed overseer of that part, And that the Tithables within five Miles on each side thereof from Mill Creek to the County Line do work thereon under Evan Jones who is appointed overseer of that part --

8 May 1771, FOB 15, p. 198
Upon the Petition of Sundry Inhabitants praying for a Road from Hurst's ford to the Fork of the Road leading to Funk's Mill. Ordered that James M^c.Kay, Henry Netherton William Nelson and

Abraham Keller or any three of them being first sworn do view the Ground and report the Conveniences and Inconveniences that may attend the opening a Road thereon to the Court --

8 May 1771, FOB 15, p. 200
Benjamin Taylor is Appointed Overseer of the Road from Winchester Commons to Littler's run in the room of Thomas White, Ordered that the usual Tithables do work thereon under him --

8 May 1771, FOB 15, p. 200
Michael Davis is Appointed Overseer of the Road from the Warm Springs to Combs's Mill and from thence to the Mouth of Sleepy Creek, Ordered that the Tithables within three Miles on each side thereof and those within three Miles of the said Springs do work thereon under him --

8 May 1771, FOB 15, p. 200
John Wolfenberger is appointed Overseer of the Road from Miller's Town to Stony Creek. Ordered that the usual Tithables do work thereon under him --

8 May 1771, FOB 15, p. 200
Ordered that the Tithables within two Miles on each side of the Road whereof John Rout is Overseer do work thereon under him --

10 May 1771, FOB 15, p. 212
Upon the Petition of Lewis Neill praying for a Road from his Mill into the road leading to Helms's Mill at the head of the dry Marsh, Ordered that John Kyser, Peter Luke Mayberry Evans and James Carter or any three of them being first sworn do view the Ground and report the Conveniences and Inconveniences that may attend the opening a Road thereon to the Court --

7 August 1771, FOB 15, p. 235
Thomas Allen, William Miller and Joseph Baker having been Appointed to view the Ground from Henry Funk's Mill to William Ashby's made their report. Ordered that a road be opened as laid off by them and that the Tithables within two Miles on each side thereof do work thereon from the said Mill to Abraham Kendricks upper ford, under Abraham Kendrick who is appointed overseer of that part, and that the Tithables within two and an half Miles on each side thereof do work thereon from the said Ford to William Ashby's under the said William Ashby who is Appointed overseer of that part --

7 August 1771, FOB 15, p. 238
Ordered that Thomas Hart, Edward Lucas, William Dark and Henry Loyd or any three of them being first sworn do view the Ground from Jacob Hites House to William Fosters Ferry and report the Conveniences and Inconveniences that may attend the opening & clearing a Road thereon --

7 August 1771, FOB 15, p. 239
Ordered that the Inhabitants within three Miles on the West side of the road leading thro' Woodstock to the County Line do for the future keep the same in repair and that the other Tithables on the West side be exempted from working on that road --

7 August 1771, FOB 15, p. 239
Upon the Petition of Sundry Inhabitants praying to have a road opened from Helms Mill into the road leading to Watkins's Ferry at Blackburn's Plantation, Ordered that Benjamin Blackburn Thomas M^c.Clunn Joseph Parrell & Andrew Millburn or any three of them being first sworn do view the Ground and report the Conveniences & Inconveniences that may attend the opening a road thereon --

7 August 1771, FOB 15, p. 239
Upon the Petition of George Keller &^{c}. praying that a Road may be opened from Peter Sharrobz to Snapp's Mill, Ordered that John Tipton Laurence Snapp Leonard Baltis and Christley Hockman or any three of them being first sworn do view the Ground and report the Conveniences and inconveniences that may attend the opening a road thereon --

7 August 1771, FOB 15, p. 240
John Rice is appointed Overseer of the Road from McCormicks to the Widow Lindseys in the room of George Rice Ordered that the usual tithables do work thereon under him

7 August 1771, FOB 15, p. 240
Francis Slaughter is appointed Overseer of the Road from the County Line to Mauk's Mill Ordered that the Tithables within Seven Miles on the East side thereof and to the Massanutting mountain on the West side do work thereon under him --

7 August 1771, FOB 15, p. 240
George Rice is appointed Overseer of the [blank in book] Road from his House to the Main road at the dry Marsh, Ordered that the Tithables within two and half Miles on each side thereof do work thereon under him --

7 August 1771, FOB 15, p. 240
John Lyndsey is appointed Overseer of the Road from Thomas Lyndsey's Plantation to Samuel Morris's. Ordered that the Tithables within one Mile on each side thereof do work thereon under him --

7 August 1771, FOB 15, p. 241
Upon the Petition of Sundry Inhabitants praying for a Road from John Nevill's Mill into Doctor Briscoes Mill Road, Ordered that Francis Lillburne, Nathaniel Morrison, Jonah Seaman, and Bartholomew Fryett or any three of them being first Sworn do view the Ground & Report the Conveniences and Inconveniences that may attend the opening a road thereon

7 August 1771, FOB 15, p. 241
Upon the Petition of the Inhabitants praying for a Road from John Spoar's Plantation to Col.^{o} Stephen's Mill, Ordered that John Spoar, John Keywood, John Strode & John Vanmetre or any three of them being first Sworn do view the Ground, and report the Conveniences & Inconveniences that may attend the opening a Road thereon --

7 August 1771, FOB 15, p. 241
Upon the Petition of the Inhabitants praying that a Road may be opened from Col°. Stephen's Mill to Edward Strode's by Matthew Allison's Ordered that James Blair, Robert Hogdon, Matthew Allison and Edward Strode or any three of them being first sworn do view the Ground and report the Conveniences and Inconveniences that may attend the opening a Road thereon --

7 August 1771, FOB 15, p. 242
Upon the Petition of the Inhabitants praying that a Road may be opened from Col.° Stephen's Mill to James Strode's Ordered that James Strode, Dugall Campbell, William Burns and Jonathan Edwards or any three of them being first sworn do view the Ground and report the Conveniences and Inconveniences that may attend the same --

7 August 1771, FOB 15, p. 242
Upon the Petition of the Inhabitants praying that a road may be opened from Hugh Lyle's Plantation to Col°. Stephens Mill, Ordered that Hugh Lyle, Benjamin Thornberry, John Evans and John Tate or any three of them being first Sworn do view the Ground & report the Conveniences and Inconveniences that may attend the opening a road thereon --

1 October 1771, FOB 15, p. 267
John Ariss is appointed overseer of the road, from the Flat Rock to the Ford on Bullskin in the room of Thomas Mason, Ordered that the usual tithables do work thereon under him --

1 October 1771, FOB 15, p. 267
Robert Watt is appointed Overseer of the road from Watkins's Ferry to Caton's Stone House, Ordered that the Tithables within three Miles on each side thereof do work thereon under him --

1 October 1771, FOB 15, p. 267
Thomas Thornberry is appointed Overseer of the Road from Mecklenburg to Opeckon, Ordered that the usual tithables do work thereon under him --
[Note: The name is indexed as "Thornbrugh."]

1 October 1771, FOB 15, p. 268
Daniel Barton is Appointed Overseer of the [blank in book] Road from Opeckon to the Warm Springs, Ordered that the usual Tithables do work thereon under him --

1 October 1771, FOB 15, p. 268
Henry Vanmetre is appointed Overseer of the Warm Spring Road through Henry Lloyd's Plantation Ordered that the usual Tithables do work thereon under him --

1 October 1771, FOB 15, p. 268
Matthew Allison James Blair and Robert Stocton having been appointed to view the Ground from Colo. Stephens Mill to Jeremiah Strode's plantation made their report -- Ordered that a Road be opened as laid off by them and that the Tithables within two Miles on each side thereof do work thereon under Jeremiah Strode who is appointed Overseer of the same

1 October 1771, FOB 15, p. 268
Daniel Morris is appointed Overseer of the Warm spring road in the room of Mercer Babb Ordered that the usual Tithables do work Thereon under him --

5 November 1771, FOB 15, p. 270
Jonathan Brittain is appointed Overseer of the road leading from Worthington's Marsh to Harper's Ferry in the room of John Crow, Ordered that the usual Tithables do work thereon under him --

6 November 1771, FOB 15, p. 274
John Timmons is appointed overseer of the Road from Berry's Ferry to Howell's Ford, Ordered that the Tithables on the road side do work thereon under him --

6 November 1771, FOB 15, p. 275
Francis Lillburn Bartholomew Fryett and Nathaniel Morrison having been appointed to View the ground from Nevill's Mill into Briscoe's Road made their report, Ordered that a Road be opened as laid off by them and that the Tithables within two Miles on each side thereof do work thereon under William Merchant who is appointed overseer of the same --

6 November 1771, FOB 15, p. 275
Robert Goldsberry is Appointed Overseer of the Road from Vestall's ford & Keyes's Ferry to the top of the Mountain Ordered that the usual Tithables do work thereon under him --

6 November 1771, FOB 15, p. 275
Magnus Tate is Appointed Overseer of the Road from the Muster Ground to Vestall's Ford Ordered that the Tithables within two Miles on each side thereof, (excepting those who Work upon the Mountain Road) do work thereon under him --

6 November 1771, FOB 15, p. 275
Thomas Hart is Appointed Overseer of the Road from Henry Lloyd's to Keyes's Ferry and from the Ferry up to the Ford. Ordered that the Tithables within three Miles on each side thereof do work thereon under him Except those who work upon the Mountain Road --

6 November 1771, FOB 15, p. 277
Upon the Petition of sundry Inhabitants praying that the Road from Shepherds Town to Keyes's Ferry may be reviewed, Ordered that William Darke, Willam Morgan, John Tayler, and Samuel Tayler do view the same and report what alterations in the said Road may be necessary, and whether they will be attended with Inconveniences --

6 November 1771, FOB 15, p. 277
Upon the Petition of sundry Inhabitants praying that the Road leading from Barretts Mill to the Warm Springs may be turned to go by Sexton's Mill, Ordered that William Hancher, Zadok Springer, Aaron Hackney and James Barrett do view the same and report the Conveniences and Inconveniences that may attend the Alteration --

6 November 1771, FOB 15, p. 277
Benjamin Blackburn, Thomas McClunn and Andrew Millburn having been appointed to view the Ground from Helm's Mill into the Road leading from Winchester to Watkins's Ferry at Blackburns Plantation made their report, It is ordered that a Road be opened as laid off by them and that the Tithables within two miles on each side thereof do work thereon under John Albin who is appointed overseer of the same --

6 November 1771, FOB 15, p. 278
John Lupton, Joseph Covill, and David Brown having been Appointed to view the Ground from Opeckon ford at Col.^{o} Hite's Tanyard to Hoop Petticoat Gap made their Report, Ordered that a Road be opened as laid off by them and that the Tithables within one and an half Miles on each side thereof do work thereon under Joseph Covill who is appointed Overseer of the same, And that the Road from Hite's Mill to Beckets be stopped --
[Note: The name is indexed as "Colvin."]

6 November 1771, FOB 15, p. 278
William Chinoweth is appointed Overseer of the Road from Littlers Lane to the Ford at Lewis Neill's in the room of Samuel Littler, Ordered that the usual Tithables do work thereon under him

6 November 1771, FOB 15, p. 279
Upon the Petition of sundry Inhabitants praying to have a Road opened from Strasburgh to Marlborough Forge, Ordered that Isaac Zane, Woolrick Subinger, Cronimous Baker & Samuel Beam or any three of them being first sworn do view the ground and report the conveniences and inconveniences that may attend the same --

6 November 1771, FOB 15, p. 280
James Green Martin is appointed Overseer of the Road from Bruce's Mill to McCormacks Road, Ordered that the usual Tithables do work thereon under him --

7 November 1771, FOB 15, p. 282
Philip Bush is appointed Overseer of Loudon Street and the Cross Streets and other Streets Back of It, in the room of Peter Helphingstone, Ordered that the usual Tithables do work thereon under him --

7 November 1771, FOB 15, p. 287
James Strode, Dugall Campbell and Jonathan Edwards having been appointed to view the Ground from Stephen's Mill to James Strode's plantation made their report, Ordered that a Road be opened as laid off by them, and that the Tithables within two miles on each side thereof do work thereon under James Strode who is appointed Overseer of the same --

8 November 1771, FOB 15, p. 300
Upon the Petition of Ralph Wormley Esqr praying that the Road leading from Snickers' to Vestalls' may be turned at his plantation, Ordered that Edward Snickers, Taliaferro Stribling Alexander Lang and Daniel M^c.Pherson or any three of them being first Sworn do view the

Ground and report the Conveniences and inconveniences that may attend the turning the said Road --

8 November 1771, FOB 15, p. 317
Woolrick Subinger, Cronimous Baker & Samuel Beam having been appointed to view the Ground from Stratsburg to Marlborough Forge made their report. Ordered that a Road be opened as laid off by them and that the Tithables within three Miles on each side thereof from the Forge to the Creek do work thereon under Isaac Zane who is appointed Overseer of that part, and that the Tithables within three Miles on each side thereof, and the Tithables of the Town, do work thereon from the Creek to the said Town, under Wolrick Subinger who is appointed Overseer of that part --

8 November 1771, FOB 15, p. 317
John Canrood, John Spore, John Strode, and John Vanmetre having been appointed to view the Ground from John Spore's Plantation to Col.º Stephens's Mill made their report. Ordered that a Road be opened as laid off by them and that the Tithables within two Miles on each side thereof do work thereon under John Canrood who is appointed Overseer of the same --
[Note: The name appears as "Conrood" in the margin and is indexed as "Conrad."]

4 December 1771, FOB 15, p. 317
County Levy
To John Lindsay for Timber to repair the bridge on Long Marsh   [£] [0.] 15. 0.

5 December 1771, FOB 15, p. 319
Upon the Petition of the Inhabitants praying for a Road from David Miller's old Plantation to Col.º Stephens's Mill, Ordered that Benjamin Thornberry, Andrew Mc.Donald, John Lyles & John Tate or any three of them being first sworn do view the Ground and report the conveniences and Inconveniences that may attend the same --

4 March 1772, FOB 15, p. 325
Upon the Petition of the Inhabitants praying that the Road may be turned at the River Ford near Burr Harrison's, Ordered that Jackson Allen, George Riddle, Edwin Young & Casper Hoop or any three of them being first Sworn do view the same and report the Conveniences and Inconveniences that may attend the same --

4 March 1772, FOB 15, p. 326
Lott Ridgway is appointed Overseer of the Road from Littler's to the Widow Cunningham's Ordered that the usual Tithables do work thereon under him --

4 March 1772, FOB 15, p. 326
Nathaniel Morrison is Appointed Overseer of the Road from Nevill's Mill into Briscoe's Mill Road Ordered that the usual Tithables do work thereon under him --

7 April 1772, FOB 15, p. 346
John Adams is appointed Overseer of the Road from the Forks of the Warm Spring Road to White's Mill Ordered that the usual Tithables do work thereon under him --

7 April 1772, FOB 15, p. 346
Stephen Ross is appointed Overseer of the road from White's Mill to William Frost's Middle plantation on Back Creek, Ordered that the usual Tithables do work thereon under him --

7 April 1772, FOB 15, p. 346
Robert Crosby is appointed Overseer of the Road from the Plantation of Dennis Springer decd. to the Top of the Mountain at Mill's Gap. Ordered that the usual Tithables do work thereon under him --

7 April 1772, FOB 15, p. 346
Ordered that Robert Brownfield, Thomas Berry, John Hancher & Abel Walker or any three of them being first sworn do view the Ground from the Warm Spring road at Joseph Bridges's into the Main Road by John Nevill's and report the conveniences and inconveniences that may attend the opening a road thereon --

7 April 1772, FOB 15, p. 346
Ordered that Angus McDonald and Edward McGuire do agree with some person to Build a Bridge over the Run in Main Street --

7 April 1772, FOB 15, p. 347
John Bell is appointed Overseer of the Road from Nation's plantation to the Ford at Berry's Ordered that the usual Tithables do work thereon under him --

7 April 1772, FOB 15, p. 347
Upon the Petition of William Hancher Ordered that Thomas Rees, David Gerrard, William Chinowith and William Boyd or any three of them being first Sworn do view the Ground from his Mill to the North Mountain near John Gerrard's and report the conveniences and Inconveniences that may attend the opening a road thereon --

7 April 1772, FOB 15, p. 347
Upon the petition of William Hancher Ordered that David Morgan, Jonah Seaman, Thomas Cowen and Isaac Eaton or any three of them being first sworn do view the Ground from the South Branch Road to his Mill and from thence into the road leading to Watkin's Ferry and report the Conveniences and Inconveniences that may attend the opening a road thereon --

7 April 1772, FOB 15, p. 347
Ordered that Marquis Calmes and John Bell do employ one or more Waggon's to haul Materials to repair the Ford at the Crossing place at Berry's --

7 April 1772, FOB 15, p. 347
Meshack Sexton is appointed Overseer of the Warm Spring Road from the Back Creek Road to the Buffaloe Lick, Ordered that the usual Tithables do work thereon under him --

7 April 1772, FOB 15, p. 347
Ordered that Isaac Larew, Jacob Larew, Warner Washington & John Lindsey or any three of them being first Sworn do view the Ground from the Flat rock by M.r Thruston's by the Head of Kate's Spring, into the road leading to the Bloomery below M.r Ariss's and report the Conveniences and Inconveniences that may attend the Opening a Road thereon --

2 June 1772, FOB 15, p. 348
Ordered that Isaac Zane, John Nisewanger Jun.r Nicholas Pitman and David Brown or any three of them being first Sworn do view the Ground from Stephensburg into the road leading from Winchester to Marlbro' Forge. And report the Conveniences and inconveniences that may attend the opening a road thereon --

2 June 1772, FOB 15, p. 348
Upon the Petition of Sundry Inhabitants praying that a Road may be opened from the road leading through Edmund Taylor's Plantation towards M.r Wormley's Mill as far as the County line, Ordered that Edward Snickers Edmund Taylor, Joseph Hampton and George Hampton or any three of them being first Sworn do view the Ground and report the Conveniences and Inconveniences that may attend the opening the road thereon --

2 June 1772, FOB 15, p. 348
A report of the road leading from the Warm Spring Road into the main road by John Nevill's was returned, Ordered that the road be opened as laid off by the viewers and that the Tithables within two miles on each side thereof do work thereon under Thomas Baldwin who is appointed Overseer of the same --

3 June 1772, FOB 15, p. 350
A Report of the viewers appointed to view the road leading from Snicker's Gap thro' M.r Wormley's Plantation to Vestal's Gap made their report. Ordered that the road be turned agreeable to the said report as far as the County line and that the Tithables within two miles on each side thereof do work thereon under Thomas Winkfield who is appointed Overseer of the same --
[Note: The name appears in the margin and is indexed as "Wingfield."]

3 June 1772, FOB 15, p. 350
Ordered that the Tithables within three miles on each side of the road leading from Opeckon to Battletown do work under Elijah Isaacs the Overseer thereof. And that the Tithables living on the other side of the road leading to the Chappel and the Long Marsh be exempted from Working on the same --

3 June 1772, FOB 15, p. 350
Edmund Taylor is Appointed Overseer of the road leading from Battletown to Shannandoah River in the room of George Hampton, Ordered that the usual Tithables do work thereon under him --

3 June 1772, FOB 15, p. 350
Upon the Petition of Meshack Sexton praying to have the road leading from Barretts Mill to the Warm Springs turned to go by his Mill, Ordered that William Hancher, James Barrett, Josiah Jackson and Jesse Falkner or any three of them being first sworn do view the Ground and report the Conveniences and Inconveniences that may attend the altering the said road --

3 June 1772, FOB 15, p. 352
Upon the Petition of Mary Wood leave is Granted her to alter the road leading from Luptons into the Town as it is already cleared by Thomas Rutherford's Pasture adjoining the Town

7 July 1772, FOB 15, p. 355
Joseph Bridges is appointed Overseer of the Warm Springs Road, from the South Branch Road near Ballenger's to the County Line, Ordered that the Tithables within five miles on each side thereof do work thereon under him --

4 August 1772, FOB 15, p. 357
Upon the Petition of David Brown praying that the Road leading from Lord Fairfax's to Winchester may be turned at his plantation, Ordered that James Willson Samuel Vance David Gilkison & David Wright or any three of them being first sworn do view the Ground and report the Conveniences and Inconveniences that may attend the altering the said --

4 August 1772, FOB 15, p. 357
Upon the Petition of David Brown praying that a road may be opened from his Mill down Opeckon Creek by James Knight's and Edward Reed's into the Chapel Road, Ordered that James Knight, William Kearfoot Peter Catlett and Joseph Roberts or any three of them being first sworn do view the Ground and report the conveniences and Inconveniences that may attend the opening the said Roads

4 August 1772, FOB 15, p. 357
David Wright is Appointed Overseer of the Road from David Brown's to the Forks of the road below the said Wright's House, Ordered that the Tithables within three Miles on each side thereof do work thereon under him --

4 August 1772, FOB 15, p. 357
George Williams is appointed Overseer of the Road from Burks Bridge along the Chapel Road to Spout Run, Ordered that the usual Tithables do work thereon under him --

4 August 1772, FOB 15, p. 357
George Vance is appointed Overseer of the road from Chrisman's Place to Cedar Creek in the room of Thomas Black, Ordered that the usual Tithables do work thereon under him --

5 August 1772, FOB 15, p. 358
David Hackney is appointed overseer of the Road from Gregory's Ford to Manassey's Gap in the room of William Ashby. Ordered that the Tithables within three and an half miles on each side & at the upper End thereof do work thereon under him --

5 August 1772, FOB 15, pp. 361-362
Isaac Zane, David Brown, John Nisewanger Junr & Nicholas Pitman having been appointed to view the Ground from Stephensburg into the road leading from Winchester to the Marlbro' Forge made their report, Ordered that a Road be opened as laid off by them only at Lewis Stephens's Fence, where It is to be Altered to go round the said Fence, and that the Tithables within one and an half miles on each side thereof and the Inhabitants of the Town do work thereon under Christian Fogglesong who is appointed overseer of the same --

5 August 1772, FOB 15, p. 362
Joseph Berry is appointed Overseer of the road from his Ford and Ferry to the Top of the Ridge, Ordered that the Tithables as low as Wright's Branch and to the head of it do work thereon under him --

5 August 1772, FOB 15, p. 364
Edmund Taylor, Edward Snickers and Joseph Hampton having been appointed to view the Ground from the road leading through Edmund Taylors Plantation to the County line towards M^r. Wormley's Mill made their report. Ordered that a road be opened as laid off by them, and that the Tithables within two Miles on each side thereof do work thereon under Edmund Taylor who is appointed Overseer of the same --

5 August 1772, FOB 15, p. 365
Charles Smith and George Jump are appointed Overseers of the road from Battletown to Snickers's Ford on Shanandoah River, Ordered that the Tithables within three Miles each side thereof do work thereon under them --

6 August 1772, FOB 15, p. 365
James Barnett and Samuel Morris are appointed Overseers of the Road from Battletown to Opeckon in the room of Elijah Isaacs, Ordered that the Tithables within four Miles each side thereof do work thereon under them --

1 September 1772, FOB 15, pp. 398-399
Peter Babb is appointed Overseer of the road from the Widow Ballenger's to the Forks of the Winchester road, Ordered that the Tithables within three Miles on each side thereof do work thereon under him --

2 September 1772, FOB 15, p. 399
James Willson, Samuel Vance & David Wright, having been appointed to view the Ground at David Brown's Plantation, and report whether the road might be turned without disadvantage made their report, Ordered that the said road be turned according to the report --

2 September 1772, FOB 15, p. 399
John McDonald & John Jolliffe are appointed Overseers of the road from the Winchester Out Lots to the Run at Littler's in the room of Benjamin Taylor Ordered that the Usual Tithables do work thereon under them --

2 September 1772, FOB 15, p. 405
James Carter Junr is Appointed Overseer of the road from Lewis Neills' old place to Winchester in the room of Philip Carter, Ordered that the usual Tithables do work thereon under him --

3 September 1772, FOB 15, p. 414
Jacob Steerly is appointed Overseer of the road from the dry Marsh to Helms' Mill in the room of Thomas Helm, Ordered that the Usual Tithables do work thereon under him --

3 September 1772, FOB 15, p. 415
Joseph Bridges is appointed Overseer of the road from Ballenger's to the Tub Mill and George Ruble from thence to the County line, Ordered that the Tithables within two miles on each side thereof do work thereon under them --

7 October 1772, FOB 15, pp. 435-436
Benjamin Morris is appointed Overseer of the road leading from Bucks Marsh to the Bloomery from the Run to the County line, Ordered that such part of the Tithables formerly working thereon who are now within the County do work thereon under him --

8 October 1772, FOB 15, p. 444
Joseph Anderson is appointed Overseer of the road from Snickers Ferry Landing to the County line on the road leading to Jacob Hite's, in the room of Taliaferro Stribling, Ordered that the usual Tithables do work thereon under him --

8 October 1772, FOB 15, p. 446
Upon the Petition of Henry Chrisman praying that the road leading from Stephensburg to Jacob Chrisman's Spring, may be turned at his plantation Ordered that Robert Throckmorton, Robert Allen, Edward Cartmill and Julius Spickard or any three of them being first Sworn do view the Ground and the Conveniences and inconveniences that may attend the altering the said Road --

8 October 1772, FOB 15, p. 449
Peter Catlett, James Knight, and Joseph Roberts having been appointed to View the Ground from David Brown's Mill down the Opeckon by James Knights' and Edward Reeds' into the Chapel Road made their report. Ordered that a road be opened as laid off by them and that the Tithables within three Miles on each side thereof do work thereon under James King who is appointed Overseer of the same --

10 October 1772, FOB 15, p. 463
Upon the Petition of Joseph Watson praying that he may have a Road opened from the South Branch road near Jeremiah Smith's to the Warm Springs near Henry Frys, Ordered that Jeremiah

Smith, Harrison Taylor, Joseph Wilkinson and John Caper or any three of them being first Sworn do view the Ground and report the conveniences and inconveniences that may attend the opening of a road thereon –

10 October 1772, FOB 15, p. 463
James Ware is appointed Overseer of the Road leading from Berry's Ferry to Winchester in the room of Daniel Morgan, Ordered that the usual Tithables do work thereon under him --

10 October 1772, FOB 15, p. 463
Samuel Blackburn is appointed Overseer of the road leading from Lord Fairfax's to Cunningham's Chapel in the room of Daniel Morgan. Ordered that the usual Tithables do work thereon under him --

4 November 1772, FOB 15, p. 465
Robert Allen is appointed Overseer of the Road leading to Marlbrough Forge from Perkin's Mill as far as Opeckon, Ordered that the usual Tithables do work thereon under him --

4 November 1772, FOB 15, p. 466
County Levy
To Baylis Earle one wagon for repairing a road   [£] [0.] 10. 0

To Jacob Groves Ditto for Ditto   [0.] 10. 0.

To John Hiller his Account for Building a Bridge
upon his giving Security to keep the same in repair
seven years   15. 0. 0.

4 November 1772, FOB 15, p. 467
Upon the Petition of Robert Glass praying that the Road leading from Marlbrough Forge to Winchester may be turned to run upon the line between him and the Rev^d. M^r. Hoge, Ordered that John Snapp, Richard Fawcett, John Fawcett and Joseph Longacre or any three of them being first Sworn do view the Ground and report the conveniences and inconveniences that may attend the turning the said Road.

4 November 1772, FOB 15, p. 467
Benjamin Fry is appointed Overseer of the Road leading from Opeckon to Fry's Mill, in the room of Joseph Glass, Ordered that the usual Tithables do work thereon under him --

Frederick County Order Book 16 (1772-1778)

3 December 1772, FOB 16, p. 10
Upon the Petition of Sundry Inhabitants seting forth that David Brown had formerly obtained an Order for opening a road from his Mill down Opeckon by James Knights and Edward reeds, and that the said road is not of public Utility or for the Convenience of more than a few individuals, and praying that the same may be stopped, On hearing It is the opinion of the Court that the said

road is necessary for the use of the Petitioners who have now prayed that the same may be continued. Therefore it is Ordered that the said road be kept in repair by them & that they do work thereon under William Kearfoot who is appointed overseer thereof.

4 December 1772, FOB 16, p. 16
William Gibbs & John Rogers are appointed overseers of the road from Jolliffes' Store to Opeckon Ford, in the room of James Hagan, Ordered that the usual Tithables do work thereon under them --

[Note: Last road order entry in the year 1772.]

INDEX

This index is arranged by subject: Bridges and Causeways; Ferries and Fords; Land Features; Meeting Houses, Chapels, Churches, and Glebes; Mills and Mill Dams; Miscellaneous Subjects; Personal Names; Rivers, Runs, Springs, Creeks, and other Water Features; and Roads

Bridges and Causeways
Bridge over Bruce's Mill Run/Bruise's Mill Run (bridge at Bruce's mill), 118, 125, 128, 147
The bridge over Bulskin Run, 152
Burk's bridge, 168
Stone bridge in Cameron Street (bridge over Cameron Street), 138, 139, 145
Bridge built by John Hiller, 171
Jacob Hite's bridge, 133
Bridge at John Hite, Gent.'s mill, 50
Jumping Run bridge, 153, 159
Bridge at/on the Long Marsh, 77, 165
the bridge between Doctor McCormack's and the Muster Ground, 139
bridge over the Run in Main Street, 166
The causeway by Onan's, 141
New bridge at Opeckon, 79
Bridge over Opeckon Creek/Opeckon bridge, 84, 88, 116
Bridge near the head of the Great Pond on Shanando, 50
Causeway over the Swamp in Smith's Marsh (bridge on Smith's Creek), 41, 44
Smith's bridge, 70, 91, 98
The bridge between Edward Thomas's and John Smith's fences (Edward Thomas's bridge/bridge at Edward Thomas's), 94, 106, 133
Stony bridge, 41
Sturman's bridge, 50
The bridge between Edward Thomas's and John Smith's fences (Edward Thomas's bridge/bridge at Edward Thomas's), 94, 106, 133
Bridge over Tuscarora Creek, 21
Bridge at Worthington's Marsh, 84

Ferries and Fords
Abril's ford (on Opecken Creek), 5
Armstrong's ford (on Opeckon), 123(2)
Ashby's ferry, 64
Ashby's ford, 76
Ford at Ashby's Gap, 130
Thomas Ashby, Jr.'s ferry (at his house), 34(2)
Thomas Ashby's ferry over Shenandoah River, 57
Barnes's/Joseph Barnes's ford, 124, 133
The ford and ferry at Berry's/(Joseph) Berry's ferry and ford, 136, 140, 169
Berry's ferry, 153, 157, 163, 171

The ford at Berry's/ford at the crossing place at Berry's, 166(2)
Christian Blank's ford on the North River, 103
The Brush Bottom ford, 74, 106
The ford upon Bulskin (above Mr. Pyke's), 136, 162
Cannill's/Stephen Cannil's ferry (over Shanando River at Col. Burwell's land), 78, 80
Carsey's [Kersey's] ferry, 58
Caton's ford, 76
Ceeder Run Creek ford, 2(2)
Thomas Cherry's ford, 143
Chester's ferry, 1, 2, 14, 16
Chester's ford, 77, 111, 121, 134
Claud's ford, 94
Combs's/Coombs's ferry/ferry landing at Combs's/Coombs's (Joseph Coombs's ferry [across Shenandoah]) 91, 93(2), 95, 100, 103, 106, 108(2), 111, 113, 118(2), 121, 122, 128
Coombs's ford/the ford at Combs's, 87, 101, 118
The ford below Mason Combs's and John Morrice's old plantation, 81
County ferry (across Shannando [Shenandoah] between the plantation where John Kersey now lives and Christopher Marr's plantation), 37(2)
County ferry over Shanando [Shenandoah] River from William Francom's plantation to John Melton's plantation (County ferry over Shanando River at John Melton's plantation), 45, 47, 48, 49, 51
The ford of Crooked Run, 81
Cunningham's ferry, 104
Edge's ford (on Shannadore [Shenandoah] River), 12, 21, 50
The ferry, 57
The ferry at the ford, 135
The ferry (near Mecklenburg), 126
The ferry landing, 83
The ferrying water (near the ford of the Potomac), 148
The ford, 135
William Foster's ferry, 160
William Frost's ford, 65
Goony Run ford, 153
Gregorie's/Gregory's ford, 2, 6, 11, 12, 38, 47, 63, 76, 91, 109, 110(2), 138, 148, 157, 169
Mark Hardin's ford (on Shanando River), 38, 51(2)
Harper's/Robert Harper's ferry (over Potomac River), 79, 126, 163
River ford near Burr Harrison's, 165
Hogeland's/Hogland's/Richard Hogland's/Hougland's/Houghland's ferry, 97, 99, 100, 102, 106, 131, 140, 143, 145[?], 147, 148, 150, 156, 157, 158
Lewis Hogg's ferry, 7
Howel's/Howell's ford, 1, 11, 29, 32(2), 37, 40, 56, 91, 92, 93, 108(2), 111, 122, 163
Hurst's ford, 159
Jay's ferry, 6(2)
Kellor's ford, 151
Abraham Kendrick's upper ford, 158, 160
Kersey's ferry, 4(2), 9, 14, 17, 19, 21, 23, 38, 41, 43, 51, 61, 65, 66(2), 68, 86

Ferry near Kersey's [Kersey's ferry?], 49
[Kersey's?] ferry near Foxtrap Point, 50
John Kersey's ferry (over Shenandoah River), 1
Kersey's ford, 9
[Kersey's?] ford near Foxtrap Point, 50
Keyes's/Keys's ferry/ferry at Keys's/Gershom Keys's ferry (ferry on Gershom Keys Gent.'s land and crossing Shanando River to the land of the Hon. William Fairfax Esq.), 72(2), 78, 80, 82, 113(2), 118, 124, 125, 126, 127, 130, 137, 139, 163(3)
The ford (near Keyes's ferry), 163
Keys's/Keyes's ford, 122, 126, 139
Linder's ford/ford at Linder's/Lynder's ford (on Opecken Creek), 53, 74, 116, 117
The old fording place at/near Linder's, 75
James McCoy's ford, 81
The ferry (near Mecklenburg), 126
Ford at Mill Creek[?], 76
Mitchell's ford, 66
Ford on the River above Rocky Moor's, 78
The ford below Mason Combs's and John Morrice's old plantation, 81
Ford near the Muster Ground [Vestall's ford?], 134
Neill's ford (on Opeckon), 82
Opecken ford (by John Neil's mill), 4, 17, 19
John Neill's ford (on Opecken by his house), 23, 53
Lewis Neill's ford (on Opeckon at his house), 48, 59(2), 164
The North River ford, 81, 158, 159
Opeckon ford/ford on Opeckon, 114, 147, 155, 164, 172
John Neill's ford (on Opecken by his house), 23, 53
Lewis Neill's ford (on Opeckon at his house), 48, 59(2), 164
Opecken ford (by John Neil's mill), 4, 17, 19
Ford of Opeckon on the Main road at Edward Stroade's, 131
The ferrying water (near the ford of the Potomac), 148
Sand ford/Sandy ford (on Opeckon), 56, 65, 69, 71, 98(2), 99, 129
Seaborn's/Seaburn's ford, 108, 118, 157
Sheppard's ferry, 7
Snickers's/Edward Snickers's ferry/ferry at Edward Snickers's house/Snigers's/Sniggers's ferry (ferry from the land of Lord Fairfax crossing Shanando River to the land of John Mercer, Gent.), 72(2), 88, 89, 104, 113, 128, 130, 134, 135, 144, 170
Snickers's ferry landing, 170
[Snigers's?] ferry, 83
Snickers's/Edward Snickers's ford/Snigers's ford (over Shanando River), 81, 106(2), 169
South River ford, 72(2)
Sutherland's ford, 144
Swearengen's/Swearingen's/Mr. Swearingen's ferry, 62, 70, 85, 97, 100, 107, 108, 113
The Swift Shoal ford on Shenandoah, 124, 132, 136
Tidwell's ford, 134
Ferry at Vestal's Gap, 54
Vestal's ferry, 49

Vestal's/Vestall's ford (on Sharando [Shenandoah] River), 25, 50, 53, 60(2), 83, 121, 134, 136, 139, 142, 144, 163(2)

Watkins's/Evan Watkins's ferry, 13, 28, 40, 47, 56(2), 57, 61, 65, 70, 73, 77, 78, 85, 100, 103, 104, 112, 133, 161, 162, 164, 166

The Wagon ford, 50, 58, 91, 93, 111

The Wagon ford on Shanando, 92

Land Features

Ashby's Gap/Ashby's Bent Gap, 1, 11, 56, 57, 128, 129, 130

The Bear Garden Ridge, 60, 61

The Blue Ridge, 68

Top of the [Blue] Ridge at Ashby's Bent, 23

Top of the Blue Ridge at the head of Menasses [Manasses] Run, 109

Top of the Blue Ridge at Thorn's/Thornton's Gap, 84, 129

Top of the Blue Ridge/top of the mountain at Vestal's Gap, 38, 55, 69

Top of the Blue Ridge/ top of the mountain at Williams's Gap, 12, 59, 76, 83

Top of the Blue Ridge/top of the Ridge, 6, 7, 10, 15, 32, 37, 40, 49, 60, 72, 73, 81, 91(2), 92, 93, 99, 108, 111, 113, 121, 122, 139, 148, 169

Branston's Gap, 2(2)

Brock's Gap, 123, 159

Cape Capon Mountain, 138

Chester's Gap, 55, 77, 91, 113, 117, 121, 137

Curtis's Gap, 103

Desponet's/Disponet's Gap, 53, 57, 69, 86

The Flat Rock, 136, 162

The Flat Rock by Mr. Thruston's by the head of Kate's Spring, 167

Foxtrap Point on the south side of Shanando, 29, 43, 50, 58

The Great Plain, 72

The first Gap in Guard Hill, 16

Hogland's Neck by Barnet Newkirk's, 77

The Hollow near Kersey's, 41, 43

Hoop Petticoat/Hoop Pettycoat Gap, 45(2), 47, 67, 104, 154(2), 155, 164

The Hunting Ridge, 97, 151, 158

Top of the Hunting Ridge, 151

Ephram Leith's hollow, 94

The Little Mountain, 38, 93, 138, 152

The Long Bottom, 73, 75

McCoy's Ridge, 80

Manassas/Mannassip's Run Gap, 70, 156

Manasset's/Manassey's [Manassas] Gap (on the Blue Ridge), 150, 169

Massanuting/Massanutting/Massinutting/Messanuting/Messanutting/Messnuting/Massanutten [Mountain], 85, 86, 93, 114, 120, 123, 127, 128, 132, 133, 135(2), 137(2), 149(2), 150, 156, 159, 161

The top of Massanutting [Massanutten] Mountain, 127, 128, 137, 149(2), 150

Mill's/Mills's Gap, 111, 112, 116, 140, 141, 166

The Gap of the Little Mountain /top of the Little Mountain, 38, 93, 138, 152
The Mountain/the mountain, 30, 42, 53, 81, 104, 110(2), 112, 127, 130, 132, 143, 144, 151, 155
The Mountains, 102
The foot of the mountain, 78
The top of the Mountain, 110, 113, 122, 124, 125, 143, 150, 163
The top of the mountain at Mills's Gap, 112, 116, 166
The North Mountain, 44, 81(2), 94, 101, 104(2), 106, 143, 153, 166
The Gap of the Mountains above Hugh Paul's, 21, 26
The Pignut Ridge, 10, 23
Robinson's/Israel Robinson's Gap, 3, 4, 24, 54
The Sleepy Creek Mountain, 126, 127
Snickers's Gap, 167
Thorn's/Thornton's Gap, 84, 106, 108, 115, 123, 129, 151
The Thorough fare [gap?] at the Pignut Ridge, 10
The Three Top Mountain, 140
The Timber Ridge, 94, 113, 126
Trough Hill, 69
Vestals/Westalls Gap, 3, 14, 19, 26, 35, 38, 47, 54, 55, 56, 69, 76, 84, 100, 102, 115, 167
John Vestal's Gap at Shenandoah River, 52, 54
Williams's Gap, 12, 33, 52, 79, 83(2), 85, 86, 87
The rock/rocks at Williams's Gap, 83, 85
Wood's Plain(s), 94, 102

Meeting Houses, Chapels, Churches, and Glebes
The Baptist meeting house, 115, 117, 146, 147
The Chapel, 1, 4, 6(2), 20, 157, 167, 168, 170
The Chapel [McCoy's?], 124
The Chapel at (James) Cunningham's/Cuningham's Chapel, 17, 20, 22, 23, 25, 26, 28, 33(2), 34,
    39, 40, 42, 46, 48, 49, 51, 53(2), 55(2), 56, 58, 76, 84, 87, 88, 89, 92, 95, 98, 101, 109,
    128, 130(2), 132, 133, 134, 140, 153(2), 171
The Chapel at (Robert) McCoy's Spring(s)/ McCoy's/McKay's/McKoy's Chapel, 26, 27, 28(2),
    30, 34, 37, 44, 55, 62, 73, 79, 82, 95, 98, 101(2), 102, 104, 109, 113, 122, 138, 145
Morgan Morgan's Chapel/Morgan's Chapel, 25, 49, 54, 69, 76, 77, 84, 97, 105, 111
Frederick Parish, 118
The Glebe, 95, 98, 101(2)
The late Glebe, 134
The Meeting House, 70
The Meeting House at the Gap of the Mountains above Hugh Paul's/the Meeting House on the
    mountain, 21, 26, 31, 42
The Meeting House on Back Creek, 153
The Meeting House between Buckles's and Lucas', 119
The Presbyterian Meeting House at the head of Tuscarora, 153
The Quaker Meeting House, 95, 102, 141

Mills and Mill Dams
Allan's/Allen's/Benjamin Allin's mill, 74(2), 85, 99
Anderson's mill, 6
Barrett's mill, 131(2), 163, 168
Pugh's and Barrett's mill, 126
Edward Beason's/Beeson's mill, 22, 52
Beelor's/Christopher Beelor's mill, 121, 130, 144
Berry's mill, 121 *[Note: Possibly Perry's mill]*
George Bowman's mill/Bowman's mill, 88, 92
Branson's/Thomas Branson's mill/Branson's mill place, 28, 32, 38, 42, 44, 46, 48, 62, 65
Bridger's mill, 134
Joseph Bridges's mill, 135
Briscoe's/Dr. Briscoe's/John Briscoe's mill (on Opeckon), 127, 129, 132(2), 143, 161, 165
David Brown's mill, 168, 170, 171
Bruce's/Bruise's/George Bruce's mill, 118, 125, 128(2), 134, 147, 156, 158, 164
Buck's/Charles Buck's mill, 85, 96, 103, 104
Burwell's/Col. Burwell's/Burwill's mill (on Shanando River), 50(3), 57, 58, 87
The mill above Charles Thompson's on Col. Carlyle's land, 115
Combs's mill, 160
Cooper's mill, 146, 148
Cunningham's/Robert Cunningham's mill, 69, 78, 93, 97, 98, 101, 108, 111, 118, 130, 131, 156
Charles Dick's mill, 113
Eaton's mill, 141, 144
Earl's mill, 122
Fallis's mill, 141, 144
Follis's mill, 111, 112
Free's mill, 62, 63(2)
Froman's/Paul Froman's/Paul Froman, Jr.'s mill, 65, 69, 71, 90, 98, 99, 129
John/Jno. Frost's mill (Capt. Frost's mill), 1, 3, 20, 28, 44, 65
Funk's mill, 17, 42(2), 64(2), 69, 79, 85(2), 93, 159
Henry Funk's mill, 153
Henry Funk's mill (on Passage Creek), 158, 160
John Funk's mill, 1, 2(3), 7, 26, 35
The mill seat near the Furnace, 130
Fry's mill, 171
Gilliland's mill, 82
William Hall's mill, 72
Hampton's/Noah Hampton's mill, 1, 6, 8, 41, 63
William Hancher's mill, 166(2)
Hardin and Keys's mill, 83, 84(2)
Helm's/Thomas Helm's mill, 155, 157, 160, 161, 164, 170
Hite's mill, 5, 42, 45(2), 46, 47, 51, 63, 67, 129, 164
Capt. Hite's mill dam, 82
Capt. Hite's mill, 78
Col. Hite's mill dam, 90
Isaac Hite's mill, 156, 159

Jacob Hite's mill, 100(2), 102(2), 103, 119, 134, 135, 136, 137, 139
(Capt.) John Hite's mill, 7, 9, 30, 34, 36, 44, 50, 64, 70, 81, 93,
John Hogland's/Houghland's mill, 99, 100, 117
Isaac Hollingsworth's mill/mill race, 52, 53
Hume's mill/Thomas Hume's mill (on Sugar Tree Run), 117, 121
Caleb Job's mill, 84
(George) Johnston's mill [formerly Scot's/Scott's'], 14, 15, 17, 33
Elizabeth Jolliffe's/Widow Jolliffe's mill, 154, 155
Keith's/James Keith's mill (on Bulskin), 139(2), 141, 142, 144(2)
Hardin and Keys's mill, 83
Lewis's/Col. Lewis's mill, 121, 128, 157
Fielding Lewis's mill, 125(2)
Littler's/John Littler's/Widow Littler's mill, 9, 29, 36, 38, 41, 44, 68, 105
Mauk's mill, 132, 133, 151, 161
Mandanhall's/Mendenall's mill, 78, 101
Thomas Morgan's mill, 7
Neavill's/Nevill's/John Neavill's/Nevill's mill, 155, 156, 161, 163, 165
[John] Neill's mill dam, 3, 7
John Neill's/Neil's mill, 4, 17, 19
The mill formerly belonging to John Neill, dec., 106
Place where John Neil's old mill formerly stood (on Opeckon), 66
Lewis Neill's mill, 119(3), 120, 123(2), 158(2), 160
Perkins's/Isaac Parkins's/Perkins's's mill (on Opecken), 3, 5, 14, 16, 17, 19, 20, 33, 56, 64(2), 66, 72, 88, 98
Patterson's mill/William Patterson's mill, 156, 159
Pennewith's mill, 94
Perkins's mill, 171
Perrie's/Perry's/Thomas Perry's mill, 114, 115, 120, 121, 123, 124
Pugh's and Barrett's mill, 126
Pugh's mill, 151
Jesse/Jessee Pugh's mill, 149, 151, 154(2)
Isaac Ruddell's mill, 90
Scot's/Scott's mill [later Johnston's] (on Shanando/Sharrando), 5, 7, 11
Selser's mill, 72(2), 94, 102
Sexton's/Meshack Sexton's mill, 163, 168
Thomas Shepard's/Sheppard's mill, 4, 5, 6, 32, 47
Sink's mill, 138
Cutlip Sink's mill on Stoney Creek, 133
Snapp's mill, 161
Thomas Sperry's mill, 120 *[Note: Probably Perry's mill]*
Col. Stephens's mill, 161, 162(4), 164, 165(2)
Stephens's/Lewis Stephens's/Stevens's mill(s), 17, 29, 30, 35(2), 37, 39, 42, 44, 47, 53, 57, 63, 64(2), 69, 78, 82, 85, 86, 98, 104(2), 117, 118,
Lewis Stevens's mill (at the Narrow Passage), 77, 79, 81
Swearingen's mill, 145, 148, 149
Andrew Swearingen's mill, 140, 142

Van Swearingen's mill on Tunis's Branch (near Houghland's ferry)/ Van Swearingen's mill at Houghland's [ferry?], 140, 142, 145
(Thomas) Thornbury's mill, 25
The Tub mill, 170
Henry Vanmetre's mill (on Tuscarora), 41, 149, 152
Walker's mill dam, 7
White's mill, 166(2)
Widow Wood's mill, 57
Mr. Wormley's mill, 167, 169

Miscellaneous Subjects (houses, landmarks, neighborhoods, plantations, quarters, stores, towns, etc.)
Allen's cabin, 154(2)
The old field formerly Benjamin Allen's, 95
Jackson Allen's, 90, 91
John Allen's field/plantation, 150(2)
Robert Allen's house, 142, 145
Matthew Allison's, 162
Thomas Anderson's, 6
Mr. Ariss's, 167
Armstrong's place (on Opeckon), 126
John Armstrong's house, 114
Thomas Ashby, Jr.'s house, 34
William Ashby's, 158, 160
Ichebud Ashcraft's/Ashcroft's, 131, 135
August[a], 93
Augusta [County]/the Augusta [County] line, 42, 43, 112, 157, 158
[Augusta] County line below Brock's Gap, 159
Augusta [County] line on the South River above John Breeding's fence, 123
The upper inhabitants of Augusta on Woods River, 10
Phillip Babb's, 95
Mercer Babb's land/plantation, 147, 150
Thomas Babb's plantation, 121(2)
Thomas Babb, Jr.'s plantation, 96
Phillip Peter Backer's/Baker's house/land, 118, 153
Joseph Baker's plantation, 153
William Baldwin's, 143, 147
Mary Ballanger's, 84
Ballenger's meadow, 86
Ballenger's land/plantation, 42, 168, 170
Widow Ballenger's/Ballinger's, 105, 110, 169
The house of Josiah Ballinger, 17
Battletown, 167, 168, 169(2)
Becket's, 164
John Becket/Beckett's house, 78, 109

Robert Beckett's, 152
Belhaven, 80
Berry's, 166(2)
Thomas Berwick's, 26
Moses Bird's, 120(2)
Mounts Bird's, 125, 131
Benjamin Blackburn's plantation, 107
Blackburn's plantation, 161, 164
The Bloomery, 130, 167, 170
The Blue Ball, 1, 2
John Bosser's field, 3
Henry Bowen's, 131
Bradley's, 130
Caspere Branner's, 137
Thomas Branson's land/plantation, 11, 16
John Breeding's fence, 123
Joseph Bridges's, 138, 156, 158, 166
Briscoe's plantation, 130
Briscoe's new ground, 130
John Briscoe's plantation, 127
Mr. Briscoe's, 44
(Place) where Dr. John Brisco now lives, 57
Henry Brooks's, 137
David Brown's land/plantation, 155, 168(2), 169
John Bryan's house, 80
Charles Buck's, 109(2)
Buckles's, 119
Buffinton's, 16
Willm. Buffington's, 63
Peter Burr's, 141
Burwell's quarter, 32, 40
Burwell's quarter where Peter Catlet is overseer, 91, 93
Burwell's Spout Run, 59, 60
The Island (land of Col. Burwell), 32, 40
Charles Burwell, Esq.'s quarters, 34
Col. Burwell's land (on Shanando River), 78
Andrew Caldwell's, 19, 64
Jane Caldwell's plantation, 111, 112
Widow Caldwell's/Calwell's, 144, 155, 156
The Muster Ground above the Widow Caldwell's/Calwell's, 155, 156
Capt. Calmees's, 128
Marquis Calmes's (and Gent.), 15, 75, 87, 109, 142
Mr. Calmes's, 66
Andrew Campbell, Gent.'s, 21, 22, 24, 28, 30(2), 82
Capt. Campbel's/Campbell's, 6(2)
Col. Carlyle's land, 115

Carney's old house, 59(2)
Francis Carnaham's/Carnie's/Carney's, 12, 16, 22, 31, 50
Carrol's place on Patterson's Creek, 16
Simon Carson's fence, 100, 101
Cartmill's, 82
Edward Cartmill's, 109
Caton's stone house, 162
Capt. Caton's, 110
Mr. Caton's, 94
Thomas Caton's (and Capt. and Gent. and Mr.) house/land/plantation, 47, 65, 67, 92, 97, 99, 100, 101, 112, 115
Thomas Cherry's, 26
Chester's, 48
Thomas Chester's (and Gent.), 8, 13, 28, 32, 42
Chrisman's place *[Note: See also Crisman; Cristman.]*, 168
Jacob Christman's plantation, 114
William Clark's at Mount Pleasant, 91
William Cockrain's/Cockraine's, 127, 132
The settlement under the [North] mountain (by William Cockrain's/Cockraine's), 127, 132, 143
James Coddy's/Cody's, 1, 6(2), 8
Combs's/Coombs's, 91, 93, 100, 101, 103
Mason Combs's, 81
The Common *[Note: See also Common/Commons of Winchester.]*, 148
Darby Conely's land/fence, 10
The upper inhabitants of the county, 30
The County line, 10, 11, 17, 29, 35, 39, 52, 55, 63(3), 64, 69, 75, 79, 81, 85, 93, 96, 102(2), 104, 105, 110, 112, 120, 21, 123, 127, 128, 137, 139, 148, 149(2), 150, 151(2), 158, 160, 161, 167, 168, 169, 170(3)
The County line on Cape Capon Mountain, 138
The County line near Jeremiah Lewis's, 81
The County line by Thomas Little's, 29
The County line in Massanutting, 132, 133
The County line on the North Mountain, 104, 106
The County line at Williams's Gap, 79
The County line at Woods Plain, 94
The old County line, 74, 88
The Court house *[Note: See also the Town; the town of Winchester/Winchester Town.]*, 3, 4, 5, 7, 9(2), 10, 11(4), 12(2), 13, 14, 15(2), 16(2), 17(3), 20(2), 23, 25, 27(2), 29, 30(2), 31, 32, 33(2), 34, 36(2), 40(2), 42, 45, 54
Thomas Cowen's meadow/plantation, 141, 144, 145
Crawford's Muster Ground, 107
Henry Crisman's plantation, 170
Jacob Cristman's *[Note: See also Chrisman; Christman.]*, 81
Culpepper [Culpeper] (Co.)/Culpepper line, 77, 91

Cunningham's/Cuningham's/Cuninghem's *[Note: Most or all of these apparently refer to James Cunningham's.]*, 17, 20, 22, 23, 25, 26, 27, 28, 33(2), 37, 39, 48, 56
James Cunningham's, 23, 26, 27, 28
Mr. Robert/Robert Cuningham's/Cunningham's land/house, 57, 68, 73, 77, 101, 103, 104, 105, 132, 138
Widow Cunningham's, 71, 165
Jonathan Curtis's house, 22
Abraham Darst's smith shop *[Note: See also Durst.]*, 137, 138
James Daugherty's, 127
John Dauven's, 137
David Dedrick's/Diddrick's land, 96, 97
Christian Dellinger's *[Note: See also Dilliner]*, 133, 159
David Denny's, 144, 146
John Denton's, 127, 133
Barnett Desponet's, 117
Charles Dick's land, 105, 110
Christian Dilliner's *[Note: See also Dellinger.]*, 81(2)
[Joseph] Dillon's plantation, 126
Widow Dillon's, 3
William Dillon's land/plantation, 110, 135
Edward Dodd's, 89
Charles Donahue's house, 24(2)
Thomas Doster's land/plantation, 110(2), 111
John Duckworth's land/house, 48, 82
Widow Duckworth's land/plantation, 104, 114, 115
Abraham Durst's smith shop *[Note: See also Darst.]*, 135, 149(2)
Samuel Earl's meadows, 157
Samuel Earl/Earle's (and Gent.) dwelling house, 9, 108, 113, 115, 116
Samuel Earle's (and Gent.) quarter, 9, 108
Isaac Eaton's, 156
Robert Edge's, 30
Joseph Edwards's land, 25
Joseph Edwards, Jr.'s., 84
Enos Ellis's plantation, 150, 156
Mathias Elmore's, 3
Henry Enochs's, 79(2)
Evans's, 43
Isaac Evans's land/plantation, 143, 149, 152
John Evans's, 1, 4, 100, 103
John Evans's fence, 135, 137, 139
Joseph Evans's, 22, 40
Fairfax/Fairfax County, 20, 23, 46, 59, 60, 73, 74, 83 *[Note: These entries apparently relate to Fairfax County, although some may relate to Lord Fairfax's property.]*
Col. Fairfax's quarter, 83(2)
His Lordship [Lord Fairfax]'s house, 73, 75
Lord Fairfax's land, 72, 120, 153, 168, 171

[Lord Fairfax's] land office, 138, 141(2)
His Lordship [Lord Fairfax]'s line, 74, 85
His Lordship [Lord Fairfax]'s seat, 47
The Hon. Thomas Lord Fairfax's/His Lordship's quarter, 6, 71(2), 113
His Lordship [Lord Fairfax]'s quarter in the Long Bottom, 73, 75
Lord Fairfax's quarter where Nation formerly lived/Fairfax's plantation called Nation's *[Note: See also Nation's.],* 101, 114
Lord Fairfax's upper quarter, 138, 141(2)
Land of the Hon. William Fairfax Esq., 72
Falkner's land *[Note: See also Felkner.],* 158
Jesse Felkner's plantation *[Note: See also Falkner],* 157
The Forge/the Forge on Cedar creek *[Note: See also Marlborough forge.],* 129(2), 142, 144, 146
[Isaac Zane's] forge, 156
John Fosset's, 47
Foster's land, 148
James Fowler's house/land, 109(2), 122
William Francom's plantation, 45, 48
Fredericksburg, 158
Frederick Town, 43
Neals Friend's, 55, 60
Frost's, 126
William/Wm. Frost's plantation, 3, 44, 110
William Frost's plantation on Back Creek, 134
William Frost's middle plantation on Back Creek, 166
Benjamin Fry's, 146
Henry Fry's, 170
Joseph Fry's plantation on Cedar Creek, 118
Fryer's, 109
Alexander Fryer's, 109, 119, 126(2)
Capt. Jacob Funk's, 81, 82
John Funk's, 113
The Furnace *[Note: See also Marlborough furnace; Semple's furnace.],* 130, 138, 146
The Furnace on the north branch of Pembroke, 118, 129(2)
William Gaddis's/Gaddy's plantation, 9, 36, 68
Gates (across the road), 48, 110, 124
John Gerrard's, 166
Moses Gess's/Guess's, 71
Line between Robert Glass and the Rev. Mr. Hoge, 171
John Glenn's plantation, 156
William Glenn's plantation, 156
Moses Guess's upper quarter, 87
Goldin's, 10
John Gregory's, 7
John Grimes's land/fence, 10
Guess *[Note: See Gess.]*
James Hagan's, 154, 155

Hugh Hains's (on Opecken), 54(2)
John Hamman's land/tobacco ground, 10
Thomas Hamman's land/fence/yard, 10
Line of Hampshire County, 154
Noah Hampton's house, 93
Hancher's, 157
William Hancheir's/Hancheire's, 143, 146, 147(2), 148
Murty Handley's, 127, 132
Timothy Haney's land/fence, 10
Hardin's, 18
Mark Hardin's, 32
Robert Harper's at the mouth of Shanando, 72
Burr Harrison's, 165
Thomas Hart's, 53, 69, 80
The Signpost at the Hawks bill, 77
the Haybottom/Hay Bottom, 2, 31, 34, 55, 78
Robert Hayes', 10
Power Hazel's, 40
Henry Heath's, 148
Hedge's, 142
George Henry's, 122, 130
Hews's, 55
James Hill's, 23
Hite's land/house, 47, 88
Capt. Hite's, 51, 75, 79, 80
Col. Hite's, 89, 90(2), 91, 109, 125, 129, 152
Col. Hite's tanyard, 155, 164
Isaac Hite's, 93, 153
Jacob Hite's (and Gent. and Mr.) land/plantation, 5, 6, 20, 21, 25, 32, 38, 47, 49, 62(2), 65, 67, 70, 85, 90, 97, 106, 107, 118, 120, 128, 131, 148, 160, 170
John Hite's/John Hite's house/land (and Capt. and Col.), 4, 8, 10, 14, 16, 26, 27, 28, 29, 32, 38, 50(2), 54, 68, 73, 93, 94, 115, 120, 124, 132, 136
The Race Grounds below John Hite's house, 124, 132, 136
Mr. Hite's, 64, 65, 66(2)
Abraham Hollingsworth's, 4
Isaac Hollingsworth's, 38, 51(2)
William Hog's, 8
Line between Robert Glass and the Rev. Mr. Hoge, 171
James Hoge's plantation, 135
William Hoge, Jr.'s land/plantation, 15, 24, 27(2)
Lewis Hogg's house, 7
Lucas Hood's, 143, 145, 148
Rachell Hood's, 57
Thomas Hooper's, 32
Houghland's *[Note: May be Hougland's ferry]*, 145
Howard's old field, 149

Howards Town, 11
Devault Hulberger's, 129
Ralph Humfrey's, 17
The Indian Grave (on the main road), 54
The Iron Works, 83, 105
The Island (land of Col. Burwell), 32, 40, 93
Thomas Postgate's Island/Islands, 8, 13
Plantation formerly John Jayeas [Jaye's], 28
George/Capt. George Johnston's house/plantation, 33, 46
Jefrey Johnston's at the Pignut Ridge, 23
William Joleff's/Jolliff's/Jollyffe's land, 65, 84, 88, 89, 94, 120, 143, 147
Jolliffe's store, 172
Mr. Jolliffe's, 158
William Jolliffe, Jr.'s, 116
Mr. Gabriel Jones's plantation/place, 33, 35, 42, 44, 64(2), 66, 68
George Julian's on Passage Creek (George Julian's in Powell's fort), 85, 96
Francis Karney's, 28
Kersey's, 41, 43, 49
(Place) where John Kersey lives (at Shenandoah River near the Wagon road), 1
Plantation on which John Kersey now lives, 37
Keys's, 113
James Knight's, 168, 170, 171
Benjamin Kuykendal's, 69
Joseph Langdon's land/plantation, 116, 117
Lemon's, 70
Robert Lemen's/Lemon's house/land/plantation, 69, 107(2), 115
Col. Fielding Lewis's quarter, 100, 103
Jeremiah/Jeremh. Lewis's, 79, 81
Hugh Lile's, 42
Linder's, 74, 75
Simon Linder's, 37
Edmond Lindsey, Jr.'s, plantation, 119
John/Jno./Mr. John Lindsey/Linsey's, Gent.'s house, 20, 22, 23, 59
Thomas Lindsey's/ Lindsay's/Lyndsey's house/land/plantation, 87(2), 113, 118, 122, 123, 139, 161
Widow Lindsey's, 161
Thomas Linsey's on the Long Marsh, 22
John Little's, 150, 155, 157, 159
Thomas Little, Gent.'s, 29
Widow Little's, 47
Littler's land/place, 47, 112, 165, 170
Littler's/John Littler's plantation, 1, 3, 4, 5, 6, 20(2), 28, 31, 32
Litler's/Littler's/John Littler's old place/old plantation/late dwelling house, 4, 5(2), 27, 33, 36(2), 40, 41, 61, 62, 71, 73(2), 117, 118
John Littler's New Design, 5
Samuel Littler's, 101, 107

The Long Bottom, 73, 75
His Lordship's land, quarter, etc. *[Note: See Fairfax.]*
Loyd's, 55
David Loyd's, 24, 38, 49
Henry Loyd's/Lloyd's house/land/plantation, 99, 125, 126, 136(2), 162, 163
Old Loyd's, 37
Lucas's, 119
Lupton's, 168
John Lupton's meadow, 144, 146
Hugh Lyle's plantation on Back Creek, 103, 104
John Lyle's plantation, 156, 159
Hugh Lyle's/Lysle's land/plantation, 143, 147, 148, 162
Dr. McCormack's, 46, 147
(Mr.) John McCarmack's/McCormack's/ McCormick's house/land, 7, 14, 20, 37, 49, 54, 67, 87, 105, 107(3), 139(2)
Widow McCormack's, 140
McCormick's, 161
James McCoy's, 74
Robert McCoy Jr.'s, 2
Robert McCoy's fence, 113
Angus McDonald's, 121
James McGill's, 119
John McMachen's old place, 158
Robert McKay Jr.'s, 2
Richard McMachen's, 94
William McMachen's, 121
John Madden's, 18
Maidston/Maidstone, 75, 94
The Mannor line, 63
William Marks's plantation, 147
Marlborough/Marlbro forge, 150(3), 151, 153, 164, 165, 167, 169, 171(2)
Marlbro furnace, 152, 154(2)
Christopher Marr's plantation, 37
Maryland, 56
The town of McLenburgh/Mecklenburg/Mecklenburgh/Mecklinburgh, 116, 117, 119, 122, 123, 124(3), 126, 133, 137, 140, 142, 148, 162
John Melton's land/plantation, 33, 45, 47, 48
Col. Mercer's upper quarter, 128, 130
Col. George Mercer's land, 108
Land of John Mercer Gent., 72
John Milbourn's/Milburn's land/plantation, 1, 3, 20, 28
Miller Town/Miller's Town, 146, 150, 155, 160
David Miller's plantation, 104
David Miller's old plantation, 156, 165
John Miller's plantation, 156
The inhabitants living about Mills's Gap, 111

William Mitchel's/Mitchell's, 6, 20, 22, 24, 25, 30, 46
Henry Moore's/Moor's (and Gent.) plantation, 92, 143
Reiley Moor's, 77, 78
Col. Morgan's, 43, 44, 71, 86, 103, 105(2)
Morgan Morgan's, (and Col. and Gent.) house/land, 9, 17, 24, 30, 32, 40, 71, 115, 117
John Morrice's old plantation, 81
Samuel Morris's, 161
James Morrison's plantation, 156
(Mr.) Robert/Robt. Moseley's/Mosely's land/place/plantation, 66(2), 68, 86, 88, 89, 90, 93
Samuel Mount's (on Bullskin), 128
Samuel Mounts's, 134, 136
(William Clark's at) Mount Pleasant, 91
The Muster Ground, 134(2), 136, 137, 139, 163
The Muster Ground (above the Widow Caldwell's/Calwell's), 155, 156
(Crawford's) Muster Ground, 107
Nation's land/plantation, 51, 58, 92, 96, 130, 136, 140, 144, 145, 166
John Nation's house, 9(2), 30,
John Nealan's/Nealand's/Neeland's on Sharrando/Sherrando River, 9
Capt. Neill's, 100, 107
John Neill's house/land, 23, 33, 39
Lewis Neill's/Neil's/Niell's (and Capt. and Gent.; including house/land at Opeckon), 12(2), 13,
    14, 22, 23(2), 29, 30, 31, 67, 73, 81, 83, 86, 88, 94, 98, 102, 103, 104, 110, 151, 158, 164
Lewis Neill's old place, 170
William Neill's (upon Opeckon), 120
John Nevill's, 166, 167
Barnet Newkirk's, 77
John Newman's, 137
The New Town *[Note: See Stephens Town/Stephensburgh.]*
John Nisewanger's, 137
Mark Oiler's, 137
Onan's, 141
Orange County Court, 1, 3, 10
Jonathon Osborn's plantation, 144
Park's graveyard, 25
John Parks's, 106, 148
Parker's on the North River of Cacapon, 41
Thomas/Tho. Parker's, 62, 68
Hugh Parrel's land, 4
Samuel Patton's, 73
George Paul's, 140
Hugh Paul's, 21, 26
Widow Paul's, 49, 105
Capt. Pearis's, 102
Richard Pearis's, 141, 142
Richard Pearis's plantation by the head of the Swan Ponds, 124(2)
Robert Pearis's land/plantation, 62(2), 66, 77

Job Pearsall's/Pearsal's, 39, 46
Job Pearsall's plantation at the South Branch, 48
Pearson's Neck of land, 10
Elizabeth Pearson's land/fence, 10
Enoch Pearson's, 78, 81
(Mr.) Isaac Perkins's/Parkins's land/plantation, 50, 64, 147, 149(2), 151
George Pemberton's dwelling house, 46
Mr. Pyke's, 136
Thomas Postgate's Islands, 8, 13
The Inhabitants of Potomac River, 21
George Potts's plantation, 61(2), 68
Powell's fort/the great fort of Powell's, 96, 104, 127, 133
Prince William County/County Court, 10, 23, 70
Pritchet's place, 97
Jesse Pugh's, 132
Mr. Pugh's land/plantation, 111, 116
The Signpost at/near Quintin's/Quinton's, 58, 78
Quintin's/Quinton's, 58(2), 78
John Racklies's, 47
The Race grounds, 57
The Race Grounds below John Hite's house, 124
Edward Reed's, 168, 170, 171
Patrick Reiley's, 71
John Reno's fence/plantation, 85(2)
William Reynolds's land/plantation, 68, 95, 96
George Rice's house, 161
Patrick Rice's house, 107(2)
William Richey's, 52, 54, 75
Josiah Ridgway's land, 85
Place (on Opeckon) where Joseph Robbins/Robins formerly lived, 57, 59(2)
Daniel Rose's, 26
Ross's/Alexander Ross's fence/field/land, 21, 45, 61, 70, 91
Israel Robinson, Gent.'s house, 14, 19
Jacob Rush's/Rushe's land/plantation, 127, 133
Capt. Rutherford's land/plantation, 46, 87
Mr. Rutherford's, 49
Reubin Rutherford's, 80
Thomas/Tho: Rutherford (and Gent.)'s house/land/plantation, 6, 12, 24, 37, 38, 49, 68
Thomas Rutherford's pasture adjoining the town, 168
Patrick Ryley's, 27, 40
The School House on the River/old School House on Shanando, 17, 55, 76
Seabin's quarter, 32
James Seabin's gate, 34
Jonah Seaman's, 155, 156
Jonathan Seaman's/Seamon's house/land (on Opeckon), 105, 120, 131
Sebastian's quarter, 83, 84

The Secretary's office, 136
George Sellers's, 104
Semple's furnace, 141, 144, 145, 147, 152
Peter Sharrobz's, 161
John Shepard's/Sheppard's, 3, 7
Shepherds Town *[Note: See also Mecklenburgh.]*, 108, 115(2), 163
Land of Walter Shirley, 79, 82
The Signpost, 80, 83
The Signpost (at intersection of the road from Armstrong's ford and Littler's road), 123
The Signpost at the Hawks bill, 77
The Signpost at/near Quintin's/Quinton's, 58, 78, 87
Joseph Sively's, 137
John Skean's, 90
Smith's fence, 21(2)
Capt. Smith's, 104
(Capt.) Jeremiah Smith's house/land/plantation, 8, 24, 54, 55, 62(2), 71(2), 75, 77, 106, 132, 154(2), 170
John Smith's land, 32, 49, 50, 126(2), 134
John Smith's fence/fences, 94, 106
The line between Edward Thomas and John Smith, 112
John Smith's old place, 61, 62
John Smith, dec.'s, late dwelling place, 5
Matthew Smith's plantation, 145
John Snap's/Snapp's, 130
Laurence/Lawrence Snapp's house, 137, 140
Snickers's, 164
Edward Snicker's/Sniger's land/house, 71, 76, 77, 113
Edward Snickers's on Shanando, 73
Snigers's house, 78
Snigers's (on the River), 79
Thomas Speak's/Speakes's/Speaks's land/plantation, 103, 134, 135
Capt. Spears's, 109
Henry Spears's, 93
John Spears's, 145
John Spenceley's house, 151, 155
John Spoars's/Spore's land/plantation, 161, 165
David Springer's, 3
Plantation of Dennis Springer, dec., 166
Stephens Town/Stephensburgh/Stephensburg/Stevensburgh (town laid out on Lewis Stephens's plantation), 90, 92(3), 93, 94, 96, 103, 114, 120, 144, 145, 167, 169, 170
Lawrence Stephens's, 87
(Capt.) Lewis Stephens's/Stevens's fence/house/land/plantation, 68, 79, 89, 169
Lewis Stevens's old plantation, 71, 87
Lands of Joseph Vance and Peter Stephens, 86
Peter Stoufer's, 92
Stoufer's Town/Stover's Town, 102, 114, 115

Strasburgh/Stratsburg, 164, 165
Stribling's quarter, 42, 51
Capt. Stribling's, 10
Toliafero Stribling's, 152
Edward Stroade's/Strode's/Stroud's (on Opeckon), 25, 131, 162
James Strode's land/plantation, 162, 164
Jeremiah Strode's plantation, 162
(Mr.) John Sturman's land/house, 31, 33, 36
Mr. John Sturman's old place, 60(2)
Mr. Sturman's, 51
Richard Sturman's house, 42
Swearingen's, 102, 113
John Swim's, 49
(Col. Hite's) tanyard, 155
Edmund Taylor's plantation, 167, 169
George Telener's [Dellener], 2
Edward Thomas's land/plantation, 90, 128, 133
Edward Thomas's fence/fences, 94, 106
The line between Edward Thomas and John Smith, 112
Plantation where Isaac Thomas did live, 96(2)
Charles Thompson's, 115
Benjamin Thornbrough's/Thornbrugh's plantation, 150, 156
Mr. Thruston's by the head of Kate's Spring, 167
Andrew Tilleroy's, 136(2)
Tostee's, 61
Peter Tostee's/Tostie's land/plantation, 52, 61, 62, 63, 67, 73, 80
The plantation late Peter Tostee's, 69
The Town *[Note: See also the Courthouse; Winchester.]*, 19, 20, 27, 36, 43, 44, 46, 49, 50, 66, 67, 88, 89, 93, 168, 169
the Trough, 41, 62, 63(2)
Lands of Joseph Vance and Peter Stephens, 86
Place where Henry Vanmetre did live, 41
Place where Henry Vanmetre now lives, 41
Vestal's/Vestall's, 49, 164
Vestal's Ironworks, 44
William Vestal's, 9, 10
Jonathan Walker's land/field, 10
Robert Warth's, 30, 63(2)
Watkins's fence, 61
Watts's ordinary, 70
Dr. Wells's, 125, 128(2)
Humphrey Wells's house, 128
Place where Humphrey Wells lives, 125
Westchester [Winchester], 122
White's bottom, 91
John White's, 154

The White House, 108, 114, 115, 127, 128, 132
The White Post, 133, 140
Joseph Wilkinson's, 12
Samuel Wilson's/Willson's house/land, 130, 156
The town of Winchester/Winchester Town *[Note: See also the Courthouse; the Town.]*, 55, 59(2), 60, 62(2), 65, 66, 67, 68, 72(2), 73(2), 74, 77, 79(3), 80(2), 81, 86(3), 88(2), 89(2), 90(3), 91, 94(3), 95, 96(2), 98(2), 100(3), 101, 102(4), 103(2), 104(2), 105, 106(3), 107(2), 108(2), 110, 111, 112(3), 114(3), 115(3), 117(2), 118, 119, 120(2), 122(2), 123, 124, 125, 126, 128, 132, 133, 136, 142, 143(2), 145, 147(3), 148(2), 149, 150(4), 151(2), 152, 154(2), 155, 156, 157, 159, 160, 164, 167, 168, 169(2), 170, 171(2)
The Common/Commons of Winchester *[Note: See also The Common.]*, 89(2), 123, 127(2), 151, 152, 160
The Winchester Out Lots, 170
Christopher Windel's/Windle's (near Stoney Lick), 111, 116
Owin Wingfield's land, 119
John Wisecarver's, 146, 148
William Wood's, 118
The town of Woodstock, 114, 116, 117, 125, 160
Wormley's quarter, 50
Mr. Wormley's plantation, 167
Ralph Wormley, Esq.'s plantation, 164
The inhabitants on Worthington's Marsh, 84
David Wright's house, 168
George/Geo. Wright's land/house, 73, 79
Isaac Zane's forge, 156

Personal Names
Sir John *[Note: See Sinclair(e), Sir John.]*
Abril, 5
Abrell, John, 88(2)
Abril, John, 70, 112
Abrill, John, 91
Acklin, Christopher, 17
Adams, John, 166
Albin, John, 164
Albin, William, 20, 119, 120
Alebin, William, dec., 123
Alexander, Thomas, 8, 11, 13
Alderson, Curtis, 135, 137
Aldred, Christopher, 114
Aldrick, Christopher, 115
Aldridge, Robert, 114, 155
Alford, John/Jno., 5, 7, 11, 31, 33
Allan, 85
Allan, Robert, 34, 38, 71

Allen, 74(2), 154(2)
Allen, Benja., 95
Allen, Jackson, 90, 91, 165
Allen, John, 97, 145, 150
Allen, Joseph, 90
Allen, Robert/Robt., 47, 67, 69, 89, 142, 145, 170, 171
Allen, Thomas, 153, 159, 160
Allin, Benjamin, 99
Allison, Matthew, 162(2)
Anderson, 6
Anderson, Abner, 40
Anderson, Colvert/Culbert, 18, 20, 25
Anderson, James, 6
Anderson, Joseph, 170
Anderson, Thomas, 6
Anderson, William, 40
Arledge, John, 11
Armstrong, 123(2), 126
Armstrong, John, 58, 80, 114
Arnold, Josiah, 25
Arnold, Richard, 3
Ariss, John, 162
Ariss, Mr., 167
Ashbey, John, 72, 76, 78, 95
Ashbey, Robert, 51(2), 78
Ashbey, Thomas, 43, 44, 76
Ashbey, Thomas, Jr., 43, 44
Ashbie, 1
Ashby, 1, 2, 11, 23, 56, 57, 64, 76, 128, 129, 130
Ashby, David, 142, 153
Ashby, John, 34, 55
Ashby, Robert, 1, 11
Ashby, Thomas, 57, 58
Ashby, Thomas, Jr., 32, 34(2)
Ashby, William, 148, 150, 158(2), 160, 169
Ashcraft, Achebud/Ichebud, 126, 131(2)
Ashcroft, Ichebud, 135
Babb, Mercer, 135, 147, 150, 163
Babb, Peter, 132, 169
Babb, Phillip, 95
Babb, Thomas, 119, 121(2), 131, 141, 142
Babb, Thomas, Jr., 96
Bachelder, John, 53
Backer, Phillip Peter, 118
Bailey, William, 85
Bails, John, 19

Baker, Charles, 8
Baker, Cronimous/Heronimus, 146, 148, 164, 165
Baker, Joseph, 153, 159, 160
Baker, Philip Peter, 150, 153, 155
Baldwin, Francis, 65
Baldwin, Thomas, 156, 158, 167
Baldwin, William/Wm., 22, 130, 143, 147, 156
Baldwin, William, Jr., 140
Bales, John, 30
Ballanger, Mary, 84
Ballenger, 42, 86, 168, 170
Ballenger, James, 147
Ballenger, Josiah, dec., 32
Ballenger, Widow, 110, 169
Ballinger, Josiah, 17
Ballinger, Widow, 105
Baltis, Leonard, 161
Bann, Christopher, 40
Bardin, Rynard, 111
Barnes, 133
Barnes, Charles, 86
Barnes, Joseph, 124
Barnett, James, 155, 157, 169
Barrett, 126, 131(2), 163, 168
Barrett, Benjamin, 138
Barrett, James, 138, 163, 168
Barton, Daniel, 162
Bauer [Baver?], John, 40
Bayes, Hugh, 118
Bayles, James, 26
Beale, Taverner, 150
Bealer, Christopher, 27
Bealer, Joseph, 87
Beall, Samuel, 148
Beall, Taverner, 133, 157
Beals, John, 4
Beam, Samuel, 108, 129, 146, 148, 164, 165
Beason, Benjamin, 22
Beason, Edward, 22
Beason, Isaac, 69, 74, 80
Beason, John, 81
Beason, Richard, 4, 61, 67, 69
Becket, 164
Becket, John, 56, 71, 78
Beckett, John, 109
Beckett, Robert, 152

Bedinger, Henry *[Note: See also Pedinger.]*, 137
Beelah (Bullah?), John, 17
Beeler, Christopher, 25, 30
Beeler, Frederick, 105
Beeler, Joseph, 100, 102, 109
Beelor, 130, 144
Beelor, Benjamin, 130, 144
Beelor, Christopher, 121
Beeson, 52
Beeson, Richard, 24
Bell, John, 129, 166(2)
Bell, Nathaniel, 147
Bennett, Robert, 40
Berry, 121, 136, 140, 153, 157, 163, 166(2), 171
Berry, Benjan., 108
Berry, Joseph, 118, 124, 132, 135, 169
Berry, Thomas, 108(2), 115, 132, 166
Berwick, Thomas, 21, 26
Bethell, William, 73, 77
Bethell, William, dec. 84
Biggerstaff, William, 43
Bilbroaw, William, 121
Bird, Moses, 112, 120(2)
Bird, Mounts, 99, 102, 125, 131
Black, Thomas, 137, 168
Blackbourn, William, 85
Blackburn, 161, 164
Blackburn, Archibald, 29
Blackburn, Benjamin, 29, 107, 121, 161, 164
Blackburn, James, 29
Blackburn, John, 29
Blackburn, Robert, 134
Blackburn, Samuel, 171
Blackburn, William, 29
Blackburn, William Jr., 29, 64
Blackburne, Samuel, 133
Blackmore, Thomas, 155, 157
Blair, James, 110, 112, 162(2)
Blank, Christian, 103
Booth, Caleb, 141, 144
Borden, 26, 27, 55
Borden, Joseph, 108
Borden, Reynold, 116
Borden, Widow, 6
Bosser, John, 3
Bounds, George, 85, 103

Bounds, James, 8(2)
Bowen, Henry, 131
Bowen, Henry (Jr.), 28, 36(2)
Bower, Henry, 111
Bowen, Richard, 136(2)
Bowman, 88
Bowman, Andrew, 133(2)
Bowman, George, 2(2), 15, 18, 19, 34, 35, 92
Bowman, Jacob, 93, 104
Boyd, John, 148
Boyd, Samuel, 90, 93
Boyd, William, 141, 146, 147, 166
Boyl, James, 21
Boyle, James, 70
Bradford, Charles Darnald, 114
Bradley, 130
Brake, Jacob, 86
Branner, Caspere, 137
Branson, 32, 38, 42, 44, 46, 48, 62, 65
Branson, John, 8, 11, 16, 42, 75, 113
Branson, Thomas/Thos., 8, 11(2), 14(2), 16, 23, 26(2), 27, 28(3), 29, 35, 46, 48
Branston, 2(2)
Braughton, Jesse, 117
Breakly, Jacob, Jr., 53
Breakly, Jacob, Sr., 53
Breed, Ebearm, 40
Breeding, John, 123
Bridger, 134
Bridges, Joseph, 135, 138, 156, 158, 166, 168, 170
Brinker, George, 156, 159
Brinker, Henry, 44, 73, 74, 86, 88, 89, 94, 95, 102, 103(2), 112, 117, 118, 122, 151
Briscoe, 130(2), 143, 163, 165
Briscoe, Dr., 161
Briscoe, George, 143
Briscoe, John, 66, 90, 112, 126, 127(2), 128, 129, 132(2)
Briscoe, Mr., 44
Brisco, Dr. John, 57
Brittain, Jonathan, 163
Brock, 123, 159
Brook, Henry, 137
Brooks, Jacob, 6, 12, 21, 22, 24, 40, 41, 62
Brooks, Matthew, 61
Broughten, Jesse, 116
Brown, David, 129, 136, 145, 155, 164, 167, 168(3), 169(2), 170, 171
Brown, James, 63
Brown, John, 10, 23

Brown, Thomas, 19, 24
Brownfield, Robert, 166
Bruce, 125, 128(2), 134, 147, 158, 164
Bruce, George, 50, 125, 156
Bruce, James, 12, 13(2), 16, 44, 86, 88, 89(3), 90, 94, 95, 114, 115
Bruin, Bryan, 108, 114
Bruise, 118
Bryan, John, 59, 80, 86
Bryant, Bartholomew, 56
Bryant, John, 36
Buck, 85, 96, 104, 170
Buck, Charles (and Mr.), 38, 62, 73, 75, 77, 103, 109(2), 153
Buck, Thomas, 78, 134
Buckles, 80, 119
Buckles, Robert, 76, 113
Buffington, William/Willm., 63, 69
Buffinton, 16
Buffinton, William, 39
Bullah (Beelah?), John, 17
Burckam, John, 149
Burckham, Joseph, 1
Burden, 37, 55, 56, 58, 84
Burk, 168
Burket, George, 158
Burkham, Joseph, 3
Burn, James, 6, 13
Burner, Jacob, 119, 127, 128, 132, 133
Burner, James, 141, 153
Burnett, Alexander, 130
Burns, James, 138
Burns, William, 139, 149, 162
Burr, Peter, 141
Burwell, 32, 40, 50, 57, 59, 60, 87, 91, 93
Burwell, Charles (and Esq.), 34
Burwell, Col., 32, 50(2), 78
Burwill, 58
Bush, Daniel (and Gent.), 94, 98, 99, 114
Bush, Phillip/Philip, 93, 95, 108, 114, 138, 145, 164
Butherfield, Thomas, 156
Butterfield, Thomas, 158
Butler, Pearce, 112, 135
Caldwell, Andrew/Andrw., 19, 33, 44, 64
Caldwell, Jane, 111, 112
Caldwell, Widow *[Note: See also Calwell.]*, 155
Calfee, William, 111
Callfee, John, 117, 121

Calmees, Capt., 128
Calmees, Marquis/Marquise, 9, 10
Calmees, William, 125(2)
Calmes, Marquis (and Gent.), 15, 17, 18, 35, 37, 48, 55, 56, 57, 58, 75, 78, 87(2), 109, 142, 166
Calmes, Mercy, 76
Calmes, Mr., 66
Calmes, William, 83, 86, 87, 100, 104
Calvin, Joseph, 155
Calwell, Widow, 144, 156
Campbel, Capt., 6
Campbell, Andrew, (and Gent. and Major), 3, 4, 21, 22, 24, 27, 28, 30(2), 40, 54, 61, 82, 143
Campbell, Capt., 6
Campbell, Dougall/Dugal/Dugall, 141, 150, 156, 162, 164
Campbell, Joseph, 39
Campbell, Richard, 150, 155
Campbell, William, 92, 143
Caneday, Hugh, 11
Cannil, Stephen, 78
Cannill, 80
Canrood, John, 165
Caper, John, 171
Capper, John, 71
Carlyle, Col., 115
Carneham, Francis, 16
Carney, 59(2), 73, 82, 83, 100, 104, 136
Carney, Francis, 12, 31, 50
Carnie, Francis, 22
Carr, Nathaniel/Nathl., 38, 71
Carrol, 16
Carsey, 58
Carsine, John, 28
Carson, Simon, 98, 100, 101
Carter, Benjamin, 5
Carter, James, 107, 110, 151, 160
Carter, James, Jr., 170
Carter, Joseph, 3, 23, 33
Carter, Philip, 170
Carter, Richard, 33, 114
Cartmell, Edward, 17, 30
Cartmell, Martin, 17, 33, 35
Cartmell, Nathaniel, 17, 45
Cartmell, Nathaniel, dec., 39
Cartmill, 82
Cartmill, Edward, 79, 109, 156, 170
Cartmill, Nathan, 71
Cartmill, Nathaniel, 56, 65, 71, 98, 99, 142, 150

Carver, Philip, 151, 158
Casey, Peter, 63
Cassine, John, 50
Castleman, David, 109, 123, 140, 157
Castleman, William, 40
Catlet, James *[Note: See also Cattlet.]*, 11
Catlet, Peter, 91, 93
Catlett, James, 132
Catlett, Peter, 124, 132, 133, 140(2), 168, 170
Catlett, Robert, 11
Catlett, William, 119
Caton, 76, 162
Caton, Capt., 110
Caton, Mr., 94
Caton, Thomas (and Capt. and Gent. and Mr.), 47(2), 65, 67, 77(2), 78, 82, 92, 97, 99, 100, 101, 112, 115
Cattlet, James, 29
Chambers, William, 104
Champion, John, 145
Chandler, Jacob, 97, 101(2)
Chaplin, William, 82
Chenowith, John, 68
Cherry, 149
Cherry, Thomas/Thos., 21, 26, 143
Cherry, William, 105
Chester, 1, 2, 14, 16, 43, 44, 48, 55, 77, 91, 92, 111, 113, 115, 117, 121(2), 134, 137
Chester, David, 101, 121
Chester, Thomas (and Gent.), 1, 2(2), 8, 9, 10, 13, 14, 28, 32, 42, 100, 109
Chew, Jacob, 155
Chew, James, 156
Childs, Henry, 107
Chinoth, William, 117
Chinoweth, William, 164
Chinowith, William, 166
Chinworth, John, 111
Chinwoth, John, 112
Chrisma, 137
Chrisman, 125, 129, 168
Chrisman, Henry, 170
Chrisman, Jacob, 170
Christman, Jacob, 34, 114
Churchman, Edward, 11
Cinacome, John, 39
Clark, William, 91
Claud, 94
Cobourn, Jonathan/Jona., 1, 5(2), 6, 13, 41

Cobourne, Jonathan, 4
Coburn, Jonathan, 2
Coddy, James, 1, 6, 25
Cody, James 3, 6, 8
Cochrain, William, 112
Cochran, William, 107
Cockendal, Abra:, 39
Cockendal, Abra: Jr.,39
Cockendal, Benjamin, 39
Cockendal, John, 39(2)
Cockendal, Nathl., 39
Cockendal, Peter, 39
Cockendall, James, 39
Cockrain, William, 132
Cockraine, William, 127
Coffield, Peter, 133
Coffman, Augustine, 157, 159
Coffman, Martin, 132
Cofman, Martin, 133
Collet, Abraham, 74, 85
Collings, John, 30
Collins, John, 41
Collins, Luke, 122
Colson, Thomas, 12, 16, 22, 23(2), 30, 31, 59(2), 82, 98, 125(2)
Colven, James, 30
Colvill, Joseph, 142, 164
Colvin, John, 6, 39
Colvin, Joseph, 164
Comber, Frederick, 123
Combes, 113, 118
Combs, 91, 100, 101, 103, 108(2), 118, 122, 128, 160
Combs, Joseph, 58, 106, 122
Combs, Mason, 81
Conely, Darby, 10
Connel, William, 115
Conrad, John, 165
Conrood, John, 165
Cook, John, 71
Cook, William, 104
Cooke, William, 132
Coombes, 121
Coombs, 87, 93(2)
Coombs, Joseph, 49, 95
Cooper, 146, 148
Cooper, Jacob, 17, 53, 71
Cooper, James, 138

Cooper, Thomas, 48, 91, 110, 113, 115, 138, 141
Corder, Edward/Edwd. 6, 9, 145
Cordery, Thomas, 80, 101
Cordit, Edward, 11
Corn, George, 39
Counts, Nicholas, 53
Covill, Joseph, 145
Cowen, Thomas, 141, 144, 145, 166
Cox, Friend, 43
Craik, James, 100
Crandon, Abraham, 11
Crane, John, 130
Crawford, 107
Crawford, Valentine, 103, 118, 142
Crawford, William, 78, 81, 105, 118, 121
Creamer, Oliver, 40
Crisman, 70(2), 86, 90, 91
Crisman, Jacob, 91
Crist, Nichl., 40
Cristman, Jacob, 81, 82
Croles, John, 72
Cromley, James, 32, 71(2), 86
Crosby, Robert, 166
Cross, Philip/Phillip, 53, 71
Crow, John, 163
Crumley, William, 117
Crunk, Richard, 11
Cryder, Martin, 53
Cuningham, 33, 34, 40, 42, 56, 58, 84
Cuningham, John, 40
Cuningham, Robert, 57
Cunningham, 46, 48, 49, 51, 53(2), 55(2), 69, 76, 78, 87, 88, 89, 92, 93, 95, 98, 101, 104, 108, 109, 111, 118, 128, 130(3), 131, 132, 133, 134, 140, 153(2), 156, 171
Cunningham, Adam, 151
Cunningham, George, 105, 108
Cunningham, (James), 17, 20, 22, 23, 25, 26, 27, 28, 37
Cunningham, Robert/Robt. (and Mr.), 54, 68, 69, 73, 77, 85, 89, 97, 98, 101(2), 103, 104, 105, 110(2), 111(2), 132, 138
Cunningham, Widow, 71, 165
Cunninghame, George, 155, 156
Currey, Daniel, 85
Curry, Daniel, 118, 153
Curry, Nathaniel, 109
Curtis, 103
Curtis, Jonathan, 22
Dacker, John, 39

Daker, Garrat, 39
Daker, Luke, 39
Dark, William, 141, 148, 160
Darke, William, 163
Darst, Abraham *[Note: See also Durst.]*, 137, 138
Daugherty, James, 126, 127, 131(2), 135
Dauven, John, 137
Davis, David, 155
Davis, Edward, 149
Davis, James, 106, 117, 140, 143, 147
Davis, John, 54, 83, 84(3), 106, 149
Davis, Michael, 160
Davis, Robert, 26, 28, 81, 82
Davis, Theodore, 39
Davis, Walter, 108
Davis, Wm., 3, 7, 12
Dawkins, John, 126(2), 140
Dawson, Isaac, 127
Dayle, Simon *[Note: See also Doyle.]*, 151
Dedrick, David *[Note: See also Diddrick.]*, 97
Delheryea, James, 1
Dellener, George 2, 17, 35
Delling, 25
Dellinger, Christian, 133, 138, 159
Demoss, Charles, 127, 132
Demose, William, 55, 60
Demosse, William, 60
Denny, David, 144, 146, 147, 149
Denton, Abraham, 74, 111, 116
Denton, Benjamin, 85
Denton, John, 96, 104, 127, 133
Denton, Robert, 8
Desponet, 57, 86
Desponet, Barnett, 117
Deveney, Charles, 117
Devinner, Charles, 116
Diddrick, David *[Note: See also Dedrick.]*, 96
Dick, Charles, 105, 110, 113
Dillan, William, 1
Dillback, Abraham, 127
Dillener, George, 42
Dilliner, Christian, 81(2)
Dilliner, George, 26
Dillon, Joseph, 126
Dillon, Widow, 3
Dillon, William, 3, 20, 28, 110, 135

Disponet, 53, 69
Disponet, Barnet, 53, 104
Disponet, Christopher, 53
Disponet, Jacob, 53
Dodd, Edward, 89, 116, 125, 128, 134, 143, 147, 154, 155
Doke, John, 149
Donahue, Charles, 24(2), 40
Doster, Thomas, 42, 56, 103(2), 105, 110(2), 111, 138(2), 149
Doster, William, 131(2)
Doston, Richard, 40
Dothertay, Gervas, 78
Doud, Caleb, 40
Dowley, Patrick, 119
Downton, John, 11
Dowther, John, 39
Doyle, Simon [Note: See also Dayle.], 151, 155
Draper, William, 72
Drening, Walter, 25
Duckworth, John, 8, 11, 34, 35, 48, 82
Duckworth, Widow, 104, 114, 115
Duckworth, William, 61, 68, 77, 84, 93, 101(2)
Duckworth, William, dec., 105
Durst, Abraham, 135, 149
Dyer, Elizabeth, 28
Dyer, John, 53, 71
Dyer, William, 53
Earl, 122
Earl, Samuel, 115, 157
Earle, Bayles/Baylis, 124, 130, 132, 133, 140(2), 150, 153, 156, 171
Earle, Samuel/Saml. (and Gent.), 6, 9, 10, 11, 13, 26, 27(2), 34(2), 37(2), 38, 41, 43, 47, 55(2), 56, 108, 110, 113, 115, 116
Earles, Bayles, 136
Earles, William, 39
Earnest, Henry, 96
Eaton, 141, 144
Eaton, Isaac, 144, 156, 166
Eger, George, 29
Edge, 12, 21, 50
Edge, Robert, 30
Edwards, Jonathan, 162, 164
Edwards, Joseph, 8, 13, 14, 25, 48, 54, 62, 70, 75, 91, 132
Edwards, Joseph, Jr., 84, 127
Ellis, Enos, 150, 156
Elmore, Mathias, 3
Elsey, William (and Mr.), 67
Emry, Stephen, 60, 77

Enochs, Henry, 45, 79(2)
Evans, 43
Evans, Isaac/Issac, 30, 78, 100, 135, 137, 143, 149, 152
Evans, John, 1, 4, 29, 61, 100, 103, 135, 137, 139, 162
Evans, Joseph, 22, 40
Evans, Mayberry, 160
Evans, William, 63, 82
Evine, William, 30
Ewing, William, 32
Ewings, William, 44, 54
Ewins, Isaac, 24
Fairfax, Col., 83(2)
Fairfax, the Right Hon[ora]ble. Thomas Lord/Lord Fairfax/His L[or]dship (and Baron of Cameron), 6, 47, 51, 56, 57, 58, 64, 66, 71(2), 72, 73, 74, 75, 85, 101, 113, 114, 120, 138, 141(2), 153, 168, 171
Fairfax, the Hon[ora]ble. William (and Esq.), 72
Falkenborough, Andrew, 2
Falkner, 158
Falkner, Jesse, 168
Fallis, 141, 144
Fallis, Richard, 84
Fallon, William, 40
ffannen, James, 39
Farnley, Thomas, 124, 153
Farrington, Samuel, 25
Farrow, George, 93
Fauhelm, John, 53
Fawcett, John, 17, 38, 118, 129(2), 146, 150, 156, 171
Fawcett, Joseph, 17, 38, 118, 129(2)
Fawcett, Richard, 17, 38, 171
Fawcett, Richard, Sr., 152
Fawcett, Thos., 17
Fawcit, Joseph, 30
Fearnley, William, 11
Felkner, Jesse, 157
Felson, Rober, 97
Ferguson, Hugh, 5, 7, 11
Fillson, Robert, 133, 145
ffinch [ffinell?], John, 40
Fisher, Barack, 147, 149(2), 151
Fleming, John, 145
Flemming, John, 97
Fogglesong, Christian, 169
Follis, 111, 112
Follis, George, 112
Foman, Matthias, 39

Foreman, James, 142
Forman, Benjamin, 69
Forman, Benjamin, Jr., 39
Forman, James, 75, 140, 142
Fosset, John, 47, 90
Fosset, Joseph, 71
Fosset, Richard, 71
Foster, 148
Foster, Peter, 25
Foster, William, 160
Fowler, Francis, 69, 84
Fowler, James, 109(2), 122
Franceway, Joseph, 140, 142
Francom, William, 45, 48
Frasier, Benoni, 50
Fravell, Henry, 131
Frazier, Benja., 10
Free, 62, 63(2)
ffreland, Richard, 39
Freitley, Andrew, 114, 115
Frey, Abram., 71
Frey, Benjamin, 71
Frey, Jacob, 71, 129
Frey, Joseph, 71
Frey, Samuel, 129
Friend, John, 43
Friend, Neals/Neils, 55, 60(2)
Froma, 65
Froman, 69, 71
Froman, Paul, 17, 35, 71, 90, 99, 129
Froman, Paul, Jr., 71, 98, 99
Frost, 126
Frost, Capt., 3, 20
Frost, John/Jno., 1, 3, 28, 44, 65
Frost, William/Wm., 3, 44, 65, 110, 134, 166
Fry, 171
Fry, Abraham, 104
Fry, Benjamin, 146, 171
Fry, Henry, 55, 170
Fry, Jacob *[Note: See also Frey.]*, 129
Fry, Joseph, 90, 104, 106, 118
Fry, Samuel, 118
Fryatt, Bartholomew, 127
Fryett, Bartholomew, 132, 161, 163
Fryer, 109
Fryer, Alexander, 109, 119, 126(2)

Fugate, Randolph, 121
Fugett, Randolph, 117
Funck, Jacob, 1
Funk, 42(2), 64(2), 69, 79, 85(2), 93, 159
Funk, Adam, 84
Funk, Henry, 153, 158, 160
Funk, Jacob (and Capt.), 2, 23, 81, 82
Funk, John (and Capt. and Gent.), 1, 2(3), 7, 17, 26, 35, 63, 88(2), 92, 113
Funk, John, Jr. 30, 42(2)
Funk, Martin, 88, 102, 114
Fussey, 133
Fussey, Peter, 133
Gabbert, Frederick, 17, 42
Gaddis, William, 36, 68
Gaddy, William, 9
Gallasby, Patrick, 4
Gardener, John, 87
Garrat, Edward, 21, 29
Garrets, Edward, 31
Garrett, David, 146
Garrett, Edward, 12
Geestin [Gustin?], John, 139
George, Joseph, 122
Gerrard, David, 147, 166
Gerrard, John, 166
Gess, Moses, 78
Gess, Moses, dec., 100, 103
Ghosney, Henry, 157
Gibbs, William, 172
Gibson, Christopher, 8
Giles, Henry, 121
Gilkison, David, 168
Gillaspy, Patrick, 19
Gilliland, 82
Gist, William, 130, 153
Glass, David, 17
Glass, Joseph, 17, 71, 78, 129, 150, 171
Glass, Robert, 71, 97, 150, 171
Glass, Samuel, 17, 71
Glenn, John, 156
Glenn, William, 156
Glover, William, 34, 36, 43, 96, 114
Goldin, 10
Goldsberry, Robert, 155, 163
Good, Jacob, 40
Gore, Henry, 137, 150

Gosne, Henry, 157
Gosney, Henry, 157
Gram, John, 123
Grantom, John, 128(2), 129
Grantum, John, 133
Grayham, James, 143
Green, Robert (and Gent.), 10
Greenfield, John (and Gent.), 91, 94, 95
Gregorie, 2
Gregory, 6, 11, 12, 32, 38, 47, 63, 76, 91, 109, 110(2), 138, 148, 157, 169
Gregory, Benja./Benjn., 6, 11
Gregory, John, 6, 7, 8, 11, 13
Gregory, Richd., 6
Grider, Martin, 69, 71, 86
Grigsby, John, 153
Grimes, John, 10
Gross, Isaac, 9
Groves, Jacob, 171
Grub, Benjamin, 49, 54, 76, 87
Grubb, Benjamin, 67, 78
Guess, Moses, 60, 71, 87
Guest, William, 128
Gustin [Geestin?], John, 139
Hackney, Aaron, 163
Hackney, David, 169
Hagan, James, 143, 154, 155, 172
Haines, Bathanay/Bathany/Bathonia/Bethany/Bethony, 8, 9, 10, 11(2), 16, 23, 26
Haines, Hugh, 107
Haines, Robert, 113, 158
Hains, Hugh, 54(2)
Hains, Robert, 141
Halfpenny, Robert, 13
Hall, William, 72
Hamilton, Francis, 144
Hamman, John, 10
Hamman, Thomas, 10
Hammer, John, 68
Hampton, 41, 63
Hampton, George, 125(2), 128, 167, 168
Hampton, John 6(2), 20
Hampton, Joseph, 167, 169
Hampton, Noah, 1, 2, 6, 8, 93
Hampton, Thomas, 66
Hancheir, William, 146, 147(2), 148
Hancheire, William, 143
Hancher, 157

Hancher, Nicholas, 28
Hancher, John, 166
Hancher, William, 131, 163, 166(2), 168
Hand, William, 77
Handley, Michael, 90
Handley, Murty, 127, 132
Handshaw, Nicholas, 19
Hanger, Peter, 125, 131, 146
Haney, Timothy, 10
Hankins, Joseph, 11
Hankins, Thomas/Thos., 8, 9, 11
Harbinson, Matthew, 29
Hardin, 18, 83, 84(2)
Hardin, Henry, 31, 34, 41, 43(3), 44, 55
Hardin, John (and Gent.), 1, 2, 3, 9, 10, 26, 27(2), 30, 40, 41, 45, 47, 49(2), 51, 52, 53, 60, 81, 105, 110
Hardin, Mark, 32, 38, 51(2)
Hardinger, John, Jr., 139
Harihill, Philip, 71
Harland, George, 82
Harman, George, 57, 58
Harper, 79, 163
Harper, Michael, 71, 78, 88, 89
Harper, Robert, 72, 126
Harrison, Burr (and Gent.), 112, 120, 122, 123, 165
Harrison, George, 133, 135
Harrison, Lawrence, 87, 113
Harrison, Thomas, 113, 115
Harrold, Richard, 91
Hart, Peter, 40
Hart, Thomas, 3, 24, 53, 56, 69, 80, 113, 136(2), 141, 143, 144, 145, 160, 163
Hartley, John, 105, 110
Hasel, Power, 46
Hawkins, Joseph, 123
Hayes, Robert, 10
Hays, John, 143
Haymaker, Adam, 122, 127
Hazell, Power, 40
Hazell, Richard, 40
Heath, Henry, 62, 67, 95, 100, 118, 139, 147, 148, 152, 157, 158
Hedge, 142
Hedge, Jonas, 24, 56, 57, 58, 70, 74, 77, 81, 142, 148
Hedge, Peter, 57, 58, 74, 75, 77, 78
Hedge, Solomon, 63, 69
Hedges, Jonah, 147
Hedges, Jonas, 106, 117, 131(2), 143

Hedges, Peter, 70
Hedges, Solomon (and Gent.), 13, 16, 39
Helm, 157, 160, 161, 164, 170
Helm, John, 147
Helm, Leonard, 31, 49, 78, 87
Helm, Meredith (and Gent.), 37, 47, 49, 58
Helm, Thomas, 105, 125, 129, 155, 157, 170
Helm, William, 87, 98
Helmes, George, 138
Helms, Joseph, 23
Helms, Leonard (and Mr.), 3, 15(2), 18, 41, 43(2), 50, 67, 68
Helms, Meredith/Mered. (and Gent.), 5, 15, 44, 51
Helms, P., 37
Helms, William, 123
Helphingston, Peter, 142
Helphingstone, Peter, 164
Helsley, Jacob, 159
Hendricks, James, 145, 148
Henry, George, 122, 130, 153
Hentine, Michael, 99
Herin, John, 38
Herrin, John, 12
Heth, Henry, 148, 150
Hews, 55
Hiat, William, 32, 39(2)
Hiatt, Semion, 133
Hickman, Ezekiel, 115
Hide, Thomas, 40
Hill, 23
Hill, James, 23, 33
Hiller, John, 171
Hinton, Thomas, 157
Hite, 5, 42, 45(2), 46, 47(2), 51, 63, 67, 70, 88, 129, 164
Hite, Abraham, 36, 42
Hite, Capt., 51, 75, 78, 79, 80, 82
Hite, Col., 89, 90(3), 91, 109, 125, 129, 152, 155, 164
Hite, Isaac, 93, 109, 134, 153, 156, 159
Hite, Jacob (and Gent. and Mr.), 4, 5, 6(3), 11, 13, 20, 21, 25, 27, 32, 38, 40, 41, 45, 47, 49, 62(2), 65, 66, 67, 70, 77, 85, 90, 97, 100(2), 102(2), 103, 105, 106, 107, 109, 110, 118, 119, 120, 128, 131, 133, 134, 135, 136, 137, 139, 146, 148, 160, 170
Hite, John/Jno. (and Capt. and Col. and Gent.), 4(2), 7, 8, 9, 10, 14, 16(2), 26, 27, 28, 29, 30, 32, 34, 36, 38, 44, 47, 50(2), 52(2), 53, 54, 64, 66, 67, 68, 73, 81, 89, 92, 93(2), 94, 96, 115, 120, 124, 132, 136(2), 145, 150(2), 156
Hite, Joseph, 24, 87
Hite, Mr., 64, 65, 66(2), 153
Hite, Wm., 40

Hobson, George, 5, 9, 36
Hobson, G_____, Jr., 25
Hockman, Christley, 161
Hodge, Jonas, 57
Hodgson, Robert, 71, 146
Hog, William, 8
Hogdon, Robert, 162
Hoge, George (and Gent.), 3, 25, 29, 68, 126, 145, 149, 151, 154
Hoge, James, 30, 48, 109, 134, 135
Hoge, the Rev. Mr., 171
Hoge, William, 149, 151
Hoge, William, Jr., 15(2), 24, 27(2)
Hogeland, 97
Hogeland, Jacobus/Cobus, 13, 21, 24(2)
Hogeland, John, 97
Hogg, Lewis, 7
Hogland, 77, 102, 106, 131, 147, 148
Hogland, Henry, 100
Hogland, John, 99, 100
Hogland, Richard, 99, 100
Holbrook, William, 84
Holdman, Daniel, 137, 138
Holdman, Jacob, 135, 137, 157, 159
Holliday, Samuel, 76
Hollingsworth, Abraham, 4, 5
Hollingsworth, George, 9, 17, 42, 66, 107(2), 121
Hollingsworth, Isaac/Isc., 38, 43, 50, 51(2), 52, 53
Holler, Peter, 159
Hollow, Peter, 157
Holman, 137
Holman, Daniel, 77, 78, 82, 85, 95, 149
Hood, Lucas, 143, 145, 148, 149
Hood, Rachell, 57
Hood, Tunis, 131(2), 149
Hoop, Casper, 165
Hooper, Thomas, 6, 32, 34
Hopkins, John, 43, 45
Hopkins, Samuel, 43
Hotsenpella, Stephen, 69, 71
Hotzenbella, Stephen, 38
Hough, William, 145
Houghland, 143, 145, 150, 156, 158
Houghland, John, 117, 145, 148
Hougland, 140, 157
Hougland, John, 140, 142
Howard, 149

Howard, John, 20, 23
Howel, 1, 29, 32, 37
Howell, 11, 32, 40, 56, 91, 92, 93, 108(2), 111, 122, 163
Huddle, George/Geo., 69, 85
Hulberger, Devault, 129
Hulls, Josiah, 139
Huls, Josiah, 49
Hulse, Josiah, 105
Hults, Josiah, 143
Humbart, Godfrey, 114
Humbert, Godfrey, 108
Hume, 121
Hume, Thomas, 117, 153
Humfrey, Ralph, 17
Hunter, Adam, 53, 57, 69, 71
Hurst, 159
Hurst, Henry, 86, 144(2)
Hurst, William, 87, 91
Hutchins, Robert, 144
Hysle, Hugh, 135
Ilor, Adolph, 81
Inglis, Melchiah, 113
Ireson, Richard, 38, 71
Irishman, Simon, 40
Isaac, 97, 113
Isaac, Elijah, 104
Isaacs, Elijah, 167, 169
Jack, James, 145
Jack, Jeremiah, 40, 61
Jackman, Richard, 149
Jackson, Josiah, 168
Jackson, Robert, 135, 140
Jay, 6(2)
Jayeas[?], Jonathan, 28
Jee, ffredk., 40
Jenkins, Aaron, 14(2), 16, 19
Job, Caleb, 84, 91
Johnson, Abraham/Abra:, 39, 69
Johnson, Isaac, 39, 125, 128, 138
Johnson, Zophar, 156
Johnston, 14, 17, 33, 53
Johnston, Capt., 53
Johnston, Daniel, 134, 135
Johnston, G., 37
Johnston, George/Geo. (and Gent. and Capt. and Mr.), 14, 15, 17, 18, 23, 33, 34, 46, 54, 70
Johnston, Isaac, Sr., 118

Johnston, Jefrey, 23
Johnston, William, 40
Johnstone, George (and Gent.), 11, 12
Joleff, William, 120
Jolliff, William, 84, 88, 89, 94, 143, 147
Jolliffe, 172
Jolliffe, Elizabeth, 154
Jolliffe, John, 170
Jolliffe, Mr., 158
Jolliffe, Widow, 155
Jolliffe, William, 89, 97, 98, 99, 125(2)
Jolliffe, William, Jr., 73, 93, 116
Jollyffe, William, 65
Jollyffe, William, Jr. 67
Jones, Evan, 157, 159
Jones, Gabriel/Gabl. (and Gent. and Mr.), 18(6), 19, 33, 35(4), 39, 42(2), 43, 44, 45, 46(2), 51, 52, 53(2), 64(2), 65, 66, 67(2), 68, 151
Jones, James, 121, 124(2), 150
Jones, John, 17, 29, 32, 36, 50, 81, 85, 104
Jones, Joseph, 97
Jones, Spencer, 8, 11
Jones, William, 66, 157
Jons, Spencer, 9
Joredon, Saml., 8
Julian, George, 68, 85, 96
Julian, Peter, 55, 60, 61, 68(2), 71(2), 79
Jump, George, 169
Jump, William, dec., 28
Jumpes, Wm., 12
Karney, Francis, 28
Kearfoot, William, 129, 159, 168, 172
Keith, 141, 142, 144
Keith, James, 139(2), 144
Keller, Abraham, 160
Keller, Charles, 40
Keller, George, 161
Kellor, 151
Kempes, James, 11
Kendrick, 146
Kendrick, Abraham, 134, 137, 158, 160
Kennedy, David, 140, 144
Kennedy, John, 153
Kersey, 4(2), 9(2), 14, 17, 19, 21, 23, 38, 41, 43(2), 49, 51, 65, 66(2), 68, 86
Kersey, John, 1, 37
Kersey, Patrick, 23
Kersey, William/Wm., 13, 14

Keye, 124
Keye, Humphrey, 114
Keyes, 118, 125, 127, 130, 137, 139, 163(3)
Keyes, Gersham/Gershom (and Gent.), 49, 53, 54, 111, 113
Keyes, Humphrey, 113, 125, 151, 155
Keykendal, John, 50, 52
Keykendal, Peter, 6
Keys, 49, 78, 80, 82, 83, 84(2), 122, 126
Keys, Gersham/Gershom/Gresham (and Gent. and Mr.), 49, 55, 56(2), 57, 60, 65, 68, 69, 72(2), 76, 79
Keys, Humphrey, 80, 82, 122, 124
Keywood, John, 161
King, James, 170
King, Joseph, 148, 156
Knight, James, 101, 129, 168, 170, 171
Kuykendal, Benjamin, 69
Kuykendal, John, 41, 69
Kuykendal, Peter, 1
Kuykendall, John, 62
Kyser, John, 160
Lahew, Isaac *[Note: See also Larew.]*, 119
Lambert, Christopher, 134, 139
Lang, Alexander, 164
Langdon, Jonathan, 116, 117
Langdon, Joseph, 29, 74, 84, 117
Larew, Isaac, 167
Larew, Jacob, 167
Larick, John, Jr., 104
Large, John, 40
Laubinger, George Michael, 114, 146
Leith, Ephram, 94(2)
Leith, George, 115
Lemen, James, 62
Lemen, Robert, 107(2)
Lemen, Thomas, 61
Lemon, 70
Lemon, James, 72, 86
Lemon, Robert, 56, 69, 70, 115
Lerew, Isaac, 123
Levingood, Harmon, 146
Lewis, 121, 157
Lewis, Col., 128
Lewis, David, 21, 40, 45, 127, 132
Lewis, David Sr., 31
Lewis, Fielding (and Col.), 100, 103, 125
Lewis, Jeremiah/Jeremh., 79, 81

Lewis, John, 79, 85, 86, 104
Lilbourn, Francis, 69, 76, 77
Lilbourne, Frances/Francis, 127, 132
Lilburn, Frances, 61
Lile, Hugh, 42
Lillburn, Francis, 155, 163
Lillburne, Francis, 156, 161
Linder, 53, 74, 75
Linder, Simon, 37
Lindsay, James, 118
Lindsay, John, 165
Lindsay, Thomas, 87(2)
Lindsey, Edmond, 119
Lindsey, Edmond, Jr., 107, 119, 123, 136
Lindsey, James, 109, 127, 134
Lindsey, John (and Gent. and Mr.), 47, 53, 59, 68, 77, 83(3), 84(3), 85, 98, 118, 125, 167
Lindsey, Thomas, 66, 113, 119, 122, 123, 139
Lindsey, Widow, 161
Linsey, John (and Gent.), 9, 10, 12, 20, 21, 22(2), 23, 28, 30
Linsey, Thomas/Thos., 22, 27
Lisher, John, 130
Litler, 117
Little, John, 150, 155, 157, 159
Little, Jonas, 77, 78
Little, Thomas (and Gent.), 29
Little, Widow, 47
Littler, 23, 36(3), 38, 40, 41(2), 47, 59(2), 61, 62, 68, 71, 73(2), 97, 98, 100, 101, 105(2), 107, 112, 118, 123, 125, 129, 138, 151, 159, 160, 164, 165, 170
Littler, James, 111
Littler, John, 1, 2, 3, 4(3), 5(2), 9, 11, 13, 20(2), 21, 27, 28, 29, 31, 32, 33, 154, 155
Littler, Samuel, 101(2), 107, 108, 129, 154, 164
Littler, Widow, 44
Lloyd, Henry, 136(2), 142, 144, 145, 162, 163
Lloyd, James, 136, 141, 143
Lloyd, Thomas, 136
Lockmiller, George, 29
Loftin, Thomas, 40
Logan, David, 30, 37
Long, Cristana, 39
Long, John Adam, 39
Long, Nicholas, 133
Long, Philip/Phillip, 72, 123
Longacre, Andrew/Andrw., 38, 71
L[or]dship, His *[Note: See Fairfax.]*
Loudeback, David, 151
Low, Thomas, 20, 46, 49, 51, 71(2), 75, 78

Lowder, Robert, 39
Lowe, Thomas, 24, 25
Loyd, 55
Loyd, David, 24, 38, 49
Loyd, Henry, 99, 111, 125, 126, 160
Loyd, Old, 37
Lucas, 119
Lucas, 92
Lucas, Edward, 62, 160
Lucus, Edward, 32
Luke, Peter, 155, 157, 160
Lupton, 168
Lupton, John, 144, 145, 146, 147, 149, 154(2), 155, 164
Lupton, Jonathan/Jonathon, 119, 125, 138, 148, 152
Lupton, Joseph, 123, 126
Lupton, William, 148
Lyle, Hugh, 103, 104, 137, 156, 162
Lyle, John, 156, 159
Lyles, John, 165
Lyndsey, John, 161
Lyndsey, Thomas, 161
Lysle, Hugh, 143, 147, 148, 150
Lynder, 116
McCarmack, John, 37
McCarty, Darby, 117, 153
McClunn, Thomas, 161, 164
McCool, John, 154
McCormack, 125, 164
McCormack, Dr., 46, 128, 139(2), 147
McCormack, Francis, 134
McCormack, James, 121, 128, 129, 139, 144
McCormack, John (and Mr.), 7(2), 20, 21, 22(2), 25, 27, 31(2), 46, 49, 54, 67, 83, 84(2), 87, 152
McCormack, Widow, 140
McCormack, William, 139
McCormick, 161
McCormick, John, 3, 14, 103, 105, 107(3)
McCoy, 28, 34, 44, 62, 73, 79, 80, 82, 113, 145
McCoy, James, 74, 77, 81
McCoy, Joseph, 159
McCoy, Moses, 74
McCoy, Robert/Robt., 2, 15, 18, 26, 27, 30, 35, 63, 113(2), 124
McCoy, Robert, Jr., 2, 8, 12
McDaniel, Alexander, 95
McDonald, Andrew, 156, 165
McDonald, Angus, 121, 141, 166
McDonald, John, 141, 142, 157, 170

McDowell, Joseph, 63, 70, 86(2), 94
McGill, James, 97, 119, 151, 158
McGrew, James, 25
McGuire, Edward, 108, 114, 166
McGuire, Thomas, 40
McIntire, Nicholas, 133
McKamie, John, 122, 127
McKamurs, John, 123
McKay, 55, 98, 101, 102, 104, 109, 122, 138
McKay, Andrew, 141
McKay, James, 159
McKay, Joseph, 153
McKay, Robert, 10, 16, 104, 109, 115, 138
McKay/ M^ckay, Robert/Robt., Jr., 2, 8, 9, 11, 28
McKeaver, Darby, 25
McKee, James, 22, 25, 130
McKee, William/Wm., 5, 7, 19, 27
McKenney, James, 79
McKever, Darby, 55
McKey, James, 127
McKoy, 37, 95
Mackoy, Robert, 92
McMachen, John, 103, 158
McMachen, William/Wm. (and Gent.), 9, 10, 11, 15, 17, 27, 94, 105, 121
McNish, 84, 100
McPherson, Daniel, 164
M^cpherson, Robert, 8
Madden, John, 18, 33, 34, 35, 36(2), 50
Mafuse, George, 159
Mandanhall, 101
Manfield, Joseph, 113
Marks, Thomas, 45, 47
Marks, William, 147
Marley, John, 27, 28
Marney, Robt., 53
Marques, Thomas, 67
Marquis, James, 142, 145
Marquis, Thomas, 78
Marquis, William, 142, 145
Marr, Christopher, 29, 32, 37(2), 52, 55, 77
Martin, Col., 87
Martin, James Green, 164
Martin, Thomas Bryan (and Gent. and Esq.), 56, 57, 61, 65, 71, 101, 113, 116, 130, 136
Mason, Thomas, 136, 162
Matterley, Mark, 50, 51
Matterly, Mark, 60, 71

Matthews, Patrick, 28
Mauk, 132, 133, 151, 161
Melton, John, 29, 33, 45, 47, 49
Melton, John, dec. 48(2), 51
Mendenal, John, 92
Mendenall, 78
Mendenhal, Mordecai, 29
Mendenhall, Mordacai/Mordecai, 19, 21
Mercer, Col., 128, 130
Mercer, Edward, 96(2), 102, 103, 117, 119
Mercer, George (and Col.), 108
Mercer, John (and Gent.), 72
Mercer, Nicholas/Nichs., 24, 37
Merchant, William, 132, 163
Merchants, William, 127
Meton [Melton], John, dec. 48
Milbourn, John 3, 54, 73(2), 88
Milbourn, Robert, 88
Milburn, John, 1, 20, 28, 29, 34
Millburn, Andrew, 161, 164
Millburn, John, 65, 66, 67
Millburne, Robert, 120
Miller, 74(2), 146, 160
Miller, Abraham, 96
Miller, David, 103, 104, 150, 156, 165
Miller, Jacob, 120
Miller, Jacob, dec., 125
Miller, James, 100, 101
Miller, John, 156
Miller, Peter, 71
Miller, William, 13, 14(2), 16, 41, 92, 93, 100, 101, 109, 141, 159, 160
Miller, William, Jr., 153
Mills, 111, 112(2), 116, 141
Mills, Henry, 36, 61, 65
Mills, John, 24, 56
Mitchel, William, 20, 24
Mitchell, 66
Mitchell, William 6, 18, 22, 25, 26, 30, 43, 46
Moody, 151(2)
Moon, Simon, 25
Moon, Jacob, 150, 156
Moor, Henry, 143
Moor, Reiley/Reily, 77, 78
Moore, Henry (and Gent.), 84, 90, 91, 92
Moore, Jacob, 122
Moore, John, 159

Moore, Lewis, 85, 88, 89, 110(2), 118
Morgan, 49, 54, 69, 76, 77, 84, 97, 105, 111, 138, 143, 147, 148
Morgan, Col., 43, 44, 71, 86, 105(2)
Morgan, Daniel, 128, 133, 140, 153, 171(2)
Morgan, David, 166
Morgan, Ezekiel, 117, 121
Morgan, Jacob, 124(2)
Morgan, John, 112
Morgan, Morgan, (and Col. and Gent.), 9, 17, 24, 25, 30, 32, 40, 71, 79, 103, 115, 116, 117(2), 146, 157, 158
Morgan, Morgan. Jr., 115, 117
Morgan, Richard (and Capt.), 4, 62, 70, 102
Morgan, Thomas, 7
Morgan, William, 97, 107, 119, 124(2), 133, 147, 163
Morgan, Zacquel/Zac'quell/Zacquell/Zacquil, 97, 110(2), 111(2), 112
Morrice, John, 81
Morris, Benjamin, 170
Morris, Daniel, 163
Morris, John, 22, 27, 30
Morris, Joseph, 113, 148
Morris, Samuel, 12, 20[?], 25, 27, 161, 169
Morrison, James, 156
Morrison, Nathaniel, 161, 163, 165
Morriss, James, 100
Moseley, Robert/Robt.(and Mr.), 68, 86, 88, 90, 93
Mosely, Robert, 66(2), 89
Mount, Samuel, 71, 128, 136
Mounts, Samuel, 134, 139, 140, 141
Murphey, Darby, 9
Musgrove, Edward, 38, 39, 49
Myles, George, 102, 117, 140, 142, 145, 148
Nash, Enoch, 111, 112
Nation, 42, 45, 51(3), 58, 64(2), 92, 96, 101, 114, 130, 136, 140, 144, 145, 166
Nation, Christopher, 11
Nation, John, 9(2), 11, 27, 30, 36, 47, 51, 58
Naylor, William, 25
Neal, Lewis, 43
Nealan[d], John, 9, 10
Neavill, 156
Neavill, John, 125, 137, 155
Neavill, Joseph, 121
Neeland, John, 10
Neil, John, 3, 4, 66
Neil, Lewis (and Gent.), 14, 158
Neill, 80, 82
Neill, Capt., 100, 107

Neill, John (and Gent.), 3, 7, 17, 19, 27, 33, 39
Neill, John, dec., 48, 53, 106
Neill, Lewis, (and Capt. and Gent. and Mr.), 12(2), 13, 20, 21, 22(2), 23(3), 29, 30, 31, 34, 35, 36, 48, 59(2), 67, 73(3), 83, 86, 88, 94, 98, 101, 102, 103, 104, 110, 119(3), 120, 123(2), 151, 158, 159, 160, 164, 170
Neill, William, 100, 101, 107, 120, 123
Neilly, George, 124
Niell, Lewis, 81
Nelson, Henry, 74, 151
Nelson, William, 159
Netherton, Henry, 159
Netherton, Thomas, 109
Nevill, 163, 165
Nevill, John, 95, 161, 166, 167
Newkird, Henry, 131
Newkirk, Barnet, 77, 99
Newkirk, Henry *[Note: See also Newkird.]*, 106, 131, 140, 142, 145, 148, 149
Newman, John, 137
Newman, Samuel, 93, 97, 102, 123
Newport, John, 10
Newton, John, 43
Newton, Joseph, 43
Nicewanger, Jacob, 15
Nicholls, George, 85
Nicholas, John, 158
Nisenwanger, Jacob, 50
Nisewanger, Abraham, 129
Nisewanger, Jacob, 19, 42, 45, 51(2), 61, 65, 71(2)
Nisewanger, John, 86, 137
Nisewanger, John, Jr., 167, 169
Niswanger, John, 7
North, John, 92
Nowland, Andrew, 39
Odell, Caleb, 85, 104
Odell, Elijah, 127, 133
Oiler, Mark, 137
Oldrages, John, 6
Onan, 141
O'Neal, Daniel, 39
Oney, Benjamin, 145
Osborn, Jonathon, 144
Osborne, Jonathon, 143
Osbourn, Nicholas, 48, 53, 71
Osburn, Jonathan, 132
Pain, Adam, 70
Painter, John, 6, 11, 13, 75, 92, 101, 113(2), 115

Painter, John, Sr., 138
Painter, John, Jr., 141
Painter, Robert, 141
Parker, 41
Parker, Benjamin, 39
Parker, George, 39, 40, 46
Parker, George Jr., 39
Parker, John, 40, 153
Parker, Thomas, 62(2), 68
Parkins, 72, 98
Parkins, Mr., 88
Parkins, Charles, 56
Parkins, Isaac (and Gent.), 50, 56, 64(2), 65(2), 66, 67(2)
Parks, 25
Parks, John, 25, 103, 104, 106, 148, 159
Parlour, Shadraik, 106
Parrel, Hugh, 4, 25, 49
Parrell, Hugh, 31
Parrell, John, 119, 120, 121, 123, 124
Parrell, Joseph, 119, 120, 121, 161
Patterson, 6, 16, 40, 41, 46, 63(3), 156
Patterson, William, 101, 110, 159
Patton, James, 39
Patton, Samuel, 73
Paul, George, 140
Paul, Hugh, 19, 21, 26, 31, 42, 43,
Paul, Hugh, dec., 49
Paul, Robert, 106
Paul, Widow, 49, 105
Pearall, Job, 39
Pearis, Capt. 102
Pearis, Richard, 110(2), 112(2), 124, 125, 141, 142, 148(2)
Pearis, Robert, 62(2), 66, 77, 80, 111, 119
Pearsall, Job, 39, 48
Pearsal, Job, 46
Pearson, 10
Pearson, Elizabeth, 10
Pearson, Enoch, 10, 26, 35, 44, 56, 78, 81
Pearson, James, 134
Pearson, Samuel, 79, 100, 102, 136
Peck, Jacob, 6
Pedinger, Henry *[Note: See also Bedinger.]*, 119, 122, 126
Pemberton, George, 46, 100
Pemberton, Isaiah, 136
Pence, Lewis, 129
Pences, Jacob, 123

Penington, Isaac, 12, 22, 33, 40, 41
Penington, Jacob, 14, 22, 25
Pennewith, 94
Pennington, 66
Pennington, Isaac, 21, 46
Perkins, 14, 171
Perkins, Isaac (and Gent.), 3, 4, 5(2), 12, 16, 17, 19, 20, 33, 35, 38, 39, 147, 149(2), 151, 154
Perkins, Isaac, Jr., 145, 146
Perkins, Mr., 64
Perrill, Hugh, 20
Perrie, 115
Perry, 119, 124
Perry, Thomas, 114, 115, 120, 121, 123, 124
Peteat, John, 22
Peterson, Peter, 40
Petite, John, 21
Phipps, Benjamin, 3
Pickering, William, 151
Pierce, Hugh, 30
Pierceful, Richard, 9
Pike, Michael (and Gent. and Mr.), 59, 76, 83, 84, 86, 87
Pikering, William, 126
Pilcher, Stephen, 59, 67
Pitman, Nicholas, 167, 169
Pitts, 7, 28
Poker, Michael, 53
Porterfeild, William, 133(2), 145
Postgate, Thomas/Thos. 6, 8(3), 10, 11(2), 12, 13(2)
Poulson, Richd., 43
Potts, George, 25, 61(2), 68
Powel, 127
Powell, 96, 104, 133
Powell, Joseph, 90
Prichard, Samuel, 64, 66, 67
Prince, John, 101(2), 102, 108, 113, 116, 122, 124
Pritchard, Samuel, 39, 67, 69, 71, 76, 89, 97(2), 143
Pritchet, 97
Provan, John, 110
Provan, Thomas, 110(3)
Provin, Thomas/Thos., 28, 44
Province, John, 126
Province, Thomas/Thos., 1, 2
Pugh, 126, 151
Pugh, Asariah, 111
Pugh, Jesse/Jessee, 132, 149, 151, 154(3)
Pugh, Job, 148, 151

Pugh, Joseph, 114, 154
Pugh, Mr., 111, 116
Pyke, Mr., 136
Quintin, 58
Quintin, William, 55, 56, 58
Quinton, 78
Quinton, William, 83, 84, 92
Racklies, Jacob, 47
Radden, John, 39
Rain, John, 13
Rainey, James, 75
Raisner, Nicholas, 39, 40
Ramor, William, 11
Rankin, Benjamine, 130
Rankin, David, 112
Rankin, William, 40, 44, 126(2), 129, 157
Ranking, William, 45
Rankins, David, Jr., 126(2)
Rankins, William, 39, 41, 112
Rawlings, Stephen, 110
Read, John, 9
Reece, Thomas, 5, 19, 86
Reed, Edward, 168, 170, 171
Reed, John, 125, 129, 147
Reed, Widow, 44
Rees, John, 147
Rees, Thomas/Thos., 15, 18, 105, 111, 148, 166
Rees, Thomas, Jr., 105
Reese, John, 125, 128
Reese, Henry, 138
Reeth, Edward, 40
Reiley, Patrick, 49, 71
Reily, Patrick, 54
Remy, William, 6, 11
Rennolds, William, 15
Reno, John, 80, 85(2), 95, 106
Rentfro, William, 28
Rentfroe, William/Wm., 8, 16
Reynolds, William, 68, 89, 90, 95, 96, 121
Rice, Edmond/Edmund, 139, 141
Rice, George, 121, 139(2), 141, 161(2)
Rice, John, 161
Rice, Patrick, 20, 23, 107(2), 119
Rice, Simeon, 69, 82, 113
Rice, Simeon, dec., 99
Richards, Henry, 150, 156

Richardson, Abraham, 39
Richardson, Benjamin, 76
Richey, William, 52, 54, 56, 75
Riddle, George, 135, 153, 165
Ridgway, Josiah, 85, 89
Ridgway, Lott, 165
Rief, Jacob, 116
Rinker, Casper/Gasper, 149, 158
Rinker, Henry, 95
Rinker, Jacob, 138, 159
Rion, John, 39
Robbins, Joseph, 57
Roberts, Joseph, 51, 58, 64, 86, 168, 170
Roberts, William, 17, 21, 38, 85(2), 95, 102, 139
Roberts, William, Sr., 98, 101
Robins, Joseph, 59
Robinson, 4, 24, 54
Robinson, Edward/Edwd., 14, 19, 21, 88
Robinson, Israel (and Gent.), 3, 14, 19, 21, 28, 42, 43
Robinson, James, 103, 104, 112, 153
Robinson, Joseph, 40
Robinson, Thomas, 89, 104, 112, 116
Robinson, William, 141, 144
Rogers, Bagman, 40
Rogers, Edward, 1, 2, 6, 38, 47, 51(2), 55, 95, 98, 101, 102, 122, 145
Rogers, Evan 45, 126
Rogers, John, 55, 172
Rogers, Matthew, 40
Rogers, Owen, 60, 61, 96
Rose, Daniel, 26
Rose, Jonathon, 143(2)
Ross, 45, 61, 70, 91
Ross, Alexander, 17, 21, 31, 156, 158
Ross, Alexander, dec., 32, 38
Ross, ffrancis, 40
Ross, George, 36, 41, 66, 71
Ross, James, 40
Ross, John, 4, 5, 40
Ross, Stephen, 166
Rout, John 6, 156, 157, 160
Rout, John, Sr., 76
Routt, John, 110
Ruble, George, 143, 147, 148, 170
Ruble, Peter, 89, 97, 111(2)
Ruckner, Peter, 72
Ruddell, Isaac, 90, 100

Ruddell, Cornelius, 95
Ruddle, Cornelius, 74, 85, 91
Ruddull, George, 137
Rufner, Benjamin, 132
Rufner, Peter, 93, 108
Rumsey, Thomas, 40
Rush, Jacob, 127, 133
Rush, Leonard, 156
Russell, William, 53, 104, 117
Rutherford, Benjamin, 49, 69, 98, 119, 159
Rutherford, Capt., 46, 87
Rutherford, Mr., 49
Rutherford, Reuben/Reubin, 38, 39, 80, 81
Rutherford, Robert, 107, 114
Rutherford, Thomas/Tho: (and Gent.), 3, 4, 5, 6(2), 7, 12, 14, 24(2), 38, 49(2), 68, 72, 120, 122, 136, 147, 152, 168
Rutherford, Thomas, dec., 107
Ryley, Patrick, 1, 27, 40
Sadin, James, 11
Saveir, John, 123
Scot, 5, 7, 11, 14
Scott, 7
Seabern, James, 6
Seabin, 32
Seabin, James, 34
Seaborn, 157
Seaburn, 108, 118
Seaburn, James, 109
Seale, William (and Mr.), 81
Seaman, Jonah, 141, 155, 156, 161, 166
Seaman, Jonas, 84, 105
Seaman, Jonathan, 105, 131, 141
Seamon, Jonathan/Jonathon, 120
Sears, Jams., 53
Seaton, James, 157
Seaton, Joseph, 158
Sebastian, 83, 84
Seller, George, 29, 111, 116
Sellers, George, 104
Selser, 72(2), 94, 102
Selser, Matthias, 72
Selser, Matthias, dec., 119
Semple, 141, 144, 145, 147, 152
Sexton, 163
Sexton, George, 127, 138
Sexton, Meshack, 167, 168

Sharrobz, Peter, 161
Sharp, Thomas/Thos., 8, 29, 46, 112
Sharp, Thomas, Sr., 11
Sharp, Thomas, Jr., 11
Sharpe, Thomas, 116
Sharpe, Thomas, Sr., 102
Shearer, John, 13, 47, 56(2), 57, 94
Shely, John, 130
Shepard, John, 3
Shepard, Thomas, 4, 5, 16, 76, 85
Shepherd, 108, 115(2), 163
Shepherd, David, 115
Shepherd, Thomas, 32, 97, 102, 119
Shepherd, William, 52, 53, 56, 57, 137
Sheppard, 7, 47
Sheppard, John, 7, 13
Sheppard, Thomas, 6
Sheppard, William, 47
Shinn, Samuel, 30
Shipley, Peter, 119
Shirley, James, 136
Shirley, Walter, 79, 82
Shirly, James, 136
Shunaman, George, 58
Simmons, Jonathan, 119
Simmons, Samuel, 1
Sinclair[e], John/Sir John (also Sir John [no surname]), 95, 96(3), 97(2), 102, 111, 112, 113, 116,
    119, 121(2), 127, 132, 135, 138, 140(2), 142, 152
Sink, 138
Sink, Cutlip, 133
Sively, Joseph, 137
Siver, Barnet, 104
Skean, John, 85, 90(2), 95
Skeane, John (and Gent.), 93, 94
Skeen, John (and Gent.), 97
Slaughter, Francis, 151, 161
Smith, 21(2), 40, 41, 70, 91(2), 94, 98, 137(2)
Smith, Benjamin, 17, 56
Smith, Capt., 104
Smith, Charles (and Gent.), 100, 118, 120, 122, 125, 169
Smith, Gerard/Gerrard, 120, 122
Smith, Jeremiah (and Capt.), 8, 24, 54, 55, 62(2), 71(2), 75, 77, 80, 104, 105, 106, 132, 151,
    154(2), 170
Smith, John, 32, 38, 49, 50, 61, 62, 94, 106, 112, 121, 126, 128, 129, 134
Smith, John, dec., 5
Smith, Joseph, 30, 36

Smith, Matthew, 145
Smith, Samuel, 154
Smith, Thomas, 25
Smith, William/Willm., 8, 11, 43
Snap, John, 38, 130
Snap, John, Jr., 38, 90, 93
Snap, John, Sr., 90, 93
Snap, Lawrence, 54, 93, 95
Snapp, 161
Snapp, _____ , 17
Snapp, John, 96, 130, 171
Snapp, Laurence/Lawrence, 103, 113, 125, 137, 140, 161
Snickers, 88, 89, 104, 128, 130, 132, 135, 164, 167, 169, 170
Snickers, Edward, 71, 73, 106(2), 108, 113, 134, 135, 164, 167, 169
Snigers, 78, 81
Sniggers, 134, 144
Snigers, Edward, 72(2), 74, 76, 77, 83(2)
Sniggers, Edward, 50(2), 59
Snodgrass, David, 153
Sobinger, Woolrick, 146, 148
Southard, Benjamin, 108
Speake, Thomas (and Gent.), 83, 84(2), 85, 98, 103, 134, 135
Speakes, Thomas, 121
Spears, Capt., 109
Spears, Henry, 75, 93, 94, 96, 134, 148
Spears, John, 145
Spenceley, John, 151, 155
Spencer, Francis, 43
Sperry, Nicholas, 156, 159
Sperry, Thomas *[Note: See also Perry.]*, 120
Spickard, Julius, 170
Spoar, John, 161
Spore, John, 165
Springer, David, 3
Springer, Dennis, 44
Springer, Dennis, dec., 166
Springer, Josias, 112, 116
Springer, Levi/Levy, 141, 144
Springer, Zadock/Zadok, 131(2), 138, 141, 144, 163
Stanly, Isaac, 141
Steer, Joseph, 141, 142
Steerly, Jacob, 170
Stepenson, Richard, 135
Stephen, Adam (and Gent.), 120
Stephens, 85, 86, 104, 117, 164
Stephens, Col., 161, 162(4), 165(2)

Stephens, Lawrence, 8, 26(2), 32, 46, 82, 91
Stephens, Lewis (and Gent. and Maj.), 17, 29, 30, 35(2), 37, 39, 42(2), 44, 47, 53, 79, 87, 89, 96, 98, 99, 104, 109, 118, 129, 142, 146, 169
Stephens, Peter, 86, 114
Stephens, Richard, 116
Stephenson, Hugh, 139, 144(2)
Stephenson, Richard, 49, 105
Stephenson, William, 29
Stevens, 57, 63, 77, 79, 82
Stevens, Henry, 87
Stevens, Lawrence, 70, 87
Stevens, Lewis (and Gent. and Capt.), 61, 64(2), 65(2), 66(2), 68(2), 69, 71, 76, 78, 81, 82, 88
Stevens, Peter, 61, 65
Stevens, William, 48(2)
Stevenson, James, 59
Stevenson, Richard/Richd., 24, 37, 53, 54, 56(2), 57, 65, 78
Stevenson, William, 47, 48
Steward, Robert, 91, 94
Stewart, Robert, 89, 96, 98
Stickley, Christian, 79, 138
Stinson, James, 57, 75, 101
Stinson, Richard, 3, 103
Stocton, Robert, 162
Stockdon, Robert, Sr., 112
Stogdon, Robert, 110, 112, 124(2)
Stomp, Adam, 39
Stone, Ulrick, 85, 93
Stoufer, Peter, 92, 102
Stover, 115
Stover, Daniel, 132, 133
Stover, Peter, 79, 155
Stribling, 42, 51
Stribling, Capt., 10
Stribling, Taliaferro/Talliaferro/Toliafero, 108, 134, 135, 152, 164, 170
Strickler, Benjamin, 151
Strickler, Joseph, 132, 133
Stripling, William, 31
Stroad, James, 135
Stroad, Jeremiah, 131
Stroade, James, 137
Stroade, Jeremiah, 131, 133
Stroade, Edward, 131
Strode, Edward, 25, 162
Strode, James, 143, 149, 152, 159, 162, 164
Strode, Jeremiah, 133, 134, 162

Strode, John, 161, 165
Stroop, William, 80
Stroud, Edward, 25
Stroud, James, 69, 75, 78, 100, 103
Stroud, Jeremiah, 92
Stroud, Samuel, 70, 75, 81
Sturges, Daniel (and Gent.), 137
Sturman, 50,
Sturman, John (and Mr.), 31, 33(3), 36, 42, 52, 60(2)
Sturman, Mr., 51
Sturman, Richard, 42, 50, 51, 85
Subinger, Woolrick/Wolrick, 164, 165
Sullivan, Gilles, 39
Sutherland, 144
Sutten, Jasper, 40
Sutton, 115
Sutton, Abraham, 141, 144
Swearangen, 85
Swearengen, 70
Swearengen, Van (and Gent.), 47, 92
Swearengen, Thomas (and Gent.), 74, 84
Swearingen, 97, 100, 102, 107, 108, 109, 113, 145, 148
Swearingen, Andrew, 140, 142
Swearingen, Mr., 62
Swearingen, Thomas (and Gent.), 26, 102, 119, 124
Swearingen, Van, 133, 140, 142, 145
Swearingen, Van, Jr., 124
Swearingham, Thomas (and Gent.), 5, 16
Swift, Godwin, 144, 145
Swim, John, 49
Tapp, William, 92
Tate, John, 162, 165
Tate, Magnes/Magness/Magnus, 125, 130, 139, 163
Tates, Magnes, 127
Tayler, John, 163
Tayler, Jonathan/Jonathon, 120, 147
Tayler, Samuel, 163
Taylor, Benjamin, 160, 170
Taylor, Edmund, 167, 168, 169
Taylor, Harrison, 171
Taylor, John, 132, 147, 148
Taylor, Jonathan/Jonathon, 71, 105
Taylor, Samuel, 147
Taylor, Simeon, 20, 25(2)
Teague, Abraham, 85
Teague, Edward, 70

Tebalt, George, 40
Teebolt, Michael, 40
Teeter, Jacob, 2(2)
Tegurden, Abra:, 39
Telener, George 2
Thomas, Edward, 5, 6, 21, 62, 79, 84, 90, 94, 106, 112, 128, 133
Thomas, Ellis, 47
Thomas, Evan, 84, 89
Thomas, Isaac, 1, 96
Thomas, John, 45, 47, 61, 71, 154(2)
Thomas, Owen, 8, 24, 139, 144
Thomas, Nathaniel, 79
Thompson, Charles, 115
Thorn, 84, 106, 108, 115, 123, 151
Thornberry, Benjamin, 141(2), 144, 159, 162, 165
Thornberry, Thomas, 116, 117, 162
Thornbrough, Benjamin, 150
Thornbrough, Thomas, 143
Thornbrugh, Benjamin, 156(2)
Thornbrugh, Thomas, 162
Thornbury, Thomas, 25
Thornton, 129
Thornton, Thomas, 8
Thorntown, Thomas, 11
Throckmorton, Robert, 170
Thruston, Mr., 167
Thorp, Zebulon, 80
Tidwell, 134
Tidwell, William, 2
Tilleroy, Andrew, 136(2)
Tillery, Andrew, 126
Timmons, John, 57, 91, 92(2), 108, 163
Timmons, Samuel, 41, 43(2)
Tipton, John, 161
Tomson, David, 39
Tomson, Frank, 39
Tostee, 61
Tostee, Peter, 61, 62, 63, 67, 69, 73, 80
Tostie, Peter, 52
Tuckerman, John, 71
Tunis, 140, 142
Turner, Anthony, 82, 92
Turner, Anthony, dec., 115
Turner, Thomas, 140
Tyler, Edward, 140, 142
Tyler, John, 114

Undergrest, George, 40
Valentine, Zachariah, 44, 49
Vance, Alexander, 118
Vance, David (and Gent. and Mr.), 4, 7, 9, 65, 68
Vance, George, 168
Vance, James, 30, 42
Vance, John, 139, 144
Vance, Joseph, 79, 86(2)
Vance, Samuel, 17, 30, 35, 71, 168, 169
Vance, William, 30
Vandeveir, William, 139
Vandevere, William, 151
Vanmeter, Abraham, 75
Vanmeter/Van Meter, Henry, 63, 110, 112
Vanmeter, Jacob, 65, 76
Vanmetre, Abraham, 37, 135, 137, 152
Vanmetre, Henry, 8, 39, 41, 149, 152, 162
Vanmetre, Jacob, 116, 117, 124, 133, 149
Vanmetre, John, 161, 165
Vecory, Marmaduke, 8
Vestal, 3, 19, 25, 26, 35, 38, 44, 47, 49(2), 50, 53, 54, 56, 69, 76, 81, 83, 84, 100, 102, 115, 121, 139, 142, 167
Vestal, John, 52, 72, 81, 83, 155
Vestal, William, 3, 9, 10
Vestall, 60, 136, 144, 163(2), 164
Vestall, John, 134, 139, 142, 151
Vickory, Marmaduke, 9, 11
Violet, Edward, 136
Violett, Edward, 130
Wadlington, Thomas, 79, 82, 83(3), 86, 87, 88
Wager, Archibald, 114, 116
Walker, 7
Walker, Abel, 166
Walker, Mordecai, 147, 150
Walker, Jonathan, 10
Walton, Moses, 134, 136
Warden, William, 3
Ware, James, 171
Warf, Robert, 15
Warner, Adam, 39
Warren, William, 148
Warth, George, 159
Warth, Robert/Robt., 7, 18, 30(3), 37, 63(2)
Washington, Warner, 167
Waters, Thomas/Thos., 21, 35, 36, 50, 57, 85(2), 86, 95
Waters, Thomas, dec. 96

Watkins, 28, 40(2), 47, 56(2), 57, 61, 65, 70, 73, 77, 78, 85, 100, 103, 104, 112, 133, 161, 162, 164, 166
Watkins, Evan, 13, 99
Watson, David, 147
Watson, John, 115, 117, 146
Watson, John, Jr., 149
Watson, Joseph, 150, 153, 170
Watt, Robert, 162
Watts, 70
Wattson, Joseph, 155
Weathers, Ralph, 8, 14
Wells, Dr., 125, 128(2)
Wells, Humphrey, 125(2), 128, 142, 155
Westall, 14
Whison, Jon, 116
White, 91, 166(2)
White, Isaac, 29
White, John, 154
White, Michael, 47
White, Robert, 104, 106, 147, 149, 151, 154, 155
White, Thomas, 151, 160
White, William/Wm., 29, 77, 78, 82, 95
Whitson, William, 74
Widell, Christopher [Note: See also Windel, etc.], 116
Wilcox, John, 1, 2(2)
Wilcox, John, dec., 31
Willf, Jacob, 40
Wilkinson, Joseph, 12, 121, 126, 171
Willett, Edward, 127
Williams, 12, 33, 52, 59, 76, 83, 85, 86, 87
Williams, George, 168
Williams, James, 39
Williams, Joseph, 56, 57
Williams, Providence, 43
Williams, Vincent, 39
Williams, William, 56
Willson, James, 168, 169
Willson, Robert, 124, 126
Willson, Samuel, 156
Wilson, John, 24, 52, 54
Wilson, Robert, 5, 12
Wilson, Samuel, 130
Wilson, William, 29
Windel, Christopher [Note: See also Widell.], 116
Windle, Augustine, 47
Windle, Christopher, 111, 157

Wingfield, Owen/Owin, 100, 103, 107, 119
Wingfield, Thomas, 167
Winkfield, Thomas, 167
Windle, Christopher, 64, 69
Wisecarver, John, 146, 148
Wiseman, Abraham, 39
Wiseman, Rodolph, 53
Withers, Ralph, 11, 16, 28, 32, 42, 73, 75, 108, 116, 138, 141, 145
Wodron, Alexander, 100
Wolf, Peter, 83, 84
Wolfe, Lewis, 139
Wolfe, Peter, 116, 133
Wolfenberger, John, 160
Wood, 102
Wood, Jame/James (and Gent.), 15(2), 27(2), 67, 68, 120, 122
Wood, James, dec., 146
Wood, John, 1, 2, 37, 40
Wood, Mary, 168
Wood, Robert, 148, 154(3), 155
Wood, Widow, 57
Wood, William, 118
Woolf, Peter, 9, 27, 37, 108
Wormley, 50
Wormley, Mr., 167(2), 169
Wormley, Ralph, Esq., 164
Worth, John, 156
Worthington, 49, 84(2), 87, 100, 102, 103, 163
Worthington, Robert/Robt., 49, 50, 52
Worthington, Robert, Jr., 118, 127, 134
Worthington, Samuel, 134, 136
Wright, 86, 169
Wright, David, 120, 168(2), 169
Wright, George/Geo., 66, 73, 79, 120
Wright, George, Sr., 88
Wright, James, 116
Wright, John, 148
Yoakam, Matthias, 6
Yoakham, Matthias, 8
Young, Edwin, 159, 165
Young, James, 29
Young, John, 30
Young, Matthew, 29
Zane, Isaac, 142, 143, 144(2), 145, 146, 156, 164, 165, 167, 169
Zane, Isaac, Jr., 150

Rivers, Runs, Springs, Creeks, and other Water Features
Abrahams Run, 39
(Benjamin) Allan's/Allen's/Allin's Mill Creek, 74(2), 85, 99
Ashbys Bent Branch, 1, 2
Babbs Creek, 68(2)
Spring by the road between William Reynolds's and Thomas Babb, Jr.'s plantations, 96
Back Creek, 42, 81, 103, 104, 134, 141, 153, 166, 167
Borden's/Burden's (Great) Spring *[Note: See also Burden's Marsh; Burden's Run.]*, 26, 27, 37, 55(2), 58
The Branch, 63
Bruce's/Bruise's Mill Run, 118, 125, 147
Buck Marsh/Buck's Marsh, 142, 170
Buckles's Marsh, 80
Buffaloe Run, 131, 138, 149
Bufflaoe Lick/Buffler Lick, 3, 167
The head spring of Bulskin, 140
Bulskin/Bullskin [Run]/Bullskin Marsh, 3, 7(2), 10, 24, 25, 31(2), 66(2), 77, 98, 107, 109(2), 123, 126(2), 128, 130(2), 136(2), 139, 152, 154, 155, 162
South fork of Bulskin, 22, 25
Burden's Marsh *[Note: See also Borden's/Burden's Great Spring.]*, 56
Burden's Run, 84
James Burner's Run, 153
Cabbin Run, 29, 32
Calebs Run, 73, 74, 75 *[Note: See also Caleb Job's Run.]*
Cape Capon Water, 25
Great Cape Capon, 1, 6, 8
North Branch/North River of Cape Capon/Cacapon/Great Cacapon, 3, 41, 48
Carney's Pond, 73
Carney's Spring, 82, 83, 100, 104, 136
Cedar Creek/Ceder Creek/Ceeder Creek/Ceeder Creek Run, 2(2), 15, 17, 26, 35(2), 42, 44, 48, 63(2), 70, 86, 102, 118, 124, 129(2), 137, 142, 144, 168
The spring by the Chapel, 1, 4
Cherry's Run, 149
(Jacob) Christman's/Crisman's/Cristman's Spring, 34, 70(2), 82, 86, 90, 91, 125, 129, 137, 170
Connigocheague [Creek], 112
Crooked Run, 8, 9, 10(2), 11, 16, 26, 29, 54, 63(2), 68, 75, 80, 81, 108, 110, 158(2)
Dellings Run, 25
Dry Marsh, 98, 155, 157, 160, 161, 170
The Dry Run, 114, 129, 132
Earl's Mill Run, 122
[Mathias] Elmor[e]s Creek, 3
Elk Branch, 143
The Falling Springs, 60(2)
The falling water, 40
The Fork, 134
Funk's Mill Creek/Funk's Mill Run, 64(2), 69, 85(2), 93

Fussey's/Peter Fussey's Big Spring/Large Spring, 133(2)
Goony Run, 153
Happy Creek, 52, 146
Hawk's Bill (Creek), 77, 128
George Henry's Spring, 153
Hill's Marsh, 23
William Hite's Spring, 40
Hog/Hog's/Hoge/Hoge's Creek, 80(2), 105, 111, 119, 121, 125, 126, 147, 148, 149(2), 151, 154(2), 155
Isaac Hollingsworth's mill race, 52
Holman's Creek, 137
The Horse Ponds, 134
Horse pond(s) in Dr. McCormick's road, 125, 128
The drafts of the Indian Run, 32
Melchiah Inglis's Branch, 113
Isaac's Creek, 97, 113, 148
Jeremiah's Run, 106(2)
Caleb Job's Run, 91
Johnston Run, 31
Jumping Run, 153, 159
Kate's Spring, 167
Lick Branch, 116
Littler's Branch/Littler's Run/the Run at Littler's, 97, 98, 151, 160, 170
John Littler's Mill Run, 29
Samuel Littler's Run, 108
Mr. George Johnston's Long Marsh, 54
The Long Marsh/Long Marsh Run, 22(2), 25, 26, 33, 35, 44, 49, 60(2), 77, 98, 107, 121, 139, 141, 165, 167
Lucas's Marsh, 92
Robert McCoy's Run, 35
(Robert) McCoy's/McKay's Spring(s), 16, 26, 27, 28, 30, 34
McNishes Run, 84, 100
Magneturs Run, 120
The Run in Main Street, 166
Manasses Run (Manaseh's/Manasseh's/Manassers/Manasses's/Mannassip's/Manassits/ Manassus/Menasses Run), 1, 2, 10, 31, 34, 40, 43, 44, 55, 70, 109, 110, 111; 156
Mandanhall's Mill Run, 101
Creek near Marlborough forge, 165
Messanuting Run, 93
Middle Creek, 24, 29, 56
Mill Creek/Mills Creek/Mill Run, 5, 24, 28, 36, 61(2), 76, 85, 90, 97, 102(2), 135, 140(2), 141, 148, 159
Moody's Run, 151(2)
Mountain Run, 144
The Narrow Passage [Creek], 77, 79, 95, 104, 131, 159
Run at John Nation's house/John Nation's Run/Nation's Run, 9, 30, 36, 42, 45, 51, 64(2)

The North Branch, 62
The North River, 2, 50, 54, 62(2), 69, 78, 79, 81, 86, 94, 103, 120, 137, 146, 147, 148, 149, 153, 158, 159
Opecken Creek/Opecken River/Opecken/Opeken/Opeckon/Oppecan, 3(2), 4, 5(3), 12, 13, 20, 22, 23, 24(2), 25, 28, 29, 30, 31(3), 33, 34(2), 35, 36(3), 41, 43, 45, 47, 48, 49, 50(3), 51, 53, 54(2), 56, 57, 58, 59(3), 65, 66, 67(2), 69(2), 70(3), 71(2), 73(2), 75(2), 78(2), 79, 80, 81, 82, 83, 84(2), 86(3), 87(3), 88(2), 90, 91, 92, 94(2), 96, 98(4), 99, 100(2), 101(2), 105(2), 107(2), 110(2), 112, 115, 116, 117(2), 120, 123(2), 125, 126, 127, 129(2), 130, 131(3), 132(2), 133(2), 136, 140, 142, 143(2), 144, 147(2), 155, 158, 159, 162(2), 164, 167, 168, 169, 170, 171(3), 172
Pasage/Passage Creek *[Note: See also Narrow Passage Creek.]*, 85, 147, 158, 159
Patterson's Creek, 6, 16, 39, 40, 41, 46, 63(3)
The north branch of Pembroke, 118, 129(2)
Pennewith's Mill Creek, 94
Pennington's Marsh, 66(2)
Percimmon Pond, 74, 75
Pitts's Marsh, 7, 28
Potomack River [Potomac], 7, 12, 21, 24, 38, 60(2), 75, 80, 107, 126
South Branch of Potomack, 43, 60
Rappahannock [River], 3
Spring by the road between William Reynolds's and Thomas Babb, Jr.'s plantations, 96
The River, 2, 17, 26, 28, 32(2), 50, 58(2), 59(2), 72, 78(2), 79, 81, 83(2), 87, 91(2), 93, 94, 106, 112, 114(2), 135, 137(2), 139, 148, 150, 155, 165
The Riverside, 88, 89
The Run, 170
Thomas Rutherford's Spring, 24
Selser's Mill Run, 72(2), 94, 102
Shenandoah River (Shanando/Shanandoah/Shannandah/Shannando/Shannadore/Sharando/Sharrando/Sherrando), 1, 5, 7, 9, 10, 12(2), 15, 25, 29, 35, 37, 40, 43(2), 45, 47, 48, 49(2), 51(2), 52, 55, 57(2), 72(5), 73, 76, 78, 80, 83, 92(2), 93, 106(2), 124, 132, 150, 155, 168, 169
Forks of the [Shenandoah] River, 146
The Great Pond on Shanando River, 50(2)
North River of Sharrando, 34
South river of Shannondoah [Shenandoah], 146
Sleepy Creek, 21, 26, 49, 70, 105, 110, 112, 143, 160
Smith's Creek, 44, 91, 94, 137(2)
The Swamp in Smith's Marsh, 40, 41
The Southwest Pond, 129
The South Branch, 6, 27, 40, 41(2), 45, 50, 55(2), 61, 62, 63, 68, 104(2), 106, 144, 146, 147, 149, 166, 168, 170
The South River, 72, 77, 109, 123, 137
The Southwest Marsh, 51
Spout Run, 36, 59, 60, 92, 100, 101, 109, 159, 168
Stoney/Stony Creek/Run, 72, 74(2), 84, 85, 90, 99, 100, 102, 112, 133, 146, 153, 159, 160
Stoney/Stony Lick, 111, 116

Pond at Capt. Stribling's, 10
Pond at Stribling's quarter, 51
John Sturman's Run, 33
Sugar Tree Creek/Sugar Tree Run, 117, 121
Sutton's Run, 115
The Swan Ponds, 124
Three Miles Lick, 153
Toms Brook, 114(2), 137, 140
Tunis's Branch, 140, 142
Tuscarora/Tuscoaora/Tuscorora/Tusegroro Creek, 4, 13, 21, 24, 29, 54, 61(2), 67, 69(2), 80, 110, 112, 149, 153
The Warm Spring(s), 21, 26, 31, 70, 112, 124(2), 126, 127, 131(2), 135, 136(2), 138(2), 139, 141, 142, 143, 144, 145(2), 147, 148, 149(2), 152(2), 156(2), 160, 162(2), 163(2), 166(2), 167(2), 168(2), 170
West Run, 12, 15
John White's Run, 154
Woods River, 10
Worthington's Marsh, 49, 84(2), 87, 100, 102, 103, 163
Wright's Branch, 86, 169

Roads

Roads are cross-indexed to all locations and persons mentioned. Descriptions have been standardized to simplify the preparation of this index. Descriptions of roads and landmarks in the early Frederick County records vary greatly, and it appears that at times road overseers were assigned or changed without being recorded in the court order books. Positive identification of many of these roads will require additional in-depth research into local history, landmark and settlers' names, and land ownership patterns.

Road from the Chapel at Cunningham's to John Neill's, Gent., to be continued to Abrahams Run (road crossing Opeckon at John Neill's ford to Cunningham's Chapel), 39, 53

Road from John Littler's to Thomas Shepard's/Sheppard's mill (road from John Littler's late dwelling house to the said Littler's New Design thence to Opecken Creek over Abril's ford thence to the late dwelling place of John Smith's dec. thence to Jacob Hite's thence to Thomas Shepard's mill), 4, 5
Sections:
- Road from John Littler's to Thomas Sheppard's mill, 6
- Road from Thomas Shepherd's mill to Jacob Hite, Gent.'s, 32
- Road from John Smith's to John Littler's, 32

[Note: See also:
Road from Alexander Ross's fence to the corner of Smith's fence, 21 (etc.)
and
Road from Smith's fence/John Smith's old place to Jacob Hite's, 21, 62, 90, 106, 128, 133
and
Road from William Hite's Spring to the middle of the Swamp in Smith's Marsh and from the Swamp to Littler's mill, 40, 41.]

[Note: Entries for Allen and Allin are combined.]

Road from the South Branch road near Capt. Smith's through Hoop Petticoat Gap to Winchester (road from Winchester through Hoop Petticoat Gap), 104, 106, 154(2)
Sections:
- Road as far as Allen's Cabin, 154
- From Allen's Cabin to the road leading from Winchester to Jeremiah Smith's, 154

Road from his Lordship's line to (Benjamin) Allen's Mill Creek, 74, 85

Road from (Benjamin) Allen's/Allin's Mill Creek to Stoney Creek, 74, 99

Road from Stoney Creek to the County line (road leading from Augusta to Winchester, from the County line to Stony Creek), 102, 112
[Note: Possibly the same as:
Road from Stoney Creek to Benjamin Allin's Mill Creek, 74, 99.]

Road from the Old field formerly Benjamin Allen's to the Narrow Passage, 95

Road from Isaac Ruddell's mill into the Main road between Jackson <u>Allen's</u> and John Skean's, 90

Road from Jackson <u>Allen's</u> crossing the mouth of Smiths Creek thence through White's Bottom to William Clark's at Mount Pleasant, 91

Road from Winchester to Marlborough forge 150(2), 171
Alterations:
- To be turned round John <u>Allen's</u> plantation, 150(2)
- To be turned to run upon the line between Robert Glass and the Rev. Mr. Hoge, 171

Road from Robert <u>Allen's</u> house to the road leading to Winchester, 142, 145

Road from Col. Stephens's mill to Edward Strode's by Matthew <u>Allison's</u>, 162

Road from the Chapel to Jay's ferry (road from the Chapel by <u>Anderson's</u>/Thos. <u>Anderson's</u> mill by William Mitchell's and Jacob Hite Gent.'s land, and thence into the road that goes from Capt. Campbell's to the ferry, near Capt. Thomas Rutherford's plantation), 6(2)

Road from the Flat Rock by Mr. Thruston's by the head of Kate's Spring, into the road leading to the Bloomery below Mr. <u>Ariss's</u>, 167

Road from Opeckon ford at John <u>Armstrong's</u> house to Winchester (road from Winchester to Opeckon at <u>Armstrong's</u> place; road from Winchester to Opeckon at <u>Armstrong's</u> ford), 114, 123, 126

Road from <u>Armstrong's</u> ford upon Opeckon to the Signpost at Littler's road, 123

Road from the Blue Ball to <u>Ashby's Bent Branch</u>, 1, 2

Road from Howel's/Howell's ford to <u>Ashby's Bent</u> Gap, 1, 11, 56

(Request to the Court of Prince William County for a) Road from Jefrey Johnston's at the Pignut Ridge to the top of the [Blue] Ridge at <u>Ashby's Bent</u>, 23

Road leading into Shanandore River (road that leads through <u>Ashby's</u> Gap below where Thomas Ashby keeps ferry over the River), 57

Road from Samuel Mount's upon Bullskin to the road leading to <u>Ashby's</u> Gap, 128

Road from John Briscoe's mill upon Opeckon to <u>Ashby's</u> Gap, 129

Road from Nation's plantation to the ford at <u>Ashby's</u> Gap (road from Nation's plantation to the ford and ferry at Berry's), 130, 136, 140, 166

Road from Nation's Run to Ashby's ferry, 64

Road from Gregory's ford to Ashby's ford, 76

Road from James Seabin's gate to Thomas Ashby, Jr.'s ferry, 34

Road leading into Shanandore River (road that leads through Ashby's Gap below where Thomas Ashby keeps ferry over the River), 57

Road from Henry Funk's mill on Passage Creek to Abraham Kendrick's upper ford and from thence to William Ashby's, 158, 160
Sections:
- From Henry Funk's mill to Abraham Kendrick's upper ford, 160
- From Abraham Kendrick's upper ford to William Ashby's, 160

Road from Pugh's and Barrett's mill by the end of the Sleepy Creek Mountain to the Warm Springs (road from the Warm Springs to Barrett's mill), 126, 131(2), 163, 168
Sections:
- From the [Warm] Springs to Ichebud Ashcraft's, 131, 135
- From Ashcraft's to the Buffaloe Run, 131
- From the Buffaloe Run to the end (from the Buffaloe Run as far as laid off by the veiwers from the Warm Springs; road from Buffaloe Run to Howard's old field, 131, 138, 149

Alteration:
- Road from Barrett's mill to the Warm Springs (to be turned to go by Meshack Sexton's mill), 163, 168

(Petition to the Court of Orange County for) a road from the County line of Frederick to the upper inhabitants of Augusta on Woods River, 10

Road from Ceedar Creek to (John) Funk's mill and from Funk's mill to the County line, 17
Sections:
- Road from John Funk's mill to Cedar Creek, 17, 26, 35, 42
- Road from Funk's mill/Funk's Mill Creek/Funk's Mill Run to the (Augusta) County line, 17, 42, 64, 69, 85, 93

Road from Manasses Run road to Chester's old road and from thence to Augusta line, 43, 44

Road from the Main county road to August[a?] where the Messnuting [Massanutten] road crosses the same to Messanuting Run, 93

Road from Stoney Creek to the County line (road leading from Augusta to Winchester, from the County line to Stony Creek), 102, 112
[Note: Possibly the same as:
Road from Stoney Creek to Benjamin Allin's Mill Creek, 74, 99.]

Road from the Augusta line on the South River above John Breeding's fence to the road crossing Thorn's Gap, 123

Road from John Little's to the Augusta [County] line (road from the [Augusta] County line below Brock's Gap to John Little's), 157, 159
Sections:
- From Little's to Narrow Passage Creek, 159
- From [Narrow] Passage Creek to Stoney Creek, 159
- From Stoney Creek to Christian Dellinger's, 159
- From Christian Dellinger's to Mill Creek, 159
- From Mill Creek to the [Augusta] County line, 159

Road from Crooked Run to the Main County road leading from Augusta County, 158

Road from the fork of the road on William Reynolds's land to Babbs Creek, 68

Road from Babbs Creek to George Potts's plantation, 68

Road from Winchester to Mercer Babb's plantation, 147, 150

Road from Sir John's road by the Quaker Meeting House and through the lane between William Reynolds and Phillip Babb (road between the plantations of William Reynolds and Thomas Babb, Jr. and into Sir John's road; road from Capt. Pearis's to Sir John's road at the Quaker Meeting House), 95, 96, 102

Road from Sir John's road by Thomas Babb's down by William McMachen's (and) Angus McDonald's and down to Berry's mill, 121
[Note: May be the same as:
Road from Sir John's road above Thomas Babb's plantation to Thomas Perry's mill, 121.]

Road from Sir John's road above Thomas Babb's plantation to Thomas Perry's mill, 121

Road from the Meeting House on the mountain to Hugh Lile's on Back Creek, 42

Road from Enoch Pearson's to the mouth of Back Creek, 81

Road from Hugh Lyle's plantation on Back Creek through Curtis's Gap, to Robert Cunningham's (road from Robert Cunningham's to Hugh Lyle's on Back Creek), 103, 104
Sections:
- From Robert Cunningham's to David Miller's plantation, 104
- From David Miller's to the foot of the North Mountain, 104
- From the foot of the North Mountain to Hugh Lyle's on Back Creek, 104

Road from William Frost's plantation on Back Creek to Bridger's mill, 134

Road from the Presbyterian Meeting House at the head of Tuscarora to the Meeting House on Back Creek, 153

Road from White's mill to William Frost's middle plantation on Back Creek, 166

The Warm Spring/Warm Springs road, 136(2), 162, 163, 167, 168, 170
Sections:
- From Andrew Tilleroy's to Henry Lloyd's, 136(2)
- Through Henry Lloyd's plantation, 162
- From the Back Creek road to the Buffaloe Lick, 167
- From the South Branch road near Ballenger's to the County line (road from Ballenger's to the County line), 168, 170
- From Ballenger's to the Tub mill, 170
- From the Tub mill to the County line, 170

[Note: Entries for Backer and Baker are combined.]

Road leading from Isaac Hite's, through Joseph Baker's plantation, to Henry Funk's mill (to be turned round Baker's plantation), 153

Road from Lewis Stephens's mill to Phillip Peter Backer's house, 118

Road from Marlbro [Marlborough] forge to Philip Peter Baker's, 153

Road from Hogland's/Houghland's ferry via Hugh Lysle's, William Baldwin's, and William Hancheire's to fall into Morgan's road leading to Winchester, 143, 147
Sections:
- From Hogland's ferry to John Parks's, 148
- From Hugh Lysle's to Mill Creek, 148
- From Mill Creek to William Hancheir's, 148
- From William Hancheir's to Morgan's road, 148

[Note: Entries for Ballanger, Ballenger, and Ballinger are combined.]

The Warm Spring/Warm Springs road, 136(2), 162, 163, 167, 168, 170
Sections:
- From Andrew Tilleroy's to Henry Lloyd's, 136(2)
- Through Henry Lloyd's plantation, 162
- From the Back Creek road to the Buffaloe Lick, 167
- From the South Branch road near Ballenger's to the County line (road from Ballenger's to the County line), 168, 170
- From Ballenger's to the Tub mill, 170
- From the Tub mill to the County line, 170

Road from Morgan Morgan Gent.'s house/Col. Morgan's to the Courthouse/Winchester (road from the Courthouse to the house of Josiah Ballenger and to Morgan Morgan's), 9, 17, 32, 103
Sections:
- Road from the Courthouse to the house of Josiah Ballenger (road from the Courthouse to Ballenger's plantation), 17, 42
- Road from Josiah Ballenger's to Morgan Morgan's (road from Col. Morgan's to Ballenger's meadow; road from Col. Morgan's to the widow Ballinger's), 17, 86, 105

Road from William Jolliff's to Mary Ballanger's, 84

Road from Morgan Morgan Gent.'s house/Col. Morgan's to the Courthouse/Winchester (road from the Courthouse to the house of Josiah Ballenger and to Morgan Morgan's), 9, 17, 32, 103
Sections:
- Road from the Courthouse to the house of Josiah Ballenger (road from the Courthouse to Ballenger's plantation), 17, 42
- Road from Josiah Ballenger's to Morgan Morgan's (road from Col. Morgan's to Ballenger's meadow; road from Col. Morgan's to the widow Ballinger's), 17, 86, 105

Road from Thomas Doster's to the Main road near the Widow Ballenger's, 110, 111

Road from the Widow Ballenger's to the forks of the Winchester road, 169

Road from the Baptist Meeting House to the Great road leading from Morgan Morgan's to the Town of Winchester, 115, 117

Road from the Baptist Meeting House to William Hancheir's, 146, 147

Road from the High Street in Mecklenburgh to Joseph Barnes's ford (road from Mecklenburg to Barnes's ford), 124, 133

Road from Pugh's and Barrett's mill by the end of the Sleepy Creek Mountain to the Warm Springs (road from the Warm Springs to Barrett's mill), 126, 131(2), 163, 168
Sections:
- From the [Warm] Springs to Ichebud Ashcraft's, 131, 135
- From Ashcraft's to the Buffaloe Run, 131
- From the Buffaloe Run to the end (from the Buffaloe Run as far as laid off by the veiwers from the Warm Springs; road from Buffaloe Run to Howard's old field, 131, 138, 149

Alteration:
- Road from Barrett's mill to the Warm Springs (to be turned to go by Meshack Sexton's mill), 163, 168

Road leading from Opeckon to Battletown, 167, 169

Road from Battletown to (Snickers's ford on) Shannandoah River, 168, 169

Road from the Falling Springs to the Bear Garden Ridge, 60

Road from the Bear Garden Ridge to George Potts's plantation 61

[Note: For Beason, see Beeson.]

Road from Beckett's/John Becket's house to Capt. Hite's/Col. Hite's mill, 78, 109, 164
[Note: Probably the same as:
Road from Col. Hite's to Robert Beckett's, 152.]

Road from Col. Hite's to Robert Beckett's, 152

Road from Beelor's mill into the Main road at Bradley's (continued along the old road to the mill, and going through a corner of Briscoe's new ground), 130

Roads to Christopher Beelor's mill:
- Road from Vestal's ford to Christopher Beelor's mill, 121 *[Note: See also Road from Beelor's mill to Vestal's ford (section of the road from Keith's mill to Vestal's ford), 144.]*
- Road from the Long Marsh to Christopher Beelor's mill, 121

Road from Keith's mill/James Keith's mill to Vestal's ford, 139, 142, 144
Sections:
- From Keith's mill to Beelor's mill, 144
- From Beelor's mill to Vestall's ford, 144 *[Note: See also Road from Vestal's ford to Christopher Beelor's mill, 121.]*

[Note: Entries for Beason and Beeson are combined.]

Road from Jonathan Curtis's house to Edward Beason's mill, 22

Road from Beeson's mill to Peter Tostie's, 52

The Belhaven road, 80

Road from Nation's plantation to the ford at Ashby's Gap (road from Nation's plantation to the ford and ferry at Berry's), 130, 136, 140, 166

Road from the forks of the road leading to Berry's ferry, to Cunningham's Chapel, 153

Road from Lewis's mill to Berry's ferry, 157

Road from Berry's ferry to Howell's ford, 163

Road leading from Berry's ferry to Winchester, 171

Road from Sir John's road by Thomas Babb's down by William McMachen's (and) Angus McDonald's and down to Berry's mill, 121
[Note: May be the same as:
Road from Sir John's road above Thomas Babb's plantation to Thomas Perry's mill, 121.]

Road from Joseph Berry's ford and ferry to the top of the Ridge, 169

Road from the Meeting House at the gap of the Mountains above Hugh Paul's to the Warm Spring(s) (Road from the Meeting House at the gap of the Mountains to Hugh Paul's from thence to Thomas Cherry's and by Daniel Rose's up the bottom to Thomas Berwick's, and from Berwick's to the Warm Springs), 21, 26, 31
Sections:
- From the Warm Spring(s) to Sleepy Creek, 21, 26, 70, 112
- From Sleepy Creek to the Meeting House, 21, 26
- From Sleepy Creek to the Widow Paul's, 49, 105

Road leading from Magneturs Run to Moses Bird's, 120

Road leading from Moses Bird's to the County line, 120

Road from Woodstock to Mounts Bird's (road from the Narrow Passage to Mounts Bird's), 125, 131

Road from Helm's mill into the road leading from Winchester to Watkins's ferry, at Blackburn's plantation, 161, 164

Road from the place where the Bullskin road intercepts Littler's old road to fall into the Potomac road before it comes to Benjamin Blackburn's plantation, 107

Road from Charles Buck's mill to Christian Blank's ford on the North River, and from thence to Stephensburg, 103

Road from Bullskin to the Bloomery, 130

Road from the Flat Rock by Mr. Thruston's by the head of Kate's Spring, into the road leading to the Bloomery below Mr. Ariss's, 167

Road leading from Bucks Marsh to the Bloomery, from the Run to the County line, 170

Road from the Blue Ball to Ashby's Bent Branch, 1, 2

[Note: In some entries, the Blue Ridge Mountains are called the Ridge; both entries should be checked.]

Road from Gregory's ford to the top of the Ridge/Blue Ridge (road from Gregory's ford to the top of the Blue Ridge at the head of Menasses [Manasses] Run; road from Gregory's ford to

Menasses Run at the County line; road from Gregory's ford to Manassey's Gap), 6, 91, 109, 110, 148, 169

(Petition to the Court of Prince William County to meet Frederick County with) a road from the Thorough fair at the Pignut Ridge to the top of the Blue Ridge at the head of Manasses Run, 10

Road from this Courthouse [Winchester] to the top of the Blue Ridge of Mountains at Williams's Gap (road from Capt. Neill's off and on the old road to Joseph Wilkenson's and thence off on the same road to Francis Carney's and from thence to Edge's ford and from thence off and on the old road to the top of the said Mountain), 12
Sections:
- From Capt. Lewis Neill's/Lewis Neill Gent.'s to Francis Carney's/Carnie's (road from Francis Carney's/Carney's Spring to Lewis Neill's/Opeckon at Neill's ford/Opeckon Creek by Capt. Neill's/ Opecken by Lewis Neill's, Gent), 12, 22, 31, 82, 100, 104
- From Carney's to Edge's ford on Shannadore River (road from Shanando River to Carney's Spring, 12, 50, 83
- From Edge's ford to the top of the Blue Ridge on Williams's Gap, 12

Probable later sections:
- Road from Winchester Town to Lewis Neill's/Lewis Neill's ford on Opeckon, 59, 67
- Road from the ford at Lewis Neill Gent.'s house to Littler's road, 59
- Road from Littler's road to Carney's old house, 59
- Road from Carney's old house to the River, 59
- Road from the River to the top of the mountain at Williams's Gap (road from Edward Snigers's [on Shanando] to the top of the Mountain at Williams's Gap; road from the River at Snigers's to the County line at Williams's Gap; road from the top of the Ridge to Edward Snickers's/Snigers's ford/ferry/ferry at Snicker's house; road from the Ferry road [Snigers's] to the top of the Ridge at Williams's Gap), 59, 76, 79, 81, 83, 113

(Request to the Court of Prince William County for a) Road from Jefrey Johnston's at the Pignut Ridge to the top of the [Blue] Ridge at Ashby's Bent, 23

Road from Howel's/Howell's ford to the top of the [Blue] Ridge, 32, 37, 40, 91, 92, 93, 111, 122
Associated roads:
- Road from the ferry landing (at Combs's) to the said road (Main road), and road from the Wagon ford into the said road (road to the Wagon ford and ferry landing), 91, 93, 111

Road from David Loyd's to the top of the Blue Ridge at Vestal's Gap (road from David Loyd's crossing Shannando River and from thence to the top of the ridge), 38, 49, 55
Section:
- Road from the River to the top of the mountain, 55

Road from the Blue Ridge to Thomas Rutherford's, 68

Road from the South River ford to the top of the Blue Ridge, 72

Road from the top of the Blue Ridge to Calebs Run (road from the top of the Blue Ridge at Thorn's Gap to Caleb Job's mill), 73, 84

Road from the top of the Mountain/top of the Blue Ridge to the ferry at Keys's/Keys's ferry/Keyes's ferry (including the ford), 113, 124, 125, 139

Road from Marlborough forge to Manasset's [Manasses] Gap upon the Blue Ridge, 150

[Note: Entries for Borden and Burden are combined.]

Road from the Chapel at James Cunningham's to the Chapel at Robert McCoy's Spring, 26
Sections:
- Road from the Chapel at Cunningham's to Borden's/Burden's Great Spring/Marsh/Run, 26, 27, 37, 55, 56, 58, 84
- Road from Borden's Great Spring to the Chapel at McCoy's Spring, 26, 55

Road from John Frost's mill to the main road between John Littler's plantation and John Milbourn's/Milburn's plantation, (road from Capt. Frost's mill thence to Buffler lick thence through the lands of John Bosser, and David Springer, thence to the ford, thence through the lands of William Frost and Mathias Elmore, along Elmor[e]'s Creek to Widow Dillon's, and thence to the main road leading to Rappahannock between John Littler's and John Milbourn's), 1, 3, 20, 28
Probable sections:
- Road from John Frost's mill to William Frost's/William Frost's ford, 44, 65
- The other part of the said road, from William Frost's to Col. Morgan's road (road from William Frost's to William Dillon's), 44, 110
- Road from Frost's to Dillon's (alteration round the north side of Dillon's plantation into a lane), 126

Road from Cunningham's mill to Henry Bowen's, 131

Road from Bowman's mill to the old County line, 88

Road from Peter Stoufer's to George Bowman's mill, 92

Road from Beelor's mill into the Main road at Bradley's (continued along the old road to the mill, and going through a corner of Briscoe's new ground), 130

Road from Branson's mill to Gregory's ford, 38

Road from Capt. John Hite's mill to Widow Reed's path leading to Branson's mill and McCoy's Chapel, 44

Road from Branson's mill/Branson's mill place to Hite's mill, 46, 65

Sections:
- Road from Branson's mill to the dividing branch, 46
- Road from the dividing branch to Hite's mill, 46

Road from Branson's mill place to the Main road from McCoy's Chapel, 62

Road from the mouth of Crooked Run to the Courthouse (road from the mouth of Crooked Run and crossing the run the upper side of Thomas Branson's plantation and thence to the Courthouse), 9, 10, 11

Road from Chester's ferry to the Courthouse (road from Chester's ferry to John Hite's; road from the ferry landing and thence via the first gap in Guard Hill, crossing Crooked Run, thence on the upper side of Robert McKay's spring, crossing Crooked Run above Thomas Branson's, thence along the road laid off by Bethany Haines to John Hite's), 14, 16

Road from John Hite's to the Chapel at McCoy's Springs (the part which was altered by Thomas Branson), 27, 28

Road from (Thomas) Branson's mill to (Thomas) Chester's, 28, 32, 42, 48

Road from John Funk's mill across Ceeder Run Creek ford to Robert McKay/McCoy Jr.'s. and to Branston's Gap (Road from Funk's mill back of George Telener's, thence to Ceedar Creek ford and Robert McCoy's, and thence to Gregorie's ford upon the river), 2(2)

Road from the Augusta line on the South River above John Breeding's fence to the road crossing Thorn's Gap, 123

Road from William Frost's plantation on Back Creek to Bridger's mill, 134

Road from Joseph Bridges's mill to William Dillon's plantation, 135

Road from where Morgan's road crosses Sir John's road, to the Warm Springs road at Joseph Bridges's, 138

Road from the Warm Spring road at Joseph Bridges's to George Bruce's mill, 156, 158

Road from the Warm Spring road at Joseph Bridges's into the Main road by John Nevill's, 166, 167

Road from Beelor's mill into the Main road at Bradley's (continued along the old road to the mill, and going through a corner of Briscoe's new ground), 130

Road from the Town to Mr. Briscoe's, 44

Road between Robert Cunningham's and where Dr. John Brisco now lives, 57

Road leading through John Briscoe's plantation to Keyes's ferry (alteration), 127, 130

Road from John Briscoe's mill upon Opeckon to the settlement under the [North] mountain (by William Cockrain's/Cockraine's), 127, 132, 143

Road from John Briscoe's mill upon Opeckon into the Mountain road by Murty Handley's, 127, 132

Road from John Briscoe's mill upon Opeckon to Ashby's Gap, 129

Road from John Nevill's mill into Dr. Briscoe's mill road, 161, 163, 165

Road from the Massanutten Mountain to the County line leading to Brock's Gap, 123

Road from John Little's to the Augusta [County] line (road from the [Augusta] County line below Brock's Gap to John Little's), 157, 159
Sections:
- From Little's to Narrow Passage Creek, 159
- From [Narrow] Passage Creek to Stoney Creek, 159
- From Stoney Creek to Christian Dellinger's, 159
- From Christian Dellinger's to Mill Creek, 159
- From Mill Creek to the [Augusta] County line, 159

Road from the ford of Opeckon by David Brown's near Col. Hite's tanyard to the Hoop Petticoat Gap, 155, 164

Road leading from Lord Fairfax's to Winchester (alteration at David Brown's plantation), 168, 169

Road from David Brown's to the forks of the road below David Wright's house, 168

Road from David Brown's mill down Opeckon Creek by James Knight's and Edward Reed's into the Chapel road, 168, 170, 171

The Main road where it crosses Bruise's [Bruce's] Mill Run, 118

Road from the Horse Pond in Dr. McCormack's road to George Bruce's mill, 125, 128, 134, 164

Road from the Warm Spring road at Joseph Bridges's to George Bruce's mill, 156, 158

Road from Calebs Run to the Brush bottom ford and from thence to the Percimmon Pond above James McCoy's, 74, 75

Road from Jeremiah's Run to the Brush Bottom ford, 106

Road from Opeckon near John Bryan's house to Winchester (road to be cleared on the top of the ridge to avoid the swampy part of the road), 80

Road from Humphrey Wells's house to Capt. Calmees's (road from the head of Buck Marsh to Marquis Calmes's), 128, 142

Road leading from Bucks Marsh to the Bloomery, from the Run to the County line, 170

Road from George Julian's on Passage Creek to Buck's mill (road from George Julian's in Powell's fort to Buck's mill; road from Buck's mill to Powell's fort), 85, 96, 104

Road from Charles Buck's mill to Christian Blank's ford on the North River, and from thence to Stephensburg, 103

Road from Capt. Spears's to the fork of the road that leads to Charles Buck's, 109

Road from the South River to the fork of the road that leads to Charles Buck's, 109

Road from Buckles's Marsh to where it intercepts the road leading to Reubin Rutherford's, 80

Road from the Town of Mecklinburgh to the Meeting House between Buckles's and Lucas's, 119

[Note: Entries for Buffaloe and Buffler are combined.]

Road from John Frost's mill to the main road between John Littler's plantation and John Milbourn's/Milburn's plantation, (road from Capt. Frost's mill thence to Buffler lick thence through the lands of John Bosser, and David Springer, thence to the ford, thence through the lands of William Frost and Mathias Elmore, along Elmor[e]'s Creek to Widow Dillon's, and thence to the main road leading to Rappahannock between John Littler's and John Milbourn's), 1, 3, 20, 28
Probable sections:
- Road from John Frost's mill to William Frost's/William Frost's ford, 44, 65
- The other part of the said road, from William Frost's to Col. Morgan's road (road from William Frost's to William Dillon's), 44, 110
- Road from Frost's to Dillon's (alteration round the north side of Dillon's plantation into a lane), 126

The Warm Spring/Warm Springs road, 136(2), 162, 163, 167, 168, 170
Sections:
- From Andrew Tilleroy's to Henry Lloyd's, 136(2)
- Through Henry Lloyd's plantation, 162
- From the Back Creek road to the Buffaloe Lick, 167
- From the South Branch road near Ballenger's to the County line (road from Ballenger's to the County line), 168, 170
- From Ballenger's to the Tub mill, 170

- From the Tub mill to the County line, 170

Road from Pugh's and Barrett's mill by the end of the Sleepy Creek Mountain to the Warm Springs (road from the Warm Springs to Barrett's mill), 126, 131(2), 163, 168
Sections:
- From the [Warm] Springs to Ichebud Ashcraft's, 131, 135
- From Ashcraft's to the Buffaloe Run, 131
- From the Buffaloe Run to the end (from the Buffaloe Run as far as laid off by the veiwers from the Warm Springs; road from Buffaloe Run to Howard's old field, 131, 138, 149

Alteration:
- Road from Barrett's mill to the Warm Springs (to be turned to go by Meshack Sexton's mill), 163, 168

Road from Buffinton's to Carrol's Place on Pattersons Creek (road from Willm. Buffington's to Pattersons Creek, 16, 63

[Note: Entries for Bullskin, Bull Skin, and Bulskin are combined.]

Road from John Shepard's/Sheppard's to the head of Bulskin (road from Potomac River from Sheppards ferry through the land of Thomas Rutherford, over Walker's mill dam and by the head of Pitts's Marsh and to the head of Bulskin through the lands of Mr. John McCormack), 3, 7
Sections:
- Road from Potomac River to Thomas Rutherford Gent.'s, 12, 38
- The remaining part of the road, 13
- Road from Thomas Rutherford Gent.'s to the head of Bullskin, 24
- Road from Thomas Rutherford's house to John McCarmack's, 37

Road from the head of Bulskin over John Neill's mill dam to the Courthouse, 3, 7

Road from John Nealan[d]'s/Neeland's on Sharrando to William Vestal's on the same river (road from John Nealand's down the river by the lands of John Grimes, Capt. Stribling, Timothy Haney, Darby Conely, Goldin, John Hamman, Thomas Hamman, and Elizabeth Pearson, across Pearson's Neck of Land to Jonathan Walker's, over Bulskin, and by Robert Hayes's and along Hayes's path to Vestal's), 9, 10

Road from John McCormack's house to Opecken Creek and from Opecken Creek to the Courthouse/the Town (road from the head of the south fork of Bullskin to Opecken and thence to the Courthouse), 20, 25
Sections:
- Road from the head of the south fork of Bullskin to Opecken (road from John McCormack's to the Main road to Town; road from John McCormack's house to Opecken Creek which leads to town), 20, 25, 49, 67, 87, 107 *[Note: This section appears to be different than the section from Opecken to the head to Bullskin (pp. 22, 31) of the road from Maj. Andrew Campbell Gent.'s to the Chapel at Cunningham's, 22.]*

- Road from Opecken to the Courthouse (road from Opeckon Creek to the Main road leading to Winchester), 20, 25, 107

Road from Maj. Andrew Campbell Gent.'s to the Chapel at Cunningham's (Road from Maj. Campbell's to Joseph Evans's thence to William Mitchell's then across Opecken thence to the head of the south fork of the Bulskin, thence to Thomas Linseys's on the Long Marsh, thence to John Linsey Gent.'s and from thence to the Chapel at Cunningham's), 22
Sections:
- From Campbell's to Opecken (from Andrew Campbell Gent.'s to William Mitchell's), 22, 30
- From Opecken to the head of Bulskin, 22, 31
- From the head of Bulskin to the Long Marsh, 22, 25
- From the Long Marsh to Fairfax road, 22
- From the Fairfax road to the Chapel), 22, 25

Road from Mitchell's ford to the head of Bullskin, 66

Road from the head of Bullskin to Pennington's Marsh, 66

Road from the head of Bullskin to Watkins's ferry, 77

Road from the head of Bullskin Marsh running by the head of Long Marsh into the road at the Dry Marsh below Capt. Lewis Neill's, 98

Road from the place where the Bullskin road intercepts Littler's old road to fall into the Potomac road before it comes to Benjamin Blackburn's plantation, 107

Road from James Fowler's house to the head of Bullskin, 109

Road from the head of Bullskin to the Main road by Fryer's (road from Alexander Fryer's to the head of Bullskin, 109, 126(2)
Alteration:
- Where the road passes through John Smith's land, 126(2)

Road from the head of Bullskin to the Main road from Winchester to McLenburgh [Mecklenburgh], 123

Road from Samuel Mount's upon Bullskin to the road leading to Ashby's Gap, 128

Road from Snickers's ferry to Bullskin, 130

Road from Bullskin to the Bloomery, 130

Road from the cross roads at Carney's Spring to the Head of Bullskin, 136

Road from the Flat Rock to the ford upon Bullskin (above Mr. Pyke's), 136, 162

Road from the head of Long Marsh to James Keith's mill upon Bulskin, 139, 141

Road from the Widow McCormack's to the head spring of Bulskin, 140

Road from Toliafero Stribling's to Bulskin (including the whole bridge over the run), 152

Road from James Hogan's to Elizabeth Jolliffe's mill and thence into the Bull Skin road (road from James Hagan's by the Widow Jolliffe's mill into the Bull Skin road), 154, 155

Road from Burk's bridge along the Chapel road to Spout Run, 168

Road from George Henry's Spring to James Burner's Run, 153

Road from Semple's furnace to the Warm Springs road above Peter Burr's, 141, 144, 145, 147, 152

Road from Opecken to Sherando River (road from Opeckon Creek to Col. Burwell's mill; road from Opeckon where Joseph Robbins lived to Burwell's mill on Shanando), 35, 50, 57

Road from Col. Burwell's mill to the fork of the road at Foxtrap Point, 50, 58
Associated roads:
- The [wagon] ford road, 50, 58
- The ferry road, 50

Road from Sturman's bridge to Burwell's mill, 50

Road from Burwell's mill to Cunningham's Chapel, 87

Road from Spout Run to Mr. John Sturman's (road from Burwell's Spout Run to Mr. John Sturman's old place), 36, 60

Road from Opeckon where Joseph Robins formerly lived to Burwell's Spout Run, 59

[Note: Entries for Caldwell and Calwell are combined.]

Road from Isaac Perkins's mill through the Town [Winchester] to the line thereof by Andrew Caldwell's (road from Isaac Perkins's mill to the north end of the Town; road(s) through the town to Parkins's mill; the Main Street of the Town), 19, 20, 64, 88

Road from Mills's Gap to Follis's mill and the Main road at Jane Caldwell's plantation, 111, 112

Road from the Widow Calwell's to the Mountain, 144

Road from the Muster Ground above the Widow Caldwell's/Calwell's to John Neavill's mill and thence into the Main road by Jonah Seaman's, 155, 156

Road from the top of the Blue Ridge to Calebs Run (road from the top of the Blue Ridge at Thorn's Gap to Caleb Job's mill), 73, 84

Road from Calebs Run to the Brush bottom ford and from thence to the Percimmon Pond above James McCoy's, 74, 75

Road from Pennington's Marsh to Mr. Calmes's, 66

Road from Marquis Calmes's to Opeckon Run, 75

Road from Thomas Lindsey's house to Marquis Calmes's, 87

Road from James Fowler's to Marquis Calmes's, 109

Road from Humphrey Wells's house to Capt. Calmees's (road from the head of Buck Marsh to Marquis Calmes's), 128, 142

Road from the Chapel to Jay's ferry (road from the Chapel by Anderson's/Thos. Anderson's mill by William Mitchell's and Jacob Hite Gent.'s land, and thence into the road that goes from Capt. Campbell's to the ferry, near Capt. Thomas Rutherford's plantation), 6(2)

Road from Andrew Campbell Gent.'s to Kersey's ferry, 21

Road from Maj. Andrew Campbell Gent.'s to the Chapel at Cunningham's (road from Maj. Campbell's to Joseph Evans's thence to William Mitchell's then across Opecken thence to the head of the south fork of the Bulskin, thence to Thomas Linseys's on the Long Marsh, thence to John Linsey Gent.'s and from thence to the Chapel at Cunningham's), 22
Sections:
- From Campbell's to Opecken (from Andrew Campbell Gent.'s to William Mitchell's), 22, 30
- From Opecken to the head of Bulskin, 22, 31
- From the head of Bulskin to the Long Marsh, 22, 25
- From the Long Marsh to Fairfax road, 22
- From the Fairfax road to the Chapel), 22, 25

Bridle road/road from Morgan Morgan Gent.'s to Andrew Campbell Gent.'s), 24, 30

Public road leading from Andrew Campbell Gent.'s to Watkins's ferry (alteration by the plantation formerly Jonathan Jayeas [Jayes?], dec., now in the possession of Elizabeth Dyer), 28

Road from Gilliland's mill to Andrew Campbell's, 82

Road from the Signpost to Cannill's ferry, 80

[Note: Entries for Cape Capon and Cacapon are combined.]

Road from Noah Hampton's mill, into the road on Great Cape Capon near James Coddy's/Cody's, 1, 6, 8

Road from the North Branch of Cape Capon to James Cody's road, 3

Road from Parks's graveyard near Cape Capon Water, over Dellings Run into the Wagon road on Joseph Edward's land, 25

Road from Stony bridge to Parker's on the North River of Cacapon, 41

Road from the North River of Great Cacapon, 48

Road from the County line on Cape Capon Mountain by Sink's mill to Abraham Darst's smith shop, 138

Road from the White House to Thorn's Gap, 108, 115
Section:
- Part from Suttons Run to a mill above Charles Thompson's on Col. Carlyle's land, 115

[Note: All variations of Carney/Carnaham are combined. See also Karney.]

Road from the cross roads at Carney's Spring to the Head of Bulskin, 136

Road from this Courthouse [Winchester] to the top of the Blue Ridge of Mountains at Williams's Gap (road from Capt. Neill's off and on the old road to Joseph Wilkenson's and thence off on the same road to Francis Carney's and from thence to Edge's ford and from thence off and on the old road to the top of the said Mountain), 12
Sections:
- From Capt. Lewis Neill's/Lewis Neill Gent.'s to Francis Carney's/Carnie's (road from Francis Carney's/Carney's Spring to Lewis Neill's/Opeckon at Neill's ford/Opeckon Creek by Capt. Neill's/ Opecken by Lewis Neill's, Gent), 12, 22, 31, 82, 100, 104
- From Carney's to Edge's ford on Shannadore River (road from Shanando River to Carney's Spring, 12, 50, 83
- From Edge's ford to the top of the Blue Ridge on Williams's Gap, 12

Probable later sections:
- Road from Winchester Town to Lewis Neill's/Lewis Neill's ford on Opeckon, 59, 67
- Road from the ford at Lewis Neill Gent.'s house to Littler's road, 59
- Road from Littler's road to Carney's old house, 59
- Road from Carney's old house to the River, 59
- Road from the River to the top of the mountain at Williams's Gap (road from Edward Snigers's [on Shanando] to the top of the Mountain at Williams's Gap; road from the River at Snigers's to the County line at Williams's Gap; road from the top of the Ridge to Edward Snickers's/Snigers's ford/ferry/ferry at Snicker's house; road from

the Ferry road [Snigers's] to the top of the Ridge at Williams's Gap), 59, 76, 79, 81, 83, 113

Road from Francis Carnaham's to the Courthouse, 16

Road from Buffinton's to Carrol's Place on Pattersons Creek (road from Willm. Buffington's to Pattersons Creek, 16, 63

Road round Simon Carson's fence (alteration), 98, 100, 101

Road from Stevens's/Lewis Stephens's mill to the road to McCoy's/McKoy's Chapel (near Cartmill's), 37, 82
Alterations, 79

Road from McKay's Chapel to Edward Cartmill's, 109

Road from Mr. Caton's to Maidston, 94

Road from Thomas Caton's house to Mr. Jacob Hite's, 47, 65, 67

Road from Caton's ford/Thomas Caton's to Vestal's Gap, 76, 115
Section:
- Part from Opeckon Creek to Shepherds Town, 115

Road passing through the plantation of Thomas Caton, Gent. (alterations), 92

Road from Hogeland's ferry to Thomas Caton's (road from Richard Hogland's ferry to go by John Hogland's mill to Capt. Thomas Caton's), 97, 99, 100

Road from Mandanhall's Mill Run to Capt. Thomas Caton's, 101

(Main) road from the Courthouse/town of Winchester to Watkins's ferry, 40, 65, 112
- To be turned where it passes through William Jollyffe's land, 65

Sections:
- From Tuscarora to Capt./Mr. (Thomas) Caton's plantation, 110, 112
- From Watkins's ferry to Caton's Stone House, 162

Road from John Funk's mill across Ceeder Run Creek ford to Robert McKay/McCoy Jr.'s. and to Branston's Gap (road from Funk's mill back of George Telener's, thence to Ceedar Creek ford and Robert McCoy's, and thence to Gregorie's ford upon the river), 2(2)

Road from Ceder Creek to West Run, 15

Road from Ceedar Creek to (John) Funk's mill and from Funk's mill to the County line, 17
Sections:
- Road from John Funk's mill to Cedar Creek, 17, 26, 35, 42

255

- Road from Funk's mill/Funk's Mill Creek/Funk's Mill Run to the (Augusta) County line, 17, 42, 64, 69, 85, 93

Road from Cedar Creek to Robert McCoy's Run, 35

Road from Cedar Creek to the crossroad at John Duckworth's, 48

Road from Hite's mill to Cedar Creek, 63

Road from Cedar Creek to the County line, 63

Road from Crisman's Spring/Chrisman's place to Cedar Creek, 70, 86, 137, 168

Road from Cedar Creek to Stoufers Town, 102

Road from Joseph Fry's plantation on Cedar Creek to the Furnace being erected on the north branch of Pembroke, 118

Road from the Chapel to Cedar Creek (alteration to return to its earlier route), 124

Road from the furnace erecting on the north branch of Pembroke to the forge erecting on Cedar Creek (road from the forge to the furnace), 129(2), 146
Sections:
- From the furnace to Devault Hulberger's, 129
- From Hulberger's to the forge (from Opeckon to the forge upon Cedar Creek), 129, 142, 144

Road from the head of the spring by the Chapel to John Evans's and from thence to Tuscorora, 4
Section:
- Road from the head of the spring by the Chapel to John Evans's, 1

Road from the Chapel to Jay's ferry (road from the Chapel by Anderson's/Thos. Anderson's mill by William Mitchell's and Jacob Hite Gent.'s land, and thence into the road that goes from Capt. Campbell's to the ferry, near Capt. Thomas Rutherford's plantation), 6(2)

Road from the Chapel to Cedar Creek (alteration to return to its earlier route), 124

The Chapel road from Samuel Earl's meadows to Gregory's ford and Seaborn's ford, 157

Road leading to the Chapel and the Long Marsh, 167

Road from David Brown's mill down Opeckon Creek by James Knight's and Edward Reed's into the Chapel road, 168, 170, 171

Road from Burk's bridge along the Chapel road to Spout Run, 168

[Note: For roads associated with a specific chapel (e.g., Cunningham's Chapel, Morgan's Chapel, McCoy's Chapel), see the entries for the particular chapel.]

Road from the Meeting House at the gap of the Mountains above Hugh Paul's to the Warm Spring(s) (road from the Meeting House at the gap of the Mountains to Hugh Paul's from thence to Thomas Cherry's and by Daniel Rose's up the bottom to Thomas Berwick's, and from Berwick's to the Warm Springs), 21, 26, 31
Sections:
- From the Warm Spring(s) to Sleepy Creek, 21, 26, 70, 112
- From Sleepy Creek to the Meeting House, 21, 26
- From Sleepy Creek to the Widow Paul's, 49, 105

Road from Van Swearingen's mill upon Tunis's Branch to the Warm Springs road near Hedges's (approved as: road from Swearingen's mill into the Warm Springs road at Lucas Hood's), 142, 145, 148
Sections:
- From Swearingen's mill to Cherry's Run, 149
- From Cherry's Run to the Warm Spring road (from Thomas Cherry's ford to the Warm Springs road by Lucas Hood's), 143, 149

Road from John Funk's mill to Chester's ferry and from thence to where the road takes out of Chester's road to Manasses Run, 1, 2
Sections:
- From John Funk's mill to the North River, 2, 79
- From the North River to the Haybottom, 2, 78
- From the Haybottom to where the road takes off to Manasses Run, 2, 31, 34, 55
- Road to be continued to Manasses Run, 31

Road from Chester's ferry to the Courthouse (road from Chester's ferry to John Hite's; road from the ferry landing and thence via the first gap in Guard Hill, crossing Crooked Run, thence on the upper side of Robert McKay's spring, crossing Crooked Run above Thomas Branson's, thence along the road laid off by Bethany Haines to John Hite's), 14, 16

Road from the Culpeper road at Chester's Gap to Chester's ford, 77

Road from Chester's ford to Manasseh's [Manasses] Run, 111

Road from Chester's ford to the top of the Ridge, 121

Road from Tidwell's ford to Chester's ford in the fork, 134

Road to the County line through Chester's Gap, 55

Road from the Culpeper road at Chester's Gap to Chester's ford, 77

Road from Caleb Job's Run to the Culpeper line at Chester's Gap, 91

Road from Samuel Earle's house into the road leading from Chester's Gap at Manasses Run (road from Samuel Earl's house into the road called Chester's road Manaseh's Run), 113, 115

Road from Hume's/Thomas Hume's mill on Sugar Tree Creek/ Sugar Tree Run into the road leading to Chester's Gap, 117, 121

Road from the North River leading to Chester's Gap to the South River, 137

Road from John Funk's mill to Chester's ferry and from thence to where the road takes out of Chester's road to Manasses Run, 1, 2
Sections:
- From John Funk's mill to the North River, 2, 79
- From the North River to the Haybottom, 2, 78
- From the Haybottom to where the road takes off to Manasses Run, 2, 31, 34, 55
- Road to be continued to Manasses Run, 31

Road from Manasses Run road to Chester's old road and from thence to Augusta line, 43, 44

Road from the New Town [Stephensburgh/Stevensburgh] into Chester's road, 92

Road from Samuel Earle's house into the road leading from Chester's Gap at Manasses Run (road from Samuel Earl's house into the road called Chester's road Manaseh's Run), 113, 115

Road from Thomas Postgate's Islands/Island into the road that comes from Thomas Chester Gent.'s, 8, 13

Road from (Thomas) Branson's mill to (Thomas) Chester's, 28, 32, 42, 48

[Note: Entries for Christman, Crisman, Cristman, etc., are combined.]

Road from Stephensburg to Jacob Chrisman's Spring (to be turned at Henry Chrisman's plantation, 170

Road from John Hite Gent.'s mill/mill dam/Hite's mill/Col. Hite's to Jacob Cristman's/Jacob Christman's Spring/Crisman's Spring, 34, 70, 81, 82, 90, 91, 125, 129

Road from Crisman's Spring/Chrisman's place to Cedar Creek, 70, 86, 137, 168

Road leading from Jacob Christman's plantation to the Widow Duckworth's plantation, 114

Road from Stephensburg to Jacob Chrisman's Spring (to be turned at Henry Chrisman's plantation, 170

Road from Jackson Allen's crossing the mouth of Smiths Creek thence through White's Bottom to William Clark's at Mount Pleasant, 91

Road from Ephram Leith's hollow to Claud's ford, 94

Road from John Briscoe's mill upon Opeckon to the settlement under the [North] mountain (by William Cockrain's/Cockraine's), 127, 132, 143

Road from Noah Hampton's mill, into the road on Great Cape Capon near James Coddy's/Cody's, 1, 6, 8

Road from the North Branch of Cape Capon to James Cody's road, 3

[Note: Entries for Combs, Combes, Coombes, and Coombs are combined.]

Road from Howel's/Howell's ford to the top of the [Blue] Ridge, 32, 37, 40, 91, 92, 93, 111, 122
Associated roads:
- Road from the ferry landing (at Combs's) to the said road (Main road), and road from the Wagon ford into the said road (road to the Wagon ford and ferry landing), 91, 93, 111

Road above Noah Hampton's house from Coombs's ferry up Shanando River (proposed alteration rejected), 93

Road from Col. Fielding Lewis's quarter to the ferry landing at Combs's, 100, 103

Road from Lord Fairfax's quarter where Nation formerly lived to the ford at Comb's (road from the Right Honourable Thomas Lord Fairfax's quarter to Combes's ferry), 101, 113

Road from the forks of the River to the ferry landing [at Combs's?], 106

Road from Seaburn's ford to Combs's ferry, 108, 118

Road from Combs's ferry to the top of the Ridge, 108

Road from John Lindsey's to the ford at Combs's ferry, 118

Road from Coombes's ferry to Lewis's mill, 121

Road from Combs's ferry at [to?] the Town of Winchester, 122

Road from Combs's ferry to the forks leading to Winchester, 128

Road from the Warm Springs to Combs's mill and from thence to the mouth of Sleepy Creek, 160

Road from John Nealan[d]'s/Neeland's on Sharrando to William Vestal's on the same river (road from John Nealand's down the river by the lands of John Grimes, Capt. Stribling, Timothy Haney, Darby Conely, Goldin, John Hamman, Thomas Hamman, and Elizabeth Pearson, across

Pearson's Neck of Land to Jonathan Walker's, over Bulskin, and by Robert Hayes's and along Hayes's path to Vestal's), 9, 10

Road from Winchester to Samuel Littler's (road leading to Connigocheague, section from the Town of Winchester to Littler's place), 107, 112

Road from John Wisecarver's to Cooper's mill by Benjamin Fry's, 146, 148

Road for the upper inhabitants of the County, 30

[Note: For County line entries, see also under specific county names (i.e., Augusta, Culpeper, Frederick, Hampshire, Orange).]

Road from Gregory's ford to the top of the Ridge/Blue Ridge (road from Gregory's ford to the top of the Blue Ridge at the head of Menasses [Manasses] Run; road from Gregory's ford to Menasses Run at the County line; road from Gregory's ford to Manassey's Gap), 6, 91, 109, 110, 148, 169

(Petition to the Court of Orange County for) a road from the County line of Frederick to the upper inhabitants of Augusta on Woods River, 10

Road from the County line through Howards Town to join the new road to the Courthouse, 11

Road from this Courthouse [Winchester] to the top of the Blue Ridge of Mountains at Williams's Gap (road from Capt. Neill's off and on the old road to Joseph Wilkenson's and thence off on the same road to Francis Carney's and from thence to Edge's ford and from thence off and on the old road to the top of the said Mountain), 12
Sections:
- From Capt. Lewis Neill's/Lewis Neill Gent.'s to Francis Carney's/Carnie's (road from Francis Carney's/Carney's Spring to Lewis Neill's/Opeckon at Neill's ford/Opeckon Creek by Capt. Neill's/ Opecken by Lewis Neill's, Gent), 12, 22, 31, 82, 100, 104
- From Carney's to Edge's ford on Shannadore River (road from Shanando River to Carney's Spring, 12, 50, 83
- From Edge's ford to the top of the Blue Ridge on Williams's Gap, 12

Probable later sections:
- Road from Winchester Town to Lewis Neill's/Lewis Neill's ford on Opeckon, 59, 67
- Road from the ford at Lewis Neill Gent.'s house to Littler's road, 59
- Road from Littler's road to Carney's old house, 59
- Road from Carney's old house to the River, 59
- Road from the River to the top of the mountain at Williams's Gap (road from Edward Snigers's [on Shanando] to the top of the Mountain at Williams's Gap; road from the River at Snigers's to the County line at Williams's Gap; road from the top of the Ridge to Edward Snickers's/Snigers's ford/ferry/ferry at Snicker's house; road from the Ferry road [Snigers's] to the top of the Ridge at Williams's Gap), 59, 76, 79, 81, 83, 113

Road from the County line by Thomas Little Gent.'s to Lewis Stephens's mill, 29, 35, 39

Road from Ceedar Creek to (John) Funk's mill and from Funk's mill to the County line, 17
Sections:
- Road from John Funk's mill to Cedar Creek, 17, 26, 35, 42
- Road from Funk's mill/Funk's Mill Creek/Funk's Mill Run to the (Augusta) County line, 17, 42, 64, 69, 85, 93

Road from the County line to Happy Creek, 52

Road to the County line through Chester's Gap, 55

Road from the Manor line to the County line, 63

Road from Cedar Creek to the County line, 63

Road from Miller's foot path to the old County line, 74

Road from the County line to Jeremiah Smith's house, 75

Road leading from Winchester to Henry Enochs's, 79(2)
Section:
- From the beginning of the new road [i.e., the road from the new bridge at Opeckon into the road leading from Winchester to Henry Enochs's], to the County line, 79

Road from Jeremiah Lewis's (at/near the County line) to Stephens's/Stevens's mill at/on the Narrow Passage, 79, 104
Sections:
- Road from the County line near Jeremiah Lewis's to Christian Dilliner's, 81
- Road from Christian Dillener's to Lewis Stevens's mill at the Narrow Passage, 81

Road from Bowman's mill to the old County line, 88

Road from Selser's Mill Run to the County line at Woods Plain (Mountain road from Wood's Plains over the mountains to Selser's Mill Run), 94, 102

Sir John's road (road called Sir John Sinclaire's road), 96, 97, 113, 119, 127, 132
Sections:
- From Winchester to the plantation where Isaac Thomas did live, 96
- From the place where the road from Robert Cunningham's falls into it to the forks where the road leads to Winchester, 132
- From the plantation where Isaac Thomas did live to the County line, 96
- From the Hunting Ridge to Isaac's Creek at Pritchet's place, 97
- Sir John's road leading from the Timber Ridge to Isaac's Creek, 113
- From the forks to James McGill's, 119

- Sir John's road from the end of the Sleepy Creek Mountain where the Warm Spring road crosses it to James Daugherty's, 127

Probable sections:
- Road from Isaac's Creek to the County line, 148
- Road from (the top of) the Hunting Ridge to the County line, 151, 158

Road from Stoney Creek to the County line (road leading from Augusta to Winchester, from the County line to Stony Creek), 102, 112
[Note: Possibly the same as:
Road from Stoney Creek to Benjamin Allin's Mill Creek, 74, 99.]

Road from Hoge Creek/Hog Creek to the County line, 105, 121

Road from Winchester to the South Branch at the County line on the North Mountain (road from the place marked by the viewers to the County line on the North Mountain), 104, 106

Road leading from Moses Bird's to the County line, 120

Road from the Massanutten Mountain to the County line leading to Brock's Gap, 123

Road from the County line in Massanutting to Mauk's mill, 132, 133

Road from Abraham Durst's Shop to the road on this side of the Massanuting Mountain (road from Abraham Darst's Smith's Shop to the top of the Massanutting [Massanutten] Mountain), 135, 137, 149(2)

Sections/related roads:
- Road from the North River to the County line, 149
- Road from the County line as the Main road now goes till it intersects the road leading from Abraham Durst's Smith Shop to the top of the [Massanutten] Mountain, 149

Road from the [top of] Massanutting Mountain to the County line [at the River], 137, 150

Road from the County line on Cape Capon Mountain by Sink's mill to Abraham Darst's smith shop, 138

Road from the Warm Springs to the County line, 139

Road from the Main road near Mauk's mill to the County line, 151, 161

Road leading through Woodstock to the County line, 160

Road leading from Snickers's Gap to Vestall's Gap (to be turned at Ralph Wormley Esq.'s plantation/as far as the County line), 164, 167

Road from the road leading through Edmund Taylor's plantation towards Mr. Wormley's mill as far as the County line, 167, 169

The Warm Spring/Warm Springs road, 136(2), 162, 163, 167, 168, 170
Sections:
- From Andrew Tilleroy's to Henry Lloyd's, 136(2)
- Through Henry Lloyd's plantation, 162
- From the Back Creek road to the Buffaloe Lick, 167
- From the South Branch road near Ballenger's to the County line (road from Ballenger's to the County line), 168, 170
- From Ballenger's to the Tub mill, 170
- From the Tub mill to the County line, 170

Road leading from Bucks Marsh to the Bloomery, from the Run to the County line, 170

Road from Snickers's ferry landing to the County line on the road leading to Jacob Hite's, 170

[Note: The term "County road" signifies a major or important road in a given area; the following entries are references to various routes, not a single road.]

Road from Robert Warth's; to be taken from the head of the road which leads from the Chapel at Robert McCoy's Spring, to Lewis Stephen's mills (road from the County road near Robert Warth's to Stevens's mill), 30, 63

Road from the County road to the Chapel at McCoy's Spring, 34

Road to and from the ferry (across Shannando between John Kersey's and Christopher Marr's plantations) in the County road, 37

Road from the Race Ground(s) below John Hite's house to the Swift Shoals ford on Shenandoah and thence down the River to the County road, 124, 132, 136

Mill road from John Spencely's house to the County road leading over the Mountain (road from John Spenceley's to the Main road leading over the mountain), 151, 155

Road from Crooked Run to the Main County road leading from Augusta County, 158

[Note: In addition to entries for the Courthouse, see also entries for the Town and Winchester.]

Road from the head of Bulskin over John Neill's mill dam to the Courthouse, 3, 7

Road from John Littler's old place by the Courthouse to Capt. John Hite's, 4

Bridle road/road from Scot's/Scott's [later Johnston's] mill on Shanando/Sharrando to the Courthouse, 5, 7, 11, 14, 15, 17

Road from Chester's ferry to the Courthouse (road from Chester's ferry to John Hite's; road from the ferry landing and thence via the first gap in Guard Hill, crossing Crooked Run, thence on the upper side of Robert McKay's spring, crossing Crooked Run above Thomas Branson's, thence along the road laid off by Bethany Haines to John Hite's), 14, 16

Road from Morgan Morgan Gent.'s house/Col. Morgan's to the Courthouse/Winchester (road from the Courthouse to the house of Josiah Ballenger and to Morgan Morgan's), 9, 17, 32, 103
Sections:
- Road from the Courthouse to the house of Josiah Ballenger (road from the Courthouse to Ballenger's plantation), 17, 42
- Road from Josiah Ballenger's to Morgan Morgan's (road from Col. Morgan's to Ballenger's meadow; road from Col. Morgan's to the widow Ballinger's), 17, 86, 105

Road from the mouth of Crooked Run to the Courthouse (road from the mouth of Crooked Run and crossing the run the upper side of Thomas Branson's plantation and thence to the Courthouse), 9, 10, 11

Road from the County line through Howards Town to join the new road to the Courthouse, 11

Road from the Courthouse to Gregory's ford, 11

Road from this Courthouse [Winchester] to the top of the Blue Ridge of Mountains at Williams's Gap (road from Capt. Neill's off and on the old road to Joseph Wilkenson's and thence off on the same road to Francis Carney's and from thence to Edge's ford and from thence off and on the old road to the top of the said Mountain), 12
Sections:
- From Capt. Lewis Neill's/Lewis Neill Gent.'s to Francis Carney's/Carnie's (road from Francis Carney's/Carney's Spring to Lewis Neill's/Opeckon at Neill's ford/Opeckon Creek by Capt. Neill's/ Opecken by Lewis Neill's, Gent), 12, 22, 31, 82, 100, 104
- From Carney's to Edge's ford on Shannadore River (road from Shanando River to Carney's Spring, 12, 50, 83
- From Edge's ford to the top of the Blue Ridge on Williams's Gap, 12

Probable later sections:
- Road from Winchester Town to Lewis Neill's/Lewis Neill's ford on Opeckon, 59, 67
- Road from the ford at Lewis Neill Gent.'s house to Littler's road, 59
- Road from Littler's road to Carney's old house, 59
- Road from Carney's old house to the River, 59
- Road from the River to the top of the mountain at Williams's Gap (road from Edward Snigers's [on Shanando] to the top of the Mountain at Williams's Gap; road from the River at Snigers's to the County line at Williams's Gap; road from the top of the Ridge to Edward Snickers's/Snigers's ford/ferry/ferry at Snicker's house; road from the Ferry road [Snigers's] to the top of the Ridge at Williams's Gap), 59, 76, 79, 81, 83, 113

Road from the Courthouse/Winchester to Lewis Neill Gent.'s/ Lewis Neill's old place/Lewis Neill's ford on Opeckon, 12, 13, 23, 29, 30, 59, 67, 73, 81, 88, 94, 102, 103, 110, 151, 170

Road from William Hoge Jr.'s to the Courthouse, 15(2)

Road from Francis Carnaham's to the Courthouse, 16

Road from Lewis Stephens's mills to the Courthouse, 17

Road from John Linsey Gent.'s house into the road which leads from the Courthouse to Fairfax County (road from the Fairfax road to John Linsey Gent.'s/Mr. John Lindsey's, 20, 23, 59

Road from John McCormack's house to Opecken Creek and from Opecken Creek to the Courthouse/the Town (road from the head of the south fork of Bullskin to Opecken and thence to the Courthouse), 20, 25
Sections:
- Road from the head of the south fork of Bullskin to Opecken (road from John McCormack's to the Main road to Town; road from John McCormack's house to Opecken Creek which leads to town), 20, 25, 49, 67, 87, 107 *[Note: This section appears to be different than the section from Opecken to the head to Bullskin (pp. 22, 31) of the road from Maj. Andrew Campbell Gent.'s to the Chapel at Cunningham's, 22.]*
- Road from Opecken to the Courthouse (road from Opeckon Creek to the Main road leading to Winchester), 20, 25, 107

Road from the Courthouse to the South Branch, 27(2), 40
Alteration:
- To go around William Hoge Jr.'s plantation, 27(2)

Road from the Courthouse to Robert Edge's, 30

Road from the Courthouse to John Littler's old place (road from Litler's/Littler's old place/plantation to Winchester Town), 33, 62, 117

Road from Capt. George Johnston's plantation on the Long Marsh into the road which leads from Williams's Gap to the Courthouse (road from George Johnston Gent.'s house to the road from Town to Fairfax County), 33, 46, 54

Road from the Courthouse/Winchester to Opecken Creek/Opecken ford, 34, 36(2), 43, 50

Road from the lower part of Pattersons Creek by Power Hazel's into the wagon road which leads from the Courthouse to the South Branch, 40

Road laid off from Cunningham's Chapel to the Main road from the Courthouse and from thence to Watkins's ferry, 40

(Main) road from the Courthouse/town of Winchester to Watkins's ferry, 40, 65, 112
- To be turned where it passes through William Jollyffe's land, 65

Sections:
- From Tuscarora to Capt./Mr. (Thomas) Caton's plantation, 110, 112
- From Watkins's ferry to Caton's Stone House, 162

Road from Frederick Town [Courthouse] to the mouth of the South Branch of Potomac, 43
*[Note: This appears to be a separate road from the following:
Road from the mouth of the South Branch to the Courthouse, 45.]*

Road from the mouth of the South Branch to the Courthouse, 45

Road running through Thomas Cowen's meadow (road through Thomas Cowen's plantation), 141, 144, 145

Road from John McCormick's house to Crawford's Muster Ground (road from Dr. McCormack's to the Muster Ground, including the bridge), 107, 139

[Note: For Crisman, Cristman, etc., see Christman.]

Road from Crooked Run/the mouth of Crooked Run to (Capt.) John Hite's, 8, 10, 26, 29, 54, 68, 75, 80

Road from the mouth of Crooked Run to the Courthouse (road from the mouth of Crooked Run and crossing the run the upper side of Thomas Branson's plantation and thence to the Courthouse), 9, 10, 11

Road from Chester's ferry to the Courthouse (road from Chester's ferry to John Hite's; road from the ferry landing and thence via the first gap in Guard Hill, crossing Crooked Run, thence on the upper side of Robert McKay's spring, crossing Crooked Run above Thomas Branson's, thence along the road laid off by Bethany Haines to John Hite's), 14, 16

Road from the Main road near Robert Warth's to Crooked Run, 63

Road from Crooked Run to Gregory's ford, 63, 110

Road from the North River ford to the ford of Crooked Run, 81, 158

Road from Crooked Run to Howell's ford, 108

Road from Crooked Run to the Main County road leading from Augusta County, 158

Road from Caleb Job's Run to the Culpeper line at Chester's Gap, 91

Road from the Culpeper road at Chester's Gap to Chester's ford, 77

Road from the School House/old School House on Shannando River to the Chapel at Cunningham's, 17, 55, 76

Road from Opecken Creek to the Chapel by James Cunningham's (road from John Neill's house to the Chapel at Cunningham's; road from Opecken Creek at John Neill's ford near his house, thence along the old path that formerly went to James Hill's, to the forks of the old wagon road commonly called Littler's Wagon road, and thence along Hill's Marsh to Cunningham's house and so to the Chapel), 20, 23, 33
[Note: May be the same as:
Road from the Chapel at Cunningham's to John Neill's, Gent., to be continued to Abrahams Run (road crossing Opeckon at John Neill's ford to Cunningham's Chapel), 39, 53.]
[Note: See also:
Road from the forks of the road at Cunningham's Chapel to Opecken Creek, 34 (Note: Road order entries appear to indicate that this road is different from the road noted on pp. 20, 23, 33.).]

Road from Maj. Andrew Campbell Gent.'s to the Chapel at Cunningham's (road from Maj. Campbell's to Joseph Evans's thence to William Mitchell's then across Opecken thence to the head of the south fork of the Bulskin, thence to Thomas Linseys's on the Long Marsh, thence to John Linsey Gent.'s and from thence to the Chapel at Cunningham's), 22
Sections:
- From Campbell's to Opecken (from Andrew Campbell Gent.'s to William Mitchell's), 22, 30
- From Opecken to the head of Bulskin, 22, 31
- From the head of Bulskin to the Long Marsh, 22, 25
- From the Long Marsh to Fairfax road, 22
- From the Fairfax road to the Chapel), 22, 25

Road from the Chapel at James Cunningham's to the Chapel at Robert McCoy's Spring, 26
Sections:
- Road from the Chapel at Cunningham's to Borden's/Burden's Great Spring/Marsh/Run, 26, 27, 37, 55, 56, 58, 84
- Road from Borden's Great Spring to the Chapel at McCoy's Spring, 26, 55

Road from the head of Pitts's Marsh to the Chapel at James Cunningham's, 28

Road from the Chapel at Cunningham's into the River road, 33

Road from the forks of the road at Cunningham's Chapel to Opecken Creek, 34 *[Note: Road order entries appear to indicate that this road is different from the road noted on pp. 20, 23, 33.]*

Road from the Chapel at Cunningham's to John Neill's, Gent., to be continued to Abrahams Run (road crossing Opeckon at John Neill's ford to Cunningham's Chapel), 39, 53

Road laid off from Cunningham's Chapel to the Main road from the Courthouse and from thence to Watkins's ferry, 40

Road from Richard Sturman's house to Stribling's quarter and from that road to Cunningham's Chapel (road from the head of the pond at Stribling's quarter to Mr. Sturman's and from thence to Cunningham's Chapel), 42, 51

Road from the Chapel to the old road which leads to William Mitchel's (road from Morgan Morgan's Chapel to William Mitchell's), 20, 25
[Note: This appears to be the same as:
Road from William Mitchell's to Cunningham's Chapel (road continued to the Creek and the bank to be cut down), 46.]

Road from William Mitchell's to Cunningham's Chapel (road continued to the Creek and the bank to be cut down), 46

Road from the Chapel at Cunningham's to Mr. Lewis Neill's ford on Opeckon, 48

Road from Mr. Rutherford's towards Cunningham's Chapel, 49

Road from the end of Johnston's road to Cunningham's Chapel, 53

Road from Burwell's mill to Cunningham's Chapel, 87

Road from Snickers's ferry/ford up the riverside to Cunningham's Chapel (road from Snickers's ferry to Cunningham's ferry), 88, 89, 104, 132

Road from Spout Run to Cunningham's Chapel, 92, 109

Roads from the Glebe:
- From the Glebe to Cunningham's Chapel, 95, 101, 134
- From the late Glebe to Cunningham's Chapel, 134
- From the Glebe to McCoy's/ McKay's Chapel, 95, 98

Sections:
- Road from the Glebe as far as the Dutch road towards McKay's Chapel, 101
- Road from the Dutch road to McKay's Chapel, 101, 102
- From the Glebe into the Main road that leads to Winchester, 98

Road from Col. Mercer's upper quarter to Cunningham's Chapel, 128, 130

Road from Cunningham's Chapel to George Henry's, 130

Road from the White Post to the cross roads near Cunningham's Chapel (road from Cunningham's Chapel to Lord Fairfax's), 133, 140, 153, 171

Road from the forks of the road leading to Berry's ferry, to Cunningham's Chapel, 153

Road from Cunningham's to Middle Creek, 56

Road from Snickers's ferry/ford up the riverside to Cunningham's Chapel (road from Snickers's ferry to Cunningham's ferry), 88, 89, 104, 132

Road from Mill Creek to Tuscarora (road from Cunningham's mill to Tuscarora), 61, 69

Road from Mendenall's mill to Cunningham's mill, 78

Road from Cunningham's mill to that part of the road opposite to Samuel Wilson's house, 130, 156

Road from Cunningham's mill to Henry Bowen's, 131

Road between Robert Cunningham's and where Dr. John Brisco now lives, 57

Road from Mr. Robert Cunningham's/Cunningham's mill to Mr. Robert Moseley's, 68, 93

Road from Robert Cunningham's to Samuel Patton's, 73

Road from Morgan's Chapel to the Main road (alteration: marked from the Chapel to Robert Cunningham's house), 77

Road from Littler's/Samuel Littler's/Samuel Littler's Run/Littler's Branch/Littler's mill/Littler's old place/ Littler's lane to Robert Cunningham's/Robert Cunningham's mill/Widow Cunningham's, 98, 101(2), 105, 108, 118, 138, 165

Sir John's road (road called Sir John Sinclaire's road), 96, 97, 113, 119, 127, 132
Sections:
- From Winchester to the plantation where Isaac Thomas did live, 96
- From the place where the road from Robert Cunningham's falls into it to the forks where the road leads to Winchester, 132
- From the plantation where Isaac Thomas did live to the County line, 96
- From the Hunting Ridge to Isaac's Creek at Pritchet's place, 97
- Sir John's road leading from the Timber Ridge to Isaac's Creek, 113
- From the forks to James McGill's, 119
- Sir John's road from the end of the Sleepy Creek Mountain where the Warm Spring road crosses it to James Daugherty's, 127

Probable sections:
- Road from Isaac's Creek to the County line, 148
- Road from (the top of) the Hunting Ridge to the County line, 151, 158

Road from Cunningham's/Robert Cunningham's mill and Morgan's Chapel into/to the road called Sir John's road, 97, 111

Road from Hugh Lyle's plantation on Back Creek through Curtis's Gap, to Robert Cunningham's (road from Robert Cunningham's to Hugh Lyle's on Back Creek), 103, 104
Sections:

- From Robert Cunningham's to David Miller's plantation, 104
- From David Miller's to the foot of the North Mountain, 104
- From the foot of the North Mountain to Hugh Lyle's on Back Creek, 104

Road from Opeckon to the Widow Cunningham's, 71

Road from Littler's/Samuel Littler's/Samuel Littler's Run/Littler's Branch/Littler's mill/Littler's old place/ Littler's lane to Robert Cunningham's/Robert Cunningham's mill/Widow Cunningham's, 98, 101(2), 105, 108, 118, 138, 165

Road from Hugh Lyle's plantation on Back Creek through Curtis's Gap, to Robert Cunningham's (road from Robert Cunningham's to Hugh Lyle's on Back Creek), 103, 104
Sections:
- From Robert Cunningham's to David Miller's plantation, 104
- From David Miller's to the foot of the North Mountain, 104
- From the foot of the North Mountain to Hugh Lyle's on Back Creek, 104

Road from Jonathan Curtis's house to Edward Beason's mill, 22

[Note: For Darst, see Durst.]

Sir John's road (road called Sir John Sinclaire's road), 96, 97, 113, 119, 127, 132
Sections:
- From Winchester to the plantation where Isaac Thomas did live, 96
- From the place where the road from Robert Cunningham's falls into it to the forks where the road leads to Winchester, 132
- From the plantation where Isaac Thomas did live to the County line, 96
- From the Hunting Ridge to Isaac's Creek at Pritchet's place, 97
- Sir John's road leading from the Timber Ridge to Isaac's Creek, 113
- From the forks to James McGill's, 119
- Sir John's road from the end of the Sleepy Creek Mountain where the Warm Spring road crosses it to James Daugherty's, 127

Probable sections:
- Road from Isaac's Creek to the County line, 148
- Road from (the top of) the Hunting Ridge to the County line, 151, 158

Road that leads through David Dedrick's/Diddrick's land (alteration), 96, 97

[Note: For Dellinger, see Dilliner.]

Road from Parks's graveyard near Cape Capon Water, over Dellings Run into the Wagon road on Joseph Edward's land, 25

Road from the head of John Lupton's meadow to the South Branch road above David Denny's, 144, 146

Road from John Denton's [to] Jacob Rush's/Rushe's plantation in the upper end of Powells Fort, 127, 133

Road from Desponet's/Disponet's Gap/Barnet Desponet's to Lewis Stephens's/Stevens's mill, 53, 57, 69, 86, 117

Road through Charles Dick's land (alteration), 105, 110

Road from Charles Dick's mill to Thomas Lindsey's, 113

[Note: Entries for Dellinger and Dillener are combined; see also Telener.]

Road from Jeremiah Lewis's (at/near the County line) to Stephens's/Stevens's mill at/on the Narrow Passage, 79, 104
Sections:
- Road from the County line near Jeremiah Lewis's to Christian Dilliner's, 81
- Road from Christian Dillener's to Lewis Stevens's mill at the Narrow Passage, 81

Road from Christian Dellinger's to Cutlip Sink's mill on Stoney Creek, 133

Road from John Little's to the Augusta [County] line (road from the [Augusta] County line below Brock's Gap to John Little's), 157, 159
Sections:
- From Little's to Narrow Passage Creek, 159
- From [Narrow] Passage Creek to Stoney Creek, 159
- From Stoney Creek to Christian Dellinger's, 159
- From Christian Dellinger's to Mill Creek, 159
- From Mill Creek to the [Augusta] County line, 159

Road from John Frost's mill to the main road between John Littler's plantation and John Milbourn's/Milburn's plantation, (road from Capt. Frost's mill thence to Buffler lick thence through the lands of John Bosser, and David Springer, thence to the ford, thence through the lands of William Frost and Mathias Elmore, along Elmor[e]'s Creek to Widow Dillon's, and thence to the main road leading to Rappahannock between John Littler's and John Milbourn's), 1, 3, 20, 28
Probable sections:
- Road from John Frost's mill to William Frost's/William Frost's ford, 44, 65
- The other part of the said road, from William Frost's to Col. Morgan's road (road from William Frost's to William Dillon's), 44, 110
- Road from Frost's to Dillon's (alteration round the north side of Dillon's plantation into a lane), 126

Road from Joseph Bridges's mill to William Dillon's plantation, 135

Bridle road from Edward Dodd's to the Main road, 89

Road from Evan Watkins's ferry [on Potomac River] to Tuscorora, 13
Sections:
- From Charles Donahue's house to Potomac River, 24
- From Charles Donahue's house to Tuscorora Creek, 24

Road through Thomas Doster's plantation (alterations), 110

Road from Thomas Doster's to the Main road near the Widow Ballenger's, 110, 111

Road from the head of Bullskin Marsh running by the head of Long Marsh into the road at the Dry Marsh below Capt. Lewis Neill's, 98

Road from the Dry Marsh to (Thomas) Helm's mill, 155, 157, 170

Road from Lewis Neill's mill into the road leading to Helms's mill at the head of the Dry Marsh, 160

Road from George Rice's house to the Main road at the Dry Marsh, 161

Road leading to Messanutting from the White House to the Dry Run, 114, 132

Road from Dry Run to the top of the Ridge at Thornton's Gap, 129

Road from Cedar Creek to the crossroad at John Duckworth's, 48

Road from Capt. Jacob Funk's to John Duckworth's house, 82

Road from McKay's Chapel to the Widow Duckworth's, 104

Road leading from Jacob Christman's plantation to the Widow Duckworth's plantation, 114

Road leading from the plantation of the Widow Duckworth to Stover's Town, 115

[Note: Entries for Darst and Durst are combined.]

Road from Abraham Durst's Shop to the road on this side of the Massanuting Mountain (road from Abraham Darst's Smith's Shop to the top of the Massanutting [Massanutten] Mountain), 135, 137, 149(2)
Sections/related roads:
- Road from the North River to the County line, 149
- Road from the County line as the Main road now goes till it intersects the road leading from Abraham Durst's Smith Shop to the top of the [Massanutten] Mountain, 149

Road from the County line on Cape Capon Mountain by Sink's mill to Abraham Darst's smith shop, 138

Road from Peter Stevens's lane to the <u>Dutch</u> road leading to Kersey's ferry, 61, 65

Road from his Lordship's quarter into the <u>Dutch</u> road (Col. Martin's road), 71

<u>Dutch</u> road from Kersey's ferry to Wrights Branch, 86

Roads from the Glebe:
- From the Glebe to Cunningham's Chapel, 95, 101, 134
- From the late Glebe to Cunningham's Chapel, 134
- From the Glebe to McCoy's/ McKay's Chapel, 95, 98

Sections:
- Road from the Glebe as far as the <u>Dutch</u> road towards McKay's Chapel, 101
- Road from the <u>Dutch</u> road to McKay's Chapel, 101, 102
- From the Glebe into the Main road that leads to Winchester, 98

Public road leading from Andrew Campbell Gent.'s to Watkins's ferry (alteration by the plantation formerly Jonathan Jayeas [Jayes?], dec., now in the possession of Elizabeth <u>Dyer</u>), 28

McKay's Chapel road, 122
Section:
- From the forks of <u>Earl's Mill Run</u> to George Henry, 122

Road from Samuel <u>Earle</u> Gent.'s dwelling house to his quarter, 9
Alteration, 108

Road from Samuel <u>Earle's</u> house into the road leading from Chester's Gap at Manasses Run (road from Samuel <u>Earl's</u> house into the road called Chester's road Manaseh's Run), 113, 115

Roads leading from Samuel <u>Earle's</u> house, 116
- The old road, 116
- The road lately opened by Samuel <u>Earle</u>, 116

The Chapel road from Samuel <u>Earl's</u> meadows to Gregory's ford and Seaborn's ford, 157

Road from <u>Eaton's</u> mill through Mill's Gap to Fallis's mill, 141, 144
Alteration:
- From the place opposite Sutherland's ford to the Mountain Run, 144

Road from Winchester to Hougland's ferry, leading through Benjamin Thornbrugh's and Enos Ellis's plantations (proposed alteration at Benjamin Thornbrugh's and Enos Ellis's plantations), 150, 156
Section:
- From David Miller's old plantation to Isaac <u>Eaton's</u>, 156

Road from this Courthouse [Winchester] to the top of the Blue Ridge of Mountains at Williams's Gap (road from Capt. Neill's off and on the old road to Joseph Wilkenson's and thence off on the

same road to Francis Carney's and from thence to Edge's ford and from thence off and on the old road to the top of the said Mountain), 12
Sections:
- From Capt. Lewis Neill's/Lewis Neill Gent.'s to Francis Carney's/Carnie's (road from Francis Carney's/Carney's Spring to Lewis Neill's/Opeckon at Neill's ford/Opeckon Creek by Capt. Neill's/ Opecken by Lewis Neill's, Gent), 12, 22, 31, 82, 100, 104
- From Carney's to Edge's ford on Shannadore River (road from Shanando River to Carney's Spring, 12, 50, 83
- From Edge's ford to the top of the Blue Ridge on Williams's Gap, 12

Probable later sections:
- Road from Winchester Town to Lewis Neill's/Lewis Neill's ford on Opeckon, 59, 67
- Road from the ford at Lewis Neill Gent.'s house to Littler's road, 59
- Road from Littler's road to Carney's old house, 59
- Road from Carney's old house to the River, 59
- Road from the River to the top of the mountain at Williams's Gap (road from Edward Snigers's [on Shanando] to the top of the Mountain at Williams's Gap; road from the River at Snigers's to the County line at Williams's Gap; road from the top of the Ridge to Edward Snickers's/Snigers's ford/ferry/ferry at Snicker's house; road from the Ferry road [Snigers's] to the top of the Ridge at Williams's Gap), 59, 76, 79, 81, 83, 113

Road from the Courthouse to Robert Edge's, 30

Road from Parks's graveyard near Cape Capon Water, over Dellings Run into the Wagon road on Joseph Edward's land, 25

Road from Joseph Edwards Jr.'s to the Main road at the bridge over Opeckon Creek, 84

Road from Henry Moor's to the Elk Branch, 143

Road from Winchester to Hougland's ferry, leading through Benjamin Thornbrugh's and Enos Ellis's plantations (proposed alteration at Benjamin Thornbrough's and Enos Ellis's plantations), 150, 156
Section:
- From David Miller's old plantation to Isaac Eaton's, 156

Road from John Frost's mill to the main road between John Littler's plantation and John Milbourn's/Milburn's plantation, (road from Capt. Frost's mill thence to Buffler lick thence through the lands of John Bosser, and David Springer, thence to the ford, thence through the lands of William Frost and Mathias Elmore, along Elmor[e]'s Creek to Widow Dillon's, and thence to the main road leading to Rappahannock between John Littler's and John Milbourn's), 1, 3, 20, 28
Probable sections:
- Road from John Frost's mill to William Frost's/William Frost's ford, 44, 65

- The other part of the said road, from William Frost's to Col. Morgan's road (road from William Frost's to William Dillon's), 44, 110
- Road from Frost's to Dillon's (alteration round the north side of Dillon's plantation into a lane), 126

Road from the new bridge at Opeckon into the road leading from Winchester to Henry Enochs's, 79

Road leading from Winchester to Henry Enochs's, 79(2)
Section:
- From the beginning of the new road [i.e., the road from the new bridge at Opeckon into the road leading from Winchester to Henry Enochs's], to the County line, 79

Road through Isaac Evans's plantation (alteration), 143

Road from Isaac Evans's to Henry Vanmetre's mill on Tuscarora and from thence to the Warm Springs road, 149, 152

Road from the head of the spring by the Chapel to John Evans's and from thence to Tuscorora, 4
Section:
- Road from the head of the spring by the Chapel to John Evans's, 1

Road from Jacob Hite's mill to the Main road (leading to Watkins's ferry) at John Evans's (road from John Evans's fence to Jacob Hite's mill [including alterations]), 100, 103, 135, 137, 139

Road from Maj. Andrew Campbell Gent.'s to the Chapel at Cunningham's (road from Maj. Campbell's to Joseph Evans's thence to William Mitchell's then across Opecken thence to the head of the south fork of the Bulskin, thence to Thomas Linseys's on the Long Marsh, thence to John Linsey Gent.'s and from thence to the Chapel at Cunningham's), 22
Sections:
- From Campbell's to Opecken (from Andrew Campbell Gent.'s to William Mitchell's), 22, 30
- From Opecken to the head of Bulskin, 22, 31
- From the head of Bulskin to the Long Marsh, 22, 25
- From the Long Marsh to Fairfax road, 22
- From the Fairfax road to the Chapel), 22, 25

Road from Joseph Evans's to Col. Morgan Morgan's, 40, 43

Road from John Linsey Gent.'s house into the road which leads from the Courthouse to Fairfax County (road from the Fairfax road to John Linsey Gent.'s/Mr. John Lindsey's, 20, 23, 59

Road from Maj. Andrew Campbell Gent.'s to the Chapel at Cunningham's (road from Maj. Campbell's to Joseph Evans's thence to William Mitchell's then across Opecken thence to the head of the south fork of the Bulskin, thence to Thomas Linseys's on the Long Marsh, thence to John Linsey Gent.'s and from thence to the Chapel at Cunningham's), 22

Sections:
- From Campbell's to Opecken (from Andrew Campbell Gent.'s to William Mitchell's), 22, 30
- From Opecken to the head of Bulskin, 22, 31
- From the head of Bulskin to the Long Marsh, 22, 25
- From the Long Marsh to Fairfax road, 22
- From the Fairfax road to the Chapel), 22, 25

Road from Capt. George Johnston's plantation on the Long Marsh into the road which leads from Williams's Gap to the Courthouse (road from George Johnston Gent.'s house to the road from Town to Fairfax County), 33, 46, 54

Road from Mr. John Sturman's old place to the Fairfax road, 60

Road from the Fairfax road to the north side of the Long Marsh, 60

The Fairfax road, 73, 74

Road from the Fairfax road to the ferry landing and from thence to the Fairfax road on the other side the River, 83

Road from Col. Fairfax's quarter to the Fairfax road, 83

Road from Vestal's ford to Col. Fairfax's quarter, 83

Road from Col. Fairfax's quarter to the Fairfax road, 83

[Note: Entries for Lord Fairfax and his Lordship are combined.]

Road from Gregory's ford thence near Lord Fairfax's seat and into Hite's wagon road, 47

Road from Lewis Stevens Gent.'s old plantation to his Lordship's quarter (road from Lawrence Stevens's by Lewis Stephens's old plantation to Col. Martin's road), 71, 87

Road from his Lordship's quarter into the Dutch road (Col. Martin's road), 71

Road from his Lordship's house into McCoy's Chapel road and from thence to his Lordship's quarter in the Long Bottom, 73, 75

Road from his Lordship's line to (Benjamin) Allen's Mill Creek, 74, 85

Road from the New Town (Stephensburgh/Stevensburgh) to Nations's (road leading from Stephensburgh to the Right Honourable Thomas Lord Fairfax's plantation called Nation's; road from Stephensburgh to Nation's plantation), 92, 96, 114, 144, 145

Road from Lord Fairfax's quarter where Nation formerly lived to the ford at Comb's (road from the Right Honourable Thomas Lord Fairfax's quarter to Combes's ferry), 101, 113

Road from Col. John Hite's to the forks of the road leading from Lord Fairfax's to Stephensburgh, 120

Road from the White Post to the cross roads near Cunningham's Chapel (road from Cunningham's Chapel to Lord Fairfax's), 133, 140, 153, 171

Road from Lord Fairfax's upper quarter to the Land Office, 138, 141(2)

Road leading from Lord Fairfax's to Winchester (alteration at David Brown's plantation), 168, 169

[Note: Entries for Falkner and Felkner are combined.]

(Alteration of) the part of the road from Hougland's ferry to Winchester, that goes by Hancher's, and through the plantations of Jesse Felkner and others where they enter at the Branch road (alteration of the road from Houghland's ferry and through Falkner's land), 157, 158

Road from Watkins's ferry to the falling water, 40

Road from Potomac River at Neals Friend's to the Falling Springs, 60

Road from the Falling Springs to the Bear Garden Ridge, 60

[Note: For Fallis, see Follis.]

[Note: For Felkner, see Falkner.]

Road from the Main road leading from Jacob Hite's to Mecklenburg through Foster's land to the Ferrying Water and also to the ford of Potomac, 148

Road from the Flat Rock to the ford upon Bulskin (above Mr. Pyke's), 136, 162

Road from the Flat Rock by Mr. Thruston's by the head of Kate's Spring, into the road leading to the Bloomery below Mr. Ariss's, 167

[Note: Entries for Fallis and Follis are combined.]

Road from Mills's Gap to Follis's mill and the Main road at Jane Caldwell's plantation, 111, 112

Road from Eaton's mill through Mill's Gap to Fallis's mill, 141, 144
Alteration:
- From the place opposite Sutherland's ford to the Mountain Run, 144

Road from the furnace erecting on the north branch of Pembroke to the forge erecting on Cedar Creek (road from the forge to the furnace), 129(2), 146
Sections:
- From the furnace to Devault Hulberger's, 129
- From Hulberger's to the forge (from Opeckon to the forge upon Cedar Creek), 129, 142, 144

[Note: For roads associated with a specific forge (e.g., Marlborough forge, Isaac Zane's forge), see the entries for the particular forge.]

Road from John Racklie's to John Fosset's, 47

Road from the Main road leading from Jacob Hite's to Mecklenburg through Foster's land to the Ferrying Water and also to the ford of Potomac, 148

Road from Jacob Hite's house to William Foster's ferry, 160

Road from James Fowler's house to the head of Bullskin, 109

Road from James Fowler's to Marquis Calmes's, 109

Road from James Fowler's to Thomas Lindsey's, 122

Road from Howel's ford to Foxtrap Point on the south side of Shanando, 29

Road from the landing place on the south side of Shanando River at Kersey's ferry to Foxtrap Point road (road from Kersey's to the ferry road on the south side of Shanando), 43, 49

Road from Col. Burwell's mill to the fork of the road at Foxtrap Point, 50, 58
Associated roads:
- The [wagon] ford road, 50, 58
- The ferry road, 50

(Petition to the Court of Orange County for) a road from the County line of Frederick to the upper inhabitants of Augusta on Woods River, 10

(Petition to the Court of Prince William County to meet Frederick County with) a road from the Thorough fair at the Pignut Ridge to the top of the Blue Ridge at the head of Manasses Run, 10

Road to be cleared in Prince William County from the fork of the road below Watts's ordinary to meet a road cleared in Frederick County leading through Manassas Run Gap, 70

Road from Frederick Town [Courthouse] to the mouth of the South Branch of Potomac, 43
[Note: This appears to be a separate road from the following:
Road from the mouth of the South Branch to the Courthouse, 45.]

The Fredericksburg road, 158

Road from the mouth of the South Branch and also from Neals Friend's (on Potomac River) to the town of Winchester (road from Winchester Town to Potomac River, in order for a road to be cleared to the mouth of the South Branch), 55, 60

Road from Potomac River at Neals Friend's to the Falling Springs, 60

Road from (Paul) Froman's mill to the Sand ford/Sandy ford on Opeckon, 65, 69, 71, 98, 99, 129

Road from Paul Froman's mill by the head of Opeckon into the road leading to Winchester, 90

Road from John Frost's mill to the main road between John Littler's plantation and John Milbourn's/Milburn's plantation, (road from Capt. Frost's mill thence to Buffler lick thence through the lands of John Bosser, and David Springer, thence to the ford, thence through the lands of William Frost and Mathias Elmore, along Elmor[e]'s Creek to Widow Dillon's, and thence to the main road leading to Rappahannock between John Littler's and John Milbourn's), 1, 3, 20, 28
Probable sections:
- Road from John Frost's mill to William Frost's/William Frost's ford, 44, 65
- The other part of the said road, from William Frost's to Col. Morgan's road (road from William Frost's to William Dillon's), 44, 110
- Road from Frost's to Dillon's (alteration round the north side of Dillon's plantation into a lane), 126

Road from John Frost's mill to the main road between John Littler's plantation and John Milbourn's/Milburn's plantation, (road from Capt. Frost's mill thence to Buffler lick thence through the lands of John Bosser, and David Springer, thence to the ford, thence through the lands of William Frost and Mathias Elmore, along Elmor[e]'s Creek to Widow Dillon's, and thence to the main road leading to Rappahannock between John Littler's and John Milbourn's), 1, 3, 20, 28
Probable sections:
- Road from John Frost's mill to William Frost's/William Frost's ford, 44, 65
- The other part of the said road, from William Frost's to Col. Morgan's road (road from William Frost's to William Dillon's), 44, 110
- Road from Frost's to Dillon's (alteration round the north side of Dillon's plantation into a lane), 126

Road from William Frost's plantation on Back Creek to Bridger's mill, 134

Road from White's mill to William Frost's middle plantation on Back Creek, 166

Road leading from Opeckon to Fry's mill, 171

Road from John Wisecarver's to Cooper's mill by Benjamin Fry's, 146, 148

Road from the South Branch road near Jeremiah Smith's to the Warm Springs near Henry Fry's, 170

Road from Joseph Fry's plantation on Cedar Creek to the Furnace being erected on the north branch of Pembroke, 118

Road from the head of Bullskin to the Main road by Fryer's (road from Alexander Fryer's to the head of Bulskin, 109, 126(2)
Alteration:
- Where the road passes through John Smith's land, 126(2)

Road from Jacob Hite's mill each way into the Main road leading to Swearingen's ferry (road from Alexander Fryer's to Swearingen's road), 100, 102, 109

Road from Alexander Fryer's to Jacob Hite's mill, 119

Road from Stephens's/Stevens's mill to the head of Funk's Mill Creek, 64, 85

Road from Hurst's ford to the fork of the road leading to Funk's mill, 159

Road leading from Isaac Hite's, through Joseph Baker's plantation, to Henry Funk's mill (to be turned round Baker's plantation), 153

Road from Henry Funk's mill on Passage Creek to Abraham Kendrick's upper ford and from thence to William Ashby's, 158, 160
Sections:
- From Henry Funk's mill to Abraham Kendrick's upper ford, 160
- From Abraham Kendrick's upper ford to William Ashby's, 160

Road from the road crossing the River at James McCoy's ford to Capt. Jacob Funk's, 81

Road from Capt. Jacob Funk's to John Duckworth's house, 82

Road from John Funk's mill to Chester's ferry and from thence to where the road takes out of Chester's road to Manasses Run, 1, 2
Sections:
- From John Funk's mill to the North River, 2, 79
- From the North River to the Haybottom, 2, 78
- From the Haybottom to where the road takes off to Manasses Run, 2, 31, 34, 55
- Road to be continued to Manasses Run, 31

Road from John Funk's mill across Ceeder Run Creek ford to Robert McKay/McCoy Jr.'s. and to Branston's Gap (road from Funk's mill back of George Telener's, thence to Ceedar Creek ford and Robert McCoy's, and thence to Gregorie's ford upon the river), 2(2)

Road from John Hite's mill into the road that comes from John Funk's mill to John Gregory's, 7

Road from Ceedar Creek to (John) Funk's mill and from Funk's mill to the County line, 17
Sections:
- Road from John Funk's mill to Cedar Creek, 17, 26, 35, 42
- Road from Funk's mill/Funk's Mill Creek/Funk's Mill Run to the (Augusta) County line, 17, 42, 64, 69, 85, 93

Road from John Funk's to McCoy's Chapel (alteration round Robert McCoy's fence), 113

Road from Joseph Fry's plantation on Cedar Creek to the Furnace being erected on the north branch of Pembroke, 118

Road from the furnace erecting on the north branch of Pembroke to the forge erecting on Cedar Creek (road from the forge to the furnace), 129(2), 146
Sections:
- From the furnace to Devault Hulberger's, 129
- From Hulberger's to the forge (from Opeckon to the forge upon Cedar Creek), 129, 142, 144

Road from John Snap's to the Furnace, 130

[Note: For roads associated with a specific furnace (e.g., Marlborough furnace, Semple's furnace), see the entries for the particular furnace.]

Road (starting at the Main road leading from Winchester to Watkins's ferry) from Peter Fussey's Big Spring/Fussey's Large Spring to the upper side of the mouth of Opeckon Creek, 133(2)

Road from John Littler's mill to William Gaddis's/Gaddy's plantation, 9, 36, 68

Road from William Hancher's mill to the North Mountain near John Gerrard's, 166

[Note: Entries for Gess and Guess at combined.]

Road from Edward Snickers's/Snigers's to Moses Guess's/Gess's, 71, 78

Road from Gilliland's mill to Andrew Campbell's, 82

Road from Winchester to Marlborough forge 150(2), 171
Alterations:
- To be turned round John Allen's plantation, 150(2)
- To be turned to run upon the line between Robert Glass and the Rev. Mr. Hoge, 171

Roads from the Glebe:
- From the Glebe to Cunningham's Chapel, 95, 101, 134
- From the late Glebe to Cunningham's Chapel, 134
- From the Glebe to McCoy's/ McKay's Chapel, 95, 98

Sections:
- Road from the <u>Glebe</u> as far as the Dutch road towards McKay's Chapel, 101
- Road from the Dutch road to McKay's Chapel, 101, 102
- From the <u>Glebe</u> into the Main road that leads to Winchester, 98

Road from John Lyles's by James Morrison's, John Miller's, John <u>Glenn's</u> and William <u>Glenn's</u> plantations, to Patterson's mill and from thence into the Warm Springs road, 156
[Note: See also:
Road from William Patterson's mill to John Lyle's (alternate route), 159.]

Road from John Nealan[d]'s/Neeland's on Sharrando to William Vestal's on the same river (road from John Nealand's down the river by the lands of John Grimes, Capt. Stribling, Timothy Haney, Darby Conely, <u>Goldin</u>, John Hamman, Thomas Hamman, and Elizabeth Pearson, across Pearson's Neck of Land to Jonathan Walker's, over Bulskin, and by Robert Hayes's and along Hayes's path to Vestal's), 9, 10

Road from <u>Goony Run</u> ford into Mr. Hite's road by the Three Miles Lick, 153

Road from the <u>Great Plain</u> to Selser's Mill Run, 72

Road from the <u>Great</u> road leading from Mr. Jacob Hite's to John Smith's to the head of Worthington's Marsh thence down the Marsh into the road near John Swim's called Keys's road and into the road leading by Thomas Rutherford's to Vestal's ferry, 49

Road from Hogland's Neck by Barnet Newkirk's and into the <u>Great</u> road, 77

Road from Opeckon Creek to the Main county road (road from William Neill's upon Opeckon into the <u>Great</u> road that runs by William Joleff's; road from the forks of the road leading from Winchester to William Jolliff's to Opeckon Creek), 88, 120, 147

Road from Henry Spears's to go by Isaac Hite's and thence into the Main county road (road from the <u>Great</u> road to the fork of the road that leads to Henry Spears's road), 93, 134

Road from the Baptist Meeting House to the <u>Great</u> road leading from Morgan Morgan's to the Town of Winchester, 115, 117

Road from John Funk's mill across Ceeder Run Creek ford to Robert McKay/McCoy Jr.'s. and to Branston's Gap (road from Funk's mill back of George Telener's, thence to Ceedar Creek ford and Robert McCoy's, and thence to <u>Gregorie's</u> ford upon the river), 2(2)

Road from <u>Gregory's</u> ford to the top of the Ridge/Blue Ridge (road from <u>Gregory's</u> ford to the top of the Blue Ridge at the head of Menasses [Manasses] Run; road from <u>Gregory's</u> ford to Menasses Run at the County line; road from <u>Gregory's</u> ford to Manassey's Gap), 6, 91, 109, 110, 148, 169

Road from the Courthouse to <u>Gregory's</u> ford, 11

Road from Gregory's ford to West Run, 12

Road from Branson's mill to Gregory's ford, 38

Road from Gregory's ford thence near Lord Fairfax's seat and into Hite's wagon road, 47

Road from Crooked Run to Gregory's ford, 63, 110

Road from Gregory's ford to Ashby's ford, 76

Road from McKay's Chapel to Gregory's ford, 138

The Chapel road from Samuel Earl's meadows to Gregory's ford and Seaborn's ford, 157

Road from Howel's ford to Gregory's wagon road, 32

Road from John Hite's mill into the road that comes from John Funk's mill to John Gregory's, 7

Road from John Nealan[d]'s/Neeland's on Sharrando to William Vestal's on the same river (road from John Nealand's down the river by the lands of John Grimes, Capt. Stribling, Timothy Haney, Darby Conely, Goldin, John Hamman, Thomas Hamman, and Elizabeth Pearson, across Pearson's Neck of Land to Jonathan Walker's, over Bulskin, and by Robert Hayes's and along Hayes's path to Vestal's), 9, 10

Road from Chester's ferry to the Courthouse (road from Chester's ferry to John Hite's; road from the ferry landing and thence via the first gap in Guard Hill, crossing Crooked Run, thence on the upper side of Robert McKay's spring, crossing Crooked Run above Thomas Branson's, thence along the road laid off by Bethany Haines to John Hite's), 14, 16

[Note: For Hagan, see Hogan.]

Road from Opecken at Hugh Hains's to the Indian Grave on the Main road, 54

Road from Hugh Hains's to John McCormack's, 54

Road from Chester's ferry to the Courthouse (road from Chester's ferry to John Hite's; road from the ferry landing and thence via the first gap in Guard Hill, crossing Crooked Run, thence on the upper side of Robert McKay's spring, crossing Crooked Run above Thomas Branson's, thence along the road laid off by Bethany Haines to John Hite's), 14, 16

Road from Robert Harper's at the mouth of Shanando to William Hall's mill and from thence into the road to Winchester, 72

Road from John Nealan[d]'s/Neeland's on Sharrando to William Vestal's on the same river (road from John Nealand's down the river by the lands of John Grimes, Capt. Stribling, Timothy Haney, Darby Conely, Goldin, John Hamman, Thomas Hamman, and Elizabeth Pearson, across

Pearson's Neck of Land to Jonathan Walker's, over Bulskin, and by Robert Hayes's and along Hayes's path to Vestal's), 9, 10

Road from Noah Hampton's mill, into the road on Great Cape Capon near James Coddy's/Cody's, 1, 6, 8

Road from Hampton's mill down the South Branch (road from below where Henry Vanmetre did live to where he now lives and down by his mill and Hampton's mill), 41

Road from Peter Tostee's plantation to Hampton's mill, 63

Road above Noah Hampton's house from Coombs's ferry up Shanando River (proposed alteration rejected), 93

Road from Jeremiah Smith's plantation to the Hampshire County line, 154

[Note: Entries for Hancheir, Hancheire, and Hancher are combined.]

(Alteration of) the part of the road from Hougland's ferry to Winchester, that goes by Hancher's, and through the plantations of Jesse Felkner and others where they enter at the Branch road (alteration of the road from Houghland's ferry and through Falkner's land), 157, 158

Road from Hogland's/Houghland's ferry via Hugh Lysle's, William Baldwin's, and William Hancheire's to fall into Morgan's road leading to Winchester, 143, 147
Sections:
- From Hogland's ferry to John Parks's, 148
- From Hugh Lysle's to Mill Creek, 148
- From Mill Creek to William Hancheir's, 148
- From William Hancheir's to Morgan's road, 148

Road from the Baptist Meeting House to William Hancheir's, 146, 147

Road from William Hancher's mill to the North Mountain near John Gerrard's, 166

Road from the South Branch road to William Hancher's mill and from thence into the road leading to Watkins's ferry, 166

Road from John Briscoe's mill upon Opeckon into the Mountain road by Murty Handley's, 127, 132

Road from John Nealan[d]'s/Neeland's on Sharrando to William Vestal's on the same river (road from John Nealand's down the river by the lands of John Grimes, Capt. Stribling, Timothy Haney, Darby Conely, Goldin, John Hamman, Thomas Hamman, and Elizabeth Pearson, across Pearson's Neck of Land to Jonathan Walker's, over Bulskin, and by Robert Hayes's and along Hayes's path to Vestal's), 9, 10

Road from the County line to Happy Creek, 52

Road from the Main road near Sebastian's quarter to Hardin and Keys's mill, and from thence to the Iron Works, 83
Section:
- Road from the Main road near Sebastian's quarter to Hardin and Keys's mill, 84

Road from the inhabitants on Worthington's Marsh to Hardin and Keys's mill, 84

Road from John Hardin's to Vestal's wagon road, 81

Road from Mark Hardin's ford on Shanando River to Isaac Hollingsworth's, 38, 51(2)
Sections
- Road from the River to Opeckon, 51
- Road from Opeckon to Isaac Hollingsworth's, 51

Road from Harper's ferry to Winchester (alterations where the road passes through Walter Shirley's land), 79, 82

Road leading from Worthington's Marsh to Harper's ferry, 163

Road from Robert Harper's at the mouth of Shanando to William Hall's mill and from thence into the road to Winchester, 72

(Alteration of) road at the River ford near Burr Harrison's, 165

Road from Thomas Hart's to Linder's ford and from the ford to the mountain, 53
Sections:
- Road from Thomas Hart's to Linder's ford, 53
- Road from Linder's ford to the mountain, 53

Road from Thomas Hart's to the top of the mountain at Vestal's Gap, 69

The old Wagon road at Thomas Hart's, 80

Road from the Signpost at the Hawks Bill down the South River into the road leading to Winchester, 77

Road from John Funk's mill to Chester's ferry and from thence to where the road takes out of Chester's road to Manasses Run, 1, 2
Sections:
- From John Funk's mill to the North River, 2, 79
- From the North River to the Haybottom, 2, 78
- From the Haybottom to where the road takes off to Manasses Run, 2, 31, 34, 55
- Road to be continued to Manasses Run, 31

Road from the lower part of Pattersons Creek by Power Hazel's into the wagon road which leads from the Courthouse to the South Branch, 40

Road from John Nealan[d]'s/Neeland's on Sharrando to William Vestal's on the same river (road from John Nealand's down the river by the lands of John Grimes, Capt. Stribling, Timothy Haney, Darby Conely, Goldin, John Hamman, Thomas Hamman, and Elizabeth Pearson, across Pearson's Neck of Land to Jonathan Walker's, over Bulskin, and by Robert Hayes's and along Hayes's path to Vestal's), 9, 10

Road from the end of the [Winchester] Common to Henry Heath's, 148

Road from Van Swearingen's mill upon Tunis's Branch to the Warm Springs road near Hedges's (approved as: road from Swearingen's mill into the Warm Springs road at Lucas Hood's), 142, 145, 148
Sections:
- From Swearingen's mill to Cherry's Run, 149
- From Cherry's Run to the Warm Spring road (from Thomas Cherry's ford to the Warm Springs road by Lucas Hood's), 143, 149

Road from Lewis Neill's mill into the road leading to Helms's mill at the head of the Dry Marsh, 160

Road from Helm's mill into the road leading from Winchester to Watkins's ferry, at Blackburn's plantation, 161, 164

Road from the Dry Marsh to (Thomas) Helm's mill, 155, 157, 170

McKay's Chapel road, 122
Section:
- From the forks of Earl's Mill Run to George Henry, 122

Road from Cunningham's Chapel to George Henry's, 130

Road from George Henry's Spring to James Burner's Run, 153

Road from Hews's to the South Branch road above Jeremiah Smith's, 55

Road from Opecken Creek to the Chapel by James Cunningham's (road from John Neill's house to the Chapel at Cunningham's; road from Opecken Creek at John Neill's ford near his house, thence along the old path that formerly went to James Hill's, to the forks of the old wagon road commonly called Littler's Wagon road, and thence along Hill's Marsh to Cunningham's house and so to the Chapel), 20, 23, 33
[Note: May be the same as:
Road from the Chapel at Cunningham's to John Neill's, Gent., to be continued to Abrahams Run (road crossing Opeckon at John Neill's ford to Cunningham's Chapel), 39, 53.]
[Note: See also:

Road from the forks of the road at Cunningham's Chapel to Opecken Creek, 34 (Note: Road order entries appear to indicate that this road is different from the road noted on pp. 20, 23, 33.).]

Road from Hoop Petticoat Gap to Hite's mill, 45, 47, 67

Road from Hite's to Littler's, 47

Road from Hite's house to Lewis Stevens's new road, 88

Road from Hite's mill to Cedar Creek, 63
Road from the Southwest Pond to Hite's mill, 129

Road from Gregory's ford thence near Lord Fairfax's seat and into Hite's wagon road, 47

Road from Beckett's/John Becket's house to Capt. Hite's/Col. Hite's mill, 78, 109, 164
[Note: Probably the same as:
Road from Col. Hite's to Robert Beckett's, 152.]

Road leading from Winchester and crossing Col. Hite's mill dam, 90

Road from Col. Hite's to Robert Beckett's, 152

Road from the ford of Opeckon by David Brown's near Col. Hite's tanyard to the Hoop Petticoat Gap, 155, 164

Road from Henry Spears's to go by Isaac Hite's and thence into the Main county road (road from the Great road to the fork of the road that leads to Henry Spears's road), 93, 134

Road leading from Isaac Hite's, through Joseph Baker's plantation, to Henry Funk's mill (to be turned round Baker's plantation), 153

Road from Isaac Hite's mill to the road leading to Massinutting [Massanutten], 156, 159

Road from John Littler's to Thomas Shepard's/Sheppard's mill (road from John Littler's late dwelling house to the said Littler's New Design thence to Opecken Creek over Abril's ford thence to the late dwelling place of John Smith's dec. thence to Jacob Hite's thence to Thomas Shepard's mill), 4, 5
Sections:
- Road from John Littler's to Thomas Sheppard's mill, 6
- Road from Thomas Shepherd's mill to Jacob Hite, Gent.'s, 32
- Road from John Smith's to John Littler's, 32

[Note: See also:
Road from Alexander Ross's fence to the corner of Smith's fence, 21 (etc.)
and
Road from Smith's fence/John Smith's old place to Jacob Hite's, 21, 62, 90, 106, 128, 133

and
Road from William Hite's Spring to the middle of the Swamp in Smith's Marsh and from the Swamp to Littler's mill, 40, 41.]

Road from the Chapel to Jay's ferry (road from the Chapel by Anderson's/Thos. Anderson's mill by William Mitchell's and Jacob Hite Gent.'s land, and thence into the road that goes from Capt. Campbell's to the ferry, near Capt. Thomas Rutherford's plantation), 6(2)

Road from Jacob Hite's to John Littler's/Littler's mill, 20, 38

Road from Smith's fence/John Smith's old place to Jacob Hite's (road from Edward Thomas's to Mr. Jacob Hite's; road from Mr. Jacob Hite's/Jacob Hite's bridge to Edward Thomas's bridge between the said Edward Thomas's fences and John Smith's fences), 21, 62, 90, 106, 128, 133

Road from Thomas Thornbury's mill to Opecken Creek by Edward Stroud's and from thence into the road that leads from Jacob Hite's to Vestal's ford on Sharando River, 25

Road from Thomas Caton's house to Mr. Jacob Hite's, 47, 65, 67

Road from the Great road leading from Mr. Jacob Hite's to John Smith's to the head of Worthington's Marsh thence down the Marsh into the road near John Swim's called Keys's road and into the road leading by Thomas Rutherford's to Vestal's ferry, 49

Road from (Mr.) Jacob Hite's to (Mr.) Swearingen's ferry, 62, 70, 85, 97
Sections:
- Road from Jacob Hite's to Robert Lemen's house, 107
- Road from Robert Lemen's to Swearingen's ferry, 107

Road from Jacob Hite's plantation to Keyes's ferry, 118

Road from Jacob Hite's house to William Foster's ferry, 160

Road from Jacob Hite's mill each way into the Main road leading to Swearingen's ferry (road from Alexander Fryer's to Swearingen's road), 100, 102, 109

Road from Jacob Hite's mill to the Main road (leading to Watkins's ferry) at John Evans's (road from John Evans's fence to Jacob Hite's mill [including alterations]), 100, 103, 135, 137, 139

Road from Jacob Hite's mill to the Main road leading from Winchester to Vestal's Gap near the head of Worthington's Marsh, 100, 102

Road from Alexander Fryer's to Jacob Hite's mill, 119

Road from Samuel Mounts's to Jacob Hite's mill, 134, 136

Road from Jonathan Seamon's house (on Opeckon) to Jacob Hite's, 120, 131

Road from the Main road leading from Jacob Hite's to Mecklenburg through Foster's land to the Ferrying Water and also to the ford of Potomac, 148

Road from Snickers's ferry landing to the County line on the road leading to Jacob Hite's, 170

Road from John Littler's old place by the Courthouse to Capt. John Hite's, 4

Road from Isaac Perkins's/[Isaac] Parkins's/Perkins's mill to John Hite's/John Hite's mill, 5, 16, 64

Road from John Hite's mill into the road that comes from John Funk's mill to John Gregory's, 7

Road from Crooked Run/the mouth of Crooked Run to (Capt.) John Hite's, 8, 10, 26, 29, 54, 68, 75, 80

(Part of) the road from John Hite's mill [to?] Kersey's ford, 9

Road from Chester's ferry to the Courthouse (road from Chester's ferry to John Hite's; road from the ferry landing and thence via the first gap in Guard Hill, crossing Crooked Run, thence on the upper side of Robert McKay's spring, crossing Crooked Run above Thomas Branson's, thence along the road laid off by Bethany Haines to John Hite's), 14, 16

Road from John Hite's to the Chapel at McCoy's Springs (the part which was altered by Thomas Branson), 27, 28

Road from John Hite's/Capt. Hite's mill to the Run at John Nation's house/Nation's Run/Nation's Branch, 30, 36, 42, 45, 51(2), 64

Road from Capt. John Hite's to the drafts of the Indian Run, 32

Road from John Hite Gent.'s mill/mill dam/Hite's mill/Col. Hite's to Jacob Cristman's/Jacob Christman's Spring/Crisman's Spring, 34, 70, 81, 82, 90, 91, 125, 129

Road from the Gap of the Little Mountain into the road which leads from John Hite Gent.'s to Kersey's ferry (road from the Gap on the Little Mountain to John Hite's mill), 38, 93

Road from Capt. John Hite's mill to Widow Reed's path leading to Branson's mill and McCoy's Chapel, 44

Road from Branson's mill/Branson's mill place to Hite's mill, 46, 65
Sections:
- Road from Branson's mill to the dividing branch, 46
- Road from the dividing branch to Hite's mill, 46

Road from John Hite's to a branch of Opeckon, 50

Road from John Hite Gent.'s house to Isaac Parkins's Gent., 50

Road from George Wright's to Capt. John Hite's, 73

Road from Capt. Hite's to the new road near George Wright's house, 79

Road from Col. Hite's through the Town laid out on Lewis Stephens's plantation/ Stephens Town and from thence into the Main road (road from Col. John Hite's to Stephensburgh; road between Col. John Hite's and the new town called Stevensburgh), 89, 90, 93, 94

Road leading from John Hite's house to the Town of Winchester (road from Opeckon to Winchester), 115, 136

Road from Col. John Hite's to the forks of the road leading from Lord Fairfax's to Stephensburgh, 120

Road from the Race Ground(s) below John Hite's house to the Swift Shoals ford on Shenandoah and thence down the River to the County road, 124, 132, 136

Road from Mr. Hite's to the road from Stevens's lane to Kersey's ferry, 66(2)

Road from Goony Run ford into Mr. Hite's road by the Three Miles Lick, 153

Road from William Hite's Spring to the middle of the Swamp in Smith's Marsh and from the Swamp to Littler's mill, 40, 41
Sections:
- Road from William Hite's Spring to the middle of the Swamp in Smith's Marsh, 40
- Road from the middle of the Swamp in Smith's Marsh to Littler's mill (road from the bridge on Smiths Creek to Widow Littler's mill), 41, 44

[Note: Entries for Hagan and Hogan are combined.]

Road from James Hogan's to Elizabeth Jolliffe's mill and thence into the Bull Skin road (road from James Hagan's by the Widow Jolliffe's mill into the Bull Skin road), 154, 155

[Note: Entries for Hog, Hoge and Hogg are combined.]

Road from Winchester to Hogs/Hoge Creek *[Note: Also called the South Branch road on p. 119]*, 80, 111, 119, 125, 148, 155

Road from Hogs Creek to McCoy's Ridge, 80

Road from Hoge Creek/Hog Creek to the County line, 105, 121

Road from the Timber Ridge to Hoge Creek, 126

Road from Isaac Perkins's to Hoge Creek where the road leading from Winchester to the South Branch crosses it, 147, 149

Road from Hog's Creek where the South Branch road crosses it to go by Isaac Perkins's plantation and thence to Jessee Pugh's mill (road from Hoge Creek where the Winchester road crosses it to go by Isaac Perkins's plantation and to Jessee Pugh's mill; road from Hog's Creek to Jessee Pugh's mill), 149, 151, 154(2)

Road leading through James Hoge's plantation to Massenutting, 135

Road from Thomas Morgan's mill to Lewis Hogg's house and from thence to the top of the Ridge, 7

Road from Winchester to Marlborough forge 150(2), 171
Alterations:
- To be turned round John Allen's plantation, 150(2)
- To be turned to run upon the line between Robert Glass and the Rev. Mr. Hoge, 171

Road from Jeremiah Smith's house to William Hog's/William Hoge Jr.'s, 8, 24

Road from William Hoge Jr.'s to the Courthouse, 15(2)

Road from the Courthouse to the South Branch, 27(2), 40
Alteration:
- To go around William Hoge Jr.'s plantation, 27(2)

[Note: Entries for Hogland, Hogeland, Hougland, and Houghland are combined.]

Road from Hogeland's ferry to Thomas Caton's (road from Richard Hogland's ferry to go by John Hogland's mill to Capt. Thomas Caton's), 97, 99, 100

Road from Hogland's ferry to the road leading to Winchester, 102

Road from Hogland's ferry to John Parks's, 106

Road from the fork of Opeckon on the Main road at Edward Stroad's/Stroade's to Hogland's ferry, 131(2)

Road from Sir John's road near George Paul's to Hougland's ferry and to Van Swearingen's mill on Tunis's Branch, 140

Road from Hogland's/Houghland's ferry via Hugh Lysle's, William Baldwin's, and William Hancheire's to fall into Morgan's road leading to Winchester, 143, 147
Sections:
- From Hogland's ferry to John Parks's, 148
- From Hugh Lysle's to Mill Creek, 148

- From Mill Creek to William Hancheir's, 148
- From William Hancheir's to Morgan's road, 148

Road from Winchester to Hougland's ferry, leading through Benjamin Thornbrugh's and Enos Ellis's plantations (proposed alteration at Benjamin Thornbrough's and Enos Ellis's plantations), 150, 156
Section:
- From David Miller's old plantation to Isaac Eaton's, 156

(Alteration of) the part of the road from Hougland's ferry to Winchester, that goes by Hancher's, and through the plantations of Jesse Felkner and others where they enter at the Branch road (alteration of the road from Houghland's ferry and through Falkner's land), 157, 158

Road from John Spears's to Van Swearingen's mill at Houghland's, 145

Road from Hogland's Neck by Barnet Newkirk's and into the Great road, 77

Road from Hogeland's ferry to Thomas Caton's (road from Richard Hogland's ferry to go by John Hogland's mill to Capt. Thomas Caton's), 97, 99, 100

Road from John Houghland's mill to Shannandah [Shenandoah] River, 117

Road from Hogeland's ferry to Thomas Caton's (road from Richard Hogland's ferry to go by John Hogland's mill to Capt. Thomas Caton's), 97, 99, 100

Road by Abraham Hollingsworth's, 4

Road from Mark Hardin's ford on Shanando River to Isaac Hollingsworth's, 38, 51(2)
Sections
- Road from the River to Opeckon, 51
- Road from Opeckon to Isaac Hollingsworth's, 51

Public road cut by Isaac Hollingsworth's mill race, 52, 53

Road from Van Swearingen's mill upon Tunis's Branch to the Warm Springs road near Hedges's (approved as: road from Swearingen's mill into the Warm Springs road at Lucas Hood's), 142, 145, 148
Sections:
- From Swearingen's mill to Cherry's Run, 149
- From Cherry's Run to the Warm Spring road (from Thomas Cherry's ford to the Warm Springs road by Lucas Hood's), 143, 149

Road from Rachell Hood's to the Race grounds, 57

Road from Hoop Petticoat Gap to Hite's mill, 45, 47, 67

Road from the South Branch road near Capt. Smith's through Hoop Petticoat Gap to Winchester (road from Winchester through Hoop Petticoat Gap), 104, 106, 154(2)
Sections:
- Road as far as Allen's Cabin, 154
- From Allen's Cabin to the road leading from Winchester to Jeremiah Smith's, 154

Road from the ford of Opeckon by David Brown's near Col. Hite's tanyard to the Hoop Petticoat Gap, 155, 164

Road from the Horse Pond in Dr. McCormack's road to George Bruce's mill, 125, 128, 134, 164

[Note: For Houghland, see Hogland, etc.]

Road from Pugh's and Barrett's mill by the end of the Sleepy Creek Mountain to the Warm Springs (road from the Warm Springs to Barrett's mill), 126, 131(2), 163, 168
Sections:
- From the [Warm] Springs to Ichebud Ashcraft's, 131, 135
- From Ashcraft's to the Buffaloe Run, 131
- From the Buffaloe Run to the end (from the Buffaloe Run as far as laid off by the veiwers from the Warm Springs; road from Buffaloe Run to Howard's old field, 131, 138, 149

Alteration:
- Road from Barrett's mill to the Warm Springs (to be turned to go by Meshack Sexton's mill), 163, 168

Road from the County line through Howards Town to join the new road to the Courthouse, 11

Road from Howel's/Howell's ford to Ashby's Bent Gap, 1, 11, 56

Road from Howel's ford to Foxtrap Point on the south side of Shanando, 29

Road from Howel's ford to Gregory's wagon road, 32

Road from Howel's/Howell's ford to the top of the [Blue] Ridge, 32, 37, 40, 91, 92, 93, 111, 122
Associated roads:
- Road from the ferry landing (at Combs's) to the said road (Main road), and road from the Wagon ford into the said road (road to the Wagon ford and ferry landing), 91, 93, 111

Road from Crooked Run to Howell's ford, 108

Road from Howell's ford, 108

Road from Berry's ferry to Howell's ford, 163

Road from the furnace erecting on the north branch of Pembroke to the forge erecting on Cedar Creek (road from the forge to the furnace), 129(2), 146
Sections:
- From the furnace to Devault Hulberger's, 129
- From Hulberger's to the forge (from Opeckon to the forge upon Cedar Creek), 129, 142, 144

Road from Hume's/Thomas Hume's mill on Sugar Tree Creek/Sugar Tree Run into the road leading to Chester's Gap, 117, 121

Road from Isaac Perkins's mill to Ralph Humfrey's, 17

Sir John's road (road called Sir John Sinclaire's road), 96, 97, 113, 119, 127, 132
Sections:
- From Winchester to the plantation where Isaac Thomas did live, 96
- From the place where the road from Robert Cunningham's falls into it to the forks where the road leads to Winchester, 132
- From the plantation where Isaac Thomas did live to the County line, 96
- From the Hunting Ridge to Isaac's Creek at Pritchet's place, 97
- Sir John's road leading from the Timber Ridge to Isaac's Creek, 113
- From the forks to James McGill's, 119
- Sir John's road from the end of the Sleepy Creek Mountain where the Warm Spring road crosses it to James Daugherty's, 127

Probable sections:
- Road from Isaac's Creek to the County line, 148
- Road from (the top of) the Hunting Ridge to the County line, 151, 158

Road from Hurst's ford to the fork of the road leading to Funk's mill, 159

Road from Opecken at Hugh Hains's to the Indian Grave on the Main road, 54

Road from Capt. John Hite's to the drafts of the Indian Run, 32

Road leading from Swearingen's ferry to Keys's ferry, 113
Sections:
- From Swearingen's to Melchiah Inglis Branch, 113
- From Melchiah Inglis Branch to Keys's ferry, 113

Road from the Main road near Sebastian's quarter to Hardin and Keys's mill, and from thence to the Iron Works, 83
Section:
- Road from the Main road near Sebastian's quarter to Hardin and Keys's mill, 84

Road from John McCormick's to the Iron Works, 105

Sir John's road (road called Sir John Sinclaire's road), 96, 97, 113, 119, 127, 132

Sections:
- From Winchester to the plantation where Isaac Thomas did live, 96
- From the place where the road from Robert Cunningham's falls into it to the forks where the road leads to Winchester, 132
- From the plantation where Isaac Thomas did live to the County line, 96
- From the Hunting Ridge to Isaac's Creek at Pritchet's place, 97
- Sir John's road leading from the Timber Ridge to Isaac's Creek, 113
- From the forks to James McGill's, 119
- Sir John's road from the end of the Sleepy Creek Mountain where the Warm Spring road crosses it to James Daugherty's, 127

Probable sections:
- Road from Isaac's Creek to the County line, 148
- Road from (the top of) the Hunting Ridge to the County line, 151, 158

Road from the Chapel to Jay's ferry (road from the Chapel by Anderson's/Thos. Anderson's mill by William Mitchell's and Jacob Hite Gent.'s land, and thence into the road that goes from Capt. Campbell's to the ferry, near Capt. Thomas Rutherford's plantation), 6(2)

Public road leading from Andrew Campbell Gent.'s to Watkins's ferry (alteration by the plantation formerly Jonathan Jayeas [Jayes?], dec., now in the possession of Elizabeth Dyer), 28

Road from Thorn's Gap to Jeremiah's Run, 106

Road from Jeremiah's Run to the Brush Bottom ford, 106

Road from the top of the Blue Ridge to Calebs Run (road from the top of the Blue Ridge at Thorn's Gap to Caleb Job's mill), 73, 84

Road from Caleb Job's Run to the Culpeper line at Chester's Gap, 91

Bridle road/road from Scot's/Scott's [later Johnston's] mill on Shanando/Sharrando to the Courthouse, 5, 7, 11, 14, 15, 17

Road from Johnston Run/Johnston's mill to John Sturman's/John Sturman's Run, 31, 33

Road from the end of Johnston's road to Cunningham's Chapel, 53

Road from Vestal's ford to Capt. Johnston's road, 53

Road from Capt. George Johnston's plantation on the Long Marsh into the road which leads from Williams's Gap to the Courthouse (road from George Johnston Gent.'s house to the road from Town to Fairfax County), 33, 46, 54

(Request to the Court of Prince William County for a) Road from Jefrey Johnston's at the Pignut Ridge to the top of the [Blue] Ridge at Ashby's Bent, 23

[Note: Various spellings of Jolliff, etc., are combined.]

Road from James Hogan's to Elizabeth Jolliffe's mill and thence into the Bull Skin road (road from James Hagan's by the Widow Jolliffe's mill into the Bull Skin road), 154, 155

The road leading to Mr. Jolliffe's, 158

Road from James Hogan's to Elizabeth Jolliffe's mill and thence into the Bull Skin road (road from James Hagan's by the Widow Jolliffe's mill into the Bull Skin road), 154, 155

(Main) road from the Courthouse/town of Winchester to Watkins's ferry, 40, 65, 112
- To be turned where it passes through William Jollyffe's land, 65

Sections:
- From Tuscarora to Capt./Mr. (Thomas) Caton's plantation, 110, 112
- From Watkins's ferry to Caton's Stone House, 162

Road from William Jolliff's to Mary Ballanger's, 84

Road from Opeckon/Opeckon bridge to William Jolliff's (road from the bridge on Opeckon Creek to William Jolliffe, Jr.'s; road from Jolliffe's store to Opeckon ford), 88, 116, 143, 172

Road from Opeckon Creek to the Main county road (road from William Neill's upon Opeckon into the Great road that runs by William Joleff's; road from the forks of the road leading from Winchester to William Jolliff's to Opeckon Creek), 88, 120, 147

(New) road from the lanes through the Common of Winchester to William Jolliff's, 89

Road from William Jolliff's to the middle of the bridge between Edward Thomas's and John Smith's fences, 94

Road from Isaac Perkins/Parkins's, Gent.'s mill to Mr. Gabriel Jones's plantation on Opecken River, 33, 64, 66, 67

Road from Lewis Stephen's/Stevens's house/land/mill to Mr. Gabriel Jones's place/plantation, 35, 42, 44, 64, 68

Road from George Julian's on Passage Creek to Buck's mill (road from George Julian's in Powell's fort to Buck's mill; road from Buck's mill to Powell's fort), 85, 96, 104

Road from Jumping Run bridge to Stony Creek, 153

Road from Jumping Run bridge to the North River ford, 159

Road from Francis Karney's to the River, 28
[Note: See also Carney.]

Road from the Flat Rock by Mr. Thruston's by the head of Kate's Spring, into the road leading to the Bloomery below Mr. Ariss's, 167

Roads to Christopher Beelor's mill:
- Road from Vestal's ford to Christopher Beelor's mill, 121 *[Note: See also Road from Beelor's mill to Vestal's ford (section of the road from Keith's mill to Vestal's ford), 144.]*
- Road from the Long Marsh to Christopher Beelor's mill, 121

Road from the head of Long Marsh to James Keith's mill upon Bulskin, 139, 141
Road from Keith's mill/James Keith's mill to Vestal's ford, 139, 142, 144
Sections:
- From Keith's mill to Beelor's mill, 144
- From Beelor's mill to Vestall's ford, 144 *[Note: See also Road from Vestal's ford to Christopher Beelor's mill, 121.]*

Road from Moody's Run to Kellor's ford, 151

Road from Henry Funk's mill on Passage Creek to Abraham Kendrick's upper ford and from thence to William Ashby's, 158, 160
Sections:
- From Henry Funk's mill to Abraham Kendrick's upper ford, 160
- From Abraham Kendrick's upper ford to William Ashby's, 160

Road from Opecken ford by John Neil's/Neill's mill to Kersey's ferry (other road to Kersey's ferry), 4(2), 17, 19

Road (cleared by David Vance, etc.) leading to Kersey's ferry, 4

Road from the run by Nation's/John Nation's house to Kersey's ferry, 9, 51

Road from Perkins's mill to Kersey's ferry, 14

Road from Andrew Campbell Gent.'s to Kersey's ferry, 21

Road from Lewis Neill, Gent.'s to Kersey's ferry, 23

Road from the Gap of the Little Mountain into the road which leads from John Hite Gent.'s to Kersey's ferry (road from the Gap on the Little Mountain to John Hite's mill), 38, 93

Road from Peter Stevens's lane to the Dutch road leading to Kersey's ferry, 61, 65

Road from Mr. Hite's to the road from Stevens's lane to Kersey's ferry, 66(2)

The [several] roads from Winchester Town to Kersey's ferry, 68

Dutch road from Kersey's ferry to Wrights Branch, 86

Road to and from the ferry (across Shannando between John Kersey's and Christopher Marr's plantations) in the County road, 37

Road from the hollow near Kersey's to Shanando River and Kersey's ferry (road to be cleared along the lower side of the hollow to the River), 41, 43

Road from the landing place on the south side of Shanando River at Kersey's ferry to Foxtrap Point road (road from Kersey's to the ferry road on the south side of Shanando), 43, 49

(Part of) the road from John Hite's mill [to?] Kersey's ford, 9

Roads on both sides of the River from Keys's ferry into the Main roads (roads from the Main roads to Keys's ferry; roads to and from Keys's ferry into the Main roads), 78, 80, 82

Road from the top of the Mountain/top of the Blue Ridge to the ferry at Keys's/Keys's ferry/Keyes's ferry (including the ford), 113, 124, 125, 139

Road leading from Swearingen's ferry to Keys's ferry, 113
Sections:
- From Swearingen's to Melchiah Inglis Branch, 113
- From Melchiah Inglis Branch to Keys's ferry, 113

Road from Jacob Hite's plantation to Keyes's ferry, 118

Road from Keys's ford and the ferry to Henry Loyd's (road from Henry Lloyd's to Keyes's ferry and from the ferry up to the ford), 126, 163

Road leading through John Briscoe's plantation to Keyes's ferry (alteration), 127, 130

Road from the Muster Ground to Keyes's ferry, 137

Road from Vestall's ford and Keyes's ferry to the top of the Mountain (the Mountain road), 163(3)

Road from Shepherds Town to Keyes's ferry, 163

Road from Keys's ford to the top of the Mountain, 122

Road from the Main road near Sebastian's quarter to Hardin and Keys's mill, and from thence to the Iron Works, 83
Section:
- Road from the Main road near Sebastian's quarter to Hardin and Keys's mill, 84

Road from the inhabitants on Worthington's Marsh to Hardin and Keys's mill, 84

Road from the Great road leading from Mr. Jacob Hite's to John Smith's to the head of Worthington's Marsh thence down the Marsh into the road near John Swim's called Keys's road and into the road leading by Thomas Rutherford's to Vestal's ferry, 49

The King's highway (alteration), 90

Road from David Brown's mill down Opeckon Creek by James Knight's and Edward Reed's into the Chapel road, 168, 170, 171

Roads (as first marked and now used) from Benjamin Kuykendal's to the Trough hill, 69

Road from Joseph Langdon's plantation to the Town of Woodstock, 116, 117

Road from Ephram Leith's hollow to Claud's ford, 94

[Note: Entries for Lemen and Lemon are combined.]

Road from Lemon's to Watkins's ferry, 70

Road from (Mr.) Jacob Hite's to (Mr.) Swearingen's ferry, 62, 70, 85, 97
Sections:
- Road from Jacob Hite's to Robert Lemen's house, 107
- Road from Robert Lemen's to Swearingen's ferry, 107

Road from Tuscorora Creek to Robert Lemon's, 69

Road leading from Shepherds Town to the plantation of Robert Lemon, 115

Road from Coombes's ferry to Lewis's mill, 121

Road from Lewis's mill to Berry's ferry, 157

Road from Dr. Wells's/place where Humphrey Wells lives to Fielding Lewis's/Col. Lewis's mill, 125(2), 128

Road from Col. Fielding Lewis's quarter to the ferry landing at Combs's, 100, 103

Road from Jeremiah Lewis's (at/near the County line) to Stephens's/Stevens's mill at/on the Narrow Passage, 79, 104
Sections:
- Road from the County line near Jeremiah Lewis's to Christian Dilliner's, 81
- Road from Christian Dillener's to Lewis Stevens's mill at the Narrow Passage, 81

Road from the top of the mountain at Mills's Gap into Sir John Sinclair's road (road from the top of the Mountain at Mill's Gap into the most convenient left part of Sir John Sinclair's road), 112, 116

Sections:
- From Sir John Sinclair's road to the mouth of Lick Branch, 116
- From Lick Branch to the top of the mountain, 116

[Note: For Lile, see Lyle.]

Road from Thomas Hart's to Linder's ford and from the ford to the mountain, 53
Sections:
- Road from Thomas Hart's to Linder's ford, 53
- Road from Linder's ford to the mountain, 53

Road at Linder's to a place below the old fording place, 75

Road from Simon Linder's to Old Loyd's, 37

[Note: Various spellings of Lindsay (i.e., Lindsay, Lindsey, Linsey, Lyndsey) are combined.]

Road from Lewis Neill's mill to Edmond Lindsey, Jr.'s plantation, 119

Road from John Linsey Gent.'s house into the road which leads from the Courthouse to Fairfax County (road from the Fairfax road to John Linsey Gent.'s/Mr. John Lindsey's, 20, 23, 59

Road from Maj. Andrew Campbell Gent.'s to the Chapel at Cunningham's (road from Maj. Campbell's to Joseph Evans's thence to William Mitchell's then across Opecken thence to the head of the south fork of the Bulskin, thence to Thomas Linseys's on the Long Marsh, thence to John Linsey Gent.'s and from thence to the Chapel at Cunningham's), 22
Sections:
- From Campbell's to Opecken (from Andrew Campbell Gent.'s to William Mitchell's), 22, 30
- From Opecken to the head of Bulskin, 22, 31
- From the head of Bulskin to the Long Marsh, 22, 25
- From the Long Marsh to Fairfax road, 22
- From the Fairfax road to the Chapel), 22, 25

Road from John Lindsey's to the ford at Combs's ferry, 118

Road from Maj. Andrew Campbell Gent.'s to the Chapel at Cunningham's (road from Maj. Campbell's to Joseph Evans's thence to William Mitchell's then across Opecken thence to the head of the south fork of the Bulskin, thence to Thomas Linseys's on the Long Marsh, thence to John Linsey Gent.'s and from thence to the Chapel at Cunningham's), 22
Sections:
- From Campbell's to Opecken (from Andrew Campbell Gent.'s to William Mitchell's), 22, 30
- From Opecken to the head of Bulskin, 22, 31
- From the head of Bulskin to the Long Marsh, 22, 25
- From the Long Marsh to Fairfax road, 22

- From the Fairfax road to the Chapel), 22, 25

Road from Worthington's Marsh to Thomas Lindsay's, 87

Road from Thomas Lindsey's house to Marquis Calmes's, 87

Road from Charles Dick's mill to Thomas Lindsey's, 113

Road from James Fowler's to Thomas Lindsey's, 122

Road from Lewis Neill's mill to Thomas Lindsey's, 123

Road from Dr. McCormack's to Thomas Lindsey's house (road from McCormick's to the Widow Lindsey's), 139, 161

Road from Thomas Lyndsey's plantation to Samuel Morris's, 161

Road from Dr. McCormack's to Thomas Lindsey's house (road from McCormick's to the Widow Lindsey's), 139, 161

Road from the Gap of the Little Mountain into the road which leads from John Hite Gent.'s to Kersey's ferry (road from the Gap on the Little Mountain to John Hite's mill), 38, 93

Road from the Furnace to the Gap of the Little Mountain (road from Marlbro' [Marlborough] furnace to the top of the Little Mountain), 138, 152

Road from John Little's to Miller's Town, 150, 155

Road from John Little's to the Augusta [County] line (road from the [Augusta] County line below Brock's Gap to John Little's), 157, 159
Sections:
- From Little's to Narrow Passage Creek, 159
- From [Narrow] Passage Creek to Stoney Creek, 159
- From Stoney Creek to Christian Dellinger's, 159
- From Christian Dellinger's to Mill Creek, 159
- From Mill Creek to the [Augusta] County line, 159

Road from the County line by Thomas Little Gent.'s to Lewis Stephens's mill, 29, 35, 39

Road from Lewis Stephens's mill to Widow Little's, 47

Road from Littlers Run to Mill Creek, 97

Road from the Winchester Common/Winchester Out Lots to Littler's Run, 151, 160, 170

Road from Opecken to Mill Creek/Mills Creek, 5, 28

Sections:
- Road from Mill Creek/Mills Creek to Littler's old place, 36, 61
- Road from Littler's old place to Opecken [including alterations], 36, 41, 71, 73(2)

Road from William Hite's Spring to the middle of the Swamp in Smith's Marsh and from the Swamp to Littler's mill, 40, 41
Sections:
- Road from William Hite's Spring to the middle of the Swamp in Smith's Marsh, 40
- Road from the middle of the Swamp in Smith's Marsh to Littler's mill (road from the bridge on Smiths Creek to Widow Littler's mill), 41, 44

Road from Hite's to Littler's, 47

Road from Littler's/Samuel Littler's/Samuel Littler's Run/Littler's Branch/Littler's mill/Littler's old place/ Littler's lane to Robert Cunningham's/Robert Cunningham's mill/Widow Cunningham's, 98, 101(2), 105, 108, 118, 138, 165

Road from Littler's lane to the ford at Lewis Neill's, 164

Road from Opecken Creek to the Chapel by James Cunningham's (road from John Neill's house to the Chapel at Cunningham's; road from Opecken Creek at John Neill's ford near his house, thence along the old path that formerly went to James Hill's, to the forks of the old wagon road commonly called Littler's Wagon road, and thence along Hill's Marsh to Cunningham's house and so to the Chapel), 20, 23, 33
[Note: May be the same as:
Road from the Chapel at Cunningham's to John Neill's, Gent., to be continued to Abrahams Run (road crossing Opeckon at John Neill's ford to Cunningham's Chapel), 39, 53.]
[Note: See also:
Road from the forks of the road at Cunningham's Chapel to Opecken Creek, 34 (Note: Road order entries appear to indicate that this road is different from the road noted on pp. 20, 23, 33.).]

Road from this Courthouse [Winchester] to the top of the Blue Ridge of Mountains at Williams's Gap (road from Capt. Neill's off and on the old road to Joseph Wilkenson's and thence off on the same road to Francis Carney's and from thence to Edge's ford and from thence off and on the old road to the top of the said Mountain), 12
Sections:
- From Capt. Lewis Neill's/Lewis Neill Gent.'s to Francis Carney's/Carnie's (road from Francis Carney's/Carney's Spring to Lewis Neill's/Opeckon at Neill's ford/Opeckon Creek by Capt. Neill's/ Opecken by Lewis Neill's, Gent), 12, 22, 31, 82, 100, 104
- From Carney's to Edge's ford on Shannadore River (road from Shanando River to Carney's Spring, 12, 50, 83
- From Edge's ford to the top of the Blue Ridge on Williams's Gap, 12

Probable later sections:
- Road from Winchester Town to Lewis Neill's/Lewis Neill's ford on Opeckon, 59, 67

- Road from the ford at Lewis Neill Gent.'s house to Littler's road, 59
- Road from Littler's road to Carney's old house, 59
- Road from Carney's old house to the River, 59
- Road from the River to the top of the mountain at Williams's Gap (road from Edward Snigers's [on Shanando] to the top of the Mountain at Williams's Gap; road from the River at Snigers's to the County line at Williams's Gap; road from the top of the Ridge to Edward Snickers's/Snigers's ford/ferry/ferry at Snicker's house; road from the Ferry road [Snigers's] to the top of the Ridge at Williams's Gap), 59, 76, 79, 81, 83, 113

Road called Littler's road, 100, 101, 105, 125, 129
Sections:
- From the beginning to Opeckon Creek, 105, 125
- From Opeckon Creek to the fork where it joins the Winchester road leading to Spout Run, 100, 101, 159

Road from the place where the Bullskin road intercepts Littler's old road to fall into the Potomac road before it comes to Benjamin Blackburn's plantation, 107

Road from Armstrong's ford upon Opeckon to the Signpost at Littler's road, 123

Road from John Frost's mill to the main road between John Littler's plantation and John Milbourn's/Milburn's plantation, (road from Capt. Frost's mill thence to Buffler lick thence through the lands of John Bosser, and David Springer, thence to the ford, thence through the lands of William Frost and Mathias Elmore, along Elmor[e]'s Creek to Widow Dillon's, and thence to the main road leading to Rappahannock between John Littler's and John Milbourn's), 1, 3, 20, 28
Probable sections:
- Road from John Frost's mill to William Frost's/William Frost's ford, 44, 65
- The other part of the said road, from William Frost's to Col. Morgan's road (road from William Frost's to William Dillon's), 44, 110
- Road from Frost's to Dillon's (alteration round the north side of Dillon's plantation into a lane), 126

Road from John Littler's to Thomas Shepard's/Sheppard's mill (road from John Littler's late dwelling house to the said Littler's New Design thence to Opecken Creek over Abril's ford thence to the late dwelling place of John Smith's dec. thence to Jacob Hite's thence to Thomas Shepard's mill), 4, 5
Sections:
- Road from John Littler's to Thomas Sheppard's mill, 6
- Road from Thomas Shepherd's mill to Jacob Hite, Gent.'s, 32
- Road from John Smith's to John Littler's, 32

[Note: See also:
Road from Alexander Ross's fence to the corner of Smith's fence, 21 (etc.)
and
Road from Smith's fence/John Smith's old place to Jacob Hite's, 21, 62, 90, 106, 128, 133

and
Road from William Hite's Spring to the middle of the Swamp in Smith's Marsh and from the Swamp to Littler's mill, 40, 41.]

Road from John Littler's old place by the Courthouse to Capt. John Hite's, 4

Road from Isaac Perkins's mill to John Littler's old place, 5

Road from John Littler's old place to Patrick Ryley's, 27, 40

Road from the Courthouse to John Littler's old place (road from Litler's/Littler's old place/plantation to Winchester Town), 33, 62, 117

Road from John Littler's mill to William Gaddis's/Gaddy's plantation, 9, 36, 68

Road from Jacob Hite's to John Littler's/Littler's mill, 20, 38

Road from John Littler's mill across Opecken at the mouth of his mill run, 29

Road from John Littler's to Opecken (alteration), 31

Road from Littler's/Samuel Littler's/Samuel Littler's Run/Littler's Branch/Littler's mill/Littler's old place/ Littler's lane to Robert Cunningham's/Robert Cunningham's mill/Widow Cunningham's, 98, 101(2), 105, 108, 118, 138, 165

Road from Winchester to Samuel Littler's (road leading to Connigocheague, section from the Town of Winchester to Littler's place), 107, 112

Road from William Hite's Spring to the middle of the Swamp in Smith's Marsh and from the Swamp to Littler's mill, 40, 41
Sections:
- Road from William Hite's Spring to the middle of the Swamp in Smith's Marsh, 40
- Road from the middle of the Swamp in Smith's Marsh to Littler's mill (road from the bridge on Smiths Creek to Widow Littler's mill), 41, 44

[Note: For Lloyd, see Loyd.]

Road from his Lordship's house into McCoy's Chapel road and from thence to his Lordship's quarter in the Long Bottom, 73, 75

Road from Maj. Andrew Campbell Gent.'s to the Chapel at Cunningham's (road from Maj. Campbell's to Joseph Evans's thence to William Mitchell's then across Opecken thence to the head of the south fork of the Bulskin, thence to Thomas Linseys's on the Long Marsh, thence to John Linsey Gent.'s and from thence to the Chapel at Cunningham's), 22
Sections:

- From Campbell's to Opecken (from Andrew Campbell Gent.'s to William Mitchell's), 22, 30
- From Opecken to the head of Bulskin, 22, 31
- From the head of Bulskin to the <u>Long Marsh</u>, 22, 25
- From the <u>Long Marsh</u> to Fairfax road, 22
- From the Fairfax road to the Chapel), 22, 25

Road from the <u>Long Marsh</u>/<u>Long Marsh Run</u> to Vestal's/Vestal's Gap/Vestal's Iron works, 26, 35, 44, 49

Road from Capt. George Johnston's plantation on the <u>Long Marsh</u> into the road which leads from Williams's Gap to the Courthouse (road from George Johnston Gent.'s house to the road from Town to Fairfax County), 33, 46, 54

Road from the Fairfax road to the north side of the <u>Long Marsh</u>, 60

Road from the north side of the <u>Long Marsh</u> to Vestal's ford, 60

Road from the bridge at the <u>Long Marsh</u> to Edward Snigers's, 77

Road from the head of Bullskin Marsh running by the head of <u>Long Marsh</u> into the road at the Dry Marsh below Capt. Lewis Neill's, 98

Road from the <u>Long Marsh</u> below Capt. Neill's to Patrick Rice's house, 107

Roads to Christopher Beelor's mill:
- Road from Vestal's ford to Christopher Beelor's mill, 121 *[Note: See also Road from Beelor's mill to Vestal's ford (section of the road from Keith's mill to Vestal's ford), 144.]*
- Road from the <u>Long Marsh</u> to Christopher Beelor's mill, 121

Road from the head of <u>Long Marsh</u> to James Keith's mill upon Bulskin, 139, 141

Road leading to the Chapel and the <u>Long Marsh</u>, 167

[Note: For entries for <u>His Lordship</u>, see <u>[Lord] Fairfax</u>.]

[Note: Entries for <u>Lloyd</u> and <u>Loyd</u> are combined.]

Road from Opecken to David <u>Loyd's</u>, 24

Road from David <u>Loyd's</u> to the top of the Blue Ridge at Vestal's Gap (road from David Loyd's crossing Shannando River and from thence to the top of the ridge), 38, 49, 55
Section:
- Road from the River to the top of the mountain, 55

Road from Henry Loyd's house to the top of the Ridge, 99

Road from Keys's ford and the ferry to Henry Loyd's (road from Henry Lloyd's to Keyes's ferry and from the ferry up to the ford), 126, 163

The Warm Spring/Warm Springs road, 136(2), 162, 163, 167, 168, 170
Sections:
- From Andrew Tilleroy's to Henry Lloyd's, 136(2)
- Through Henry Lloyd's plantation, 162
- From the Back Creek road to the Buffaloe Lick, 167
- From the South Branch road near Ballenger's to the County line (road from Ballenger's to the County line), 168, 170
- From Ballenger's to the Tub mill, 170
- From the Tub mill to the County line, 170

Road from Simon Linder's to Old Loyd's, 37

Road from Opeckon Creek to Lucas's Marsh, 92

Road from the Town of Mecklinburgh to the Meeting House between Buckles's and Lucas's, 119

Road leading from Lupton's into the Town (alteration as it is already cleared by Thomas Rutherford's pasture adjoining the Town), 168

Road from the head of John Lupton's meadow to the South Branch road above David Denny's, 144, 146

[Note: Entries for Lile, Lyle, Lyles, and Lysle are combined.]

Road from the Meeting House on the mountain to Hugh Lile's on Back Creek, 42

Road from Hugh Lyle's plantation on Back Creek through Curtis's Gap, to Robert Cunningham's (road from Robert Cunningham's to Hugh Lyle's on Back Creek), 103, 104
Sections:
- From Robert Cunningham's to David Miller's plantation, 104
- From David Miller's to the foot of the North Mountain, 104
- From the foot of the North Mountain to Hugh Lyle's on Back Creek, 104

Road from Hogland's/Houghland's ferry via Hugh Lysle's, William Baldwin's, and William Hancheire's to fall into Morgan's road leading to Winchester, 143, 147
Sections:
- From Hogland's ferry to John Parks's, 148
- From Hugh Lysle's to Mill Creek, 148
- From Mill Creek to William Hancheir's, 148
- From William Hancheir's to Morgan's road, 148

Road from Hugh Lyle's plantation to Col. Stephens's mill, 162

Road from John Lyles's by James Morrison's, John Miller's, John Glenn's and William Glenn's plantations, to Patterson's mill and from thence into the Warm Springs road, 156
[Note: See also:
Road from William Patterson's mill to John Lyle's (alternate route), 159.]

Road from William Patterson's mill to John Lyle's (alternate route), 159

Road from the Town of Mecklenburgh to Lynder's ford, or the most convenient ford, on Opecken Creek (road from Mecklenburg to Opeckon), 116, 117, 162

[Note: Entries for McCarmack, McCormack, and McCormick are combined.]

Road from George Pemberton's dwelling house to the road that leads from Capt. Rutherford's to Dr. McCormack's, 46

Road from John McCormick's house to Crawford's Muster Ground (road from Dr. McCormack's to the Muster Ground, including the bridge), 107, 139

Road from the Horse Pond in Dr. McCormack's road to George Bruce's mill, 125, 128, 134, 164

Road from Dr. McCormack's to Thomas Lindsey's house (road from McCormick's to the Widow Lindsey's), 139, 161

Road from the ford on Opeckon to Dr. McCormack's, 147

Road from John Shepard's/Sheppard's to the head of Bulskin (road from Potomac River from Sheppards ferry through the land of Thomas Rutherford, over Walker's mill dam and by the head of Pitts's Marsh and to the head of Bulskin through the lands of Mr. John McCormack), 3, 7
Sections:
- Road from Potomac River to Thomas Rutherford Gent.'s, 12, 38
- The remaining part of the road, 13
- Road from Thomas Rutherford Gent.'s to the head of Bullskin, 24
- Road from Thomas Rutherford's house to John McCarmack's, 37

Road from John McCormick's to Lewis Neil Gent.'s, 14

Road from John McCormack's house to Opecken Creek and from Opecken Creek to the Courthouse/the Town (road from the head of the south fork of Bullskin to Opecken and thence to the Courthouse), 20, 25
Sections:
- Road from the head of the south fork of Bullskin to Opecken (road from John McCormack's to the Main road to Town; road from John McCormack's house to Opecken Creek which leads to town), 20, 25, 49, 67, 87, 107 *[Note: This section appears to be different than the section from Opecken to the head to Bullskin (pp 22,*

31) of the road from Maj. Andrew Campbell Gent.'s to the Chapel at Cunningham's, 22.]
- Road from Opecken to the Courthouse (road from Opeckon Creek to the Main road leading to Winchester), 20, 25, 107

Road from Hugh Hains's to John M<u>cCormack's</u>, 54

Road from John M<u>cCormick's</u> to the Iron Works, 105

Road from Patrick Rice's house to John M<u>cCormick's</u>, 107

Road from John M<u>cCormick's</u> house to Crawford's Muster Ground (road from Dr. M<u>cCormack's</u> to the Muster Ground, including the bridge), 107, 139

Road from the Widow M<u>cCormack's</u> to the head spring of Bulskin, 140

[Note: Entries for M<u>cCoy</u>, M<u>cKay</u>, and M<u>cKoy</u> are combined.]

Road from Hogs Creek to M<u>cCoy's</u> Ridge, 80

Road from Calebs Run to the Brush bottom ford and from thence to the Percimmon Pond above James M<u>cCoy's</u>, 74, 75

Road from the road crossing the River at James M<u>cCoy's</u> ford to Capt. Jacob Funk's, 81

Road from John Funk's mill across Ceeder Run Creek ford to Robert M<u>cKay</u>/M<u>cCoy</u> Jr.'s and to Branston's Gap (road from Funk's mill back of George Telener's, thence to Ceedar Creek ford and Robert M<u>cCoy's</u>, and thence to Gregorie's ford upon the river), 2(2)

Road from John Funk's to M<u>cCoy's</u> Chapel (alteration round Robert M<u>cCoy's</u> fence), 113

Road from Chester's ferry to the Courthouse (road from Chester's ferry to John Hite's; road from the ferry landing and thence via the first gap in Guard Hill, crossing Crooked Run, thence on the upper side of Robert M<u>cKay's</u> spring, crossing Crooked Run above Thomas Branson's, thence along the road laid off by Bethany Haines to John Hite's), 14, 16

Road from the Chapel at James Cunningham's to the Chapel at Robert M<u>cCoy's</u> Spring, 26
Sections:
- Road from the Chapel at Cunningham's to Borden's/Burden's Great Spring/Marsh/Run, 26, 27, 37, 55, 56, 58, 84
- Road from Borden's Great Spring to the Chapel at M<u>cCoy's</u> Spring, 26, 55

Road from John Hite's to the Chapel at M<u>cCoy's</u> Springs (the part which was altered by Thomas Branson), 27, 28

Road from Robert Warth's; to be taken from the head of the road which leads from the Chapel at Robert McCoy's Spring, to Lewis Stephen's mills (road from the County road near Robert Warth's to Stevens's mill), 30, 63

Road from the County road to the Chapel at McCoy's Spring, 34

Road from Stevens's/Lewis Stephens's mill to the road to McCoy's/McKoy's Chapel (near Cartmill's), 37, 82
Alterations, 79

Road from Capt. John Hite's mill to Widow Reed's path leading to Branson's mill and McCoy's Chapel, 44

Road from Branson's mill place to the Main road from McCoy's Chapel, 62

Road from his Lordship's house into McCoy's Chapel road and from thence to his Lordship's quarter in the Long Bottom, 73, 75

Roads from the Glebe:
- From the Glebe to Cunningham's Chapel, 95, 101, 134
- From the late Glebe to Cunningham's Chapel, 134
- From the Glebe to McCoy's/ McKay's Chapel, 95, 98

Sections:
- Road from the Glebe as far as the Dutch road towards McKay's Chapel, 101
- Road from the Dutch road to McKay's Chapel, 101, 102
- From the Glebe into the Main road that leads to Winchester, 98

Road from McKay's Chapel to the Widow Duckworth's, 104

Road from McKay's Chapel to Edward Cartmill's, 109

Road from John Funk's to McCoy's Chapel (alteration round Robert McCoy's fence), 113

McKay's Chapel road, 122
Section:
- From the forks of Earl's Mill Run to George Henry, 122

Road from McKay's Chapel to Gregory's ford, 138

Road from Matthew Smith's plantation to McCoy's Chapel, 145

Road from Cedar Creek to Robert McCoy's Run, 35

Road from Sir John's road by Thomas Babb's down by William McMachen's (and) Angus McDonald's and down to Berry's mill, 121

[Note: May be the same as:
Road from Sir John's road above Thomas Babb's plantation to Thomas Perry's mill, 121.]

Sir John's road (road called Sir John Sinclaire's road), 96, 97, 113, 119, 127, 132
Sections:
- From Winchester to the plantation where Isaac Thomas did live, 96
- From the place where the road from Robert Cunningham's falls into it to the forks where the road leads to Winchester, 132
- From the plantation where Isaac Thomas did live to the County line, 96
- From the Hunting Ridge to Isaac's Creek at Pritchet's place, 97
- Sir John's road leading from the Timber Ridge to Isaac's Creek, 113
- From the forks to James McGill's, 119
- Sir John's road from the end of the Sleepy Creek Mountain where the Warm Spring road crosses it to James Daugherty's, 127

Probable sections:
- Road from Isaac's Creek to the County line, 148
- Road from (the top of) the Hunting Ridge to the County line, 151, 158

Road from Lewis Neil's mill to John McMachen's old place, 158

Road leading from Winchester by Richard McMachen's, 94

Road from Sir John's road by Thomas Babb's down by William McMachen's (and) Angus McDonald's and down to Berry's mill, 121
[Note: May be the same as:
Road from Sir John's road above Thomas Babb's plantation to Thomas Perry's mill, 121.]

Road from McNishes Run to Stoney Run, 84, 100

Road leading from Magneturs Run to Moses Bird's, 120

Road through the Main street of Maidstone to Potomac River and to the Main road, 75

Road from Mr. Caton's to Maidston, 94

[Note: The term "Main road" signifies the major road in a given area; the following entries are references to various routes, not a single road.]

Road from John McCormack's house to Opecken Creek and from Opecken Creek to the Courthouse/the Town (road from the head of the south fork of Bullskin to Opecken and thence to the Courthouse), 20, 25
Sections:
- Road from the head of the south fork of Bullskin to Opecken (road from John McCormack's to the Main road to Town; road from John McCormack's house to Opecken Creek which leads to town), 20, 25, 49, 67, 87, 107 *[Note: This section appears to be different than the section from Opecken to the head to Bullskin (pp. 22,*

31) of the road from Maj. Andrew Campbell Gent.'s to the Chapel at Cunningham's, 22.]
- Road from Opecken to the Courthouse (road from Opeckon Creek to the <u>Main</u> road leading to Winchester), 20, 25, 107

Road from Howel's/Howell's ford to the top of the [Blue] Ridge, 32, 37, 40, 91, 92, 93, 111, 122
Associated roads:
- Road from the ferry landing (at Combs's) to the said road (<u>Main</u> road), and road from the Wagon ford into the said road (road to the Wagon ford and ferry landing), 91, 93, 111

Road laid off from Cunningham's Chapel to the <u>Main</u> road from the Courthouse and from thence to Watkins's ferry, 40

(<u>Main</u>) road from the Courthouse/town of Winchester to Watkins's ferry, 40, 65, 112
- To be turned where it passes through William Jollyffe's land, 65

Sections:
- From Tuscarora to Capt./Mr. (Thomas) Caton's plantation, 110, 112
- From Watkins's ferry to Caton's Stone House, 162

Road from Opecken at Hugh Hains's to the Indian Grave on the <u>Main</u> road, 54

Road from Branson's mill place to the <u>Main</u> road from McCoy's Chapel, 62

Road from the <u>Main</u> road near Robert Warth's to Crooked Run, 63

Road from the lower part of the South Branch to the <u>Main</u> road near Thomas Parker's, 68

Road from Capt. Jeremiah Smith's to Col. Morgan Morgan's and thence into the <u>Main</u> County road near Patrick Reiley's, 71(2)

Road through the Main street of Maidstone to Potomac River and to the <u>Main</u> road, 75

Road from Morgan's Chapel to the <u>Main</u> road (alteration: marked from the Chapel to Robert Cunningham's house), 77

Road from Stevens's mill at the Narrow Passage to the <u>Main</u> road near Reiley Moor's, 77
[Note: See also:
Road from Lewis Stevens's mill to the next best ford on the River above Reily Moor's and from thence into the <u>Main</u> road, 78.]

Road from Lewis Stevens's mill to the next best ford on the River above Reily Moor's and from thence into the <u>Main</u> road, 78

Roads on both sides of the River from Keys's ferry into the <u>Main</u> roads (roads from the <u>Main</u> roads to Keys's ferry; roads to and from Keys's ferry into the <u>Main</u> roads), 78, 80, 82

Road from the Main road near Sebastian's quarter to Hardin and Keys's mill, and from thence to the Iron Works, 83
Section:
- Road from the Main road near Sebastian's quarter to Hardin and Keys's mill, 84

Road from Joseph Edwards Jr.'s to the Main road at the bridge over Opeckon Creek, 84

Road from the bridge at Worthington's Marsh to the Main road to Vestal's Gap, 84

Road from the lower corner of John Reno's plantation to some part of the road above the said plantation (road from the corner of Reno's fence into the Main road) (alteration), 85(2)

Main road through Josiah Ridgway's land towards Watkins's ferry (alteration), 85, 89

Main road running through the lands of Joseph Vance and Peter Stephens (alteration), 86

Road from Opeckon Creek to the Main county road (road from William Neill's upon Opeckon into the Great road that runs by William Joleff's; road from the forks of the road leading from Winchester to William Jolliff's to Opeckon Creek), 88, 120, 147

Bridle road from Edward Dodd's to the Main road, 89

Road from Col. Hite's through the Town laid out on Lewis Stephens's plantation/ Stephens Town and from thence into the Main road (road from Col. John Hite's to Stephensburgh; road between Col. John Hite's and the new town called Stevensburgh), 89, 90, 93, 94

Road from Isaac Ruddell's mill into the Main road between Jackson Allen's and John Skean's, 90

Road from the Main county road to August[a?] where the Messnuting [Massanutten] road crosses the same to Messanuting Run, 93

Road from Henry Spears's to go by Isaac Hite's and thence into the Main county road (road from the Great road to the fork of the road that leads to Henry Spears's road), 93, 134

Roads from the Glebe:
- From the Glebe to Cunningham's Chapel, 95, 101, 134
- From the late Glebe to Cunningham's Chapel, 134
- From the Glebe to McCoy's/ McKay's Chapel, 95, 98

Sections:
- Road from the Glebe as far as the Dutch road towards McKay's Chapel, 101
- Road from the Dutch road to McKay's Chapel, 101, 102
- From the Glebe into the Main road that leads to Winchester, 98

Road from Jacob Hite's mill to the Main road (leading to Watkins's ferry) at John Evans's (road from John Evans's fence to Jacob Hite's mill [including alterations]), 100, 103, 135, 137, 139

Road from Jacob Hite's mill each way into the Main road leading to Swearingen's ferry (road from Alexander Fryer's to Swearingen's road), 100, 102, 109

Road from Jacob Hite's mill to the Main road leading from Winchester to Vestal's Gap near the head of Worthington's Marsh, 100, 102

Road from the head of Bullskin to the Main road by Fryer's (road from Alexander Fryer's to the head of Bulskin, 109, 126(2)
Alteration:
- Where the road passes through John Smith's land, 126(2)

Road from Thomas Doster's to the Main road near the Widow Ballenger's, 110, 111

Road from Mills's Gap to Follis's mill and the Main road at Jane Caldwell's plantation, 111, 112

Road from Stoney Lick/Stony Lick by Christopher Windle's/Windel's into the Main road by Mr. Pugh's plantation, 111, 116

(Alteration of) Main road to run on the line between Edward Thomas and John Smith, 112

The Main road where it crosses Bruise's [Bruce's] Mill Run, 118

Road from the head of Bulskin to the Main road from Winchester to McLenburgh [Mecklenburgh], 123

Road from Beelor's mill into the Main road at Bradley's (continued along the old road to the mill, and going through a corner of Briscoe's new ground), 130

Road from the fork of Opeckon on the Main road at Edward Stroad's/Stroade's to Hogland's ferry, 131(2)

Road (starting at the Main road leading from Winchester to Watkins's ferry) from Peter Fussey's Big Spring/Fussey's Large Spring to the upper side of the mouth of Opeckon Creek, 133(2)

Road from Abraham Durst's Shop to the road on this side of the Massanuting Mountain (road from Abraham Darst's Smith's Shop to the top of the Massanutting [Massanutten] Mountain), 135, 137, 149(2)
Sections/related roads:
- Road from the North River to the County line, 149
- Road from the County line as the Main road now goes till it intersects the road leading from Abraham Durst's Smith Shop to the top of the [Massanutten] Mountain, 149

Road from Mecklenburgh to Andrew Swearingen's mill and from thence to the Main road that leads to the mouth of Opeckon, 140
Section:

- Road from Mecklenburgh to Andrew Swearingen's mill, 142

Road from the Main road leading from Jacob Hite's to Mecklenburg through Foster's land to the Ferrying Water and also to the ford of Potomac, 148

Road from the Main road near Mauk's mill to the County line, 151, 161

Mill road from John Spencely's house to the County road leading over the Mountain (road from John Spenceley's to the Main road leading over the mountain), 151, 155

Road from the Muster Ground above the Widow Caldwell's/Calwell's to John Neavill's mill and thence into the Main road by Jonah Seaman's, 155, 156

Road from Crooked Run to the Main County road leading from Augusta County, 158

Road from George Rice's house to the Main road at the Dry Marsh, 161

Road from the Warm Spring road at Joseph Bridges's into the Main road by John Nevill's, 166, 167

[Note: Entries for Manasses and variations (i.e., Manasseys, Menasses, etc.) are combined.]

Road from Gregory's ford to the top of the Ridge/Blue Ridge (road from Gregory's ford to the top of the Blue Ridge at the head of Menasses [Manasses] Run; road from Gregory's ford to Menasses Run at the County line; road from Gregory's ford to Manassey's Gap), 6, 91, 109, 110, 148, 169

Road to be cleared in Prince William County from the fork of the road below Watts's ordinary to meet a road cleared in Frederick County leading through Manassas Run Gap, 70

Road from Marlborough forge to Manasset's [Manasses] Gap upon the Blue Ridge, 150

Road from Isaac Zane's forge through Manassip's [Manasses] Run Gap, 156

Road from John Funk's mill to Chester's ferry and from thence to where the road takes out of Chester's road to Manasses Run, 1, 2
Sections:
- From John Funk's mill to the North River, 2, 79
- From the North River to the Haybottom, 2, 78
- From the Haybottom to where the road takes off to Manasses Run, 2, 31, 34, 55
- Road to be continued to Manasses Run, 31

Road from Gregory's ford to the top of the Ridge/Blue Ridge (road from Gregory's ford to the top of the Blue Ridge at the head of Menasses [Manasses] Run; road from Gregory's ford to Menasses Run at the County line; road from Gregory's ford to Manassey's Gap), 6, 91, 109, 110, 148, 169

(Petition to the Court of Prince William County to meet Frederick County with) a road from the Thorough fair at the Pignut Ridge to the top of the Blue Ridge at the head of Manasses Run, 10

Road from Manasses Run road to Chester's old road and from thence to Augusta line, 43, 44

Road from Chester's ford to Manasseh's [Manasses] Run, 111

Road from Samuel Earle's house into the road leading from Chester's Gap at Manasses Run (road from Samuel Earl's house into the road called Chester's road Manaseh's Run), 113, 115

The Manassits [Manasses] Run road, 146

[Note: For Mandanhall, see Mendenall.]

Road from the Manor line to the County line, 63

Road at William Marks's plantation (alteration), 147

Road from the Furnace to the Gap of the Little Mountain (road from Marlbro' [Marlborough] furnace to the top of the Little Mountain), 138, 152

Road from Winchester to Marlborough forge 150(2), 171
Alterations:
- To be turned round John Allen's plantation, 150(2)
- To be turned to run upon the line between Robert Glass and the Rev. Mr. Hoge, 171

Road from Marlborough forge to Manasset's [Manasses] Gap upon the Blue Ridge, 150

Road from Marlborough forge to Pugh's mill (road from Jessee Pugh's mill to Marlbro furnace), 151, 154(2)
Sections:
- From Pugh's mill to John White's, 154
- From John White's Run to the furnace, 154

Road from Marlbro [Marlborough] forge to Philip Peter Baker's, 153

Road from Strasburgh to Marlborough forge, 164, 165
Sections:
- From the forge to the creek, 165
- From the creek to the town, 165

Road from Stephensburg into the road leading from Winchester to Marlbro' [Marlborough] forge, 167, 169
Alteration:
- To go around Lewis Stephens's fence, 169

Road leading to Marlbrough forge from Perkins's mill as far as Opeckon, 171

Road to and from the ferry (across Shannando between John Kersey's and Christopher Marr's plantations) in the County road, 37

Road from Lewis Stevens Gent.'s old plantation to his Lordship's quarter (road from Lawrence Stevens's by Lewis Stephens's old plantation to Col. Martin's road), 71, 87

Road from his Lordship's quarter into the Dutch road (Col. Martin's road), 71

[Note: Entries for various spellings of Massanutten are combined.]

Massanuting/Messanuting/Messanutting [Massanutten] road, 85, 86, 120

Road from the Main county road to August[a?] where the Messnuting [Massanutten] road crosses the same to Messanuting Run, 93

Road leading to Messanutting from the White House to the Dry Run, 114, 132

Road from the Massanutten Mountain to the County line leading to Brock's Gap, 123

Road from the White House in Masanutting to the top of Masanutting Mountain, 127, 128

Road from the County line in Massanutting to Mauk's mill, 132, 133

Road leading through James Hoge's plantation to Massenutting, 135

Road from Abraham Durst's Shop to the road on this side of the Massanuting Mountain (road from Abraham Darst's Smith's Shop to the top of the Massanutting [Massanutten] Mountain), 135, 137, 149(2)
Sections/related roads:
- Road from the North River to the County line, 149
- Road from the County line as the Main road now goes till it intersects the road leading from Abraham Durst's Smith Shop to the top of the [Massanutten] Mountain, 149

Road from the [top of] Massanutting Mountain to the County line [at the River], 137, 150

Road from Isaac Hite's mill to the road leading to Massinutting [Massanutten], 156, 159

Road from the County line in Massanutting to Mauk's mill, 132, 133

Road from the Main road near Mauk's mill to the County line, 151, 161

[Note: Entries for various spellings of Mecklenburgh are combined.]

Road from the Town of Mecklenburgh to Lynder's ford, or the most convenient ford, on Opecken Creek (road from Mecklenburg to Opeckon), 116, 117, 162

Road from the Town of Mecklinburgh to the Meeting House between Buckles's and Lucas's, 119

The streets of Mecklenburgh, 122, 126
- High Street, 124

Road from the head of Bulskin to the Main road from Winchester to McLenburgh [Mecklenburgh], 123

Road from Mecklenburgh into the Warm Spring road at Richard Pearis's plantation (by the head of the Swan Ponds), 124(2)

Road from the High Street in Mecklenburgh to Joseph Barnes's ford (road from Mecklenburg to Barnes's ford), 124, 133

Road from the streets of Mecklenburgh to the ferry (the streets of Mecklenburg and the road leading to the River), 126, 137

Road from Mecklenburgh to Andrew Swearingen's mill and from thence to the Main road that leads to the mouth of Opeckon, 140
Section:
- Road from Mecklenburgh to Andrew Swearingen's mill, 142

Road from the Main road leading from Jacob Hite's to Mecklenburg through Foster's land to the Ferrying Water and also to the ford of Potomac, 148

Road from the Meeting House at the gap of the Mountains above Hugh Paul's to the Warm Spring(s) (road from the Meeting House at the gap of the Mountains to Hugh Paul's from thence to Thomas Cherry's and by Daniel Rose's up the bottom to Thomas Berwick's, and from Berwick's to the Warm Springs), 21, 26, 31
Sections:
- From the Warm Spring(s) to Sleepy Creek, 21, 26, 70, 112
- From Sleepy Creek to the Meeting House, 21, 26
- From Sleepy Creek to the Widow Paul's, 49, 105

Road from the Meeting House on the mountain to Hugh Lile's on Back Creek, 42

Road from the Meeting House to Opeckon, 70

Road from the Town of Mecklinburgh to the Meeting House between Buckles's and Lucas's, 119

Road from the Presbyterian Meeting House at the head of Tuscarora to the Meeting House on Back Creek, 153

Road from the Baptist Meeting House to the Great road leading from Morgan Morgan's to the Town of Winchester, 115, 117

Road from the Baptist Meeting House to William Hancheir's, 146, 147

Road from the Presbyterian Meeting House at the head of Tuscarora to the Meeting House on Back Creek, 153

Road from Sir John's road by the Quaker Meeting House and through the lane between William Reynolds and Phillip Babb (road between the plantations of William Reynolds and Thomas Babb, Jr. and into Sir John's road; road from Capt. Pearis's to Sir John's road at the Quaker Meeting House), 95, 96, 102

Road from John Melton's to John Sturman's house, 33

[Note: Entries for Mendenall and Mandanhall are combined.]

Road from Mendenall's mill to Cunningham's mill, 78

Road from Mandanhall's Mill Run to Capt. Thomas Caton's, 101

Road through Col. George Mercer's land (alteration), 108

Road from Col. Mercer's upper quarter to Cunningham's Chapel, 128, 130

Road from Middle Creek to Mill Creek, 24

Road from Tuscorora to Middle Creek, 29

Road from Cunningham's to Middle Creek, 56

Road from John Frost's mill to the main road between John Littler's plantation and John Milbourn's/Milburn's plantation, (road from Capt. Frost's mill thence to Buffler lick thence through the lands of John Bosser, and David Springer, thence to the ford, thence through the lands of William Frost and Mathias Elmore, along Elmor[e]'s Creek to Widow Dillon's, and thence to the main road leading to Rappahannock between John Littler's and John Milbourn's), 1, 3, 20, 28
Probable sections:
- Road from John Frost's mill to William Frost's/William Frost's ford, 44, 65
- The other part of the said road, from William Frost's to Col. Morgan's road (road from William Frost's to William Dillon's), 44, 110
- Road from Frost's to Dillon's (alteration round the north side of Dillon's plantation into a lane), 126

[Note: Entries for Mill Creek, Mills Creek, and Mill Run are combined.]

Road from Opecken to Mill Creek/Mills Creek, 5, 28
Sections:
- Road from Mill Creek/Mills Creek to Littler's old place, 36, 61
- Road from Littler's old place to Opecken [including alterations], 36, 41, 71, 73(2)

Road from Middle Creek to Mill Creek, 24

Road from Mill Creek to Tuscarora (road from Cunningham's mill to Tuscarora), 61, 69

Road and ford from Morgan's Chapel to Mill Creek, 76

Road from Stoney Creek to Mill Creek, 85, 90

Road from Littlers Run to Mill Creek, 97

Road from Mill Creek/Mill Run to Sir John's road, 135, 140

Road from Mill Run to Mills's Gap, 140

Road from the head of Mills Creek to the causeway by Onan's, 141

Road from John Little's to the Augusta [County] line (road from the [Augusta] County line below Brock's Gap to John Little's), 157, 159
Sections:
- From Little's to Narrow Passage Creek, 159
- From [Narrow] Passage Creek to Stoney Creek, 159
- From Stoney Creek to Christian Dellinger's, 159
- From Christian Dellinger's to Mill Creek, 159
- From Mill Creek to the [Augusta] County line, 159

Road from Hogland's/Houghland's ferry via Hugh Lysle's, William Baldwin's, and William Hancheire's to fall into Morgan's road leading to Winchester, 143, 147
Sections:
- From Hogland's ferry to John Parks's, 148
- From Hugh Lysle's to Mill Creek, 148
- From Mill Creek to William Hancheir's, 148
- From William Hancheir's to Morgan's road, 148

Road from Stoney Creek to Miller's foot path, 74

Road from Miller's foot path to the old County line, 74

Road from Miller's Town to Stoney Creek, 146, 160

Road from John Little's to Miller's Town, 150, 155

Road from Hugh Lyle's plantation on Back Creek through Curtis's Gap, to Robert Cunningham's (road from Robert Cunningham's to Hugh Lyle's on Back Creek), 103, 104
Sections:
- From Robert Cunningham's to David Miller's plantation, 104
- From David Miller's to the foot of the North Mountain, 104
- From the foot of the North Mountain to Hugh Lyle's on Back Creek, 104

Road from Winchester to Hougland's ferry, leading through Benjamin Thornbrugh's and Enos Ellis's plantations (proposed alteration at Benjamin Thornbrugh's and Enos Ellis's plantations), 150, 156
Section:
- From David Miller's old plantation to Isaac Eaton's, 156

Road from David Miller's old plantation to Col. Stephens's mill, 165

Road from John Lyles's by James Morrison's, John Miller's, John Glenn's and William Glenn's plantations, to Patterson's mill and from thence into the Warm Springs road, 156
[Note: See also:
Road from William Patterson's mill to John Lyle's (alternate route), 159.]

Road from Mills's Gap to Follis's mill and the Main road at Jane Caldwell's plantation, 111, 112

Road from the top of the mountain at Mills's Gap into Sir John Sinclair's road (road from the top of the Mountain at Mill's Gap into the most convenient left part of Sir John Sinclair's road), 112, 116
Sections:
- From Sir John Sinclair's road to the mouth of Lick Branch, 116
- From Lick Branch to the top of the mountain, 116

Road from Mill Run to Mills's Gap, 140

Road from Eaton's mill through Mill's Gap to Fallis's mill, 141, 144
Alteration:
- From the place opposite Sutherland's ford to the Mountain Run, 144

Road from the plantation of Dennis Springer dec. to the top of the mountain at Mill's Gap, 166

Road from Mitchell's ford to the head of Bullskin, 66

Road from the Chapel to Jay's ferry (road from the Chapel by Anderson's/Thos. Anderson's mill by William Mitchell's and Jacob Hite Gent.'s land, and thence into the road that goes from Capt. Campbell's to the ferry, near Capt. Thomas Rutherford's plantation), 6(2)

Road from the Chapel to the old road which leads to William Mitchel's (road from Morgan Morgan's Chapel to William Mitchell's), 20, 25
[Note: This appears to be the same as:
Road from William Mitchell's to Cunningham's Chapel (road continued to the Creek and the bank to be cut down), 46.]

Road from Maj. Andrew Campbell Gent.'s to the Chapel at Cunningham's (road from Maj. Campbell's to Joseph Evans's thence to William Mitchell's then across Opecken thence to the head of the south fork of the Bulskin, thence to Thomas Linseys's on the Long Marsh, thence to John Linsey Gent.'s and from thence to the Chapel at Cunningham's), 22
Sections:
- From Campbell's to Opecken (from Andrew Campbell Gent.'s to William Mitchell's), 22, 30
- From Opecken to the head of Bulskin, 22, 31
- From the head of Bulskin to the Long Marsh, 22, 25
- From the Long Marsh to Fairfax road, 22
- From the Fairfax road to the Chapel), 22, 25

Road from Thomas Rutherford's Spring to William Mitchel's, 24

Road from William Mitchell's to Cunningham's Chapel (road continued to the Creek and the bank to be cut down), 46

Road from Moody's Run to Thorn's Gap, 151

Road from Moody's Run to Kellor's ford, 151

[Note: Entries for Moor and Moore are combined.]

Main road near Henry Moore's plantation (alterations), 92

Road from Henry Moor's to the Elk Branch, 143

Road from Stevens's mill at the Narrow Passage to the Main road near Reiley Moor's, 77
[Note: See also:
Road from Lewis Stevens's mill to the next best ford on the River above Reily Moor's and from thence into the Main road, 78.]

Road from Lewis Stevens's mill to the next best ford on the River above Reily Moor's and from thence into the Main road, 78

Road from the Chapel to the old road which leads to William Mitchel's (road from Morgan Morgan's Chapel to William Mitchell's), 20, 25
[Note: This appears to be the same as:
Road from William Mitchell's to Cunningham's Chapel (road continued to the Creek and the bank to be cut down), 46.]

Road from Morgan's Chapel to Opeckon Creek (at Jonathan Seaman's house), 49, 54, 69, 84, 105

Road and ford from Morgan's Chapel to Mill Creek, 76

Road from Morgan's Chapel to the Main road (alteration: marked from the Chapel to Robert Cunningham's house), 77

Road from Cunningham's/Robert Cunningham's mill and Morgan's Chapel into/to the road called Sir John's road, 97, 111

Road from where Morgan's road crosses Sir John's road, to the Warm Springs road at Joseph Bridges's, 138

Road from John Frost's mill to the main road between John Littler's plantation and John Milbourn's/Milburn's plantation, (road from Capt. Frost's mill thence to Buffler lick thence through the lands of John Bosser, and David Springer, thence to the ford, thence through the lands of William Frost and Mathias Elmore, along Elmor[e]'s Creek to Widow Dillon's, and thence to the main road leading to Rappahannock between John Littler's and John Milbourn's), 1, 3, 20, 28
Probable sections:
- Road from John Frost's mill to William Frost's/William Frost's ford, 44, 65
- The other part of the said road, from William Frost's to Col. Morgan's road (road from William Frost's to William Dillon's), 44, 110
- Road from Frost's to Dillon's (alteration round the north side of Dillon's plantation into a lane), 126

Road from Hogland's/Houghland's ferry via Hugh Lysle's, William Baldwin's, and William Hancheire's to fall into Morgan's road leading to Winchester, 143, 147
Sections:
- From Hogland's ferry to John Parks's, 148
- From Hugh Lysle's to Mill Creek, 148
- From Mill Creek to William Hancheir's, 148
- From William Hancheir's to Morgan's road, 148

Road from Morgan Morgan Gent.'s house/Col. Morgan's to the Courthouse/Winchester (road from the Courthouse to the house of Josiah Ballenger and to Morgan Morgan's), 9, 17, 32, 103
Sections:
- Road from the Courthouse to the house of Josiah Ballenger (road from the Courthouse to Ballenger's plantation), 17, 42
- Road from Josiah Ballenger's to Morgan Morgan's (road from Col. Morgan's to Ballenger's meadow; road from Col. Morgan's to the widow Ballenger's), 17, 86, 105

Bridle road/road from Morgan Morgan Gent.'s to Andrew Campbell Gent.'s), 24, 30

Road from Joseph Evans's to Col. Morgan Morgan's, 40, 43

Road from Capt. Jeremiah Smith's to Col. Morgan Morgan's and thence into the Main County road near Patrick Reiley's, 71(2)

Road from the Baptist Meeting House to the Great road leading from Morgan Morgan's to the Town of Winchester, 115, 117

Road from Thomas Morgan's mill to Lewis Hogg's house and from thence to the top of the Ridge, 7

Road from Thomas Lyndsey's plantation to Samuel Morris's, 161

Road from John Lyles's by James Morrison's, John Miller's, John Glenn's and William Glenn's plantations, to Patterson's mill and from thence into the Warm Springs road, 156
[Note: See also:
Road from William Patterson's mill to John Lyle's (alternate route), 159.]

Road from Winchester Town to Robert Mosely's/Moseley's place, 66, 86, 88, 90
[Note: See also:
(New) road through the Common from Winchester to Robert Mosely's, 89.]

Road from Robert Mosely's to Opeckon Creek where John Neil's old mill formerly stood, 66

Road from Mr. Robert Cunningham's/Cunningham's mill to Mr. Robert Moseley's, 68, 93

(New) road through the Common from Winchester to Robert Mosely's, 89

Road from Samuel Mount's upon Bullskin to the road leading to Ashby's Gap, 128

Road from Samuel Mounts's to Jacob Hite's mill, 134, 136

Road from Jackson Allen's crossing the mouth of Smiths Creek thence through White's Bottom to William Clark's at Mount Pleasant, 91

Road from the Meeting House at the gap of the Mountains above Hugh Paul's to the Warm Spring(s) (road from the Meeting House at the gap of the Mountains to Hugh Paul's from thence to Thomas Cherry's and by Daniel Rose's up the bottom to Thomas Berwick's, and from Berwick's to the Warm Springs), 21, 26, 31
Sections:
- From the Warm Spring(s) to Sleepy Creek, 21, 26, 70, 112
- From Sleepy Creek to the Meeting House, 21, 26
- From Sleepy Creek to the Widow Paul's, 49, 105

Road from the Meeting House on the mountain to Hugh Lile's on Back Creek, 42

Road from Thomas Hart's to Linder's ford and from the ford to the mountain, 53
Sections:

- Road from Thomas Hart's to Linder's ford, 53
- Road from Linder's ford to the mountain, 53

Road from the mountain to Opeckon, 81
[Note: This appears to be a different road than:
Road from Opeckon Creek to the Mountain, 110, 112.]

Road from Selser's Mill Run to the County line at Woods Plain (Mountain road from Wood's Plains over the mountains to Selser's Mill Run), 94, 102

Road from the top of the Mountain to Sleepy Creek, 110, 143

Road from Opeckon Creek to the Mountain, 110, 112

Road from the top of the mountain at Mills's Gap into Sir John Sinclair's road (road from the top of the Mountain at Mill's Gap into the most convenient left part of Sir John Sinclair's road), 112, 116
Sections:
- From Sir John Sinclair's road to the mouth of Lick Branch, 116
- From Lick Branch to the top of the mountain, 116

Road from Keys's ford to the top of the Mountain, 122

Road from the Widow Calwell's to the Mountain, 144

Road from the forks of Shanondoah to the top of the mountain, 150

Road from Vestall's ford and Keyes's ferry to the top of the Mountain (the Mountain road), 163(3)

Road from the plantation of Dennis Springer dec. to the top of the mountain at Mill's Gap, 166

Road from John Briscoe's mill upon Opeckon into the Mountain road by Murty Handley's, 127, 132

Mill road from John Spencely's house to the County road leading over the Mountain (road from John Spenceley's to the Main road leading over the mountain), 151, 155

Road from Eaton's mill through Mill's Gap to Fallis's mill, 141, 144
Alteration:
- From the place opposite Sutherland's ford to the Mountain Run, 144

Road from John McCormick's house to Crawford's Muster Ground (road from Dr. McCormack's to the Muster Ground, including the bridge), 107, 139

Road from the Muster Ground to the [Vestal's] ford/Vestall's ford, 134, 136, 163

Road from the Muster Ground to the forks by John Smith's, 134

Road from the Muster Ground to Keyes's ferry, 137

Road from the Muster Ground above the Widow Caldwell's/Calwell's to John Neavill's mill and thence into the Main road by Jonah Seaman's, 155, 156

Road from Stevens's mill at the Narrow Passage to the Main road near Reiley Moor's, 77
[Note: See also:
Road from Lewis Stevens's mill to the next best ford on the River above Reily Moor's and from thence into the Main road, 78.]

Road from Jeremiah Lewis's (at/near the County line) to Stephens's/Stevens's mill at/on the Narrow Passage, 79, 104
Sections:
- Road from the County line near Jeremiah Lewis's to Christian Dilliner's, 81
- Road from Christian Dillener's to Lewis Stevens's mill at the Narrow Passage, 81

Road from the Old field formerly Benjamin Allen's to the Narrow Passage, 95

Road from Woodstock to Mounts Bird's (road from the Narrow Passage to Mounts Bird's), 125, 131

Road from John Little's to the Augusta [County] line (road from the [Augusta] County line below Brock's Gap to John Little's), 157, 159
Sections:
- From Little's to Narrow Passage Creek, 159
- From [Narrow] Passage Creek to Stoney Creek, 159
- From Stoney Creek to Christian Dellinger's, 159
- From Christian Dellinger's to Mill Creek, 159
- From Mill Creek to the [Augusta] County line, 159

Road from the run by Nation's/John Nation's house to Kersey's ferry, 9, 51

Road from John Hite's/Capt. Hite's mill to the Run at John Nation's house/Nation's Run/Nation's Branch, 30, 36, 42, 45, 51(2), 64

Road from Nation's plantation to the River, 58

Road from the New Town (Stephensburgh/Stevensburgh) to Nations's (road leading from Stephensburgh to the Right Honourable Thomas Lord Fairfax's plantation called Nation's; road from Stephensburgh to Nation's plantation), 92, 96, 114, 144, 145

Road from Lord Fairfax's quarter where Nation formerly lived to the ford at Comb's (road from the Right Honourable Thomas Lord Fairfax's quarter to Combes's ferry), 101, 113

Road from Nation's plantation to the ford at Ashby's Gap (road from Nation's plantation to the ford and ferry at Berry's), 130, 136, 140, 166

Road from Nation's Run to Ashby's ferry, 64

Road from John Nealan[d]'s/Neeland's on Sharrando to William Vestal's on the same river (road from John Nealand's down the river by the lands of John Grimes, Capt. Stribling, Timothy Haney, Darby Conely, Goldin, John Hamman, Thomas Hamman, and Elizabeth Pearson, across Pearson's Neck of Land to Jonathan Walker's, over Bulskin, and by Robert Hayes's and along Hayes's path to Vestal's), 9, 10

[Note: Entries for Neavill and Nevill are combined.]

Road from the Muster Ground above the Widow Caldwell's/Calwell's to John Neavill's mill and thence into the Main road by Jonah Seaman's, 155, 156

Road from John Nevill's mill into Dr. Briscoe's mill road, 161, 163, 165

Road from the Warm Spring road at Joseph Bridges's into the Main road by John Nevill's, 166, 167

Neill's road, 80

Road from the Long Marsh below Capt. Neill's to Patrick Rice's house, 107

Road from the head of Bulskin over John Neill's mill dam to the Courthouse, 3, 7

Road from Opecken ford by John Neil's/Neill's mill to Kersey's ferry (other road to Kersey's ferry), 4(2), 17, 19

Road from Opecken Creek to the Chapel by James Cunningham's (road from John Neill's house to the Chapel at Cunningham's; road from Opecken Creek at John Neill's ford near his house, thence along the old path that formerly went to James Hill's, to the forks of the old wagon road commonly called Littler's Wagon road, and thence along Hill's Marsh to Cunningham's house and so to the Chapel), 20, 23, 33
[Note: May be the same as:
Road from the Chapel at Cunningham's to John Neill's, Gent., to be continued to Abrahams Run (road crossing Opeckon at John Neill's ford to Cunningham's Chapel), 39, 53.]
[Note: See also:
Road from the forks of the road at Cunningham's Chapel to Opecken Creek, 34 (Note: Road order entries appear to indicate that this road is different from the road noted on pp. 20, 23, 33.).]

Road from the Chapel at Cunningham's to John Neill's, Gent., to be continued to Abrahams Run (road crossing Opeckon at John Neill's ford to Cunningham's Chapel), 39, 53.]

Road from Robert Mosely's to Opeckon Creek where John Neil's old mill formerly stood, 66

Main road by John Neill's old mill, 106

Road from this Courthouse [Winchester] to the top of the Blue Ridge of Mountains at Williams's Gap (road from Capt. Neill's off and on the old road to Joseph Wilkenson's and thence off on the same road to Francis Carney's and from thence to Edge's ford and from thence off and on the old road to the top of the said Mountain), 12
Sections:
- From Capt. Lewis Neill's/Lewis Neill Gent.'s to Francis Carney's/Carnie's (road from Francis Carney's/Carney's Spring to Lewis Neill's/Opeckon at Neill's ford/Opeckon Creek by Capt. Neill's/ Opecken by Lewis Neill's, Gent), 12, 22, 31, 82, 100, 104
- From Carney's to Edge's ford on Shannadore River (road from Shanando River to Carney's Spring, 12, 50, 83
- From Edge's ford to the top of the Blue Ridge on Williams's Gap, 12

Probable later sections:
- Road from Winchester Town to Lewis Neill's/Lewis Neill's ford on Opeckon, 59, 67
- Road from the ford at Lewis Neill Gent.'s house to Littler's road, 59
- Road from Littler's road to Carney's old house, 59
- Road from Carney's old house to the River, 59
- Road from the River to the top of the mountain at Williams's Gap (road from Edward Snigers's [on Shanando] to the top of the Mountain at Williams's Gap; road from the River at Snigers's to the County line at Williams's Gap; road from the top of the Ridge to Edward Snickers's/Snigers's ford/ferry/ferry at Snicker's house; road from the Ferry road [Snigers's] to the top of the Ridge at Williams's Gap), 59, 76, 79, 81, 83, 113

Road from the Courthouse/Winchester to Lewis Neill Gent.'s/ Lewis Neill's old place/Lewis Neill's ford on Opeckon, 12, 13, 23, 29, 30, 59, 67, 73, 81, 88, 94, 102, 103, 110, 151, 170

Road from John McCormick's to Lewis Neil Gent.'s, 14

Road from Lewis Neill, Gent.'s to Kersey's ferry, 23

Road from the Chapel at Cunningham's to Mr. Lewis Neill's ford on Opeckon, 48

Road from Littler's lane to the ford at Lewis Neill's, 164

Road from Lewis Neill's house at Opeckon to the Signpost, 83

Road from the head of Bullskin Marsh running by the head of Long Marsh into the road at the Dry Marsh below Capt. Lewis Neill's, 98

Road from Lewis Neill's mill to Edmond Lindsey, Jr.'s plantation, 119

Road from Lewis Neill's mill to Owin Wingfield's land, 119

Road from Lewis Neill's mill into Perry's road (road leading from Lewis Neill's mill into the road leading from Thomas Sperry's [Perry's] mill to the town of Winchester; road from Lewis Neill's mill to Thomas Perry's mill), 119, 120, 123

Road from Lewis Neill's mill to Thomas Lindsey's, 123

Road from Lewis Neil's mill to John McMachen's old place, 158

Road from Lewis Neill's mill, 158

Road from Lewis Neill's mill into the road leading to Helms's mill at the head of the Dry Marsh, 160

Road from Opeckon Creek to the Main county road (road from William Neill's upon Opeckon into the Great road that runs by William Joleff's; road from the forks of the road leading from Winchester to William Jolliff's to Opeckon Creek), 88, 120, 147

Road from Hogland's Neck by Barnet Newkirk's and into the Great road, 77

Road from Col. Hite's through the Town laid out on Lewis Stephens's plantation/ Stephens Town and from thence into the Main road (road from Col. John Hite's to Stephensburgh; road between Col. John Hite's and the new town called Stevensburgh), 89, 90, 93, 94

Road from the New Town (Stephensburgh/Stevensburgh) to Nations's (road leading from Stephensburgh to the Right Honourable Thomas Lord Fairfax's plantation called Nation's; road from Stephensburgh to Nation's plantation), 92, 96, 114, 144, 145

Road from the New Town [Stephensburgh/Stevensburgh] into Chester's road, 92

Road from Hugh Lyle's plantation on Back Creek through Curtis's Gap, to Robert Cunningham's (road from Robert Cunningham's to Hugh Lyle's on Back Creek), 103, 104
Sections:
- From Robert Cunningham's to David Miller's plantation, 104
- From David Miller's to the foot of the North Mountain, 104
- From the foot of the North Mountain to Hugh Lyle's on Back Creek, 104

Road from Winchester to the South Branch at the County line on the North Mountain (road from the place marked by the viewers to the County line on the North Mountain), 104, 106

Road from John Briscoe's mill upon Opeckon to the settlement under the [North] mountain (by William Cockrain's/Cockraine's), 127, 132, 143

Road from William Hancher's mill to the North Mountain near John Gerrard's, 166

Road from John Funk's mill to Chester's ferry and from thence to where the road takes out of Chester's road to Manasses Run, 1, 2
Sections:
- From John Funk's mill to the North River, 2, 79
- From the North River to the Haybottom, 2, 78
- From the Haybottom to where the road takes off to Manasses Run, 2, 31, 34, 55
- Road to be continued to Manasses Run, 31

Road from the South Branch to the North River, 50

Road from Jeremiah Smith's to the North River (near Thomas Parker's), 54, 62

Road from the North River near Thomas Parker's to Peter Tostee's plantation/Toste's late plantation, 62, 69

Road from the North River ford to the ford of Crooked Run, 81, 158

Road from Charles Buck's mill to Christian Blank's ford on the North River, and from thence to Stephensburg, 103

Road from the North River leading to Chester's Gap to the South River, 137

Road from Passage Creek to the North River, 147

Road from the North River to the forks of Henry Spears's road, 148

Road from Abraham Durst's Shop to the road on this side of the Massanuting Mountain (road from Abraham Darst's Smith's Shop to the top of the Massanutting [Massanutten] Mountain), 135, 137, 149(2)
Sections/related roads:
- Road from the North River to the County line, 149
- Road from the County line as the Main road now goes till it intersects the road leading from Abraham Durst's Smith Shop to the top of the [Massanutten] Mountain, 149

Road from Jumping Run bridge to the North River ford, 159

Road from the head of Mills Creek to the causeway by Onan's, 141

Road from Isaac Perkins's mill to Opecken, 3, 5

Road from Israel Robinson's Gap to Vestal's Gap (via Opecken Creek), 3
Section:
- Road from Robinson's Gap to Opecken, 4, 24

329

Road from John Littler's to Thomas Shepard's/Sheppard's mill (road from John Littler's late dwelling house to the said Littler's New Design thence to Opecken Creek over Abril's ford thence to the late dwelling place of John Smith's dec. thence to Jacob Hite's thence to Thomas Shepard's mill), 4, 5
Sections:
- Road from John Littler's to Thomas Sheppard's mill, 6
- Road from Thomas Shepherd's mill to Jacob Hite, Gent.'s, 32
- Road from John Smith's to John Littler's, 32

[Note: See also:
Road from Alexander Ross's fence to the corner of Smith's fence, 21 (etc.)
and
Road from Smith's fence/John Smith's old place to Jacob Hite's, 21, 62, 90, 106, 128, 133
and
Road from William Hite's Spring to the middle of the Swamp in Smith's Marsh and from the Swamp to Littler's mill, 40, 41.]

Road from Opecken ford by John Neil's/Neill's mill to Kersey's ferry (other road to Kersey's ferry), 4(2), 17, 19

Road from Opecken to Mill Creek/Mills Creek, 5, 28
Sections:
- Road from Mill Creek/Mills Creek to Littler's old place, 36, 61
- Road from Littler's old place to Opecken [including alterations], 36, 41, 71, 73(2)

Road from this Courthouse [Winchester] to the top of the Blue Ridge of Mountains at Williams's Gap (road from Capt. Neill's off and on the old road to Joseph Wilkenson's and thence off on the same road to Francis Carney's and from thence to Edge's ford and from thence off and on the old road to the top of the said Mountain), 12
Sections:
- From Capt. Lewis Neill's/Lewis Neill Gent.'s to Francis Carney's/Carnie's (road from Francis Carney's/Carney's Spring to Lewis Neill's/Opeckon at Neill's ford/Opeckon Creek by Capt. Neill's/ Opecken by Lewis Neill's, Gent), 12, 22, 31, 82, 100, 104
- From Carney's to Edge's ford on Shannadore River (road from Shanando River to Carney's Spring, 12, 50, 83
- From Edge's ford to the top of the Blue Ridge on Williams's Gap, 12

Probable later sections:
- Road from Winchester Town to Lewis Neill's/Lewis Neill's ford on Opeckon, 59, 67
- Road from the ford at Lewis Neill Gent.'s house to Littler's road, 59
- Road from Littler's road to Carney's old house, 59
- Road from Carney's old house to the River, 59
- Road from the River to the top of the mountain at Williams's Gap (road from Edward Snigers's [on Shanando] to the top of the Mountain at Williams's Gap; road from the River at Snigers's to the County line at Williams's Gap; road from the top of the Ridge to Edward Snickers's/Snigers's ford/ferry/ferry at Snicker's house; road from

the Ferry road [Snigers's] to the top of the Ridge at Williams's Gap), 59, 76, 79, 81, 83, 113

Road from Opecken to Shanandore River, 12, 35

Road from the Courthouse/Winchester to Lewis Neill Gent.'s/ Lewis Neill's old place/Lewis Neill's ford on Opeckon, 12, 13, 23, 29, 30, 59, 67, 73, 81, 88, 94, 102, 103, 110, 151, 170

Road from John McCormack's house to Opecken Creek and from Opecken Creek to the Courthouse/the Town (road from the head of the south fork of Bullskin to Opecken and thence to the Courthouse), 20, 25
Sections:
- Road from the head of the south fork of Bullskin to Opecken (road from John McCormack's to the Main road to Town; road from John McCormack's house to Opecken Creek which leads to town), 20, 25, 49, 67, 87, 107 *[Note: This section appears to be different than the section from Opecken to the head to Bullskin (pp. 22, 31) of the road from Maj. Andrew Campbell Gent.'s to the Chapel at Cunningham's, 22.]*
- Road from Opecken to the Courthouse (road from Opeckon Creek to the Main road leading to Winchester), 20, 25, 107

Road from Opecken Creek to the Chapel by James Cunningham's (road from John Neill's house to the Chapel at Cunningham's; road from Opecken Creek at John Neill's ford near his house, thence along the old path that formerly went to James Hill's, to the forks of the old wagon road commonly called Littler's Wagon road, and thence along Hill's Marsh to Cunningham's house and so to the Chapel), 20, 23, 33
[Note: May be the same as:
Road from the Chapel at Cunningham's to John Neill's, Gent., to be continued to Abrahams Run (road crossing Opeckon at John Neill's ford to Cunningham's Chapel), 39, 53.]
[Note: See also:
Road from the forks of the road at Cunningham's Chapel to Opecken Creek, 34 (Note: Road order entries appear to indicate that this road is different from the road noted on pp. 20, 23, 33.).]

Road from Maj. Andrew Campbell Gent.'s to the Chapel at Cunningham's (road from Maj. Campbell's to Joseph Evans's thence to William Mitchell's then across Opecken thence to the head of the south fork of the Bulskin, thence to Thomas Linseys's on the Long Marsh, thence to John Linsey Gent.'s and from thence to the Chapel at Cunningham's), 22
Sections:
- From Campbell's to Opecken (from Andrew Campbell Gent.'s to William Mitchell's), 22, 30
- From Opecken to the head of Bulskin, 22, 31
- From the head of Bulskin to the Long Marsh, 22, 25
- From the Long Marsh to Fairfax road, 22
- From the Fairfax road to the Chapel), 22, 25

Road from Opecken to David Loyd's, 24

Road from Thomas Thornbury's mill to Opecken Creek by Edward Stroud's and from thence into the road that leads from Jacob Hite's to Vestal's ford on Sharando River, 25

Road from John Littler's mill across Opecken at the mouth of his mill run, 29

Road from John Littler's to Opecken (alteration), 31

Road from Isaac Perkins/Parkins's, Gent.'s mill to Mr. Gabriel Jones's plantation on Opecken River, 33, 64, 66, 67

Road from the Courthouse/Winchester to Opecken Creek/Opecken ford, 34, 36(2), 43, 50

Road from the forks of the road at Cunningham's Chapel to Opecken Creek, 34 *[Note: Road order entries appear to indicate that this road is different from the road noted on pp. 20, 23, 33.]*

Road from Opecken to Sherando River (road from Opeckon Creek to Col. Burwell's mill; road from Opeckon where Joseph Robbins lived to Burwell's mill on Shanando), 35, 50, 57

Road from the Chapel at Cunningham's to John Neill's, Gent., to be continued to Abrahams Run (road crossing Opeckon at John Neill's ford to Cunningham's Chapel), 39, 53

Road from Ross's fence by the great road to Opeckon Creek, 45

Road from Watkins's ferry to Vestal's Gap, 47, 56
Sections:
- The part of the road lying on the west side of Opeckon, 47
- The road from Opeckon to the Gap, 47

Road from the Chapel at Cunningham's to Mr. Lewis Neill's ford on Opeckon, 48

Road from Morgan's Chapel to Opeckon Creek (at Jonathan Seaman's house), 49, 54, 69, 84, 105

Road from John Hite's to a branch of Opeckon, 50

Road from Mark Hardin's ford on Shanando River to Isaac Hollingsworth's, 38, 51(2)
Sections
- Road from the River to Opeckon, 51
- Road from Opeckon to Isaac Hollingsworth's, 51

Road from Opecken at Hugh Hains's to the Indian Grave on the Main road, 54

Road from Sandy ford on Opeckon to Isaac Parkins's/Perkins's mill, 56, 98

Road from Opeckon to the Signpost/the Signpost at/near Quintin's/Quinton's, 58, 78, 87

Road from Opeckon where Joseph Robins formerly lived to Burwell's Spout Run, 59

Road from Winchester Town to Opeckon where Joseph Robins formerly lived, 59

Road from (Paul) Froman's mill to the Sand ford/Sandy ford on Opeckon, 65, 69, 71, 98, 99, 129

Road from Robert Mosely's to Opeckon Creek where John Neil's old mill formerly stood, 66

Road from the Meeting House to Opeckon, 70

Road from Ross's field crossing Opeckon to the middle of Smith's bridge, 91
Sections:
- Road from Ross's field to the other side of Opeckon Creek, 70
- Road from Opeckon Creek to the middle of Smith's bridge, 70, 98

Road from Opeckon to the Widow Cunningham's, 71

Road from Marquis Calmes's to Opeckon Run, 75

Road from William Richey's to Opeckon, 75

Road from the new bridge at Opeckon into the road leading from Winchester to Henry Enochs's, 79

Road leading from Winchester to Henry Enochs's, 79(2)
Section:
- From the beginning of the new road [i.e., the road from the new bridge at Opeckon into the road leading from Winchester to Henry Enochs's], to the County line, 79

Road from Opeckon near John Bryan's house to Winchester (road to be cleared on the top of the ridge to avoid the swampy part of the road), 80

Road from the mountain to Opeckon, 81
[Note: This appears to be a different road than:
Road from Opeckon Creek to the Mountain, 110, 112.]

Road from Lewis Neill's house at Opeckon to the Signpost, 83

Road from Joseph Edwards Jr.'s to the Main road at the bridge over Opeckon Creek, 84

Road from Opeckon Creek to Capt. Rutherford's plantation, 87

Road from Opeckon/Opeckon bridge to William Jolliff's (road from the bridge on Opeckon Creek to William Jolliffe, Jr.'s; road from Jolliffe's store to Opeckon ford), 88, 116, 143, 172

Road from Opeckon Creek to the Main county road (road from William Neill's upon Opeckon into the Great road that runs by William Joleff's; road from the forks of the road leading from Winchester to William Jolliff's to Opeckon Creek), 88, 120, 147

Road from Paul Froman's mill by the head of Opeckon into the road leading to Winchester, 90

Road from Opeckon Creek to Lucas's Marsh, 92

Road leading from Maj. Lewis Stephens's mill to Opeckon Creek, 98

Road called Littler's road, 100, 101, 105, 125, 129
Sections:
- From the beginning to Opeckon Creek, 105, 125
- From Opeckon Creek to the fork where it joins the Winchester road leading to Spout Run, 100, 101, 159

Road from Opeckon Creek to the Mountain, 110, 112

Road from Opeckon ford at John Armstrong's house to Winchester (road from Winchester to Opeckon at Armstrong's place; road from Winchester to Opeckon at Armstrong's ford), 114, 123, 126

Road from Caton's ford/Thomas Caton's to Vestal's Gap, 76, 115
Section:
- Part from Opeckon Creek to Shepherds Town, 115

Road leading from John Hite's house to the Town of Winchester (road from Opeckon to Winchester), 115, 136

Road from the Town of Mecklenburgh to Lynder's ford, or the most convenient ford, on Opecken Creek (road from Mecklenburg to Opeckon), 116, 117, 162

Road from Jonathan Seamon's house (on Opeckon) to Jacob Hite's, 120, 131

Road from Armstrong's ford upon Opeckon to the Signpost at Littler's road, 123

Road from John Briscoe's mill upon Opeckon to the settlement under the [North] mountain (by William Cockrain's/Cockraine's), 127, 132, 143

Road from John Briscoe's mill upon Opeckon into the Mountain road by Murty Handley's, 127, 132

Road from the furnace erecting on the north branch of Pembroke to the forge erecting on Cedar Creek (road from the forge to the furnace), 129(2), 146
Sections:
- From the furnace to Devault Hulberger's, 129

- From Hulberger's to the forge (from <u>Opeckon</u> to the forge upon Cedar Creek), 129, 142, 144

Road from John Briscoe's mill upon <u>Opeckon</u> to Ashby's Gap, 129

Road from the fork of <u>Opeckon</u> on the Main road at Edward Stroad's/Stroade's to Hogland's ferry, 131(2)

Road (starting at the Main road leading from Winchester to Watkins's ferry) from Peter Fussey's Big Spring/Fussey's Large Spring to the upper side of the mouth of <u>Opeckon Creek</u>, 133(2)

Road from Mecklenburgh to Andrew Swearingen's mill and from thence to the Main road that leads to the mouth of <u>Opeckon</u>, 140
Section:
- Road from Mecklenburgh to Andrew Swearingen's mill, 142

Road from <u>Opeckon</u> to the Winchester road, 143

Road from the ford on <u>Opeckon</u> to Dr. McCormack's, 147

Road from the ford of <u>Opeckon</u> by David Brown's near Col. Hite's tanyard to the Hoop Petticoat Gap, 155, 164

Road from <u>Opeckon</u> to the Warm Springs, 162

Road leading from <u>Opeckon</u> to Battletown, 167, 169

Road from David Brown's mill down <u>Opeckon Creek</u> by James Knight's and Edward Reed's into the Chapel road, 168, 170, 171

Road leading to Marlbrough forge from Perkins's mill as far as <u>Opeckon</u>, 171

Road leading from <u>Opeckon</u> to Fry's mill, 171

(Petition to the Court of <u>Orange County</u> for) a road from the County line of Frederick to the upper inhabitants of Augusta on Woods River, 10

Road from Stony bridge to <u>Parker's</u> on the North River of Cacapon, 41

Road from Jeremiah Smith's to the North River (near Thomas <u>Parker's</u>), 54, 62

Road from the North River near Thomas <u>Parker's</u> to Peter Tostee's plantation/Toste's late plantation, 62, 69

Road from the lower part of the South Branch to the Main road near Thomas <u>Parker's</u>, 68

Road from Parks's graveyard near Cape Capon Water, over Dellings Run into the Wagon road on Joseph Edward's land, 25

Road from Hogland's ferry to John Parks's, 106

Road from Hogland's/Houghland's ferry via Hugh Lysle's, William Baldwin's, and William Hancheire's to fall into Morgan's road leading to Winchester, 143, 147
Sections:
- From Hogland's ferry to John Parks's, 148
- From Hugh Lysle's to Mill Creek, 148
- From Mill Creek to William Hancheir's, 148
- From William Hancheir's to Morgan's road, 148

Roads through Hugh Parrel's land, 4

Road from George Julian's on Passage Creek to Buck's mill (road from George Julian's in Powell's fort to Buck's mill; road from Buck's mill to Powell's fort), 85, 96, 104

Road from Passage Creek to the North River, 147

Road from Henry Funk's mill on Passage Creek to Abraham Kendrick's upper ford and from thence to William Ashby's, 158, 160
Sections:
- From Henry Funk's mill to Abraham Kendrick's upper ford, 160
- From Abraham Kendrick's upper ford to William Ashby's, 160

Road from Buffinton's to Carrol's Place on Pattersons Creek (road from Willm. Buffington's to Pattersons Creek, 16, 63

Road from the mouth of Pattersons Creek to Job Pearsal's/Pearsall's, 39, 46

Road from the lower part of Pattersons Creek by Power Hazel's into the wagon road which leads from the Courthouse to the South Branch, 40

Road from John Lyles's by James Morrison's, John Miller's, John Glenn's and William Glenn's plantations, to Patterson's mill and from thence into the Warm Springs road, 156
[Note: See also:
Road from William Patterson's mill to John Lyle's (alternate route), 159.]

Road from William Patterson's mill to John Lyle's (alternate route), 159

Road from Robert Cunningham's to Samuel Patton's, 73

Road from Sir John's road near George Paul's to Hougland's ferry and to Van Swearingen's mill on Tunis's Branch, 140

Road from the Meeting House at the gap of the Mountains above Hugh Paul's to the Warm Spring(s) (road from the Meeting House at the gap of the Mountains to Hugh Paul's from thence to Thomas Cherry's and by Daniel Rose's up the bottom to Thomas Berwick's, and from Berwick's to the Warm Springs), 21, 26, 31
Sections:
- From the Warm Spring(s) to Sleepy Creek, 21, 26, 70, 112
- From Sleepy Creek to the Meeting House, 21, 26
- From Sleepy Creek to the Widow Paul's, 49, 105

Road from Sir John's road by the Quaker Meeting House and through the lane between William Reynolds and Phillip Babb (road between the plantations of William Reynolds and Thomas Babb, Jr. and into Sir John's road; road from Capt. Pearis's to Sir John's road at the Quaker Meeting House), 95, 96, 102

Road from Mecklenburgh into the Warm Spring road at Richard Pearis's plantation (by the head of the Swan Ponds), 124(2)

Road from Richard Pearis's to the Quaker Meeting House (road from Richard Pearis's into Sir John's road), 141, 142

Road from Winchester Town to Robert Pearis's plantation, 62, 66

Road from Robert Pearis's to Capt. Jeremiah Smith's house, 62, 77

Road from the mouth of Pattersons Creek to Job Pearsal's/Pearsall's, 39, 46

Main road leading through Job Pearsall's plantation at the South Branch, 48

Road from John Nealan[d]'s/Neeland's on Sharrando to William Vestal's on the same river (road from John Nealand's down the river by the lands of John Grimes, Capt. Stribling, Timothy Haney, Darby Conely, Goldin, John Hamman, Thomas Hamman, and Elizabeth Pearson, across Pearson's Neck of Land to Jonathan Walker's, over Bulskin, and by Robert Hayes's and along Hayes's path to Vestal's), 9, 10

Road from Enoch Pearson's to Watkins's ferry, 78

Road from Enoch Pearson's to the mouth of Back Creek, 81

Road from George Pemberton's dwelling house to the road that leads from Capt. Rutherford's to Dr. McCormack's, 46

Road from Joseph Fry's plantation on Cedar Creek to the Furnace being erected on the north branch of Pembroke, 118

Road from the furnace erecting on the north branch of Pembroke to the forge erecting on Cedar Creek (road from the forge to the furnace), 129(2), 146

Sections:
- From the furnace to Devault Hulberger's, 129
- From Hulberger's to the forge (from Opeckon to the forge upon Cedar Creek), 129, 142, 144

Road from the head of Bullskin to Pennington's Marsh, 66

Road from Pennington's Marsh to Mr. Calmes's, 66

Road from Calebs Run to the Brush bottom ford and from thence to the Percimmon Pond above James McCoy's, 74, 75

[Note: Entries for Parkins and Perkins are combined.]

Road from Perkins's mill to Kersey's ferry, 14

Road from the end of the new street in Winchester into the Main road leading to Parkins's [Perkins's] mill, 72
[Note: See also the entries under Streets in Winchester.]

Road leading to Marlbrough forge from Perkins's mill as far as Opeckon, 171

Road from Isaac Perkins's mill to Opecken, 3, 5

Road from Isaac Perkins's/[Isaac] Parkins's/Perkins's mill to John Hite's/John Hite's mill, 5, 16, 64

Road from Isaac Perkins's mill to John Littler's old place, 5

Road from Isaac Perkins's mill to Ralph Humfrey's, 17

Road from Isaac Perkins's mill through the Town [Winchester] to the line thereof by Andrew Caldwell's (road from Isaac Perkins's mill to the north end of the Town; road through the town to Parkins's [Perkins's] mill; the Main Street of the Town), 19, 20, 64, 88

Road from Isaac Perkins/Parkins's, Gent.'s mill to Mr. Gabriel Jones's plantation on Opecken River, 33, 64, 66, 67

Road from John Hite Gent.'s house to Isaac Parkins's Gent., 50

Road from Sandy ford on Opeckon to Isaac Parkins's/Perkins's mill, 56, 98

Road from Isaac Perkins's to Hoge Creek where the road leading from Winchester to the South Branch crosses it, 147, 149

Road from Hog's Creek where the South Branch road crosses it to go by Isaac Perkins's plantation and thence to Jessee Pugh's mill (road from Hoge Creek where the Winchester road crosses it to go by Isaac Perkins's plantation and to Jessee Pugh's mill; road from Hog's Creek to Jessee Pugh's mill), 149, 151, 154(2)

Road from the Town of Winchester to Thomas Perry's mill, 114, 115, 124

Road from Lewis Neill's mill into Perry's road (road leading from Lewis Neill's mill into the road leading from Thomas Sperry's [Perry's] mill to the town of Winchester; road from Lewis Neill's mill to Thomas Perry's mill), 119, 120, 123

Road from Sir John's road by Thomas Babb's down by William McMachen's (and) Angus McDonald's and down to Berry's mill, 121
[Note: May be the same as:
Road from Sir John's road above Thomas Babb's plantation to Thomas Perry's mill, 121.]

Road from Sir John's road above Thomas Babb's plantation to Thomas Perry's mill, 121

(Petition to the Court of Prince William County to meet Frederick County with) a road from the Thorough fair at the Pignut Ridge to the top of the Blue Ridge at the head of Manasses Run, 10

(Request to the Court of Prince William County for a) Road from Jefrey Johnston's at the Pignut Ridge to the top of the [Blue] Ridge at Ashby's Bent, 23

Road from John Shepard's/Sheppard's to the head of Bulskin (road from Potomac River from Sheppards ferry through the land of Thomas Rutherford, over Walker's mill dam and by the head of Pitts's Marsh and to the head of Bulskin through the lands of Mr. John McCormack), 3, 7
Sections:
- Road from Potomac River to Thomas Rutherford Gent.'s, 12, 38
- The remaining part of the road, 13
- Road from Thomas Rutherford Gent.'s to the head of Bullskin, 24
- Road from Thomas Rutherford's house to John McCarmack's, 37

Road from the head of Pitts's Marsh to the Chapel at James Cunningham's, 28

Road from Thomas Postgate's Islands/Island into the road that comes from Thomas Chester Gent.'s, 8, 13

Road from John Shepard's/Sheppard's to the head of Bulskin (road from Potomac River from Sheppards ferry through the land of Thomas Rutherford, over Walker's mill dam and by the head of Pitts's Marsh and to the head of Bulskin through the lands of Mr. John McCormack), 3, 7
Sections:
- Road from Potomac River to Thomas Rutherford Gent.'s, 12, 38
- The remaining part of the road, 13
- Road from Thomas Rutherford Gent.'s to the head of Bullskin, 24
- Road from Thomas Rutherford's house to John McCarmack's, 37

Road from Evan Watkins's ferry [on Potomac River] to Tuscorora, 13
Sections:
- From Charles Donahue's house to Potomac River, 24
- From Charles Donahue's house to Tuscorora Creek, 24

Road from Frederick Town [Courthouse] to the mouth of the South Branch of Potomac, 43
*[Note: This appears to be a separate road from the following:
Road from the mouth of the South Branch to the Courthouse, 45.]*

Road from the mouth of the South Branch and also from Neals Friend's (on Potomac River) to the town of Winchester (road from Winchester Town to Potomac River, in order for a road to be cleared to the mouth of the South Branch), 55, 60

Road from Potomac River at Neals Friend's to the Falling Springs, 60

Road through the Main street of Maidstone to Potomac River and to the Main road, 75

Road from the place where the Bullskin road intercepts Littler's old road to fall into the Potomac road before it comes to Benjamin Blackburn's plantation, 107

Road from the Main road leading from Jacob Hite's to Mecklenburg through Foster's land to the Ferrying Water and also to the ford of Potomac, 148

Road from the Bear Garden Ridge to George Potts's plantation 61

Road from George Potts's to the South Branch road, 61

Road from Babbs Creek to George Potts's plantation, 68

Road from George Julian's on Passage Creek to Buck's mill (road from George Julian's in Powell's fort to Buck's mill; road from Buck's mill to Powell's fort), 85, 96, 104

Road from John Denton's [to] Jacob Rush's/Rushe's plantation in the upper end of Powell's fort, 127, 133

Road from the Presbyterian Meeting House at the head of Tuscarora to the Meeting House on Back Creek, 153

(Petition to the Court of Prince William County to meet Frederick County with) a road from the Thorough fair at the Pignut Ridge to the top of the Blue Ridge at the head of Manasses Run, 10

(Request to the Court of Prince William County for a) Road from Jefrey Johnston's at the Pignut Ridge to the top of the [Blue] Ridge at Ashby's Bent, 23

Road to be cleared in Prince William County from the fork of the road below Watts's ordinary to meet a road cleared in Frederick County leading through Manassas Run Gap, 70

Sir John's road (road called Sir John Sinclaire's road), 96, 97, 113, 119, 127, 132
Sections:
- From Winchester to the plantation where Isaac Thomas did live, 96
- From the place where the road from Robert Cunningham's falls into it to the forks where the road leads to Winchester, 132
- From the plantation where Isaac Thomas did live to the County line, 96
- From the Hunting Ridge to Isaac's Creek at Pritchet's place, 97
- Sir John's road leading from the Timber Ridge to Isaac's Creek, 113
- From the forks to James McGill's, 119
- Sir John's road from the end of the Sleepy Creek Mountain where the Warm Spring road crosses it to James Daugherty's, 127

Probable sections:
- Road from Isaac's Creek to the County line, 148
- Road from (the top of) the Hunting Ridge to the County line, 151, 158

Road from Pugh's and Barrett's mill by the end of the Sleepy Creek Mountain to the Warm Springs (road from the Warm Springs to Barrett's mill), 126, 131(2), 163, 168
Sections:
- From the [Warm] Springs to Ichebud Ashcraft's, 131, 135
- From Ashcraft's to the Buffaloe Run, 131
- From the Buffaloe Run to the end (from the Buffaloe Run as far as laid off by the veiwers from the Warm Springs; road from Buffaloe Run to Howard's old field, 131, 138, 149

Alteration:
- Road from Barrett's mill to the Warm Springs (to be turned to go by Meshack Sexton's mill), 163, 168

Road from Jesse Pugh's to Jeremiah Smith's, 132

Road from Hog's Creek where the South Branch road crosses it to go by Isaac Perkins's plantation and thence to Jessee Pugh's mill (road from Hoge Creek where the Winchester road crosses it to go by Isaac Perkins's plantation and to Jessee Pugh's mill; road from Hog's Creek to Jessee Pugh's mill), 149, 151, 154(2)

Road from Marlborough forge to Pugh's mill (road from Jessee Pugh's mill to Marlbro furnace), 151, 154(2)
Sections:
- From Pugh's mill to John White's, 154
- From John White's Run to the furnace, 154

Road from Stoney Lick/Stony Lick by Christopher Windle's/Windel's into the Main road by Mr. Pugh's plantation, 111, 116

Road from the Flat Rock to the ford upon Bulskin (above Mr. Pyke's), 136, 162

Road from Sir John's road by the Quaker Meeting House and through the lane between William Reynolds and Phillip Babb (road between the plantations of William Reynolds and Thomas Babb, Jr. and into Sir John's road; road from Capt. Pearis's to Sir John's road at the Quaker Meeting House), 95, 96, 102

Road from Richard Pearis's to the Quaker Meeting House (road from Richard Pearis's into Sir John's road), 141, 142

Road from Opeckon to the Signpost/the Signpost at/near Quintin's/Quinton's, 58, 78, 87

Road from the Signpost at Quintin's to the River, 58

Road from Rachell Hood's to the Race grounds, 57

Road from the Race Ground(s) below John Hite's house to the Swift Shoals ford on Shenandoah and thence down the River to the County road, 124, 132, 136

Road from John Racklie's to John Fosset's, 47

Road from John Frost's mill to the main road between John Littler's plantation and John Milbourn's/Milburn's plantation, (road from Capt. Frost's mill thence to Buffler lick thence through the lands of John Bosser, and David Springer, thence to the ford, thence through the lands of William Frost and Mathias Elmore, along Elmor[e]'s Creek to Widow Dillon's, and thence to the main road leading to Rappahannock between John Littler's and John Milbourn's), 1, 3, 20, 28
Probable sections:
- Road from John Frost's mill to William Frost's/William Frost's ford, 44, 65
- The other part of the said road, from William Frost's to Col. Morgan's road (road from William Frost's to William Dillon's), 44, 110
- Road from Frost's to Dillon's (alteration round the north side of Dillon's plantation into a lane), 126

Road from David Brown's mill down Opeckon Creek by James Knight's and Edward Reed's into the Chapel road, 168, 170, 171

Road from Capt. John Hite's mill to Widow Reed's path leading to Branson's mill and McCoy's Chapel, 44

Road from Capt. Jeremiah Smith's to Col. Morgan Morgan's and thence into the Main County road near Patrick Reiley's, 71(2)

Road from the lower corner of John Reno's plantation to some part of the road above the said plantation (road from the corner of Reno's fence into the Main road) (alteration), 85(2)

Road from the fork of the road on William Reynolds's land to Babbs Creek, 68

Road from Sir John's road by the Quaker Meeting House and through the lane between William Reynolds and Phillip Babb (road between the plantations of William Reynolds and Thomas Babb, Jr. and into Sir John's road; road from Capt. Pearis's to Sir John's road at the Quaker Meeting House), 95, 96, 102

Road from George Rice's house to the Main road at the Dry Marsh, 161

Road from the Long Marsh below Capt. Neill's to Patrick Rice's house, 107

Road from Patrick Rice's house to John McCormick's, 107

Road from William Richey's to John Vestal's Gap at Shanandoah River, 52

Road from Tuscarora to William Richey's, 54

Road from William Richey's to Opeckon, 75

[Note: In many entries, the Ridge may refer to the Blue Ridge Mountains; see also Blue Ridge.]

Road from Thomas Morgan's mill to Lewis Hogg's house and from thence to the top of the Ridge, 7

Road from Sharrando River to the top of the Ridge, 15

Road from Vestal's ford to the top of the Ridge, 60

Road from Henry Loyd's house to the top of the Ridge, 99

Road from Combs's ferry to the top of the Ridge, 108

Road from Chester's ford to the top of the Ridge, 121

Road from Dry Run to the top of the Ridge at Thornton's Gap, 129

Road from the top of a Ridge to the top of the bank of the River opposite the ferry at the ford, 135

Road from Joseph Berry's ford and ferry to the top of the Ridge, 169

Main road through Josiah Ridgway's land towards Watkins's ferry (alteration), 85, 89

Road from Francis Karney's to the River, 28

Road from Nation's plantation to the River, 58

Road from the Signpost at Quintin's to the River, 58

Road from the Chapel at Cunningham's into the River road, 33

Road from Stevens's mill at the Narrow Passage to the Main road near Reiley Moor's, 77
[Note: See also:
Road from Lewis Stevens's mill to the next best ford on the River above Reily Moor's and from thence into the Main road, 78.]

Road from Lewis Stevens's mill to the next best ford on the River above Reily Moor's and from thence into the Main road, 78

Roads on both sides of the River from Keys's ferry into the Main roads (roads from the Main roads to Keys's ferry; roads to and from Keys's ferry into the Main roads), 78, 80, 82

Road from the road crossing the River at James McCoy's ford to Capt. Jacob Funk's, 81

Road from the Fairfax road to the ferry landing and from thence to the Fairfax road on the other side the River, 83

Road from the forks of the River to the ferry landing [at Combs's?], 106

Road from the streets of Mecklenburgh to the ferry (the streets of Mecklenburg and the road leading to the River), 126, 137

Road from the top of a Ridge to the top of the bank of the River opposite the ferry at the ford, 135

Road from the [top of] Massanutting Mountain to the County line [at the River], 137, 150

(Alteration of) road at the River ford near Burr Harrison's, 165

Road from Snickers's ferry/ford up the riverside to Cunningham's Chapel (road from Snickers's ferry to Cunningham's ferry), 88, 89, 104, 132

Road from Opecken to Sherando River (road from Opeckon Creek to Col. Burwell's mill; road from Opeckon where Joseph Robbins lived to Burwell's mill on Shanando), 35, 50, 57

Road from Opeckon where Joseph Robins formerly lived to Burwell's Spout Run, 59

Road from Winchester Town to Opeckon where Joseph Robins formerly lived, 59

Road from the ferry at Vestal's Gap to the main road leading to Robinson's Gap, 54

Road from Israel Robinson's Gap to Vestal's Gap (via Opecken Creek), 3
Section:
- Road from Robinson's Gap to Opecken, 4, 24

Road from Israel Robinson, Gent.'s house into the road that goes over Vestal's/Westall's Gap, 14, 19

Road from the Meeting House at the gap of the Mountains above Hugh Paul's to the Warm Spring(s) (road from the Meeting House at the gap of the Mountains to Hugh Paul's from thence to Thomas Cherry's and by Daniel Rose's up the bottom to Thomas Berwick's, and from Berwick's to the Warm Springs), 21, 26, 31
Sections:
- From the Warm Spring(s) to Sleepy Creek, 21, 26, 70, 112
- From Sleepy Creek to the Meeting House, 21, 26
- From Sleepy Creek to the Widow Paul's, 49, 105

Road from Alexander Ross's fence to the corner of Smith's fence, 21
[Note: See also:
Road from Ross's fence by the great road to Opeckon Creek, 45
and
Road from Ross's to John Smith's old place, 61
and
Road from Ross's field crossing Opeckon to the middle of Smith's bridge, 91.]

Road from Ross's fence by the great road to Opeckon Creek, 45

Road from Ross's to John Smith's old place, 61

Road from Ross's field crossing Opeckon to the middle of Smith's bridge, 91
Sections:
- Road from Ross's field to the other side of Opeckon Creek, 70
- Road from Opeckon Creek to the middle of Smith's bridge, 70, 98.]

Road from Isaac Ruddell's mill into the Main road between Jackson Allen's and John Skean's, 90

Road from John Denton's [to] Jacob Rush's/Rushe's plantation in the upper end of Powell's fort, 127, 133

Road from George Pemberton's dwelling house to the road that leads from Capt. Rutherford's to Dr. McCormack's, 46

Road from Opeckon Creek to Capt. Rutherford's plantation, 87

Road from Mr. Rutherford's towards Cunningham's Chapel, 49

Road from Buckles's Marsh to where it intercepts the road leading to Reubin Rutherford's, 80

Road from John Shepard's/Sheppard's to the head of Bulskin (road from Potomac River from Sheppards ferry through the land of Thomas Rutherford, over Walker's mill dam and by the head of Pitts's March and to the head of Bulskin through the lands of Mr. John McCormack), 3, 7
Sections:
- Road from Potomac River to Thomas Rutherford Gent.'s, 12, 38
- The remaining part of the road, 13
- Road from Thomas Rutherford Gent.'s to the head of Bullskin, 24
- Road from Thomas Rutherford's house to John McCarmack's, 37

Road from the Chapel to Jay's ferry (road from the Chapel by Anderson's/Thos. Anderson's mill by William Mitchell's and Jacob Hite Gent.'s land, and thence into the road that goes from Capt. Campbell's to the ferry, near Capt. Thomas Rutherford's plantation), 6(2)

Road from Thomas Rutherford's Spring to William Mitchel's, 24

Road from the Great road leading from Mr. Jacob Hite's to John Smith's to the head of Worthington's Marsh thence down the Marsh into the road near John Swim's called Keys's road and into the road leading by Thomas Rutherford's to Vestal's ferry, 49

Road from the Blue Ridge to Thomas Rutherford's, 68

Road leading from Lupton's into the Town (alteration as it is already cleared by Thomas Rutherford's pasture adjoining the Town), 168

Road from John Littler's old place to Patrick Ryley's, 27, 40

Road from Sandy ford on Opeckon to Isaac Parkins's/Perkins's mill, 56, 98

Road from (Paul) Froman's mill to the Sand ford/Sandy ford on Opeckon, 65, 69, 71, 98, 99, 129

Road from the School House/old School House on Shannando River to the Chapel at Cunningham's, 17, 55, 76

Bridle road/road from Scot's/Scott's [later Johnston's] mill on Shanando/Sharrando to the Courthouse, 5, 7, 11, 14, 15, 17

Road from James Seabin's gate to Thomas Ashby, Jr.'s ferry, 34

The Chapel road from Samuel Earl's meadows to Gregory's ford and Seaborn's ford, 157

Road from Seaburn's ford to Combs's ferry, 108, 118

Road from the Muster Ground above the Widow Caldwell's/Calwell's to John Neavill's mill and thence into the Main road by Jonah Seaman's, 155, 156

Road from Morgan's Chapel to Opeckon Creek (at Jonathan Seaman's house), 49, 54, 69, 84, 105

Road from Jonathan Seamon's house (on Opeckon) to Jacob Hite's, 120, 131

Road from the Main road near Sebastian's quarter to Hardin and Keys's mill, and from thence to the Iron Works, 83
Section:
- Road from the Main road near Sebastian's quarter to Hardin and Keys's mill, 84

Road from George Sellers's to Lewis Stephens's mill, 104

Road from the Great Plain to Selser's Mill Run, 72

Road from Selser's Mill Run to the South River ford, 72

Road from Selser's Mill Run to the County line at Woods Plain (Mountain road from Wood's Plains over the mountains to Selser's Mill Run), 94, 102

Road from Semple's furnace to the Warm Springs road above Peter Burr's, 141, 144, 145, 147, 152

Road from Pugh's and Barrett's mill by the end of the Sleepy Creek Mountain to the Warm Springs (road from the Warm Springs to Barrett's mill), 126, 131(2), 163, 168
Sections:
- From the [Warm] Springs to Ichebud Ashcraft's, 131, 135
- From Ashcraft's to the Buffaloe Run, 131
- From the Buffaloe Run to the end (from the Buffaloe Run as far as laid off by the veiwers from the Warm Springs; road from Buffaloe Run to Howard's old field, 131, 138, 149

Alteration:
- Road from Barrett's mill to the Warm Springs (to be turned to go by Meshack Sexton's mill), 163, 168

Road from Peter Sharrobz to Snapp's mill, 161

[Note: Entries for all spelling variations of Shenandoah (i.e., Shanando, Sharrando, etc.) are combined.]

Bridle road/road from Scot's/Scott's [later Johnston's] mill on Shanando/Sharrando to the Courthouse, 5, 7, 11, 14, 15, 17

Road from John Nealan[d]'s/Neeland's on Sharrando to William Vestal's on the same river (road from John Nealand's down the river by the lands of John Grimes, Capt. Stribling, Timothy Haney, Darby Conely, Goldin, John Hamman, Thomas Hamman, and Elizabeth Pearson, across

Pearson's Neck of Land to Jonathan Walker's, over Bulskin, and by Robert Hayes's and along Hayes's path to Vestal's), 9, 10

Road from this Courthouse [Winchester] to the top of the Blue Ridge of Mountains at Williams's Gap (road from Capt. Neill's off and on the old road to Joseph Wilkenson's and thence off on the same road to Francis Carney's and from thence to Edge's ford and from thence off and on the old road to the top of the said Mountain), 12
Sections:
- From Capt. Lewis Neill's/Lewis Neill Gent.'s to Francis Carney's/Carnie's (road from Francis Carney's/Carney's Spring to Lewis Neill's/Opeckon at Neill's ford/Opeckon Creek by Capt. Neill's/ Opecken by Lewis Neill's, Gent), 12, 22, 31, 82, 100, 104
- From Carney's to Edge's ford on Shannadore River (road from Shanando River to Carney's Spring, 12, 50, 83
- From Edge's ford to the top of the Blue Ridge on Williams's Gap, 12

Probable later sections:
- Road from Winchester Town to Lewis Neill's/Lewis Neill's ford on Opeckon, 59, 67
- Road from the ford at Lewis Neill Gent.'s house to Littler's road, 59
- Road from Littler's road to Carney's old house, 59
- Road from Carney's old house to the River, 59
- Road from the River to the top of the mountain at Williams's Gap (road from Edward Snigers's [on Shanando] to the top of the Mountain at Williams's Gap; road from the River at Snigers's to the County line at Williams's Gap; road from the top of the Ridge to Edward Snickers's/Snigers's ford/ferry/ferry at Snicker's house; road from the Ferry road [Snigers's] to the top of the Ridge at Williams's Gap), 59, 76, 79, 81, 83, 113

Road from Opecken to Shanandore River, 12, 35

Road from Sharrando River to the top of the Ridge, 15

Road from the School House/old School House on Shannando River to the Chapel at Cunningham's, 17, 55, 76

Road from Thomas Thornbury's mill to Opecken Creek by Edward Stroud's and from thence into the road that leads from Jacob Hite's to Vestal's ford on Sharando River, 25

Road from Howel's ford to Foxtrap Point on the south side of Shanando, 29

Road from Opecken to Sherando River (road from Opeckon Creek to Col. Burwell's mill; road from Opeckon where Joseph Robbins lived to Burwell's mill on Shanando), 35, 50, 57

Road to and from the ferry (across Shannando between John Kersey's and Christopher Marr's plantations) in the County road, 37

Road from Mark Hardin's ford on Shanando River to Isaac Hollingsworth's, 38, 51(2)

Sections:
- Road from the River to Opeckon, 51
- Road from Opeckon to Isaac Hollingsworth's, 51

Road from David Loyd's to the top of the Blue Ridge at Vestal's Gap (road from David Loyd's crossing Shannando River and from thence to the top of the ridge), 38, 49, 55
Section:
- Road from the River to the top of the mountain, 55

Road from the hollow near Kersey's to Shanando River and Kersey's ferry (road to be cleared along the lower side of the hollow to the River), 41, 43

Road from the landing place on the south side of Shanando River at Kersey's ferry to Foxtrap Point road (road from Kersey's to the ferry road on the south side of Shanando), 43, 49

Road from the head of the Pond on Shanando River to Wormley's quarter, 50

Road from the bridge to the head of the Great Pond on Shanando, 50

Road from William Richey's to John Vestal's Gap at Shanandoah River, 52

Road leading into Shanandore River (road that leads through Ashby's Gap below where Thomas Ashby keeps ferry over the River), 57

Road from Robert Harper's at the mouth of Shanando to William Hall's mill and from thence into the road to Winchester, 72

Road from Shanando at the Wagon ford to the fork of the road to Stephens Town, 92

Road above Noah Hampton's house from Coombs's ferry up Shanando River (proposed alteration rejected), 93

Road leading from Winchester to Edward Snickers's ford over Shanando River, 106

Road from John Houghland's mill to Shannandah [Shenandoah] River, 117

Road from the Race Ground(s) below John Hite's house to the Swift Shoals ford on Shenandoah and thence down the River to the County road, 124, 132, 136

Road from the forks of Shanondoah to the top of the mountain, 150

Road from Battletown to (Snickers's ford on) Shannandoah River, 168, 169

Road from John Shepard's/Sheppard's to the head of Bulskin (road from Potomac River from Sheppards ferry through the land of Thomas Rutherford, over Walker's mill dam and by the head of Pitts's March and to the head of Bulskin through the lands of Mr. John McCormack), 3, 7

Sections:
- Road from Potomac River to Thomas Rutherford Gent.'s, 12, 38
- The remaining part of the road, 13
- Road from Thomas Rutherford Gent.'s to the head of Bullskin, 24
- Road from Thomas Rutherford's house to John McCarmack's, 37

Road from Sheppard's mill, 47

Road from John Shepard's/Sheppard's to the head of Bulskin (road from Potomac River from Sheppards ferry through the land of Thomas Rutherford, over Walker's mill dam and by the head of Pitts's March and to the head of Bulskin through the lands of Mr. John M°Cormack), 3, 7
Sections:
- Road from Potomac River to Thomas Rutherford Gent.'s, 12, 38
- The remaining part of the road, 13
- Road from Thomas Rutherford Gent.'s to the head of Bullskin, 24
- Road from Thomas Rutherford's house to John McCarmack's, 37

Road from John Littler's to Thomas Shepard's/Sheppard's mill (road from John Littler's late dwelling house to the said Littler's New Design thence to Opecken Creek over Abril's ford thence to the late dwelling place of John Smith's dec. thence to Jacob Hite's thence to Thomas Shepard's mill), 4, 5
Sections:
- Road from John Littler's to Thomas Sheppard's mill, 6
- Road from Thomas Shepherd's mill to Jacob Hite, Gent.'s, 32
- Road from John Smith's to John Littler's, 32

[Note: See also:
Road from Alexander Ross's fence to the corner of Smith's fence, 21 (etc.)
and
Road from Smith's fence/John Smith's old place to Jacob Hite's, 21, 62, 90, 106, 128, 133
and
Road from William Hite's Spring to the middle of the Swamp in Smith's Marsh and from the Swamp to Littler's mill, 40, 41.]

Road from Caton's ford/Thomas Caton's to Vestal's Gap, 76, 115
Section:
- Part from Opeckon Creek to Shepherds Town, 115

Road from Swearingen's ferry through Shepherds Town to the old road that leads to Winchester, 108

Road leading from Shepherds Town to the plantation of Robert Lemon, 115

Road from Shepherds Town to Keyes's ferry, 163

Road from Harper's ferry to Winchester (alterations where the road passes through Walter Shirley's land), 79, 82

Road from Opeckon to the Signpost/the Signpost at/near Quintin's/Quinton's, 58, 78, 87

Road from the Signpost at Quintin's to the River, 58

Road from the Signpost at the Hawks Bill down the South River into the road leading to Winchester, 77

Road from the Signpost to Cannill's ferry, 80

Road from Armstrong's ford upon Opeckon to the Signpost at Littler's road, 123

[Note: Entries for Sir John Sinclaire's road are combined and indexed with entries for Sir John's road.]

Road from the County line on Cape Capon Mountain by Sink's mill to Abraham Darst's smith shop, 138

Road from Christian Dellinger's to Cutlip Sink's mill on Stoney Creek, 133

Road from Sir John's road by the Quaker Meeting House and through the lane between William Reynolds and Phillip Babb (road between the plantations of William Reynolds and Thomas Babb, Jr. and into Sir John's road; road from Capt. Pearis's to Sir John's road at the Quaker Meeting House), 95, 96, 102

Sir John's road (road called Sir John Sinclaire's road), 96, 97, 113, 119, 127, 132
Sections:
- From Winchester to the plantation where Isaac Thomas did live, 96
- From the place where the road from Robert Cunningham's falls into it to the forks where the road leads to Winchester, 132
- From the plantation where Isaac Thomas did live to the County line, 96
- From the Hunting Ridge to Isaac's Creek at Pritchet's place, 97
- Sir John's road leading from the Timber Ridge to Isaac's Creek, 113
- From the forks to James McGill's, 119
- Sir John's road from the end of the Sleepy Creek Mountain where the Warm Spring road crosses it to James Daugherty's, 127

Probable sections:
- Road from Isaac's Creek to the County line, 148
- Road from (the top of) the Hunting Ridge to the County line, 151, 158

Road from Cunningham's/Robert Cunningham's mill and Morgan's Chapel into/to the road called Sir John's road, 97, 111

Road from the top of the mountain at Mills's Gap into Sir John Sinclair's road (road from the top of the Mountain at Mill's Gap into the most convenient left part of Sir John Sinclair's road), 112, 116

Sections:
- From Sir John Sinclair's road to the mouth of Lick Branch, 116
- From Lick Branch to the top of the mountain, 116

Road from Sir John's road by Thomas Babb's down by William McMachen's (and) Angus McDonald's and down to Berry's mill, 121
[Note: May be the same as:
Road from Sir John's road above Thomas Babb's plantation to Thomas Perry's mill, 121.]

Road from Sir John's road above Thomas Babb's plantation to Thomas Perry's mill, 121

Road from Mill Creek/Mill Run to Sir John's road, 135, 140

Road from where Morgan's road crosses Sir John's road, to the Warm Springs road at Joseph Bridges's, 138

Road from Sir John's road near George Paul's to Hougland's ferry and to Van Swearingen's mill on Tunis's Branch, 140

Road from Richard Pearis's to the Quaker Meeting House (road from Richard Pearis's into Sir John's road), 141, 142

Road from the Winchester Common to Sir John's road, 152

Road from Isaac Ruddell's mill into the Main road between Jackson Allen's and John Skean's, 90

Road from the Meeting House at the gap of the Mountains above Hugh Paul's to the Warm Spring(s) (road from the Meeting House at the gap of the Mountains to Hugh Paul's from thence to Thomas Cherry's and by Daniel Rose's up the bottom to Thomas Berwick's, and from Berwick's to the Warm Springs), 21, 26, 31
Sections:
- From the Warm Spring(s) to Sleepy Creek, 21, 26, 70, 112
- From Sleepy Creek to the Meeting House, 21, 26
- From Sleepy Creek to the Widow Paul's, 49, 105

Road from the top of the Mountain to Sleepy Creek, 110, 143

Road from the Warm Springs to Combs's mill and from thence to the mouth of Sleepy Creek, 160

Sir John's road (road called Sir John Sinclaire's road), 96, 97, 113, 119, 127, 132
Sections:
- From Winchester to the plantation where Isaac Thomas did live, 96
- From the place where the road from Robert Cunningham's falls into it to the forks where the road leads to Winchester, 132

- From the plantation where Isaac Thomas did live to the County line, 96
- From the Hunting Ridge to Isaac's Creek at Pritchet's place, 97
- Sir John's road leading from the Timber Ridge to Isaac's Creek, 113
- From the forks to James McGill's, 119
- Sir John's road from the end of the <u>Sleepy Creek Mountain</u> where the Warm Spring road crosses it to James Daugherty's, 127

Probable sections:
- Road from Isaac's Creek to the County line, 148
- Road from (the top of) the Hunting Ridge to the County line, 151, 158

Road from Pugh's and Barrett's mill by the end of the <u>Sleepy Creek Mountain</u> to the Warm Springs (road from the Warm Springs to Barrett's mill), 126, 131(2), 163, 168
Sections:
- From the [Warm] Springs to Ichebud Ashcraft's, 131, 135
- From Ashcraft's to the Buffaloe Run, 131
- From the Buffaloe Run to the end (from the Buffaloe Run as far as laid off by the veiwers from the Warm Springs; road from Buffaloe Run to Howard's old field, 131, 138, 149

Alteration:
- Road from Barrett's mill to the Warm Springs (to be turned to go by Meshack Sexton's mill), 163, 168

Road from William Hite's Spring to the middle of the Swamp in <u>Smith's Marsh</u> and from the Swamp to Littler's mill, 40, 41
Sections:
- Road from William Hite's Spring to the middle of the Swamp in <u>Smith's Marsh</u>, 40
- Road from the middle of the Swamp in <u>Smith's Marsh</u> to Littler's mill (road from the bridge on <u>Smiths Creek</u> to Widow Littler's mill), 41, 44

Road from Jackson Allen's crossing the mouth of <u>Smiths Creek</u> thence through White's Bottom to William Clark's at Mount Pleasant, 91

Road from Jeremiah <u>Smith's</u> house to William Hog's/William Hoge Jr.'s, 8, 24

Road from Jeremiah <u>Smith's</u> to the North River (near Thomas Parker's), 54, 62

Road from Hews's to the South Branch road above Jeremiah <u>Smith's</u>, 55

Road from Robert Pearis's to Capt. Jeremiah <u>Smith's</u> house, 62, 77

Road from Capt. Jeremiah <u>Smith's</u> to Col. Morgan Morgan's and thence into the Main County road near Patrick Reiley's, 71(2)

Road from the County line to Jeremiah <u>Smith's</u> house, 75

Road from the South Branch road near Capt. Smith's through Hoop Petticoat Gap to Winchester (road from Winchester through Hoop Petticoat Gap), 104, 106, 154(2)
Sections:
- Road as far as Allen's Cabin, 154
- From Allen's Cabin to the road leading from Winchester to Jeremiah Smith's, 154

Road from Jesse Pugh's to Jeremiah Smith's, 132

Road from Jeremiah Smith's plantation to the Hampshire County line, 154

Road from the South Branch road near Jeremiah Smith's to the Warm Springs near Henry Fry's, 170

Road from John Littler's to Thomas Shepard's/Sheppard's mill (road from John Littler's late dwelling house to the said Littler's New Design thence to Opecken Creek over Abril's ford thence to the late dwelling place of John Smith's dec. thence to Jacob Hite's thence to Thomas Shepard's mill), 4, 5
Sections:
- Road from John Littler's to Thomas Sheppard's mill, 6
- Road from Thomas Shepherd's mill to Jacob Hite, Gent.'s, 32
- Road from John Smith's to John Littler's, 32

[Note: See also:
Road from Alexander Ross's fence to the corner of Smith's fence, 21 (etc.)
and
Road from Smith's fence/John Smith's old place to Jacob Hite's, 21, 62, 90, 106, 128, 133
and
Road from William Hite's Spring to the middle of the Swamp in Smith's Marsh and from the Swamp to Littler's mill, 40, 41.]

Road from Alexander Ross's fence to the corner of Smith's fence, 21
[Note: See also:
Road from Ross's fence by the great road to Opeckon Creek, 45
and
Road from Ross's to John Smith's old place, 61
and
Road from Ross's field crossing Opeckon to the middle of Smith's bridge, 91.]

Road from Smith's fence/John Smith's old place to Jacob Hite's (road from Edward Thomas's to Mr. Jacob Hite's; road from Mr. Jacob Hite's/Jacob Hite's bridge to Edward Thomas's bridge between the said Edward Thomas's fences and John Smith's fences), 21, 62, 90, 106, 128, 133

Road from the Great road leading from Mr. Jacob Hite's to John Smith's to the head of Worthington's Marsh thence down the Marsh into the road near John Swim's called Keys's road and into the road leading by Thomas Rutherford's to Vestal's ferry, 49

Road from John Smith's to Vestal's ford, 50

Road from Ross's to John Smith's old place, 61

Road from Ross's field crossing Opeckon to the middle of Smith's bridge, 91.]
Sections:
- Road from Ross's field to the other side of Opeckon Creek, 70
- Road from Opeckon Creek to the middle of Smith's bridge, 70, 98

Road from William Jolliff's to the middle of the bridge between Edward Thomas's and John Smith's fences, 94

(Alteration of) Main road to run on the line between Edward Thomas and John Smith, 112

Road from the head of Bullskin to the Main road by Fryer's (road from Alexander Fryer's to the head of Bulskin, 109, 126(2)
Alteration:
- Where the road passes through John Smith's land, 126(2)

Road from the Muster Ground to the forks by John Smith's, 134

Road from Matthew Smith's plantation to McCoy's Chapel, 145

Road from Peter Sharrobz to Snapp's mill, 161

Road from John Snap's to the Furnace, 130

Road from Laurence/Lawrence Snapp's house to Toms Brook, 137, 140

[Note: Entries for Snickers and Sniggers are combined.]

Road from Snickers's ferry/ford up the riverside to Cunningham's Chapel (road from Snickers's ferry to Cunningham's ferry), 88, 89, 104, 132

Road from Dr. Wells's to Snickers's ferry, 128

Road from Snickers's ferry to Bullskin, 130

Road from Thomas Speaks's to Snickers's/Sniggers's ferry, 134, 135

Road from this Courthouse [Winchester] to the top of the Blue Ridge of Mountains at Williams's Gap (road from Capt. Neill's off and on the old road to Joseph Wilkenson's and thence off on the same road to Francis Carney's and from thence to Edge's ford and from thence off and on the old road to the top of the said Mountain), 12
Sections:
- From Capt. Lewis Neill's/Lewis Neill Gent.'s to Francis Carney's/Carnie's (road from Francis Carney's/Carney's Spring to Lewis Neill's/Opeckon at Neill's

ford/Opeckon Creek by Capt. Neill's/ Opecken by Lewis Neill's, Gent), 12, 22, 31, 82, 100, 104
- From Carney's to Edge's ford on Shannadore River (road from Shanando River to Carney's Spring, 12, 50, 83
- From Edge's ford to the top of the Blue Ridge on Williams's Gap, 12

Probable later sections:
- Road from Winchester Town to Lewis Neill's/Lewis Neill's ford on Opeckon, 59, 67
- Road from the ford at Lewis Neill Gent.'s house to Littler's road, 59
- Road from Littler's road to Carney's old house, 59
- Road from Carney's old house to the River, 59
- Road from the River to the top of the mountain at Williams's Gap (road from Edward Snigers's [on Shanando] to the top of the Mountain at Williams's Gap; road from the River at Snigers's to the County line at Williams's Gap; road from the top of the Ridge to Edward Snickers's/Snigers's ford/ferry/ferry at Snicker's house; road from the Ferry road [Snigers's] to the top of the Ridge at Williams's Gap), 59, 76, 79, 81, 83, 113

Road from Snickers's ferry landing to the County line on the road leading to Jacob Hite's, 170

Road from Battletown to (Snickers's ford on) Shannandoah River, 168, 169

Road leading from Snickers's Gap to Vestall's Gap (to be turned at Ralph Wormley Esq.'s plantation/as far as the County line), 164, 167

Road from Edward Snickers's/Snigers's to Moses Guess's/Gess's, 71, 78

Road from the bridge at the Long Marsh to Edward Snigers's, 77

Road leading from Winchester to Edward Snickers's ford over Shanando River, 106

Road from the Courthouse to the South Branch, 27(2), 40
Alteration:
- To go around William Hoge Jr.'s plantation, 27(2)

Road from the lower part of Pattersons Creek by Power Hazel's into the wagon road which leads from the Courthouse to the South Branch, 40

Road from Hampton's mill down the South Branch (road from below where Henry Vanmetre did live to where he now lives and down by his mill and Hampton's mill), 41

Road from Frederick Town [Courthouse] to the mouth of the South Branch of Potomac, 43
[Note: This appears to be a separate road from the following:
Road from the mouth of the South Branch to the Courthouse, 45.]

Road from the mouth of the South Branch to the Courthouse, 45

Main road leading through Job Pearsall's plantation at the South Branch, 48

Road from the South Branch to the North River, 50

Road from the mouth of the South Branch and also from Neals Friend's (on Potomac River) to the town of Winchester (road from Winchester Town to Potomac River, in order for a road to be cleared to the mouth of the South Branch), 55, 60

Road from Hews's to the South Branch road above Jeremiah Smith's, 55

Road from George Potts's to the South Branch road, 61

Road from the lower part of the South Branch to the Main road near Thomas Parker's, 68

Road from Winchester to Hogs/Hoge Creek *[Note: Also called the South Branch road on p. 119]*, 80, 111, 119, 125, 148, 155

Road from the South Branch road near Capt. Smith's through Hoop Petticoat Gap to Winchester (road from Winchester through Hoop Petticoat Gap), 104, 106, 154(2)
Sections:
- Road as far as Allen's Cabin, 154
- From Allen's Cabin to the road leading from Winchester to Jeremiah Smith's, 154

Road from Winchester to the South Branch at the County line on the North Mountain (road from the place marked by the viewers to the County line on the North Mountain), 104, 106

Road from the head of John Lupton's meadow to the South Branch road above David Denny's, 144, 146

Road from Isaac Perkins's to Hoge Creek where the road leading from Winchester to the South Branch crosses it, 147, 149

Road from Hog's Creek where the South Branch road crosses it to go by Isaac Perkins's plantation and thence to Jessee Pugh's mill (road from Hoge Creek where the Winchester road crosses it to go by Isaac Perkins's plantation and to Jessee Pugh's mill; road from Hog's Creek to Jessee Pugh's mill), 149, 151, 154(2)

Road from the South Branch road to William Hancher's mill and from thence into the road leading to Watkins's ferry, 166

The Warm Spring/Warm Springs road, 136(2), 162, 163, 167, 168, 170
Sections:
- From Andrew Tilleroy's to Henry Lloyd's, 136(2)
- Through Henry Lloyd's plantation, 162
- From the Back Creek road to the Buffaloe Lick, 167

- From the South Branch road near Ballenger's to the County line (road from Ballenger's to the County line), 168, 170
- From Ballenger's to the Tub mill, 170
- From the Tub mill to the County line, 170

Road from the South Branch road near Jeremiah Smith's to the Warm Springs near Henry Fry's, 170

Road from Selser's Mill Run to the South River ford, 72

Road from the South River ford to the top of the Blue Ridge, 72

Road from the Signpost at the Hawks Bill down the South River into the road leading to Winchester, 77

Road from the South River to the fork of the road that leads to Charles Buck's, 109

Road from the Augusta line on the South River above John Breeding's fence to the road crossing Thorn's Gap, 123

Road from the North River leading to Chester's Gap to the South River, 137

Road from the Southwest Pond to Hite's mill, 129

Road from the head of Worthington's Marsh to Thomas Speak's, 103

Road from Thomas Speaks's to Snickers's/Sniggers's ferry, 134, 135

Road from Capt. Spears's to the fork of the road that leads to Charles Buck's, 109

Road from Henry Spears's to go by Isaac Hite's and thence into the Main county road (road from the Great road to the fork of the road that leads to Henry Spears's road), 93, 134

Road from the North River to the forks of Henry Spears's road, 148

Road from John Spears's to Van Swearingen's mill at Houghland's, 145

Mill road from John Spencely's house to the County road leading over the Mountain (road from John Spenceley's to the Main road leading over the mountain), 151, 155

Road from Lewis Neill's mill into Perry's road (road leading from Lewis Neill's mill into the road leading from Thomas Sperry's [Perry's] mill to the town of Winchester; road from Lewis Neill's mill to Thomas Perry's mill), 119, 120, 123

Road from John Spoar's/Spore's plantation to Col. Stephens's mill, 161, 165

Road from Spout Run to Mr. John Sturman's (road from Burwell's Spout Run to Mr. John Sturman's old place), 36, 60

Road from Opeckon where Joseph Robins formerly lived to Burwell's Spout Run, 59

Road from Spout Run to Cunningham's Chapel, 92, 109

Road called Littler's road, 100, 101, 105, 125, 129
Sections:
- From the beginning to Opeckon Creek, 105, 125
- From Opeckon Creek to the fork where it joins the Winchester road leading to Spout Run, 100, 101, 159

Road from Burk's bridge along the Chapel road to Spout Run, 168

Road from John Frost's mill to the main road between John Littler's plantation and John Milbourn's/Milburn's plantation, (road from Capt. Frost's mill thence to Buffler lick thence through the lands of John Bosser, and David Springer, thence to the ford, thence through the lands of William Frost and Mathias Elmore, along Elmor[e]'s Creek to Widow Dillon's, and thence to the main road leading to Rappahannock between John Littler's and John Milbourn's), 1, 3, 20, 28
Probable sections:
- Road from John Frost's mill to William Frost's/William Frost's ford, 44, 65
- The other part of the said road, from William Frost's to Col. Morgan's road (road from William Frost's to William Dillon's), 44, 110
- Road from Frost's to Dillon's (alteration round the north side of Dillon's plantation into a lane), 126

Road from the plantation of Dennis Springer dec. to the top of the mountain at Mill's Gap, 166

[Note: Entries for Stephens and Stevens are combined.]

Road from John Spoar's/Spore's plantation to Col. Stephens's mill, 161, 165

Road from Col. Stephens's mill to Edward Strode's by Matthew Allison's, 162

Road from Col. Stephens's mill to James Strode's, 162, 164
Road from Col. Stephens's mill to Jeremiah Strode's plantation, 162

Road from Hugh Lyle's plantation to Col. Stephens's mill, 162

Road from David Miller's old plantation to Col. Stephens's mill, 165

Road from Lewis Stevens Gent.'s old plantation to his Lordship's quarter (road from Lawrence Stevens's by Lewis Stephens's old plantation to Col. Martin's road), 71, 87

Road from Lewis Stephens's mills to the Courthouse, 17

Road from the County line by Thomas Little Gent.'s to Lewis Stephens's mill, 29, 35, 39

Road from Robert Warth's; to be taken from the head of the road which leads from the Chapel at Robert M\u000ecCoy's Spring, to Lewis Stephen's mills (road from the County road near Robert Warth's to Stevens's mill), 30, 63

Road from Lewis Stephen's/Stevens's house/land/mill to Mr. Gabriel Jones's place/plantation, 35, 42, 44, 64, 68

Road from Stevens's/Lewis Stephens's mill to the road to McCoy's/McKoy's Chapel (near Cartmill's), 37, 82
Alterations, 79

Road from Lewis Stephens's mill to Widow Little's, 47

Road from Desponet's/Disponet's Gap/Barnet Desponet's to Lewis Stephens's/Stevens's mill, 53, 57, 69, 86, 117

Road from Stephens's/Stevens's mill to the head of Funk's Mill Creek, 64, 85

Road from Stevens's mill at the Narrow Passage to the Main road near Reiley Moor's, 77
[Note: See also:
Road from Lewis Stevens's mill to the next best ford on the River above Reily Moor's and from thence into the Main road, 78.]

Road from Lewis Stevens's mill to the next best ford on the River above Reily Moor's and from thence into the Main road, 78

Road from Jeremiah Lewis's (at/near the County line) to Stephens's/Stevens's mill at/on the Narrow Passage, 79, 104
Sections:
- Road from the County line near Jeremiah Lewis's to Christian Dilliner's, 81
- Road from Christian Dillener's to Lewis Stevens's mill at the Narrow Passage, 81

Road leading from Maj. Lewis Stephens's mill to Opeckon Creek, 98

Road from George Sellers's to Lewis Stephens's mill, 104

Road from Lewis Stephens's mill to Phillip Peter Backer's house, 118

Road from Lewis Stevens Gent.'s old plantation to his Lordship's quarter (road from Lawrence Stevens's by Lewis Stephens's old plantation to Col. Martin's road), 71, 87

Road from Mr. Hite's to the road from Stevens's lane to Kersey's ferry, 66(2)

Road from Hite's house to Lewis Stevens's new road, 88

Road from Col. Hite's through the Town laid out on Lewis Stephens's plantation/ Stephens Town and from thence into the Main road (road from Col. John Hite's to Stephensburgh; road between Col. John Hite's and the new town called Stevensburgh), 89, 90, 93, 94

Road from Stephensburg into the road leading from Winchester to Marlbro' [Marlborough] forge, 167, 169
Alteration:
- To go around Lewis Stephens's fence, 169

Road from Peter Stevens's lane to the Dutch road leading to Kersey's ferry, 61, 65

Main road running through the lands of Joseph Vance and Peter Stephens (alteration), 86

[Note: Entries for Stephens Town/Stephensburg/Stevensburgh, etc., are combined.]

Road from Col. Hite's through the Town laid out on Lewis Stephens's plantation/ Stephens Town and from thence into the Main road (road from Col. John Hite's to Stephensburgh; road between Col. John Hite's and the new town called Stevensburgh), 89, 90, 93, 94

Road from Shanando at the Wagon ford to the fork of the road to Stephens Town, 92

Road from the New Town (Stephensburgh/Stevensburgh) to Nations's (road leading from Stephensburgh to the Right Honourable Thomas Lord Fairfax's plantation called Nation's; road from Stephensburgh to Nation's plantation), 92, 96, 114, 144, 145

Road from the New Town [Stephensburgh/Stevensburgh] into Chester's road, 92

Road from Charles Buck's mill to Christian Blank's ford on the North River, and from thence to Stephensburg, 103

Road from Col. John Hite's to the forks of the road leading from Lord Fairfax's to Stephensburgh, 120

Road from Stephensburg into the road leading from Winchester to Marlbro' [Marlborough] forge, 167, 169
Alteration:
- To go around Lewis Stephens's fence, 169

Road from Stephensburg to Jacob Chrisman's Spring (to be turned at Henry Chrisman's plantation, 170

Road from Stony bridge to Parker's on the North River of Cacapon, 41

Road from (Benjamin) Allen's/Allin's Mill Creek to Stoney Creek, 74, 99

Road from Stoney Creek to Miller's foot path, 74

Road from Stoney Creek to Mill Creek, 85, 90

Road from Stoney Creek to the County line (road leading from Augusta to Winchester, from the County line to Stony Creek), 102, 112
[Note: Possibly the same as:
Road from Stoney Creek to Benjamin Allin's Mill Creek, 74, 99.]

Road from Christian Dellinger's to Cutlip Sink's mill on Stoney Creek, 133

Road from Miller's Town to Stoney Creek, 146, 160

Road from Jumping Run bridge to Stony Creek, 153

Road from John Little's to the Augusta [County] line (road from the [Augusta] County line below Brock's Gap to John Little's), 157, 159
Sections:
- From Little's to Narrow Passage Creek, 159
- From [Narrow] Passage Creek to Stoney Creek, 159
- From Stoney Creek to Christian Dellinger's, 159
- From Christian Dellinger's to Mill Creek, 159
- From Mill Creek to the [Augusta] County line, 159

Road from Stoney Lick/Stony Lick by Christopher Windle's/Windel's into the Main road by Mr. Pugh's plantation, 111, 116

Road from McNishes Run to Stoney Run, 84, 100

Road from Peter Stoufer's to George Bowman's mill, 92

[Note: Entries for Stoufers Town and Stover(s) Town are combined.]

Road from Cedar Creek to Stoufers Town, 102

Road leading from Toms Brook to Stover Town, 114

Road leading from the plantation of the Widow Duckworth to Stover's Town, 115

Road from Strasburgh to Marlborough forge, 164, 165
Sections:
- From the forge to the creek, 165
- From the creek to the town, 165

Road from Richard Sturman's house to Stribling's quarter and from that road to Cunningham's Chapel (road from the head of the pond at Stribling's quarter to Mr. Sturman's and from thence to Cunningham's Chapel), 42, 51

Road from John Nealan[d]'s/Neeland's on Sharrando to William Vestal's on the same river (road from John Nealand's down the river by the lands of John Grimes, Capt. Stribling, Timothy Haney, Darby Conely, Goldin, John Hamman, Thomas Hamman, and Elizabeth Pearson, across Pearson's Neck of Land to Jonathan Walker's, over Bulskin, and by Robert Hayes's and along Hayes's path to Vestal's), 9, 10

Road from Toliafero Stribling's to Bulskin (including the whole bridge over the run), 152

[Note: Entries for Stroad, Stroade, Strode, and Stroud are combined.]

Road from the fork of Opeckon on the Main road at Edward Stroad's/Stroade's to Hogland's ferry, 131(2)

Road from Col. Stephens's mill to Edward Strode's by Matthew Allison's, 162

Road from Col. Stephens's mill to James Strode's, 162, 164

Road from Col. Stephens's mill to Jeremiah Strode's plantation, 162

Road from Thomas Thornbury's mill to Opecken Creek by Edward Stroud's and from thence into the road that leads from Jacob Hite's to Vestal's ford on Sharando River, 25

Road from Sturman's bridge to Burwell's mill, 50

Road from Johnston Run/Johnston's mill to John Sturman's/John Sturman's Run, 31, 33

Road from John Melton's to John Sturman's house, 33

Road from Spout Run to Mr. John Sturman's (road from Burwell's Spout Run to Mr. John Sturman's old place), 36, 60

Road from Richard Sturman's house to Stribling's quarter and from that road to Cunningham's Chapel (road from the head of the pond at Stribling's quarter to Mr. Sturman's and from thence to Cunningham's Chapel), 42, 51

Road from Mr. John Sturman's old place to the Fairfax road, 60

Road from Hume's/Thomas Hume's mill on Sugar Tree Creek/Sugar Tree Run into the road leading to Chester's Gap, 117, 121

Road from Eaton's mill through Mill's Gap to Fallis's mill, 141, 144

Alteration:
- From the place opposite Sutherland's ford to the Mountain Run, 144

Road from the White House to Thorn's Gap, 108, 115
Section:
- Part from Suttons Run to a mill above Charles Thompson's on Col. Carlyle's land, 115

Road from Mecklenburgh into the Warm Spring road at Richard Pearis's plantation (by the head of the Swan Ponds), 124(2)

Road from (Mr.) Jacob Hite's to (Mr.) Swearingen's ferry, 62, 70, 85, 97
Sections:
- Road from Jacob Hite's to Robert Lemen's house, 107
- Road from Robert Lemen's to Swearingen's ferry, 107

Road from Swearingen's ferry through Shepherds Town to the old road that leads to Winchester, 108

Road from Jacob Hite's mill each way into the Main road leading to Swearingen's ferry (road from Alexander Fryer's to Swearingen's road), 100, 102, 109

Road leading from Swearingen's ferry to Keys's ferry, 113
Sections:
- From Swearingen's to Melchiah Inglis Branch, 113
- From Melchiah Inglis Branch to Keys's ferry, 113

Road from Mecklenburgh to Andrew Swearingen's mill and from thence to the Main road that leads to the mouth of Opeckon, 140
Section:
- Road from Mecklenburgh to Andrew Swearingen's mill, 142

Road from Sir John's road near George Paul's to Hougland's ferry and to Van Swearingen's mill on Tunis's Branch, 140

Road from Van Swearingen's mill upon Tunis's Branch to the Warm Springs road near Hedges's (approved as: road from Swearingen's mill into the Warm Springs road at Lucas Hood's), 142, 145, 148
Sections:
- From Swearingen's mill to Cherry's Run, 149
- From Cherry's Run to the Warm Spring road (from Thomas Cherry's ford to the Warm Springs road by Lucas Hood's), 143, 149

Road from John Spears's to Van Swearingen's mill at Houghland's, 145

Road from the Race Ground(s) below John Hite's house to the <u>Swift Shoal</u> ford on Shenandoah and thence down the River to the County road, 124, 132, 136

Road from the Great road leading from Mr. Jacob Hite's to John Smith's to the head of Worthington's Marsh thence down the Marsh into the road near John <u>Swim's</u> called Keys's road and into the road leading by Thomas Rutherford's to Vestal's ferry, 49

Road from the road leading through Edmund <u>Taylor's</u> plantation towards Mr. Wormley's mill as far as the County line, 167, 169

Road from John Funk's mill across Ceeder Run Creek ford to Robert McKay/McCoy Jr.'s. and to Branston's Gap (road from Funk's mill back of George <u>Telener's</u>, thence to Ceedar Creek ford and Robert McCoy's, and thence to Gregorie's ford upon the river), 2(2)

Road from Smith's fence/John Smith's old place to Jacob Hite's (road from Edward <u>Thomas's</u> to Mr. Jacob Hite's; road from Mr. Jacob Hite's/Jacob Hite's bridge to Edward <u>Thomas's</u> bridge between the said Edward <u>Thomas's</u> fences and John Smith's fences), 21, 62, 90, 106, 128, 133

Road from William Jolliff's to the middle of the bridge between Edward <u>Thomas's</u> and John Smith's fences, 94

(Alteration of) Main road to run on the line between Edward <u>Thomas</u> and John Smith, 112

Sir John's road (road called Sir John Sinclaire's road), 96, 97, 113, 119, 127, 132
Sections:
- From Winchester to the plantation where Isaac <u>Thomas</u> did live, 96
- From the place where the road from Robert Cunningham's falls into it to the forks where the road leads to Winchester, 132
- From the plantation where Isaac <u>Thomas</u> did live to the County line, 96
- From the Hunting Ridge to Isaac's Creek at Pritchet's place, 97
- Sir John's road leading from the Timber Ridge to Isaac's Creek, 113
- From the forks to James McGill's, 119
- Sir John's road from the end of the Sleepy Creek Mountain where the Warm Spring road crosses it to James Daugherty's, 127

Probable sections:
- Road from Isaac's Creek to the County line, 148
- Road from (the top of) the Hunting Ridge to the County line, 151, 158

Road from the White House to Thorn's Gap, 108, 115
Section:
- Part from Suttons Run to a mill above Charles <u>Thompson's</u> on Col. Carlyle's land, 115

Road from Winchester to Hougland's ferry, leading through Benjamin <u>Thornbrugh's</u> and Enos Ellis's plantations (proposed alteration at Benjamin <u>Thornbrough's</u> and Enos Ellis's plantations), 150, 156

Section:
- From David Miller's old plantation to Isaac Eaton's, 156

Road from Thomas Thornbury's mill to Opecken Creek by Edward Stroud's and from thence into the road that leads from Jacob Hite's to Vestal's ford on Sharando River, 25

Road from the top of the Blue Ridge to Calebs Run (road from the top of the Blue Ridge at Thorn's Gap to Caleb Job's mill), 73, 84

Road from Thorn's Gap to Jeremiah's Run, 106

Road from the White House to Thorn's Gap, 108, 115
Section:
- Part from Suttons Run to a mill above Charles Thompson's on Col. Carlyle's land, 115

Road from the Augusta line on the South River above John Breeding's fence to the road crossing Thorn's Gap, 123

Road from Moody's Run to Thorn's Gap, 151

Road from Dry Run to the top of the Ridge at Thornton's Gap, 129

(Petition to the Court of Prince William County to meet Frederick County with) a road from the Thorough fair at the Pignut Ridge to the top of the Blue Ridge at the head of Manasses Run, 10

Road from Goony Run ford into Mr. Hite's road by the Three Miles Lick, 153

Road from the Flat Rock by Mr. Thruston's by the head of Kate's Spring, into the road leading to the Bloomery below Mr. Ariss's, 167

Road from Tidwell's ford to Chester's ford in the fork, 134

The Warm Spring/Warm Springs road, 136(2), 162, 163, 167, 168, 170
Sections:
- From Andrew Tilleroy's to Henry Lloyd's, 136(2)
- Through Henry Lloyd's plantation, 162
- From the Back Creek road to the Buffaloe Lick, 167
- From the South Branch road near Ballenger's to the County line (road from Ballenger's to the County line), 168, 170
- From Ballenger's to the Tub mill, 170
- From the Tub mill to the County line, 170

Sir John's road (road called Sir John Sinclaire's road), 96, 97, 113, 119, 127, 132
Sections:
- From Winchester to the plantation where Isaac Thomas did live, 96

- From the place where the road from Robert Cunningham's falls into it to the forks where the road leads to Winchester, 132
- From the plantation where Isaac Thomas did live to the County line, 96
- From the Hunting Ridge to Isaac's Creek at Pritchet's place, 97
- Sir John's road leading from the <u>Timber Ridge</u> to Isaac's Creek, 113
- From the forks to James McGill's, 119
- Sir John's road from the end of the Sleepy Creek Mountain where the Warm Spring road crosses it to James Daugherty's, 127

Probable sections:
- Road from Isaac's Creek to the County line, 148
- Road from (the top of) the Hunting Ridge to the County line, 151, 158

Road from the <u>Timber Ridge</u> to Hoge Creek, 126

Road leading from the Town of Woodstock to <u>Toms Brook</u>, 114

Road leading from <u>Toms Brook</u> to Stover Town, 114

Road from Laurence/Lawrence Snapp's house to <u>Toms Brook</u>, 137, 140

[Note: Entries for <u>Toste</u>, <u>Tostee</u>, and <u>Tostie</u> are combined.]

Road from Beeson's mill to Peter <u>Tostie's</u>, 52

Road from Tuscarora to <u>Tostee's</u>/Peter <u>Tostee's</u>, 61, 67, 80

Road from Peter <u>Tostee's</u> to Watkins's ferry, 61, 73

Road from the North River near Thomas Parker's to Peter <u>Tostee's</u> plantation/<u>Toste's</u> late plantation, 62, 69

Road from Peter <u>Tostee's</u> plantation to Hampton's mill, 63

[Note: In addition to <u>Town</u> roads and streets, see also <u>Courthouse</u>; <u>Winchester</u>, and other specific towns.]

Road from Isaac Perkins's mill through the <u>Town</u> [Winchester] to the line thereof by Andrew Caldwell's (road from Isaac Perkins's mill to the north end of the <u>Town</u>; road(s) through the town to Parkins's mill; the Main Street of the <u>Town</u>), 19, 20, 64, 88

Road from Capt. George Johnston's plantation on the Long Marsh into the road which leads from Williams's Gap to the Courthouse (road from George Johnston Gent.'s house to the road from <u>Town</u> to Fairfax County), 33, 46, 54

Road from the <u>Town</u> to Mr. Briscoe's, 44

Road leading from Lupton's into the Town (alteration as it is already cleared by Thomas Rutherford's pasture adjoining the Town), 168

Roads (as first marked and now used) from Benjamin Kuykendal's to the Trough hill, 69

The Warm Spring/Warm Springs road, 136(2), 162, 163, 167, 168, 170
Sections:
- From Andrew Tilleroy's to Henry Lloyd's, 136(2)
- Through Henry Lloyd's plantation, 162
- From the Back Creek road to the Buffaloe Lick, 167
- From the South Branch road near Ballenger's to the County line (road from Ballenger's to the County line), 168, 170
- From Ballenger's to the Tub mill, 170
- From the Tub mill to the County line, 170

Road from Sir John's road near George Paul's to Hougland's ferry and to Van Swearingen's mill on Tunis's Branch, 140

Road from Van Swearingen's mill upon Tunis's Branch to the Warm Springs road near Hedges's (approved as: road from Swearingen's mill into the Warm Springs road at Lucas Hood's), 142, 145, 148
Sections:
- From Swearingen's mill to Cherry's Run, 149
- From Cherry's Run to the Warm Spring road (from Thomas Cherry's ford to the Warm Springs road by Lucas Hood's), 143, 149

[Note: Entries for Tuscarora and Tuscorora are combined.]

Road from the head of the spring by the Chapel to John Evans's and from thence to Tuscorora, 4
Section:
- Road from the head of the spring by the Chapel to John Evans's, 1

Road from Evan Watkins's ferry [on Potomac River] to Tuscorora, 13
Sections:
- From Charles Donahue's house to Potomac River, 24
- From Charles Donahue's house to Tuscorora Creek, 24

Road from Tuscorora to Middle Creek, 29

Road from Tuscarora to William Richey's, 54

Road from Mill Creek to Tuscarora (road from Cunningham's mill to Tuscarora), 61, 69

Road from Tuscarora to Tostee's/Peter Tostee's, 61, 67, 80

Road from Tuscorora Creek to Robert Lemon's, 69

(Main) road from the Courthouse/town of Winchester to Watkins's ferry, 40, 65, 112
- To be turned where it passes through William Jollyffe's land, 65

Sections:
- From <u>Tuscarora</u> to Capt./Mr. (Thomas) Caton's plantation, 110, 112
- From Watkins's ferry to Caton's Stone House, 162

Road from Isaac Evans's to Henry Vanmetre's mill on <u>Tuscarora</u> and from thence to the Warm Springs road, 149, 152

Road from the Presbyterian Meeting House at the head of <u>Tuscarora</u> to the Meeting House on Back Creek, 153

Road for the <u>upper inhabitants</u> of the County, 30

Road (cleared by David <u>Vance</u>, etc.) leading to Kersey's ferry, 4

Main road running through the lands of Joseph <u>Vance</u> and Peter Stephens (alteration), 86

Road from Hampton's mill down the South Branch (road from below where Henry <u>Vanmetre</u> did live to where he now lives and down by his mill and Hampton's mill), 41

Road from Isaac Evans's to Henry <u>Vanmetre's</u> mill on Tuscarora and from thence to the Warm Springs road, 149, 152

Road from the Great road leading from Mr. Jacob Hite's to John Smith's to the head of Worthington's Marsh thence down the Marsh into the road near John Swim's called Keys's road and into the road leading by Thomas Rutherford's to <u>Vestal's</u> ferry, 49

Road from Thomas Thornbury's mill to Opecken Creek by Edward Stroud's and from thence into the road that leads from Jacob Hite's to <u>Vestal's</u> ford on Sharando River, 25

Road from John Smith's to <u>Vestal's</u> ford, 50

Road from <u>Vestal's</u> ford to Capt. Johnston's road, 53

Road from the north side of the Long Marsh to <u>Vestal's</u> ford, 60

Road from <u>Vestal's</u> ford to the top of the Ridge, 60

Road from <u>Vestal's</u> ford to Col. Fairfax's quarter, 83

Roads to Christopher Beelor's mill:
- Road from <u>Vestal's</u> ford to Christopher Beelor's mill, 121 *[Note: See also Road from Beelor's mill to <u>Vestal's</u> ford (section of the road from Keith's mill to <u>Vestal's</u> ford), 144.]*
- Road from the Long Marsh to Christopher Beelor's mill, 121

Road from the Muster Ground to the [Vestal's] ford/Vestall's ford, 134, 136, 163

Road from Keith's mill/James Keith's mill to Vestal's ford, 139, 142, 144
Sections:
- From Keith's mill to Beelor's mill, 144
- From Beelor's mill to Vestall's ford, 144 *[Note: See also Road from Vestal's ford to Christopher Beelor's mill, 121.]*

Road from Vestall's ford and Keyes's ferry to the top of the Mountain (the Mountain road), 163(3)

Road from Israel Robinson's Gap to Vestal's Gap (via Opecken Creek), 3
Section:
- Road from Robinson's Gap to Opecken, 4, 24

Road from Israel Robinson, Gent.'s house into the road that goes over Vestal's/Westall's Gap, 14, 19

Road from the Long Marsh/Long Marsh Run to Vestal's/Vestal's Gap/Vestal's Iron works, 26, 35, 44, 49

Road from David Loyd's to the top of the Blue Ridge at Vestal's Gap (road from David Loyd's crossing Shannando River and from thence to the top of the ridge), 38, 49, 55
Section:
- Road from the River to the top of the mountain, 55

Road from Watkins's ferry to Vestal's Gap, 47, 56
Sections:
- The part of the road lying on the west side of Opeckon, 47
- The road from Opeckon to the Gap, 47

Road from William Richey's to John Vestal's Gap at Shanandoah River, 52

Road from the ferry at Vestal's Gap to the main road leading to Robinson's Gap, 54

Road from Thomas Hart's to the top of the mountain at Vestal's Gap, 69

Road from Caton's ford/Thomas Caton's to Vestal's Gap, 76, 115
Section:
- Part from Opeckon Creek to Shepherds Town, 115

Road from the bridge at Worthington's Marsh to the Main road to Vestal's Gap, 84

Road from Jacob Hite's mill to the Main road leading from Winchester to Vestal's Gap near the head of Worthington's Marsh, 100, 102

Road leading from Snickers's Gap to <u>Vestall's</u> Gap (to be turned at Ralph Wormley Esq.'s plantation/as far as the County line), 164, 167

Road from John Hardin's to <u>Vestal's</u> wagon road, 81

Road from John Nealan[d]'s/Neeland's on Sharrando to William <u>Vestal's</u> on the same river (road from John Nealand's down the river by the lands of John Grimes, Capt. Stribling, Timothy Haney, Darby Conely, Goldin, John Hamman, Thomas Hamman, and Elizabeth Pearson, across Pearson's Neck of Land to Jonathan Walker's, over Bulskin, and by Robert Hayes's and along Hayes's path to <u>Vestal's</u>), 9, 10

Road from Howel's/Howell's ford to the top of the [Blue] Ridge, 32, 37, 40, 91, 92, 93, 111, 122
Associated roads:
- Road from the ferry landing (at Combs's) to the said road (Main road), and road from the <u>Wagon</u> ford into the said road (road to the <u>Wagon</u> ford and ferry landing), 91, 93, 111

Road from Col. Burwell's mill to the fork of the road at Foxtrap Point, 50, 58
Associated roads:
- The [wagon] ford road, 50, 58
- The ferry road, 50

Road from Shanando at the <u>Wagon</u> ford to the fork of the road to Stephens Town, 92

The <u>Wagon</u> road, 1

Road from Parks's graveyard near Cape Capon Water, over Dellings Run into the <u>Wagon</u> road on Joseph Edward's land, 25

The old <u>Wagon</u> road at Thomas Hart's, 80

Road from John Hardin's to Vestal's <u>wagon</u> road, 81

Road from John Shepard's/Sheppard's to the head of Bulskin (road from Potomac River from Sheppards ferry through the land of Thomas Rutherford, over <u>Walker's</u> mill dam and by the head of Pitts's March and to the head of Bulskin through the lands of Mr. John McCormack), 3, 7
Sections:
- Road from Potomac River to Thomas Rutherford Gent.'s, 12, 38
- The remaining part of the road, 13
- Road from Thomas Rutherford Gent.'s to the head of Bullskin, 24
- Road from Thomas Rutherford's house to John McCarmack's, 37

Road from John Nealan[d]'s/Neeland's on Sharrando to William Vestal's on the same river (road from John Nealand's down the river by the lands of John Grimes, Capt. Stribling, Timothy Haney, Darby Conely, Goldin, John Hamman, Thomas Hamman, and Elizabeth Pearson, across

Pearson's Neck of Land to Jonathan Walker's, over Bulskin, and by Robert Hayes's and along Hayes's path to Vestal's), 9, 10

Road from the Meeting House at the gap of the Mountains above Hugh Paul's to the Warm Spring(s) (road from the Meeting House at the gap of the Mountains to Hugh Paul's from thence to Thomas Cherry's and by Daniel Rose's up the bottom to Thomas Berwick's, and from Berwick's to the Warm Springs), 21, 26, 31
Sections:
- From the Warm Spring(s) to Sleepy Creek, 21, 26, 70, 112
- From Sleepy Creek to the Meeting House, 21, 26
- From Sleepy Creek to the Widow Paul's, 49, 105

Sir John's road (road called Sir John Sinclaire's road), 96, 97, 113, 119, 127, 132
Sections:
- From Winchester to the plantation where Isaac Thomas did live, 96
- From the place where the road from Robert Cunningham's falls into it to the forks where the road leads to Winchester, 132
- From the plantation where Isaac Thomas did live to the County line, 96
- From the Hunting Ridge to Isaac's Creek at Pritchet's place, 97
- Sir John's road leading from the Timber Ridge to Isaac's Creek, 113
- From the forks to James McGill's, 119
- Sir John's road from the end of the Sleepy Creek Mountain where the Warm Spring road crosses it to James Daugherty's, 127

Probable sections:
- Road from Isaac's Creek to the County line, 148
- Road from (the top of) the Hunting Ridge to the County line, 151, 158

Road from Mecklenburgh into the Warm Spring road at Richard Pearis's plantation (by the head of the Swan Ponds), 124(2)

Road from Pugh's and Barrett's mill by the end of the Sleepy Creek Mountain to the Warm Springs (road from the Warm Springs to Barrett's mill), 126, 131(2), 163, 168
Sections:
- From the [Warm] Springs to Ichebud Ashcraft's, 131, 135
- From Ashcraft's to the Buffaloe Run, 131
- From the Buffaloe Run to the end (from the Buffaloe Run as far as laid off by the veiwers from the Warm Springs; road from Buffaloe Run to Howard's old field, 131, 138, 149

Alteration:
- Road from Barrett's mill to the Warm Springs (to be turned to go by Meshack Sexton's mill), 163, 168

The Warm Spring/Warm Springs road, 136(2), 162, 163, 167, 168, 170
Sections:
- From Andrew Tilleroy's to Henry Lloyd's, 136(2)

- Through Henry Lloyd's plantation, 162
- From the Back Creek road to the Buffaloe Lick, 167
- From the South Branch road near Ballenger's to the County line (road from Ballenger's to the County line), 168, 170
- From Ballenger's to the Tub mill, 170
- From the Tub mill to the County line, 170

Road from where Morgan's road crosses Sir John's road, to the Warm Springs road at Joseph Bridges's, 138

Road from the Warm Springs to the County line, 139

Road from Semple's furnace to the Warm Springs road above Peter Burr's, 141, 144, 145, 147, 152

Road from Van Swearingen's mill upon Tunis's Branch to the Warm Springs road near Hedges's (approved as: road from Swearingen's mill into the Warm Springs road at Lucas Hood's), 142, 145, 148
Sections:
- From Swearingen's mill to Cherry's Run, 149
- From Cherry's Run to the Warm Spring road (from Thomas Cherry's ford to the Warm Springs road by Lucas Hood's), 143, 149

Road from Isaac Evans's to Henry Vanmetre's mill on Tuscarora and from thence to the Warm Springs road, 149, 152

Road from the Warm Spring road at Joseph Bridges's to George Bruce's mill, 156, 158

Road from John Lyles's by James Morrison's, John Miller's, John Glenn's and William Glenn's plantations, to Patterson's mill and from thence into the Warm Springs road, 156
[Note: See also:
Road from William Patterson's mill to John Lyle's (alternate route), 159.]

Road from the Warm Springs to Combs's mill and from thence to the mouth of Sleepy Creek, 160

Road from Opeckon to the Warm Springs, 162

Road from the forks of the Warm Spring road to White's mill, 166

Road from the Warm Spring road at Joseph Bridges's into the Main road by John Nevill's, 166, 167

Road from the South Branch road near Jeremiah Smith's to the Warm Springs near Henry Fry's, 170

Road from Robert Warth's; to be taken from the head of the road which leads from the Chapel at Robert McCoy's Spring, to Lewis Stephen's mills (road from the County road near Robert Warth's to Stevens's mill), 30, 63

Road from the Main road near Robert Warth's to Crooked Run, 63

Road from Evan Watkins's ferry [on Potomac River] to Tuscorora, 13
Sections:
- From Charles Donahue's house to Potomac River, 24
- From Charles Donahue's house to Tuscorora Creek, 24

Public road leading from Andrew Campbell Gent.'s to Watkins's ferry (alteration by the plantation formerly Jonathan Jayeas [Jayes?], dec., now in the possession of Elizabeth Dyer), 28

Road from Watkins's ferry to the falling water, 40

Road laid off from Cunningham's Chapel to the Main road from the Courthouse and from thence to Watkins's ferry, 40

(Main) road from the Courthouse/town of Winchester to Watkins's ferry, 40, 65, 112
- To be turned where it passes through William Jollyffe's land, 65

Sections:
- From Tuscarora to Capt./Mr. (Thomas) Caton's plantation, 110, 112
- From Watkins's ferry to Caton's Stone House, 162

Road from Watkins's ferry to Vestal's Gap, 47, 56
Sections:
- The part of the road lying on the west side of Opeckon, 47
- The road from Opeckon to the Gap, 47

Road landings at Watkins's ferry, 56, 57

Road from Peter Tostee's to Watkins's ferry, 61, 73

Road from Lemon's to Watkins's ferry, 70

Road leading to Watkins's ferry, 104

Road from the head of Bullskin to Watkins's ferry, 77

Road from Enoch Pearson's to Watkins's ferry, 78

Main road through Josiah Ridgway's land towards Watkins's ferry (alteration), 85, 89

Road from Jacob Hite's mill to the Main road (leading to Watkins's ferry) at John Evans's (road from John Evans's fence to Jacob Hite's mill [including alterations]), 100, 103, 135, 137, 139

Road (starting at the Main road leading from Winchester to Watkins's ferry) from Peter Fussey's Big Spring/Fussey's Large Spring to the upper side of the mouth of Opeckon Creek, 133(2)

Road from Helm's mill into the road leading from Winchester to Watkins's ferry, at Blackburn's plantation, 161, 164

Road from the South Branch road to William Hancher's mill and from thence into the road leading to Watkins's ferry, 166

Road to be cleared in Prince William County from the fork of the road below Watts's ordinary to meet a road cleared in Frederick County leading through Manassas Run Gap, 70

Road from Dr. Wells's/place where Humphrey Wells lives to Fielding Lewis's/Col. Lewis's mill, 125(2), 128

Road from Dr. Wells's to Snickers's ferry, 128

Road from Dr. Wells's/place where Humphrey Wells lives to Fielding Lewis's/Col. Lewis's mill, 125(2), 128

Road from Humphrey Wells's house to Capt. Calmees's (road from the head of Buck Marsh to Marquis Calmes's), 128, 142

Road from Gregory's ford to West Run, 12

Road from Ceder Creek to West Run, 15

Road from Israel Robinson, Gent.'s house into the road that goes over Vestal's/Westall's Gap, 14, 19

Road from Jackson Allen's crossing the mouth of Smiths Creek thence through White's Bottom to William Clark's at Mount Pleasant, 91

Road from the forks of the Warm Spring road to White's mill, 166

Road from White's mill to William Frost's middle plantation on Back Creek, 166

Road from Marlborough forge to Pugh's mill (road from Jessee Pugh's mill to Marlbro furnace), 151, 154(2)
Sections:
- From Pugh's mill to John White's, 154
- From John White's Run to the furnace, 154

Road from the White House to Thorn's Gap, 108, 115

Section:
- Part from Suttons Run to a mill above Charles Thompson's on Col. Carlyle's land, 115

Road leading to Messanutting from the White House to the Dry Run, 114, 132

Road from the White House in Masanutting to the top of Masanutting Mountain, 127, 128

Road from the White Post to the cross roads near Cunningham's Chapel (road from Cunningham's Chapel to Lord Fairfax's), 133, 140, 153, 171

Road from this Courthouse [Winchester] to the top of the Blue Ridge of Mountains at Williams's Gap (road from Capt. Neill's off and on the old road to Joseph Wilkenson's and thence off on the same road to Francis Carney's and from thence to Edge's ford and from thence off and on the old road to the top of the said Mountain), 12
Sections:
- From Capt. Lewis Neill's/Lewis Neill Gent.'s to Francis Carney's/Carnie's (road from Francis Carney's/Carney's Spring to Lewis Neill's/Opeckon at Neill's ford/Opeckon Creek by Capt. Neill's/ Opecken by Lewis Neill's, Gent), 12, 22, 31, 82, 100, 104
- From Carney's to Edge's ford on Shannadore River (road from Shanando River to Carney's Spring, 12, 50, 83
- From Edge's ford to the top of the Blue Ridge on Williams's Gap, 12

Probable later sections:
- Road from Winchester Town to Lewis Neill's/Lewis Neill's ford on Opeckon, 59, 67
- Road from the ford at Lewis Neill Gent.'s house to Littler's road, 59
- Road from Littler's road to Carney's old house, 59
- Road from Carney's old house to the River, 59
- Road from the River to the top of the mountain at Williams's Gap (road from Edward Snigers's [on Shanando] to the top of the Mountain at Williams's Gap; road from the River at Snigers's to the County line at Williams's Gap; road from the top of the Ridge to Edward Snickers's/Snigers's ford/ferry/ferry at Snicker's house; road from the Ferry road [Snigers's] to the top of the Ridge at Williams's Gap), 59, 76, 79, 81, 83, 113

Road from Capt. George Johnston's plantation on the Long Marsh into the road which leads from Williams's Gap to the Courthouse (road from George Johnston Gent.'s house to the road from Town to Fairfax County), 33, 46, 54

Road through Williams's Gap, 52, 83, 85, 86, 87

Road from this Courthouse [Winchester] to the top of the Blue Ridge of Mountains at Williams's Gap (road from Capt. Neill's off and on the old road to Joseph Wilkenson's and thence off on the same road to Francis Carney's and from thence to Edge's ford and from thence off and on the old road to the top of the said Mountain), 12

Sections:
- From Capt. Lewis Neill's/Lewis Neill Gent.'s to Francis Carney's/Carnie's (road from Francis Carney's/Carney's Spring to Lewis Neill's/Opeckon at Neill's ford/Opeckon Creek by Capt. Neill's/ Opecken by Lewis Neill's, Gent), 12, 22, 31, 82, 100, 104
- From Carney's to Edge's ford on Shannadore River (road from Shanando River to Carney's Spring, 12, 50, 83
- From Edge's ford to the top of the Blue Ridge on Williams's Gap, 12

Probable later sections:
- Road from Winchester Town to Lewis Neill's/Lewis Neill's ford on Opeckon, 59, 67
- Road from the ford at Lewis Neill Gent.'s house to Littler's road, 59
- Road from Littler's road to Carney's old house, 59
- Road from Carney's old house to the River, 59
- Road from the River to the top of the mountain at Williams's Gap (road from Edward Snigers's [on Shanando] to the top of the Mountain at Williams's Gap; road from the River at Snigers's to the County line at Williams's Gap; road from the top of the Ridge to Edward Snickers's/Snigers's ford/ferry/ferry at Snicker's house; road from the Ferry road [Snigers's] to the top of the Ridge at Williams's Gap), 59, 76, 79, 81, 83, 113

Road from Cunningham's mill to that part of the road opposite to Samuel <u>Wilson's</u> house, 130, 156

Road from Morgan Morgan Gent.'s house/Col. Morgan's to the Courthouse/<u>Winchester</u> (road from the Courthouse to the house of Josiah Ballenger and to Morgan Morgan's), 9, 17, 32, 103
Sections:
- Road from the Courthouse to the house of Josiah Ballenger (road from the Courthouse to Ballenger's plantation), 17, 42
- Road from Josiah Ballenger's to Morgan Morgan's (road from Col. Morgan's to Ballenger's meadow; road from Col. Morgan's to the widow Ballinger's), 17, 86, 105

Road from this Courthouse [<u>Winchester</u>] to the top of the Blue Ridge of Mountains at Williams's Gap (road from Capt. Neill's off and on the old road to Joseph Wilkenson's and thence off on the same road to Francis Carney's and from thence to Edge's ford and from thence off and on the old road to the top of the said Mountain), 12
Sections:
- From Capt. Lewis Neill's/Lewis Neill Gent.'s to Francis Carney's/Carnie's (road from Francis Carney's/Carney's Spring to Lewis Neill's/Opeckon at Neill's ford/Opeckon Creek by Capt. Neill's/ Opecken by Lewis Neill's, Gent), 12, 22, 31, 82, 100, 104
- From Carney's to Edge's ford on Shannadore River (road from Shanando River to Carney's Spring, 12, 50, 83
- From Edge's ford to the top of the Blue Ridge on Williams's Gap, 12

Probable later sections:
- Road from <u>Winchester Town</u> to Lewis Neill's/Lewis Neill's ford on Opeckon, 59, 67
- Road from the ford at Lewis Neill Gent.'s house to Littler's road, 59

- Road from Littler's road to Carney's old house, 59
- Road from Carney's old house to the River, 59
- Road from the River to the top of the mountain at Williams's Gap (road from Edward Snigers's [on Shanando] to the top of the Mountain at Williams's Gap; road from the River at Snigers's to the County line at Williams's Gap; road from the top of the Ridge to Edward Snickers's/Snigers's ford/ferry/ferry at Snicker's house; road from the Ferry road [Snigers's] to the top of the Ridge at Williams's Gap), 59, 76, 79, 81, 83, 113

Road from the Courthouse/<u>Winchester</u> to Lewis Neill Gent.'s/ Lewis Neill's old place/Lewis Neill's ford on Opeckon, 12, 13, 23, 29, 30, 59, 67, 73, 81, 88, 94, 102, 103, 110, 151, 170

Road from Isaac Perkins's mill through the Town [<u>Winchester</u>] to the line thereof by Andrew Caldwell's (road from Isaac Perkins's mill to the north end of the Town; road(s) through the town to Parkins's mill; the Main Street of the Town), 19, 20, 64, 88

Road from John McCormack's house to Opecken Creek and from Opecken Creek to the Courthouse/the Town (road from the head of the south fork of Bullskin to Opecken and thence to the Courthouse), 20, 25
Sections:
- Road from the head of the south fork of Bullskin to Opecken (road from John McCormack's to the Main road to Town; road from John McCormack's house to Opecken Creek which leads to town), 20, 25, 49, 67, 87, 107 *[Note: This section appears to be different than the section from Opecken to the head to Bullskin (pp. 22, 31) of the road from Maj. Andrew Campbell Gent.'s to the Chapel at Cunningham's, 22.]*
- Road from Opecken to the Courthouse (road from Opeckon Creek to the Main road leading to <u>Winchester</u>), 20, 25, 107

Road from the Courthouse to John Littler's old place (road from Litler's/Littler's old place/plantation to <u>Winchester Town</u>), 33, 62, 117

Road from the Courthouse/<u>Winchester</u> to Opecken Creek/Opecken ford, 34, 36(2), 43, 50

(Main) road from the Courthouse/town of <u>Winchester</u> to Watkins's ferry, 40, 65, 112
- To be turned where it passes through William Jollyffe's land, 65
Sections:
- From Tuscarora to Capt./Mr. (Thomas) Caton's plantation, 110, 112
- From Watkins's ferry to Caton's Stone House, 162

Road from the mouth of the South Branch and also from Neals Friend's (on Potomac River) to the town of <u>Winchester</u> (road from <u>Winchester Town</u> to Potomac River, in order for a road to be cleared to the mouth of the South Branch), 55, 60

Road from <u>Winchester Town</u> to Opeckon where Joseph Robins formerly lived, 59

Road from Winchester Town to Robert Pearis's plantation, 62, 66

Road from Winchester Town to Robert Mosely's/Moseley's place, 66, 86, 88, 90
[Note: See also:
(New) road through the Common from Winchester to Robert Mosely's, 89.]

The [several] roads from Winchester Town to Kersey's ferry, 68

Road from Robert Harper's at the mouth of Shanando to William Hall's mill and from thence into the road to Winchester, 72

Road from the Signpost at the Hawks Bill down the South River into the road leading to Winchester, 77

Road from Harper's ferry to Winchester (alterations where the road passes through Walter Shirley's land), 79, 82

Road from the new bridge at Opeckon into the road leading from Winchester to Henry Enochs's, 79

Road leading from Winchester to Henry Enochs's, 79(2)
Section:
- From the beginning of the new road [i.e., the road from the new bridge at Opeckon into the road leading from Winchester to Henry Enochs's], to the County line, 79

Road from Winchester to Hogs/Hoge Creek *[Note: Also called the South Branch road on p. 119]*, 80, 111, 119, 125, 148, 155

Road from Opeckon near John Bryan's house to Winchester (road to be cleared on the top of the ridge to avoid the swampy part of the road), 80

Road from Opeckon Creek to the Main county road (road from William Neill's upon Opeckon into the Great road that runs by William Joleff's; road from the forks of the road leading from Winchester to William Jolliff's to Opeckon Creek), 88, 120, 147

(New) road from the lanes through the Common of Winchester to William Jolliff's, 89

(New) road through the Common from Winchester to Robert Mosely's, 89

Road from Paul Froman's mill by the head of Opeckon into the road leading to Winchester, 90

Road leading from Winchester and crossing Col. Hite's mill dam, 90

Road leading from Winchester by Richard M°Machen's, 94

Roads from the Glebe:
- From the Glebe to Cunningham's Chapel, 95, 101, 134
- From the late Glebe to Cunningham's Chapel, 134
- From the Glebe to McCoy's/ McKay's Chapel, 95, 98

Sections:
- Road from the Glebe as far as the Dutch road towards McKay's Chapel, 101
- Road from the Dutch road to McKay's Chapel, 101, 102
- From the Glebe into the Main road that leads to Winchester, 98

Sir John's road (road called Sir John Sinclaire's road), 96, 97, 113, 119, 127, 132
Sections:
- From Winchester to the plantation where Isaac Thomas did live, 96
- From the place where the road from Robert Cunningham's falls into it to the forks where the road leads to Winchester, 132
- From the plantation where Isaac Thomas did live to the County line, 96
- From the Hunting Ridge to Isaac's Creek at Pritchet's place, 97
- Sir John's road leading from the Timber Ridge to Isaac's Creek, 113
- From the forks to James McGill's, 119
- Sir John's road from the end of the Sleepy Creek Mountain where the Warm Spring road crosses it to James Daugherty's, 127

Probable sections:
- Road from Isaac's Creek to the County line, 148
- Road from (the top of) the Hunting Ridge to the County line, 151, 158

Road from Jacob Hite's mill to the Main road leading from Winchester to Vestal's Gap near the head of Worthington's Marsh, 100, 102

Road called Littler's road, 100, 101, 105, 125, 129
Sections:
- From the beginning to Opeckon Creek, 105, 125
- From Opeckon Creek to the fork where it joins the Winchester road leading to Spout Run, 100, 101, 159

Road from Hogland's ferry to the road leading to Winchester, 102

Road from Stoney Creek to the County line (road leading from Augusta to Winchester, from the County line to Stony Creek), 102, 112
[Note: Possibly the same as:
Road from Stoney Creek to Benjamin Allin's Mill Creek, 74, 99.]

Road from the South Branch road near Capt. Smith's through Hoop Petticoat Gap to Winchester (road from Winchester through Hoop Petticoat Gap), 104, 106, 154(2)
Sections:
- Road as far as Allen's Cabin, 154
- From Allen's Cabin to the road leading from Winchester to Jeremiah Smith's, 154

Road from Winchester to the South Branch at the County line on the North Mountain (road from the place marked by the viewers to the County line on the North Mountain), 104, 106

Road leading from Winchester to Edward Snickers's ford over Shanando River, 106

Road from Winchester to Samuel Littler's (road leading to Connigocheague, section from the Town of Winchester to Littler's place), 107, 112

Road from Swearingen's ferry through Shepherds Town to the old road that leads to Winchester, 108

Road from Opeckon ford at John Armstrong's house to Winchester (road from Winchester to Opeckon at Armstrong's place; road from Winchester to Opeckon at Armstrong's ford), 114, 123, 126

Road from the Town of Winchester to Thomas Perry's mill, 114, 115, 124

Road leading from John Hite's house to the Town of Winchester (road from Opeckon to Winchester), 115, 136

Road from the Baptist Meeting House to the Great road leading from Morgan Morgan's to the Town of Winchester, 115, 117

Road from Lewis Neill's mill into Perry's road (road leading from Lewis Neill's mill into the road leading from Thomas Sperry's [Perry's] mill to the town of Winchester; road from Lewis Neill's mill to Thomas Perry's mill), 119, 120, 123

Road from Combs's ferry at [to?] the Town of Winchester, 122

Road from the head of Bulskin to the Main road from Winchester to McLenburgh [Mecklenburgh], 123

Road from Combs's ferry to the forks leading to Winchester, 128

Road (starting at the Main road leading from Winchester to Watkins's ferry) from Peter Fussey's Big Spring/Fussey's Large Spring to the upper side of the mouth of Opeckon Creek, 133(2)

Road from Robert Allen's house to the road leading to Winchester, 142, 145

Road from Opeckon to the Winchester road, 143

Road from Hogland's/Houghland's ferry via Hugh Lysle's, William Baldwin's, and William Hancheire's to fall into Morgan's road leading to Winchester, 143, 147
Sections:
- From Hogland's ferry to John Parks's, 148
- From Hugh Lysle's to Mill Creek, 148

- From Mill Creek to William Hancheir's, 148
- From William Hancheir's to Morgan's road, 148

Road from <u>Winchester</u> to Mercer Babb's plantation, 147, 150

Road from Isaac Perkins's to Hoge Creek where the road leading from <u>Winchester</u> to the South Branch crosses it, 147, 149

Road from Hog's Creek where the South Branch road crosses it to go by Isaac Perkins's plantation and thence to Jessee Pugh's mill (road from Hoge Creek where the <u>Winchester</u> road crosses it to go by Isaac Perkins's plantation and to Jessee Pugh's mill; road from Hog's Creek to Jessee Pugh's mill), 149, 151, 154(2)

Road from <u>Winchester</u> to Marlborough forge 150(2), 171
Alterations:
- To be turned round John Allen's plantation, 150(2)
- To be turned to run upon the line between Robert Glass and the Rev. Mr. Hoge, 171

Road from <u>Winchester</u> to Hougland's ferry, leading through Benjamin Thornbrugh's and Enos Ellis's plantations (proposed alteration at Benjamin Thornbrough's and Enos Ellis's plantations), 150, 156
Section:
- From David Miller's old plantation to Isaac Eaton's, 156

(Alteration of) the part of the road from Hougland's ferry to <u>Winchester</u>, that goes by Hancher's, and through the plantations of Jesse Felkner and others where they enter at the Branch road (alteration of the road from Houghland's ferry and through Falkner's land), 157, 158

Road from Helm's mill into the road leading from <u>Winchester</u> to Watkins's ferry, at Blackburn's plantation, 161, 164

Road from Stephensburg into the road leading from <u>Winchester</u> to Marlbro' [Marlborough] forge, 167, 169
Alteration:
- To go around Lewis Stephens's fence, 169

Road leading from Lord Fairfax's to <u>Winchester</u> (alteration at David Brown's plantation), 168, 169

Road from the Widow Ballenger's to the forks of the <u>Winchester</u> road, 169

Road leading from Berry's ferry to <u>Winchester</u>, 171

Streets in <u>Winchester</u>:
- All the streets in <u>Winchester</u>/the streets in <u>Winchester</u>, 100, 108, 114, 120, 122
- The streets in Westchester [<u>Winchester</u>], 122

- Road from the end of the new street in <u>Winchester</u> into the Main road leading to Parkins's [Perkins's] mill, 72
- Road from the end of the new street in <u>Winchester</u> into the road leading to the River, 72
- <u>Winchester</u> old street/Old Street in <u>Winchester</u>, 80(2)
- Road leading through <u>Winchester</u> and Loudoun Street, 98
- Loudon/Loudoun Street, 91, 93, 94(2), 95, 118, 139, 146
- Loudon Street and associated cross streets, lanes, Commons (etc.), 123, 134, 146, 152(2), 164
- Loudon Street, the cross streets and Commons as far as Cameron Street, 127
- Cameron Street, 91, 93, 94, 118, 138(2), 142, 145
- Cameron Street and into the main road, 95
- Cameron Street and all the streets to the eastward, and the Commons, 127
- Road from the end of Cameron Street in the town of Winchester to where it joins the road leading from the end of Loudon Street, 118
- Peccadilley/Piccadilley Street, 91, 94
- Main Street, 166 *[Note: See also Road from Isaac Perkins's mill through the Town (the Main Street of the Town), 19, 20, 64, 88.]*

Road from the end of the [<u>Winchester</u>] <u>Common</u> to Henry Heath's, 148

Road from the <u>Winchester Common</u>/<u>Winchester Out Lots</u> to Littler's Run, 151, 160, 170

Road from the <u>Winchester Common</u> to Sir John's road, 152

Road from Stoney Lick/Stony Lick by Christopher <u>Windle's</u>/<u>Windel's</u> into the Main road by Mr. Pugh's plantation, 111, 116

Road from Lewis Neill's mill to Owin <u>Wingfield's</u> land, 119

Road from John <u>Wisecarver's</u> to Cooper's mill by Benjamin Fry's, 146, 148

Road from Selser's Mill Run to the County line at <u>Woods Plain</u> (Mountain road from <u>Wood's Plains</u> over the mountains to Selser's Mill Run), 94, 102

(Petition to the Court of Orange County for) a road from the County line of Frederick to the upper inhabitants of Augusta on <u>Woods River</u>, 10

Road from the Widow <u>Woods's</u> mill to the ferry, 57

Road leading from the Town of <u>Woodstock</u> to Toms Brook, 114

Road from Joseph Langdon's plantation to the Town of <u>Woodstock</u>, 116, 117

Road from <u>Woodstock</u> to Mounts Bird's (road from the Narrow Passage to Mounts Bird's), 125, 131

Road leading through Woodstock to the County line, 160

Road from the head of the Pond on Shanando River to Wormley's quarter, 50

Road from the road leading through Edmund Taylor's plantation towards Mr. Wormley's mill as far as the County line, 167, 169

Road leading from Snickers's Gap to Vestall's Gap (to be turned at Ralph Wormley Esq.'s plantation/as far as the County line), 164, 167

Road from the Great road leading from Mr. Jacob Hite's to John Smith's to the head of Worthington's Marsh thence down the Marsh into the road near John Swim's called Keys's road and into the road leading by Thomas Rutherford's to Vestal's ferry, 49

Road from the bridge at Worthington's Marsh to the Main road to Vestal's Gap, 84

Road from the inhabitants on Worthington's Marsh to Hardin and Keys's mill, 84

Road from Worthington's Marsh to Thomas Lindsay's, 87

Road from Jacob Hite's mill to the Main road leading from Winchester to Vestal's Gap near the head of Worthington's Marsh, 100, 102

Road from the head of Worthington's Marsh to Thomas Speak's, 103

Road leading from Worthington's Marsh to Harper's ferry, 163

Dutch road from Kersey's ferry to Wrights Branch, 86

Road from David Brown's to the forks of the road below David Wright's house, 168

Road from George Wright's to Capt. John Hite's, 73

Road from Capt. Hite's to the new road near George Wright's house, 79

Road from Isaac Zane's forge through Manassip's [Manasses] Run Gap, 156

www.ingramcontent.com/pod-product-compliance
Lightning Source LLC
Chambersburg PA
CBHW060505300426
44112CB00017B/2560